IFIP Advances in Information and Communication Technology

593

Editor-in-Chief

IFIP – The International Federation for Information Processing

IFIP was founded in 1960 under the auspices of UNESCO, following the first World Computer Congress held in Paris the previous year. A federation for societies working in information processing, IFIP's aim is two-fold: to support information processing in the countries of its members and to encourage technology transfer to developing nations. As its mission statement clearly states:

IFIP is the global non-profit federation of societies of ICT professionals that aims at achieving a worldwide professional and socially responsible development and application of information and communication technologies.

IFIP is a non-profit-making organization, run almost solely by 2500 volunteers. It operates through a number of technical committees and working groups, which organize events and publications. IFIP's events range from large international open conferences to working conferences and local seminars.

The flagship event is the IFIP World Computer Congress, at which both invited and contributed papers are presented. Contributed papers are rigorously refereed and the rejection rate is high.

As with the Congress, participation in the open conferences is open to all and papers may be invited or submitted. Again, submitted papers are stringently refereed.

The working conferences are structured differently. They are usually run by a working group and attendance is generally smaller and occasionally by invitation only. Their purpose is to create an atmosphere conducive to innovation and development. Refereeing is also rigorous and papers are subjected to extensive group discussion.

Publications arising from IFIP events vary. The papers presented at the IFIP World Computer Congress and at open conferences are published as conference proceedings, while the results of the working conferences are often published as collections of selected and edited papers.

IFIP distinguishes three types of institutional membership: Country Representative Members, Members at Large, and Associate Members. The type of organization that can apply for membership is a wide variety and includes national or international societies of individual computer scientists/ICT professionals, associations or federations of such societies, government institutions/government related organizations, national or international research institutes or consortia, universities, academies of sciences, companies, national or international associations or federations of companies.

More information about this series at http://www.springer.com/series/6102

Nathan Clarke · Steven Furnell (Eds.)

Human Aspects of Information Security and Assurance

14th IFIP WG 11.12 International Symposium, HAISA 2020
Mytilene, Lesbos, Greece, July 8–10, 2020
Proceedings

 Springer

Editors
Nathan Clarke (iD)
University of Plymouth
Plymouth, UK

Steven Furnell (iD)
University of Plymouth
Plymouth, UK

ISSN 1868-4238   ISSN 1868-422X (electronic)
IFIP Advances in Information and Communication Technology
ISBN 978-3-030-57406-2   ISBN 978-3-030-57404-8 (eBook)
https://doi.org/10.1007/978-3-030-57404-8

This Springer imprint is published by the registered company Springer Nature Switzerland AG
The registered company address is: Gewerbestrasse 11, 6330 Cham, Switzerland

Preface

It is now widely recognized that technology alone cannot provide the answer to security problems. A significant aspect of protection comes down to the attitudes, awareness, behavior, and capabilities of the people involved, and they often need support in order to get it right. Factors such as lack of awareness and understanding, combined with unreasonable demands from security technologies, can dramatically impede their ability to act securely and comply with policies. Ensuring appropriate attention to the needs of users is therefore a vital element of a successful security strategy, and they need to understand how the issues may apply to them and how to use the available technology to protect their systems.

With the above in mind, the Human Aspects of Information Security and Assurance (HAISA) symposium series specifically addresses information security issues that relate to people. It concerns the methods that inform and guide users' understanding of security, and the technologies that can benefit and support them in achieving protection.

This book presents the proceedings from the 2020 event, held virtually due to the COVID-19 pandemic, during July 2020. A total of 27 reviewed papers are included, spanning a range of topics including issues related directly to the pandemic and the impacts on contact-tracing applications and privacy, education and awareness, and management and modeling of security. All of the papers were subject to double-blind peer review, with each being reviewed by at least two members of the International Program Committee. We are grateful to all of the authors for submitting their work and sharing their findings.

The HAISA symposium is the official event of IFIP Working Group 11.12 on Human Aspects of Information Security and Assurance, and we would like to thank Prof. Kerry-Lynn Thomson for supporting the event as Working Group chair. We would also like to acknowledge the significant work undertaken by our International Program Committee and recognize their efforts in reviewing the submissions and ensuring the quality of the resulting event and proceedings. Finally, we would like to thank Dr. Christos Kalloniatis and the organizing team for making all the necessary arrangements to enable this symposium to take place.

July 2020

Nathan Clarke
Steven Furnell

Organization

General Chairs

Nathan Clarke   University of Plymouth, UK
Steven Furnell   University of Plymouth, UK

IFIP TC11.12 Conference Chair

Kerry-Lynn Thomson   Nelson Mandela University, South Africa

Local Organizing Chair

Christos Kalloniatis   University of the Aegean, Greece

Publicity Chair

Fudong Li   University of the Portsmouth, UK

International Program Committee

Sal Aurigemma   University of Tulsa, USA
Maria Bada   University of Cambridge, UK
Peter Bednar   University of Portsmouth, UK
Matt Bishop   UC Davis, USA
Patrick Bours   Norwegian University of Science and Technology,
                         Norway
William Buchanan   Edinburgh Napier University, UK
Mauro Cherubini   University of Lausanne, Switzerland
Jeff Crume   IBM, USA
Adele Da Veiga   University of South Africa, South Africa
Ronald Dodge   Palo Alto Networks, USA
Paul Dowland   Edith Cowan University, Australia
Jan Eloff   University of Pretoria, South Africa
Simone Fischer-Huebner Karlstad University, Sweden
Stephen Flowerday   Rhodes University, South Africa
Lynn Futcher   Nelson Mandela University, South Africa
Sarah Gordon   USA
Stefanos Gritzalis   University of Piraeus, Greece
Karen Hedström   Örebro University, Sweden
Yuxiang Hong   Hangzhou Dianzi University, China
John Howie   Cloud Security Alliance, USA
Kévin Huguenin   University of Lausanne, Switzerland

William Hutchinson	Edith Cowan University, Australia
Murray Jennex	San Diego State University, USA
Andy Jones	University of Suffolk, UK
Christos Kalloniatis	University of the Aegean, Greece
Fredrik Karlsson	Örebro University, Sweden
Vasilios Katos	Bournemouth University, UK
Sokratis Katsikas	Open University of Cyprus, Cyprus
Joakim Kavrestad	University of Skövde, Sweden
Stewart Kowalski	Norwegian University of Science and Technology, Norway
Hennie Kruger	North-West University, South Africa
Costas Lambrinoudakis	University of Piraeus, Greece
Michael Lavine	Johns Hopkins University, USA
Gabriele Lenzini	University of Luxembourg, Luxembourg
Shujun Li	University of Kent, UK
Javier Lopez	University of Malaga, Spain
George Magklaras	University of Oslo, Norway
Herb Mattord	Kennesaw State University, USA
Haris Mouratidis	University of Brighton, UK
Marcus Nohlberg	University of Skövde, Sweden
Jason Nurse	University of Kent, UK
Malcolm Pattinson	The University of Adelaide, Australia
Jacques Ophoff	Abertay University, UK
Nathalie Rebe	University of Burgundy, France
Karen Renaud	Abertay University, UK
Nader Sohrabi Safa	Coventry University, UK
Rossouw Von Solms	Nelson Mandela University, South Africa
Theo Tryfonas	University of Bristol, UK
Aggeliki Tsohou	Ionian University, Greece
Kerry-Lynn Thomson	Nelson Mandela University, South Africa
Ismini Vasileiou	De Montfort University, UK
Jeremy Ward	Security Consultant, UK
Merrill Warkentin	Mississippi State University, USA
Zihang Xiao	Palo Alto Networks, USA
Wei Yan	Trend Micro, USA
Ibrahim Zincir	İzmir University of Economics, Turkey

Contents

Privacy and COVID-19

Australian Attitudes Towards Privacy of Information: Will COVID-19
Make a Difference?. 3
   Leah Shanley, Michael N. Johnstone, Michael Crowley,
   and Patryk Szewczyk

Concern for Information Privacy: A Cross-Nation Study of the United
Kingdom and South Africa. 16
   Adéle Da Veiga and Jacques Ophoff

A Review of Information Security Aspects of the Emerging Covid-19
Contact Tracing Mobile Phone Applications. 30
   Georgios Magklaras and Lucia N. López-Bojórquez

Awareness and Training

Towards a Cross-Cultural Education Framework for Online
Safety Awareness 47
   R. Herkanaidu, S. M. Furnell, and M. Papadaki

Towards an Heuristic Approach to Cybersecurity and Online
Safety Pedagogy. 58
   Simon Marsden

ContextBased MicroTraining: A Framework for Information
Security Training 71
   Joakim Kävrestad and Marcus Nohlberg

Social Engineering

Employees' Interest in Professional Advancement on LinkedIn Increases
Susceptibility to Cyber-Social Engineering: An Empirical Test 85
   Mohammed Khaled N. Alotaibi

Does Ubuntu Influence Social Engineering Susceptibility? 97
   Ntsewa B. Mokobane and Reinhardt A. Botha

Quantifying Susceptibility to Spear Phishing in a High School Environment
Using Signal Detection Theory. 109
   P. Unchit, S. Das, A. Kim, and L. J. Camp

Security Behaviour

KidsDoodlePass: An Exploratory Study of an Authentication Mechanism
for Young Children   123
  Esra Alkhamis, Helen Petrie, and Karen Renaud

Information Security Behavioural Threshold Analysis in Practice:
An Implementation Framework   133
  D. P. Snyman and H. A. Kruger

Information Security Behavior: Development of a Measurement Instrument
Based on the Self-determination Theory   144
  Yotamu Gangire, Adéle Da Veiga, and Marlien Herselman

Education

Addressing SME Characteristics for Designing Information Security
Maturity Models   161
  Bilge Yigit Ozkan and Marco Spruit

Cyber Security Education and Training Delivering Industry Relevant
Education and Skills via Degree Apprenticeships   175
  Ismini Vasileiou

Internet Self-regulation in Higher Education: A Metacognitive Approach
to Internet Addiction   186
  Dean John von Schoultz, Kerry-Lynn Thomson, and Johan Van Niekerk

End-User Security

Bayesian Evaluation of User App Choices in the Presence of Risk
Communication on Android Devices   211
  B. Momenzadeh, S. Gopavaram, S. Das, and L. J. Camp

Exploring Information Security and Domestic Equality   224
  Marcus Nohlberg and Joakim Kävrestad

Responding to KRACK: Wi-Fi Security Awareness in Private Households . . .   233
  Jan Freudenreich, Jake Weidman, and Jens Grossklags

Usable Security

Exploring the Meaning of "Usable Security"   247
  Markus Lennartsson, Joakim Kävrestad, and Marcus Nohlberg

Dyslexia and Password Usage: Accessibility in Authentication Design   259
  Karen Renaud, Graham Johnson, and Jacques Ophoff

Securing User eXperience: A Review for the End-Users'
Software Robustness   269
   Panagiotis Zagouras and Christos Kalloniatis

Security Policy

SMEs' Confidentiality Concerns for Security Information Sharing   289
   Alireza Shojaifar and Samuel A. Fricker

Validation of an Information Privacy Perception Instrument
at a Zimbabwean University   300
   Kudakwashe Maguraushe, Adéle Da Veiga, and Nico Martins

Are We Really Informed on the Rights GDPR Guarantees?   315
   Maria Sideri and Stefanos Gritzalis

Attitudes and Perceptions

"Most Companies Share Whatever They Can to Make Money!":
Comparing User's Perceptions with the Data Practices of IoT Devices   329
   Mahdi Nasrullah Al-Ameen, Apoorva Chauhan, M. A. Manazir Ahsan,
   and Huzeyfe Kocabas

Analysis of the 'Open Source Internet Research Tool':
A Usage Perspective from UK Law Enforcement   341
   Joseph Williams and Paul Stephens

Critical Analysis of Information Security Culture Definitions   353
   Zainab Ruhwanya and Jacques Ophoff

Author Index   367

Privacy and COVID-19

Australian Attitudes Towards Privacy of Information: Will COVID-19 Make a Difference?

Leah Shanley[✉], Michael N. Johnstone, Michael Crowley, and Patryk Szewczyk

School of Science, Edith Cowan University, Perth, WA, Australia
a.shanley@ecu.edu.au

Abstract. There has always been tension between security needs (as expressed by a nation-state) and privacy needs (as expressed by the citizens of said nation-state). Achieving this balance is perhaps one of the goals of statecraft. Terrorist attacks tend to shift the balance towards security, whilst proponents of civil liberties tend to want to move the balance in the other direction. We examine Australian attitudes to privacy in the light of the COVID-19 pandemic and consider whether the effect of the pandemic is likely to change Australian's perception of their fundamental right to privacy, as determined by law, enabled by technology and shaped by human concerns.

Keywords: Privacy · Surveillance · Security · Public attitudes · COVID-19

1 Introduction

Security concerns have become heightened across Federal, State and Local government agencies alike, primarily due to the severity of international and domestic incidents that relate specifically to terrorism and cybercrime (ANZCTC 2017). Terrorism incidents such as the attacks in the United States of America on September 11, 2001 and the Bali bombings in 2002, among others, have contributed to the growing use of surveillance technologies in both the private and public sectors (Mann and Smith 2017). More recently, however, the COVID-19 pandemic has emerged and presented further privacy concerns for the public and privacy advocates. The COVID-19 response has seen an increase in the rapid deployment of surveillance devices in Australia. For instance, the use of drones and smartphone applications to enforce social distancing measures or support contact tracing methods.

The tension between privacy and security is a complex debate between privacy advocates and security proponents; however, public citizens appear to be either indifferent to, or are struggling to grasp, the effect of technological advancements on privacy erosion, especially when privacy infringements are legitimised when contextualised with the War on Terror (Broek et al. 2017) and more recently the COVID-19 pandemic. The introduction of public surveillance systems and laws that support their use appear contradictory. Juridical matters bring forth legal implications in relation to data handling, leaving little

© IFIP International Federation for Information Processing 2020
Published by Springer Nature Switzerland AG 2020
N. Clarke and S. Furnell (Eds.): HAISA 2020, IFIP AICT 593, pp. 3–15, 2020.
https://doi.org/10.1007/978-3-030-57404-8_1

room for redress with the continued trend of surveillance systems as a remedy to support national security objectives.

This paper examines the privacy-security debate through the lens of the power model developed by Turner (2005). The balance between privacy and security is at the nexus of technology, law and people. Technology enables what is legitimate under law on behalf of the people. Australians are typically mistrustful of their government with respect to personal data (Lupton 2019) - they do not like to be identified. A recent survey by the Office of the Australian Information Commissioner (OAIC) showed that this is still an issue for Australians (OAIC 2017). Witness the "Australia Card" of the 1980s and the more recent "My Health Record" (an opt-out system). Briefly, the Australia Card was a failed attempt to issue a national identity card. Further, approximately 20% of Australians have elected to opt-out of My Health Record. As noted by Hanson (2018), "The controversy over police access to the My Health Record [data] and the need to add further privacy protections in that scheme also point to heightened public awareness and concern about digitisation processes, including about losing control of personal information that might be used to cause harm". The 2017 survey administered by the OAIC showed that government access to personal data continues to concern Australians (OAIC 2017). The COVID-19 pandemic may prove to be an interesting confounding variable. The use of Bluetooth Low Energy (BLE) technology, in the case of the COVIDSafe application (Department of Health 2020) appears at first glance to potentially enhance the rapid detection of contacts with an infected person - a laudable public health goal. However, a BLE signal could produce false positives which would hinder, rather than help, the public health effort. Standing outside a closed office for 15 min could generate a "contact" where no direct exposure has occurred. This paper hereafter summarises related work on privacy, provides an extensive discussion of legal, technical and human-centred matters pertaining to privacy, shows how the discourse fits an established theory of power in groups (Turner's TPT) and concludes by suggesting that further work can be done in the form of surveying segments of the population to determine if the attitudes of Australians have changed.

2   Related Work

Privacy is recognised in fundamental documents that define human rights (Clark 2006). For example, section 12 of the Universal Declaration of Human Rights states "No one shall be subjected to arbitrary interference with his privacy, family, home or correspondence, nor to attacks upon his honour and reputation. Everyone has the right to the protection of the law against such interference or attacks." (UN General Assembly 1948). Historically, Australians have been at best, reluctant to accept government attempts to impose policies that result in universal identification. In the 1980's the Hawke Government proposed introducing a national identity card (Hawley 2005) that was quickly consigned to the waste bin of history. Recently, the Morrison Government's COVID-19 application attracted greater acceptance with citizens notwithstanding ongoing technical issues and release of draft legislation to enshrine privacy protections. While this draft legislation seems to exclude the operation of other security legislation the fact remains that Australia's security apparatus has acknowledged that it does at times carry out illegal acts in the course of fulfilling its role in protecting Australians (Moorhouse 2014). If nothing else Australians are on notice that different Australian agencies hold different approaches to the balancing act that underpins the relationship between privacy and security.

The balance between privacy and security is continually shifting and increasing discord between individual privacy rights and the collective security objectives of a nation state (Mann and Smith 2017). Goggin et al. (2017) conducted a survey of 1,600 Australians. The research explored questions about the nature of digital rights and covered four key issues, namely; (1) privacy surrounding data profiling and analytics, (2) government data matching and surveillance, (3) digital privacy relating to the work place (work), and (4) freedom of expression (speech) with an emphasis on online digital platforms (Goggin et al. 2017). Key areas of interest drawn from the research were the findings relating to privacy profiling, and government data matching and surveillance. The research revealed that Australians are genuinely concerned about their online privacy in agreeance with research conducted by the OAIC in 2017 that showed similar outcomes (OAIC 2017). 65% of participants felt they had nothing to hide, whilst 67% actively took steps to protect their online privacy. 57% of participants agreed that corporations were a threat to privacy. With regards to government data matching and surveillance, 47% were concerned about government violating their privacy, however, when questions were framed from a security perspective the percentage changed. When respondents were asked whether they are in favour of law enforcement or security agencies accessing meta data, 42% were in favour, conversely, when framed as an anti-terrorism measure 57% were in favour (Goggin et al. 2017). The change in attitudes suggests that personal views towards privacy breaches varied depending on the context–further highlighting the complexity of the issue.

A 2017 survey on Australian attitudes towards privacy conducted by the OAIC (2017) further identified that 93% of respondents do not want their personal data sent and stored overseas. The desire for personal privacy has seen an increase in the use of encryption technology by consumers and enterprises globally (Korolov 2016). The widespread use of encryption has contributed to more recent developments in law, for example, in 2018 the Australian Parliament passed the Assistance and Access Act 2018 (Cth). The Act is designed to improve the ability of Australian law enforcement and security agencies in decrypting information when investigating serious crimes (The Parliament of the Commonwealth of Australia 2018). Thus, the introduction of the Act is a contributing factor to the rising tensions between privacy advocates and security proponents. Similarly, the Identity Matching Services Bill (2019) implements the Intergovernmental Agreement (IGA) on identity matching services. Under the Intergovernmental agreement, the Commonwealth and all states and territories agree to preserve or introduce legislation to support the sharing of facial images and related identity information via a set of identity-matching services (Parliament of Australia, 2019). While privacy laws in Australia do exist at both State and Federal level, not all government agencies work in unison, furthermore, juridical issues greatly influence law enforcement. As noted by Greenleaf (2020) any COVID-19 legislation needs to avoid 'pseudo-voluntary' compliance by which voluntary uptake becomes de facto compulsory. That is, any resultant legislation should make the uptake of the COVID-19 application 'genuinely voluntary and guaranteed by enforceable laws.' (Greenleaf 2020). In contrast, the exposure draft makes it an offence to 'require another person to download the application or have the application in operation (The Parliament of the Commonwealth of Australia 2020b). The exposure draft does not use the words 'voluntary'. Section 94B (Object of this Part) could enshrine the principle of voluntary uptake.

3 Discussion

Paine et al. (2007) noted over a decade ago, that advances in technology have altered the way in which information is collected, stored and exchanged. Increasing threats to public safety, whether criminal or health related, have contributed to the accelerated implementation of surveillance technologies in both the public and private sector. An outcome is that regulators are struggling to keep abreast of technological developments and their impact on society (Mann and Smith 2017). Public trust, a domain of concern, is found to play a critical role regarding surveillance in society. Major studies, for instance, the Public perception of security and privacy: Assessing knowledge, Collecting evidence, Translating research into action (PACT) survey, found that respondents level of distrust reflected in the preferences for different security and privacy practices (Patil et al. 2015). The Australian Government is not exempt from public trust issues on multiple fronts. For example, the government's handling of the Robo Debt process wherein its use of flawed technology (Price 2019) to shift the onus of proof of financial entitlement onto those least able to look after themselves indicated either a collective lack of trust in citizens or an unhealthy focus on achieving a budget surplus at all cost.

In a not unrelated vein, the government's pursuit of journalists and whistle-blowers who, respectively, exposed government plans to secretly spy upon Australians (Ryall 2019; Tillett 2018) and revealed illegal government behaviour against a friendly neighbour during Timor Gap negotiations (Knaus 2019; Heathcote 2013) further illustrates a preoccupation with secrecy. Furthermore, the government has just introduced into parliament proposed amendments to the Australian Security and Intelligence Act 1979 (Cth) (ASIO Act). These amendments include provision for ASIO to use nonintrusive surveillance devices on Australian citizens without needing to apply to a court for a warrant and to examine articles being delivered by a delivery service provider (The Parliament of the Commonwealth of Australia 1999). These proposed amendments have been described as 'one more step towards a totalitarian state' (Barnes 2020). This same government now asks Australians to trust it on providing adequate protections of citizen's privacy within its COVID-19 smartphone application. This is the same application that has not achieved universal uptake by all federal politicians, including some ministers of the government (ABC News 2020). Importantly, one politician has given the protection of the identity of whistle-blowers as the reason why he will not download the COVID-19 application. This raises an important issue, while the draft legislation provides criminal sanctions for misuse of 'tracing application data' beyond medical contact tracing for the purposes of COVID-19, the derivative use of the outcome of such tracing might not be so easily prevented. It might not take much for a well-resourced agency to link a person of interest or to narrow its field of search to persons required to isolate following the identification of a politician, investigative journalist or lawyer who has become a recent victim of COVID-19. For clever people, knowing where to start looking is almost as good as knowing where to search.

Brown et al. (2014) confirm that transparency is indeed important to the public in Australia and the UK, thus public trust relies on increasing the responsibility of institutions to recognise and protect whistle-blowers. Brown et al. (2014) show in their research regarding transparency and whistleblowing, that public attitudes towards whistleblowing is divided. Half of the respondents (50%) surveyed felt information was kept to secret demonstrating public opinion in these domains has the potential to impact political support. Therefore, introducing intrusive means of data collection in combination with legislative amendments that threaten public trust is paramount. As such public figures, for example, Julian Assange, have potential to not only influence public opinion but contribute to the increasing pressure of trust in modern institutions.

Recent developments with respect to COVID-19 have prompted governments of the world to canvas technological solutions capable of contributing to the response effort. For instance, drone deployment has been trialed in some countries to enforce social distancing polices while other technological solutions such as GPS ankle monitoring devices have been acquired to help police track citizens who should be in quarantine or self-isolation (Sky News 2020). In contrast, automatic number plate recognition (ANPR) cameras have been purchased in the state of Western Australia to enforce state-wide travel restrictions (Hendry 2020b). Mann and Smith (2017) astutely point out that Australia is following the trend of expanding its surveillance capabilities, noting the most significant development that occurred in 2015. The National Facial Recognition Biometric Matching Capability (NFRBMC) was announced and intended to become operational in 2016. The NFRBMC provides for the sharing of facial templates across state and federal agencies. According to more recent reports, Western Australia as a case in point, at present is preparing for the upload of licence and photographs to be shared, while other states (Victoria, South Australia and Tasmania) have already supplied driver's licence details and photographs to the National Driver's Licence Facial Recognition System (NDLFRS) (Hendry 2020a). The NDLFRS, hosted on a Department of Home Affairs platform, contributes data to the NFRBMC system. The end result will probably result in the driver's licence becoming by stealth what Australian's had collectively rejected with the Hawke Government (the national identity "Australia" card). A government focused on identification and secrecy may find the lure of surreptitiously linking such data to Australians using the same phone application very tempting.

One particular technological response measure of interest is the introduction of a smartphone application for the purpose of social distancing and contact tracing. Countries around the world such as Singapore, Israel, South Korea and the United States have adopted surveillance methods leveraging mobile location data to enforce social distancing policies and contact tracing (Ng 2020). Contact tracing aims to identify citizens that have come into close contact with a COVID-19 positive case or who have tested positive, thus the data can be used to promptly notify people who may be at risk or should be in quarantine. The COVIDSafe application, released in Australia on 26 April, 2020 (Department of Health 2020), underwent some consultation prior to its release. The Department of Health released a Privacy Impact Assessment (PIA) prior to the application being released that documented recommendations yet to materialise. In addition, the

PIA performed a compliance analysis against the Australian Privacy Principles (APPs). Whilst there are rhetorical moves to enforce penalty for breach of information privacy (Dentons 2019), it is important to note that the APPs are not enforceable (Australian Law Reform Commission 2014, p. 21), in other words, legal remedy for encroachment does not currently exist in Australia. Furthermore, the Australian Privacy Act (that incorporates the APPs), provide exemptions to a number of Federal and State agencies, thus it is questionable as to what protections exist for the Australian public should a breach be realised.

As the privacy debate continues, there exists an emerging discourse with regards to public surveillance and security, or put another way, national security versus information security. The balance between privacy and surveillance for the purpose of national security - a debate that continues to gain ground, demonstrates the discourse with the introduction of Acts such as the Assistance and Access Act (2018), designed to improve the ability of Australian law enforcement and security agencies in decrypting information, is in contradiction to the advocacy of privacy. The Australian Government purportedly promotes privacy on the one hand while simultaneously implementing legislation that supports intrusive means of data collection. The primary legislation for regulating privacy in Australia is the Privacy Act 1988 (Cth). The Australian Privacy Principles (APPs), included in schedule 1 of the Privacy Act, outline how personal information should be managed and handled by entities subject to the Act. Exemptions to the Act include entitles with an annual turnover of less than three million AUD, local and state governments are also exempt (OAIC, n.d.). In addition, defence and intelligence agencies are either partially or completely exempt (Australian Law Reform Commission 2008). The Australian Law Reform Commission (2008) stated that "Australia is yet to achieve uniformity in the regulation of personal information".

Due to public concern, Australia's Federal Health Minister, Greg Hunt, shared a Determination under the Biosecurity Act 2015 (Cth) in an attempt to protect people's privacy and quell fears. The Determination restricts access to state and territory health authorities only, for the purpose of contact tracing. The Determination declares that a person must not retain the data on a database outside Australia, and the Commonwealth must cause COVID-19 application data in the National COVIDSafe data store to be deleted after the COVID-19 pandemic has concluded (Australian Government 2020). A better option would be to insert a sunset clause in the proposed legislation requiring the approval of parliament to extend the use of the COVID-19 application legislation notwithstanding a Determination can be amended or appealed at the discretion of the government anytime. Thus, the finalisation of the draft COVID-19 application legislation is crucial for clarity. As legal experts have warned, legislation would be a better instrument (Bogle 2020). Law Council of Australia president Pauline Wright stated, "there was some potential legal ambiguity around whether laws authorising the law enforcement and intelligence warrants could override the Determination's prohibition on access" (Bogle 2020). In addition to the ambiguity that exists in Australian law, international requests for data deserves the serious consideration of the current Parliamentary Joint Committee on Intelligence and Security (PJCIS) review. To illustrate further, the Department of Health has contractual agreements with Amazon Web Services (AWS) for the COVIDSafe application data store. The use of AWS, an American company, raises some juridical issues. AWS has an annual turnover of more than three million AUD qualifying AWS as an APP entity. However, a bilateral agreement between Australia and the United States following enactment of the United States CLOUD Act (Clarifying Lawful Overseas Use of Data), enacted in 2018, may or may not weaken protections afforded under Australian's Privacy Act. This agreement is subject to the outcome of the PJCIS review and is currently being negotiated (see Second Reading Speech on the Telecommunications Legislation Amendment (International Production Orders) Bill 2020 by Minister Mr Tudge (Parliament of Australia 2020). In the meantime, The PJCIS has commenced a review into the effectiveness of the Telecommunications Legislation Amendment (International Production Orders) Bill 2020 with a reporting date of 26 June 2020 (The Parliament of the Commonwealth of Australia 2020a). As recently as 14 May 2020, Taylor (2020) has canvassed concerns about US law enforcement accessing COVID-19 data making the PJCIS review crucial for those concerned with privacy.

Another issue worthy of consideration is the Archives Act 1983 (Cth), an Act that sets out requirements for the retention of data. This means that archived data needs considerable attention in relation to data access, storage, backups and retention timeframes. Other pertinent issues worthy to note include function creep and exemptions to current Australian law. Function creep in generic terms addresses the originally intended purpose of a particular surveillance system. The originally intended purpose does not necessarily mean the surveillance technology will cease to operate once the originating use case ceases. A case in point is the COVIDSafe application. Whilst the Australian Government has stated that the data store must be deleted when the pandemic ends, as noted by Ahmed et al (2020), the term "end of pandemic" is vague. Whilst use of the technology by the government of the day may have well-deserved intentions, this does not guarantee future governments will hold the same values. Therefore, legislative guarantees to protect against a host of potentially lucrative markets or temptation of the security apparatus (both public and private) require mitigation to balance the potential unforeseen effects or secondary uses.

Turning to the implication of exemptions, certain Australian laws such as the Privacy Act 1988 (Cth) allow for state and federal exemptions across agencies. Should Pauline Wright's concerns come to fruition, laws that authorise state, federal and intelligence agency warrants override the Determination's prohibition on access, therefore, requirement for entities to share information with foreign governments exists and requires rigorous investigation, fortunately this is currently part of the PJCIS review mentioned above.

Instruments to investigate data protection and information privacy are widely available. PIA's are one such mechanism designed to consider the impacts and issues that may arise due to deployment of surveillance systems, In addition, PIA's aim to bring forth alternatives or safeguards to mitigate negative impacts to stakeholders (Wright et al. 2010). The PIA officiated by the Department of Health failed to adequately address these issues relating to the COVIDSafe application data. The PIA raised concerns in the form of recommendations prior to release. However, until legislation concerning usage and contractual arrangements is enacted, information privacy related matters will continue to emerge. Moreover, public trust will continue to decline. It is not desirable that a PIA for an application critical for the health and safety of Australians, and by extension privacy, did not seek independent expert or community input prior to release. The Australian government has openly stated that returning to normal life is dependent upon the application being downloaded and used (Ruiz and Moore 2020). In contrast, Professor McLaws, a member of the WHO coronavirus response panel stated "What's not clear is who the custodian of the data is and where the data are stored. It's not true informed consent" and in another statement "Until we know what the source code is and until we know whether Amazon has to fulfil Australian law, I won't download the application" (White 2020). Amazon's relationship with Australian law in releasing data held within Australia to the United States of America will hopefully crystallise after the PJCIS review into the Telecommunications Legislation Amendment (International Production Orders) Bill 2020 is completed.

Privacy of one's information is significantly important in the pursuit of public trust, a critical factor that may impact on citizens' support for a security practice (Friedewald et al. 2016), thus acceptance of intrusive technological solutions rely heavily on trust in the institutions that advocate such practices. The aim of the Privacy and Security Mirrors: "Towards a European Framework for integrated decision making" (PRISMS) project, was to gain better understanding of the relation between surveillance, security and privacy that could inform public policy and decision makers. The PRISMS project, a relatively large study, found a strong correlation between public trust and privacy intrusive measures, thus public trust played a critical role in the acceptance of security practices (Friedewald et al. 2016). The introduction of the General Data Protection Directive in May of 2018, otherwise referred to as the GDPR, illustrates that privacy of personal data is a serious issue in the European Union. The PRISMS project successfully informed policy makers in the EU, and by implication, influenced policy makers worldwide to follow suit (van Lieshout et al. 2013).

We acknowledge that any solution that enables health professionals to effectively and efficiently detect COVID-19 transmissions is a benefit to society as a whole and that contact tracing is effective. Conflicting views are however apparent with Norway's health authority for instance ceasing to use the country's COVID-19 application and deleting existing data (Kelio 2020). Within Australia, there are concerns about the technical implications of the use of the COVIDSafe application. We have already suggested a scenario where a false positive might occur. Interesting, the OAIC recommends turning Bluetooth 'off' to preserve privacy (although the pandemic might be considered a special case). Perhaps more seriously, there have been reports of the application interfering with medical devices that also use Bluetooth. Bluetooth may also be resource-intensive and drain a phone's battery prematurely, so users might be reluctant to enable it, thus invalidating the data collected by the application. Furthermore, the application does not function correctly on Apple products. Notwithstanding the functionality issue, Apple and Google are jointly designing a different privacy-preserving contact tracing protocol. The Apple/Google solution is different to the COVIDSafe application in several respects, in that their solution does not collect location data from a user's phone, nor does it share the identities of users with each other (or with Apple/Google for that matter). Further, random Bluetooth identifiers rotate every 10–20 min, which helps prevent tracking.

We now examine the above evidence and frame it in terms of Turner's Three Process Theory (TPT) of power. Turner (2005) contends that the "standard" theory of power is really a set of general assumptions about the relationship between power and influence. He addresses this by providing a more formal model of the factors that influence power (see Fig. 1). Turner's model is interesting in that, contrary to the standard model of power, group formation or the development of a shared social identity is the catalyst for influence, and this influence (separated by the different elements of persuasion, authority and coercion) is the foundation of power.

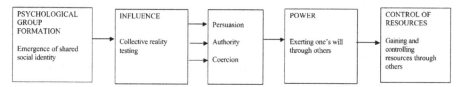

Fig. 1. Turner's power model (adapted from Turner 2005).

Applying Turner's TPT to the constructs of Fig. 1, we find evidence (or, at least the semblance) of a shared social identity (group formation), driven by the COVID-19 threat and expressed by frequent television advertising as "We are all in this together". Examining the three elements of influence, there is evidence of persuasion or convincing someone that your view is the correct one (advertising campaigns exhorting citizens to download the application), authority or the belief that someone else can control what you do (the government wants citizens to download the application) and coercion or someone can control your behaviour, even against your own interests (you may not be able to attend certain events if you have not downloaded the application). Notwithstanding concerns expressed about the security of the application's data and potential future uses (cross-matching) of said data, there is also an "appeal to the gallery" implicit in the conversation around Facebook and other social media platforms capturing more personal data than the application (therefore, why not use the application?). One could argue that end-user's perceptions of Facebook data collection processes are camouflaged through the perceived leisurely benefits of the application. Patil and Shyamasundar (2019) suggest that end-users believe they may exercise a degree of control over Facebook's data collection process, despite not actively reviewing or adjusting any controls. In contrast COVID-19 centric applications are often managed by the governing body thus minimising opportunities for end-users to exercise control. The final element of Turner's model, gaining control of resources, is evidenced by considering the data collected by the application to be a resource.

4   Conclusion

The number of private and public sector organisations deploying surveillance technologies is increasing rapidly (Mann and Smith 2017). This trend is expected to continue as new challenges emerge, for example, the outbreak of COVID-19. Recent law developments, for example, the Identity-Matching Services Bill (2019) or the Assistance and

Access Act 2018 (Cth), have generated significant concern in regard to the erosion of privacy. In Australia, the uploading of facial images and licence plate information to the National Database is now a reality with little oversight and little debate regarding the rollout of such technologies.

It is clear from the literature that privacy is important to the public. With the introduction of new surveillance methods such as the deployment of drones, GPS tracking devices and contact tracing apps, public concern will likely continue to increase. An important finding from the EU PRISMS project was that public trust was paramount. The research concluded that public trust played a critical role in the acceptance of security practices (Friedewald et al. 2016). If surveillance technologies are to be deployed as solutions to security objectives, or in the case of COVID-19, a rapid response to unforeseen circumstances, then the Australian Government has a responsibility to address the ambiguity that surrounds the public's perception of technological solutions and the laws that purport to protect privacy. A clear and definite roadmap for the reversal of intrusive technological surveillance systems would contribute to public trust, however such debate is absent from the discussion. The Australian Privacy Act offers little redress for breach of information privacy, moreover, the plethora of Acts, Bills and other Amendments provides for a contradictory landscape that is difficult to navigate leaving the average Australian often confused and mislead when new surveillance systems are introduced. It is time to consolidate these nuances surrounding law and design a solid framework for the deployment of surveillance technology. Worthy of consideration among all the newly, or otherwise predicated surveillance systems, is the continued advocacy of surveillance technology as a primary solution to national and state security objectives. The trade-off paradigm, that is, the assumption people are willing to trade privacy for more security, has been debated among scholars and academic circles for considerable time. People desire both security and privacy (Broek et al. 2017), thus finding the balance is pertinent in the pursuit of public trust. Friedewald et al. (2015) showed in research concerning the trade-off paradigm, evidence against the trade-off hypothesis and found no significant statistical correlation between people's valuation of privacy and security concern, therefore, generalising that Australian citizens are willing to trade privacy for more security is not consistent with the evidence.

We are not arguing that privacy trumps security in all cases. All nations keep secrets and it is in their national interest to do so. What we observe is that, by nature, Australians are reticent to share their personal information with any government entity. In order to test if this is true, we propose to undertake a survey of segments of the population to evaluate current Australian attitudes to privacy and to evaluate if the COVID-19 pandemic changes these attitudes in any significant way.

The COVID-19 pandemic has seen the suspension of parliamentary sittings potentially setting a precedent for future emergency protocols to be established. Laws have been passed without opposition and surveillance systems are in the process of rapid deployment, thus the absence of political safeguards reduces the potential for external scrutiny. While the gravity of the pandemic can be appreciated, and we are indeed chartering unfamiliar waters, still it is unequivocally necessary that a well-informed sense of assurance that information risks and controls are in balance is paramount, in other words, a clear and concise Business Continuity Plan on behalf of Federal and State governments is crucial to enable continuation of government and democratic debate. Furthermore, decision making without practicing due diligence and regard for the impact on the Australian public deserves criticism. As stated by Zedner (2009) "Do we want to be completely secure in a police state?".

References

ABC News. Easing coronavirus restrictions depends on the uptake of the Government's tracing app, so has your MP downloaded it? ABC News (2020). https://www.abc.net.au/news/2020-05-07/has-your-mp-downloaded-the-coronavirus-tracing-app/12215092?nw=0

Ahmed, N., Michelin, R.A., Xue, W., Ruj, S., Malaney, R., Kanhere, S.S., Seneviratne, A., Hu, W., Janicke, H., Jha, S.: A Survey of COVID-19 Contact Tracing Apps. Ithaca: Cornell University Library, arXiv.org (2020)

ANZCTC. Australia's Strategy for Protecting Crowded Places from Terrorism. Commonwealth of Australia (2017). https://www.nationalsecurity.gov.au/Media-and-publications/Publications/Documents/Australias-Strategy-Protecting-Crowded-Places-Terrorism.pdf

Australian Government. Biosecurity (Human Biosecurity Emergency) (Human Coronavirus with Pandemic Potential) (Emergency Requirements—Public Health Contact Information) Determination 2020 (2020). https://www.legislation.gov.au/Details/F2020L00480

Australian Law Reform Commission. Australian Privacy Law and Practice, vol. 3 (2008)

Australian Law Reform Commission. Serious Invasions of Privacy in the Digital Era (2014)

Barnes, G.: New ASIO law one more step towards a totalitarian state. Sydney Morning Herald, 13 May 2020. https://www.smh.com.au/national/new-asio-law-one-more-step-towards-a-totalitarian-state-20200513-p54smi.html

Bogle, A.: Will the Government's coronavirus app COVIDSafe keep your data secure Here's what the experts say. ABC News, 27 April 2020. https://www.abc.net.au/news/science/2020-04-27/covidsafe-contact-tracing-app-coronavirus-privacy-security/12186044

Van den Broek, T., Ooms, M., Friedewald, M., Lieshout, M.V., Rung, S.: Privacy and Security: Citizens' Desires for an Equal Footing Surveillance, Privacy and Security: Citizens' Perspectives. Taylor and Francis (2017)

Brown, A.J., Vandekerckhove, W., Dreyfus, S.: The relationship between transparency, whistleblowing, and public trust (2014). https://doi.org/10.4337/9781781007945.00008

Clark, R.: What's 'Privacy'? (2006)

Dentons. New tougher penalties to apply in Australia for breach of privacy (2019). https://www.dentons.com/en/insights/alerts/2019/march/28/new-tougher-penalties-to-apply-in-australia-for-breach-of-privacy

Department of Health. COVIDSafe app [Press release] (2020). https://www.health.gov.au/resources/apps-and-tools/covidsafe-app

Friedewald, M., Lieshout, M.V., Rung, S., Ooms, M., Ypma, J.: Privacy and Security Perceptions of European Citizens: A Test of the Trade-Off Model. Springer, New York (2015). WorldCat.org database

Friedewald, M., van Lieshout, M., Rung, S., Ooms, M.: The context-dependence of citizens' attitudes and preferences regarding privacy and security. In: Gutwirth, S., Leenes, R., De Hert, P. (eds.) Data Protection on the Move. LGTS, vol. 24, pp. 51–74. Springer, Dordrecht (2016). https://doi.org/10.1007/978-94-017-7376-8_3

Goggin, G., et al.: Digital Rights in Australia (2017)

Hanson, F.: Preventing another Australia Card fail. Australian Strategic Policy Institute (2018)

Heathcote, S.: Australia and Timor Leste in The Hague. The Conversation (2013)

Hendry, J.: WA prepares for national face matching database upload. IT News, 27 March 2020 (2020a). https://www.itnews.com.au/news/wa-prepares-for-national-face-matching-database-upload-539863

Hendry, J.: WA to electronically track COVID-19 patients who defy isolation orders. IT News (2020b). https://www.itnews.com.au/news/wa-to-electronically-track-covid-19-patients-who-defy-isolation-orders-546224?eid=65&edate=20200414&utm_source=20200414&utm_med ium=newsletter&utm_campaign=sc_weekly

Kelio, L.: Coronavirus: Contact-tracing apps face further hitches (2020). https://www.bbc.com/nes/technology-53051783

Knaus, C.: Witness K and the outrageous spy scandal that failed to shame Australia. The Guardian (2019). https://www.theguardian.com/australia-news/2019/aug/10/witness-k-and-the-outrageous-spy-scandal-that-failed-to-shame-australia

Korolov, M.: Study: Encryption use increase largest in 11 years. CSO (2016). https://www.csoonl ine.com/article/3088916/study-encryption-use-increase-largest-in-11-years.html

Mann, M., Smith, M.: Automated facial recognition technology: recent developments and approaches to oversight. Univ. New South Wales Law J. **40**(1), 121–145 (2017)

Moorhouse, F.: Australia Under Surveillance. Random House, Sydney (2014)

OAIC. Australian Community Attitudes to Privacy. Office of the Australian Information Commissioner (2017). https://www.oaic.gov.au/resources/engage-with-us/community-attitudes/acaps-2017/acaps-2017-report.pdf

OAIC. (n.d). Government Agencies. Office of the Australian Information Commissioner. https://www.oaic.gov.au/privacy/your-privacy-rights/government-agencies/

Ng, A.: Location data used for tracking COVID-19 has its limits, ACLU warns. CNET (2020). http://www.cnet.com/news/location-data-used-for-tracking-covid-19-has-its-limits-aclu-warns/

Parliament of Australia. Identity-matching Services Bill 2019 (2019). http://www.aph.gov.au/Par liamentary_Business/Bills_Legislation/Bills_Search_Results/Result?bId=r6387

Telecommunications Legislation Amendment (International Production Orders) Bill 2020 (2020)

Patil, S., et al.: Public Perception of Security and Privacy: Results of the comprehensive analysis of PACT's pan-European Survey. PACT Project Consortium (2015)

Patil, V., Shyamasundar, R.K.: Is privacy a myth for Facebook users? In: Proceedings of the 16th International Joint Conference on e-Business and Telecommunications (ICETE 2019), pp. 510–516 (2019)

Price, J.: Quiet Australians, it's time to ask Centrelink for your money back - loudly. The Sydney Morning Herald (2019). http://www.smh.com.au/national/quiet-australians-it-s-time-to-ask-centrelink-for-your-money-back-loudly-20191128-p53f1i.html

Ruiz, K., Moore, C.: Missing the pub this arvo? Well download the COVIDSafe app and we'll open them up, Scott Morrison says. Daily Mail Australia (2020). https://www.dailymail.co.uk/news/article-8276671/Australians-told-return-normal-life-soon-download-Covid-19-app.html

Ryall, J.: Federal police raid home of Australian journalist who revealed government's proposal to spy on the public. Business Insider (2019). http://www.businessinsider.com.au/federal-pol ice-raid-home-of-australian-journalist-who-revealed-governments-plan-to-spy-on-the-public-2019-6

Sky News. Drones Deployed to police social distancing in WA [Press release] (2020). http://www.skynews.com.au/details/_6145829434001

Taylor, J.: Questions remain over whether data collected by Covidsafe app could be accessed by US law enforcement (2020). https://www.theguardian.com/law/2020/may/14/questions-rem ain-over-whether-data-collected-by-covidsafe-app-could-be-accessed-by-us-law-enforcement

The Parliament of the Commonwealth of Australia. Australian Security Intelligence Organisation Legislation Amendment Bill 1999 (1999). https://www.legislation.gov.au/Details/C2004B 00436/Revised%20Explanatory%20Memorandum/Text

The Parliament of the Commonwealth of Australia. Telecommunications and Other Legislation Amendment (Assistance and Access) Bill 2018 - Explanatory Memorandum
(2018). https://parlinfo.aph.gov.au/parlInfo/download/legislation/ems/r6195_ems_1139bfde-
17f3-4538-b2b2-5875f5881239/upload_pdf/685255.pdf;fileType=application/pdf
The Parliament of the Commonwealth of Australia. Explanatory Memorandum: Telecommunications Legislation Amendment (International Productions Orders) Bill 2020 T
(2020a). https://parlinfo.aph.gov.au/parlInfo/download/legislation/ems/r6511_ems_0ac5ae09-
3e3e-400b-ae5e-680a68af4e45/upload_pdf/733176.pdf;fileType=application%2Fpdf
The Parliament of the Commonwealth of Australia. Privacy Amendment (Pubic Health Contact Information) (2020b). http://www.ag.gov.au/RightsAndProtections/Privacy/Documents/
exposure-draft-privacy-amendment-public-health-contact-information.pdf
Tillett, A.: Top bureaucrats deny report cyber agency wants to spy on Australians. Financial
Review (2018). http://www.afr.com/politics/top-bureaucrats-deny-report-cyber-agency-wants-
to-spy-on-australians-20180429-h0ze7a
Turner, J.C.: Explaining the nature of power: a three-process theory. Eur. J. Soc. Psychol. **35:1**,
1–22 (2005)
Universal Declaration of Human Rights (1948)
van Lieshout, M., Friedewald, M., Wright, D., Gutwirth, S.: Reconciling privacy and security.
Innovation **26**(1–2), 119 (2013)
White, N.: Australia's leading coronavirus expert at the World Health Organisation REFUSES to
download the COVIDSafe app - despite Scott Morrison saying it's our key to lifting lockdowns,
News. Daily Mail Australia (2020). http://www.dailymail.co.uk/news/article-8281393/Austra
lian-Infection-expert-REFUSES-download-COVIDSafe-app.html
Wright, D., et al.: Sorting out smart surveillance. Comput. Law Secur. Rev. **26**(4), 343–354 (2010).
https://doi.org/10.1016/j.clsr.2010.05.007
Zedner, L.: Security Key Ideas in Criminology, 3. WorldCat.org database (2009). http://public.
eblib.com/choice/publicfullrecord.aspx?p=425617

Concern for Information Privacy: A Cross-Nation Study of the United Kingdom and South Africa

Adéle Da Veiga[1]([☒]) [iD] and Jacques Ophoff[2,3] [iD]

[1] School of Computing, College of Science, Engineering and Technology,
University of South Africa (UNISA), Florida Campus, Johannesburg, South Africa
dveiga@unisa.ac.za
[2] University of Cape Town, Cape Town, South Africa
[3] Division of Cyber Security, School of Design and Informatics, Abertay University,
Dundee, Scotland
j.ophoff@abertay.ac.uk

Abstract. Individuals have differing levels of information privacy concern, formed by their expectations and the confidence they have that organisations meet this in practice. Variance in privacy laws and national factors may also play a role. This study analyses individuals' information privacy expectation and confidence across two nations, the United Kingdom and South Africa, through a survey of 1463 respondents. The findings indicate that the expectation for privacy in both countries are very high. However, numerous significant differences exist between expectations and confidence when examining privacy principles. The overall results for both countries show that there is a gap in terms of the privacy expectations of respondents compared to the confidence they have in whether organisations are meeting their expectations. Governments, regulators, and organisations with an online presence need to consider individuals' expectations and ensure that controls that meet regulatory requirements, as well as expectations, are in place.

Keywords: Information privacy · Concern · Expectation · South Africa · United Kingdom

1 Introduction

A data subject's (i.e. individual, consumer, citizen) concern for information privacy is an important topic receiving a lot of attention [1–5]. From an organisational perspective, data protection law research examines compliance and issues related to data breaches [6–11]. Consumer expectations, together with whether organisations are indeed meeting such expectations in line with regulatory requirements, is a topic receiving increasing attention. This addresses concern for information privacy [12–14], but also the enhancement of digital trust and organisational compliance [15].

© IFIP International Federation for Information Processing 2020
Published by Springer Nature Switzerland AG 2020
N. Clarke and S. Furnell (Eds.): HAISA 2020, IFIP AICT 593, pp. 16–29, 2020.
https://doi.org/10.1007/978-3-030-57404-8_2

Privacy expectations could vary across groups of citizens based on their demographic profile (such as gender, age, nationality) or varying factors such as culture or recent data breaches that occurred in a country [16]. Some studies show that privacy expectations are lower in the United States, compared to Europe and the United Kingdom, and that women are more concerned about privacy than men [17]. Surveys also show that individuals in the same data protection jurisdiction could have different perceptions and expectations towards their personal information. For example, citizens from Germany and the United Kingdom are more concerned about their personal information than the French [16]. Consumers indicate that they are becoming more concerned about the manner in which organisations are using personal information and are less likely to trust organisations with it [18]. Various studies have focused on concern for information privacy [4, 19–21, 28], but do not necessarily consider individuals' privacy expectations and confidence in whether organisations are meeting such expectations.

This study aims to holistically measure individuals' concern for information privacy by considering their expectations and, in addition, whether they have experienced that organisations do indeed meet their expectations in practice. It aims to answer the following primary research question: How do individual privacy expectations and confidence in organizational practices align? It also considers whether differences could exist between nations. The study was conducted across two nations, the United Kingdom (UK) and South Africa (SA), providing data for comparative purposes. While there is a concern of consumers toward the use of personal information by government and invasion of their privacy from that perspective [25], it was excluded from the scope of this study.

The remainder of this paper proceeds as follows. Section 2 provides an overview of relevant privacy literature and Sect. 3 briefly examines privacy legislation in the target countries. Section 4 reviews the research methodology, followed by results and a discussion of the findings in Sect. 5. Finally, this paper concludes by discussing opportunities for future research.

2 Concern for Information Privacy

Concern for information privacy relates to individuals who have certain concerns about the practices used by responsible parties when processing their personal information [22]. While individuals could have certain privacy expectations there could be risk and potential negative consequences when organisations process their personal information, resulting in concern for their information privacy [4]. Westin developed several surveys to measure concern for information privacy from perspectives such as computer fear, medical, and consumer concerns. He proposed the Concern for Information Privacy (CFIP) Index which is measured using a survey questionnaire. With the growth of the world wide web the Internet Users Information Privacy Concern (IUIPC) survey was developed [23]. The IUIPC or the CFIP of Stewart et al. [24], Smith et al. [22] and Westin [25] were further used in various studies to investigate concern for information privacy. Examples include the work of Heales et al. [20] who integrated global cultural dimensions and investigated the influence of national culture. Fodor and Brem [26] applied the CFIP and IUIPC to study the privacy concerns of millennials in Germany. Similarly, Tanantuputra et al. [27] applied the CFIP of Smith et al. [22] and tested the influence of demographic factors, self-efficacy, computer anxiety, and internet literacy in Malaysia.

The Online Information Privacy Culture Index (OIPCI) [12, 29] was developed to measure consumers' information privacy expectations and whether they experience that online organisations do indeed meet these expectations. This validated instrument was used in this study for data collection and the comparative analysis between SA and the UK.

3   Privacy Regulation

Regulating privacy through laws is a necessity to address information privacy concern of data subjects [2]. Studies show that effective enforcement of privacy laws could decrease concern for information privacy in an online context, but when data subjects perceive that the governance of privacy regulation is weak they have greater privacy concern [2]. Wu et al. [30] argue that while one needs to understand individuals' privacy needs one should also address regulatory requirements. The challenge is that each jurisdiction has its own privacy laws, which are regulated differently. In a global environment online users could be based, and their information processed, across jurisdictions making it a challenge for organisations (website owners) to comply with privacy regulations in each jurisdiction. Wu et al. [30] argues that privacy governance can aid in developing practices and policies meeting higher privacy standards across borders, however organisations could move operations to jurisdictions with no or limited regulations. While this perspective focusses on the implementation of best practices where policies meet higher privacy standards, it cannot be done in isolation of consumer expectations. A consideration is therefore that organisations should understand the privacy expectations of their customers in line with generally accepted privacy principles. They should also map this to legal requirements of the respective jurisdictions they operate in. Where a customer base is in a predominant jurisdiction the generally accepted privacy principles can be mapped to the applicable privacy laws to ensure that legal requirements are complied with whilst meeting customer expectations. From this perspective UK and SA privacy legislation is considered next.

3.1   Privacy Legislation in the UK

Through the Data Protection Act (DPA) 1984 [31] the UK implemented one of world's first measures to protect people's personal information. It was underpinned by fundamental privacy principles and introduced criminal offences for failure to comply [32]. The DPA has since been revised and in its current format, the Data Protection Act 2018, is closely aligned with the EU General Data Protection Regulation (GDPR). It has modernised data protection laws in the UK to be relevant in an online world.

While the DPA empowers citizens to take control of their data it also provides support to organisations to implement required operational changes. The Act is structured into seven parts and includes 20 schedules. In particular, Part 2 (Chapter 1 and 2) supplements GDPR by completing specific member state interpretations and implementations; this includes reference to lawfulness of processing, special categories of personal data, rights (as well as restrictions of rights) of the data subject, accreditation of certification providers, transfers of personal data to third countries, and specific processing situations. Part 5 confirms the Information Commissioner's Office (ICO) as the UK's supervisory authority. Since 2018 enforcement actions include monetary penalties, enforcement notices, prosecutions, and undertakings [33].

Industry reports indicate that the majority (57%) of UK consumers are concerned about the amount of personal data they have shared online. While consumers are concerned about data sharing many (63%) know little or nothing about their rights or legislation such as GDPR [34]. However, indications are that these are declining numbers and that consumers are becoming 'data pragmatists' who are willing to share personal information for clear rewards [35]. Contradictions between the UK public's perception of online privacy and behaviour is not unusual and this phenomenon has been widely studied in different contexts (e.g. Kokolakis [36]). An examination of the privacy paradox among consumers across four UK cities postulates that insufficient education, apathy, and underestimating risks could still be relevant in this context [37].

From an organisational perspective the introduction of GDPR has forced UK organisations to inspect their data processing practices. Research shows that many UK organisations may not be fully aware of the changes in data protection, also at the executive level [38]. This could have significant implications, considering that Section 198 of the DPA includes liability of directors. Another challenge is interpreting the 'regulation's qualitative statements' or accessing external support to do so. This issue can be acute in resource-constrained organisations, such as SMEs [39]. In an effort to support data protection the ICO has published an extensive set of organisational guidelines, specifically aimed at SMEs, that cover the DPA and GDPR as it applies in the UK [40].

3.2 Privacy Legislation in SA

South Africa has lagged in implementing comprehensive privacy legislation. While privacy is addressed to some extent in legal frameworks (e.g. section 14 of the Constitution of the Republic of South Africa (1996) [41] stipulates that all citizens have the right to privacy) the online processing of personal information has been a concerning gap. In this regard legislators have enacted the Protection of Personal Information Act (POPIA) [42] to promote the protection of individuals' data processed by organisations. POPIA incorporates some of the most effective elements from global privacy laws and parallels can be drawn with the EU's approach in implementing the GDPR [43].

The POPIA regulates the processing of personally identifiable information by public and private bodies, aligning with international standards. While exceptions and special cases to conditions exist (e.g. processing after obtaining consent from a data subject) the POPIA is a comprehensive privacy legislation. With the appointment of an information regulator in December 2016 the Act has moved one step closer to implementation. In line with global trends to establish a data protection authority [6] the information regulator will handle data subject complaints, investigations, and impose penalties.

The POPIA presents a positive step for the protection of personal information and should be welcomed by consumers. Prior research has shown that South African citizens have high privacy expectations regarding organisations processing personal information [44]. However, organisational compliance will take significant effort, unless an organisation is already compliant with similar international laws. A particular concern for organisations is how the law will be interpreted (since it is based on privacy principles) by the information regulator, and how penalties will be imposed. Practical difficulties could include change management, adapting employee culture, and implementing new security technologies [45]. It is also recognised that POPIA will impact data management professionals in particular, with several steps necessary to move towards legislative compliance [46].

4   Research Methodology

A quantitative research approach, using a survey, was followed to measure the concern for information privacy in the UK and SA. Quantitative methods are frequently questionnaire-based, which works well for descriptive research where attitude and opinion data are collected and statistically analysed to draw general conclusions [47, 48]. While qualitative methods could give more in-depth insight it was not included in the scope of this study.

4.1   Instrument and Data Collection

As instrument the Online Information Privacy Culture Index (OIPCI) was used. This questionnaire consists of four sections, starting with questions about biographical data and concern for information privacy. The next sections include expectation and confidence items based on 11 components which map to the FIPPS privacy principles, conditions in the DPA (UK), and the principles in POPIA (SA). All measures use a 5-point scale. The expectation items aim to identify whether the consumer has a high or low expectation of a specific privacy principle. The confidence questions measure whether the consumer perceives that organisations indeed conform in practice to meet the respective privacy principle.

An online research platform, Prolific [49], was used to distribute the survey to a representative sample in the UK. The survey was distributed electronically by InSites Consulting [50], a market research company, to consumers in SA. Ethical clearance was obtained prior to data collection to validate that the survey complied with research principles such as being voluntary, anonymous, and that consent was obtained to use the data for research publications.

4.2   Sample

A total of 456 responses were collected in the UK, and 1007 in SA according to the demographic profile of the country (total responses was 1463). The majority of the UK sample were female (69.96%) whereas the SA sample was relatively balanced (51.9% male). The SA participants represented the demographic profile of SA with two thirds being African (black) and in the UK two thirds of the respondents indicated that they were English, as illustrated in Table 1.

The majority of the respondents use their mobile phone (58% SA; 59% UK), followed by a laptop (22% SA; 23% UK), desktop (12%) and tablet (8% SA; 7% UK) to access the

Table 1. Responses per SA and UK demographic profile

South Africa		United Kingdom	
Demographic	Percent	Demographic	Percent
African	63.8%	English	63.7%
Coloured	11.3%	Welsh	3.2%
Indian	4.9%	Scottish	6.2%
Asian	0.2%	Northern Irish	1.7%
White	19.9%	British	8.5%
		Other	14.1%
		Missing	2.6%

Internet. Individuals in both countries mostly go online for purposes such as browsing, e-mail, social media, and banking. Respondents indicated that the scenarios in which they provide their personal information to websites are mostly when purchasing a product or for social media purposes.

5 Results

The SA respondents indicated that they obtain privacy information from the Internet/websites (71%), banks (40%), and organisations to whom they provide their information (29%). Similarly, the UK respondents indicated that they obtain privacy information from the Internet/websites (26.3%), the organisation where they work (10.2%), the government (9.6%), organisations to whom they provide their information (9.6%), and banks (9.4%). Respondents indicated that the preferred places to obtain privacy information were the Internet/websites, banks, government, organisation to whom they provide their personal information, and organisation they work for.

5.1 Expectation Versus Confidence Means

The expectation for privacy in both countries was very high, with the UK being slightly higher (mean of 4.45) than SA (4.43). This shows that consumers expect privacy when sharing their personal information on websites. This could be expected in the UK where data protection laws have been in place for a long time. However, while POPIA has not yet commenced, online users in SA still have a high expectation of privacy.

The difference in expectation versus confidence is illustrated in Fig. 1. The results for both countries show that there is a gap in terms of respondents' privacy expectation compared to the confidence they have in whether organisations are meeting this. The UK respondents were more negative (2.63) compared to the SA respondents (2.93) in terms of their confidence in whether online companies are indeed meeting the regulatory requirements and their expectation for privacy. Correspondingly, the gap between the means for expectation versus confidence questions is higher for the UK (1.82) than SA (1.5).

Fig. 1. Expectation and confidence means: SA and UK

While the DPA has been in place since 1995, UK respondents were less confident that online companies are preserving their privacy. If consumers feel that organisations are not meeting their privacy expectations it indicates that organisations might not meet regulatory requirements as the expectations are in line with the POPIA and DPA requirements.

5.2 Expectations and Confidence Regarding Privacy Principles

The majority of expectation response means for both the UK and SA were above 4.00. Only two statements with the lower means were recorded. The first was the expectation to keep personal information updated, which was higher for SA (3.67 mean, 61% expected this) than the UK (3.32 mean, 42.9% expected this). The second related to whether respondents know where to submit a complaint if they believed an online company did not protect their personal data. More people in SA (3.29, 47.5% agreed) believed they know where to submit a complaint compared to the UK (2.66 mean, 27.8% agreed).

The statement with the highest mean for SA respondents related to the expectation that online companies should only use personal information for the purposes agreed with the data subject and never for other purposes (4.64 mean, 92.2% expected this). Secondly, to use personal information in a lawful manner (4.62 mean, 91.4% expected this). Thirdly, the expectation that online companies should have all the necessary technology and processes in place to protect personal information (4.61 mean, 91% expected this) as well as to protect it when sending it to other countries (4.61 mean, 92.7% expected this). In the UK the expectation statement that had the highest mean was to correct or delete personal information upon request (4.73 mean, 91% expected this). Secondly, to honour the choice if one decides not to receive direct marketing (4.72 mean, 90.4% expected this). Thirdly, to inform the data subject if personal information was lost, damaged, or exposed publicly (4.7 mean, 89.1% expected this).

UK respondents were more negative in terms of whether online companies are meeting privacy requirements and expectations in practice (four statements with a mean below 2.5). They were most negative about whether online companies are only using their personal information for purposes they agreed (2.27 mean, 17.5% were confident). Secondly, they indicated that they are not confident that online companies are ensuring that third-party's have all the necessary technology and processes in place to protect their personal information (2.37 mean, 22.4% were confident). Thirdly, they were not confident that online companies were using their personal information in lawful ways (2.48 means, 23.7% were confident), nor collecting it with their consent (2.49 mean, 25% were confident). The lowest means in the SA data related to the confidence that online companies are informing one if personal information was lost, damaged, or exposed publicly (2.75 mean, 35% expected this). Secondly, respondents were less confident that online companies protect their information when sending it to other countries (2.81 mean, 34% were confident). Thirdly, that personal information is only used for purposes data subjects agreed to (2.84 mean, 36% were confident).

5.3 Significant Country Differences

Table 2 in Appendix A portrays the means of the items for the SA and UK data. The last column indicates the difference in means, in descending order of difference. A positive number indicates that the SA mean was higher. A negative number indicates the UK mean was higher. There were 30 items with a significant difference (indicated with "*") based on Levine's test of significance. The Sig. (2-tailed) value was 0.000 for all the question pairs (significant if $p < 0.05$) and was supported by the t-values.

The SA respondents were significantly more positive than the UK respondents for 22 of the confidence statements. This indicates that, compared to the UK, SA respondents are more confident that online companies are implementing data privacy requirements and thereby meeting their privacy expectations. A reason could be that UK respondents are more aware of the regulatory requirements, having had data privacy law in place for a long time as well as an active regulator issuing fines. In SA POPIA only commenced as of 1 July 2020, which could result in less awareness amongst consumers regarding compliance with the law. However, it could also relate to a difference in national culture or compliance of organisations. This aspect requires further investigation for influencing factors and additional data collection once POPIA has commenced.

Respondents from both countries were negative in terms of whether online companies (websites) take their responsibility to protect individuals' personal information seriously, with the UK (2.77 mean, 31.85 were confident) respondents being significantly more negative compared to the SA respondents (2.98 mean, 39% were confident). It should be noted that in the case of both countries none of the confidence-expectation item pair means correspond, indicating a gap in terms of what online users expect and how they experience their information being used in practice. Of importance is that there are statistically significant (based on the t-tests conducted) differences for all paired items in the SA and UK data. Thus, respondents from both countries have a high expectation for privacy, but are significantly less confident that online companies meet this in practice. This emphasises the concern for privacy from an expectation and compliance perspective for both countries.

6   Conclusion

This study aimed to measure individuals' concern for information privacy by considering their expectations and perceptions whether organisations do indeed meet expectations in practice. The study was conducted in two countries, the UK and SA, providing data for comparative purposes. The expectation for privacy in both countries are very high. The overall results for both countries show that there is a gap in terms of the privacy expectations of respondents compared to the confidence they have in whether organisations are meeting their expectations. The UK respondents are more concerned that online companies are not meeting expectations, which also indicates that regulatory requirements might not be met. Governments, regulators, and organisations with an online presence need to consider the expectations of individuals and ensure that controls for privacy expectations and regulatory requirements for data privacy are in place.

The results highlight the transdisciplinary nature of information privacy and that it is important to consider synergies between individual and organisational research [51]. As POPIA only recently commenced in SA the study can be repeated in future to identify whether concern for information privacy changes once legislation is in place. Further work should also focus on the concern for information privacy between biographical groups and to expand the data collection to qualitative methods.

Acknowledgements. Women in Research Grant of UNISA and NRF Incentive Funding for Rated Researchers grant number: 103965.

Appendix A

Table 2. Means and significant differences (items from [14])

Items – Experience	SA	UK	Diff.
I know where to submit a complaint if I believe an online company (website) did not protect my personal information.*	3.29	2.66	0.63
I expect online companies (websites): ...to keep my personal information updated.*	3.67	3.32	0.35
...to explicitly define the purpose for which they want to use my information.	4.59	4.51	0.08
...to inform me of the conditions for processing my personal information.	4.56	4.49	0.07
...to notify me before they start collecting my personal information.*	4.48	4.43	0.05
...to only use my personal information for purposes I agreed to and never for other purposes.	4.64	4.61	0.03
...not to collect sensitive personal information about me.	4.31	4.3	0.01
...to obtain my consent if they want to use my personal information for purposes not agreed to with them.	4.59	4.62	−0.03
...I expect privacy when an online company (website) has to processes my personal information for services or products.	4.59	4.63	−0.04

(continued)

Table 2. (*continued*)

Items – Experience	SA	UK	Diff.
…to only collect my personal information when I have given my consent; or if it is necessary for a legitimate business reason.	4.58	4.62	−0.04
…to only collect my personal information from myself and not from other sources.	4.49	4.53	−0.04
…to use my personal information in a lawful manner.	4.62	4.67	−0.05
…to have all the necessary technology and processes in place to protect my personal information.	4.61	4.66	−0.05
…to ensure that their third parties (processing my personal information) have all the necessary technology and processes in place to protect my personal information.	4.51	4.56	−0.05
…to protect my information when they have to send it to other countries.	4.61	4.67	−0.06
…to protect my personal information.*	4.56	4.65	−0.09
…to inform me if records of my personal data were lost, damaged or exposed publicly.	4.59	4.7	−0.11
…to give me a choice if I want to receive direct marketing from them.*	4.51	4.63	−0.12
…to honour my choice if I decide not to receive direct marketing.*	4.58	4.72	−0.14
…to correct or delete my personal information at my request.*	4.56	4.73	−0.17
…to only keep my personal information for as long as required for business purposes or regulatory requirements.*	4.26	4.44	−0.18
…not to collect excessive or unnecessary information from me.*	4.35	4.55	−0.2
…to tell me what records of personal information they have about me when I enquire about it.*	4.41	4.68	−0.27
Items – Confidence			
I believe that online companies (websites) are only using my personal information for purposes I agreed to and never for other purposes.*	2.84	2.27	0.57
I feel confident that online companies (websites): …ensure that their third parties have all the necessary technology and processes in place to protect my personal information.*	2.89	2.37	0.52
…are requesting only relevant and not information other than what is needed for them to offer me a service or product.*	3.04	2.54	0.5
…are collecting my personal information only with my consent, or for a legitimate business reason.*	2.92	2.49	0.43
…keep my personal information up to date.*	2.95	2.53	0.42
…are explicitly defining the purpose they want to use my information for.*	2.92	2.5	0.42
…are notifying me before collecting my personal information.*	2.92	2.51	0.41
…have all the necessary technology and processes in place to protect my personal information.*	3	2.62	0.38

(*continued*)

Table 2. (*continued*)

Items – Experience	SA	UK	Diff.
...respect my right to privacy when collecting my personal information for services or products.*	2.87	2.5	0.37
...are using my personal information in lawful ways.*	2.84	2.48	0.36
...adequately inform me of the conditions.*	2.9	2.57	0.33
...are collecting my personal information from legitimate sources. *	2.91	2.62	0.29
...protect my information if they have to send it to other countries.*	2.81	2.53	0.28
...are protecting my personal information.*	2.86	2.59	0.27
...only collect sensitive personal information.*	2.92	2.65	0.27
...are obtaining my consent to use my personal information for purposes other than those agreed to with me.*	2.88	2.62	0.26
...inform me if records of my personal data were lost, damaged or exposed publically.*	2.75	2.52	0.23
I believe that online companies (websites) take their responsibility seriously to protect my personal information.*	2.98	2.77	0.21
I feel confident that if I submit a complaint, believing that an online company (website) did not protect my personal information, that it will be dealt with appropriately by the relevant authorities.*	2.92	2.74	0.18
...will correct or delete my personal information at my request.*	2.98	2.82	0.16
can tell me what records or personal information they have about me.	2.99	2.86	0.13
I believe that online companies (websites) are keeping my personal information indefinitely.	3.26	3.14	0.12
Online companies (websites) always give me a choice to indicate if I want to receive direct marketing from them.	3.14	3.06	0.08
...honour my choice if I do not want to receive direct marketing.	2.93	2.87	0.06

* significant difference between SA and UK mean

References

1. Degirmenci, K.: Mobile users' information privacy concerns and the role of app permission requests. Int. J. Inf. Manag. **50**, 261–272 (2020). https://doi.org/10.1016/j.ijinfomgt.2019.05.010
2. Anic, ID., Škare, V., Kursan, M.I.: The determinants and effects of online privacy concerns in the context of e-commerce. Electron. Commer. Res. Appl. 36 (2019). https://doi.org/10.1016/j.elerap.2019.100868
3. Wang, Y., Herrando, C.: Does privacy assurance on social commerce sites matter to millennials? Int. J. Inf. Manag. **44**, 164–177 (2019). https://doi.org/10.1016/j.ijinfomgt.2018.10.016
4. Yun, H., Lee, G., Kim, D.J.: A chronological review of empirical research on personal information privacy concerns: an analysis of contexts and research constructs. Inf. Manag. **56**, 570–601 (2019). https://doi.org/10.1016/j.im.2018.10.001

5. Kaushik, K., Kumar Jain, N., Kumar Singh, A.: Antecedents and outcomes of information privacy concerns: Role of subjective norm and social presence. Electron. Commer. Res. Appl. **32**, 57–68 (2018). https://doi.org/10.1016/j.elerap.2018.11.003

6. Greenleaf, G.: Systems I Global data privacy laws 2019: 132 national laws & many bills (2019)

7. Custers, B., Dechesne, F., Sears, A.M., et al.: A comparison of data protection legislation and policies across the EU. Comput. Law Secur. Rev. **34**, 234–243 (2018). https://doi.org/10.1016/j.clsr.2017.09.001

8. Chua, H.N., Herbland, A., Wong, S.F., Chang, Y.: Compliance to personal data protection principles: a study of how organizations frame privacy policy notices. Telemat. Inform. **34**, 157–170 (2017). https://doi.org/10.1016/j.tele.2017.01.008

9. Politou, E., Michota, A., Alepis, E., et al.: Backups and the right to be forgotten in the GDPR: an uneasy relationship. Comput. Law Secur. Rev. **34**, 1247–1257 (2018). https://doi.org/10.1016/j.clsr.2018.08.006

10. Tosoni, L.: Rethinking privacy in the council of Europe's convention on cybercrime. Comput. Law Secur. Rev. **34**, 1197–1214 (2018). https://doi.org/10.1016/j.clsr.2018.08.004

11. Liginlal, D., Sim, I., Khansa, L., Fearn, P.: HIPAA privacy rule compliance: an interpretive study using norman' s action theory 5. Comput. Secur. **31**, 206–220 (2011). https://doi.org/10.1016/j.cose.2011.12.002

12. Da Veiga, A.: An information privacy culture instrument to measure consumer privacy expectations and confidence. Inf. Comput. Secur. **26**, 338–364 (2018). https://doi.org/10.1108/ics-03-2018-0036

13. Da Veiga, A.: An information privacy culture index framework and instrument to measure privacy perceptions across nations: results of an empirical study. In: Furnell, S., Clark, N. (eds.) Proceedings of the Eleventh International Symposium on Human Aspects of Information Security & Assurance (HAISA). Plymouth University, Adelaide (2017)

14. Da Veiga, A.: An online information privacy culture. In: Conference on Information Communications Technology and Society (ICTAS), pp. 1–6. IEEE, Durban (2018)

15. Abraham, C., Sims, R.R., Daultrey, S., Buff, A.: How digital trust drives culture change. MIT Sloan Manage. Rev. **60**(3), 1–8 (2019)

16. RSA (2019) RSA Data Privacy & Security Survey (2019)

17. Baruh, L., Secinti, E., Cemalcilar, Z.: Online privacy concerns and privacy management: a meta-analytical review. J. Commun. **67**(1), 26–53 (2017). https://doi.org/10.1111/jcom.12276

18. Sherman, E.: People are concerned about their privacy in theory, not practice, says new study. Fortune (2019)

19. Bellman, S., Johnson, E.J., Kobrin, S.J., Lohse, G.L.: International differences in information privacy concerns: a global survey of consumers. Inf. Soc. **20**, 313–324 (2004). https://doi.org/10.1080/01972240490507956

20. Heales, J., Cockcroft, S., Trieu, V.-H.: The influence of privacy, trust, and national culture on internet transactions. In: Meiselwitz, G. (ed.) SCSM 2017. LNCS, vol. 10282, pp. 159–176. Springer, Cham (2017). https://doi.org/10.1007/978-3-319-58559-8_14

21. Smith, J.H., Milberg, S., Burke, S.: Information privacy: measuring individual's concerns about organisational practice. MIS Q. 167–195 (1995)

22. Smith, H.J., Milberg, S.J., Burke, S.J.: Information privacy: measuring individuals' concerns about organizational practices. MIS Q. **20**, 167 (1996). https://doi.org/10.2307/249477

23. Malhotra, N.K., Kim, S.S., Agarwal, J.: Internet users' information privacy concerns (IUIPC): the construct, the scal. Inf. Syst. Res. **15**, 336–355 (2004)

24. Stewart, K.A., Segars, A.H.: Examination empirical for information privacy of the concern instrument. Inf. Syst. Res. **13**, 36–49 (2002)

25. Kumaraguru, P., Cranor, LF.: Privacy indexes: A survey of westin's studies. Carnegie Mellon Univ CMU-ISRI-5 (2005)

26. Fodor, M., Brem, A.: Computers in human behavior do privacy concerns matter for millennials? Results from an empirical analysis of location-based services adoption in Germany. Comput. Hum. Behav. **53**, 344–353 (2015). https://doi.org/10.1016/j.chb.2015.06.048

27. Tanantaputra, J., Chong, C.W., Rahman, M.S.: Influence of individual factors on concern for information privacy (CFIP), a perspective from Malaysian higher educational students. Libr. Rev. **66**, 182–200 (2017). https://doi.org/10.1108/lr-05-2016-0043

28. Esmaeilzadeh, P.: The effects of public concern for information privacy on the adoption of health information exchanges (HIEs) by healthcare entities. Health Commun. **34**, 1202–1211 (2019). https://doi.org/10.1080/10410236.2018.1471336

29. Da Veiga, A.: An information privacy culture index framework and instrument to measure privacy perceptions across nations: results of an empirical study. In: Proceedings of the Eleventh International Symposium on Human Aspects of Information Security & Assurance (HAISA), pp. 196–209. Plymouth University, Adelaide, Australia (2017)

30. Wu, P.F., Vitak, J., Zimmer, M.T.: A contextual approach to information privacy research. J. Assoc. Inf. Sci. Technol. **00**, 1–6 (2019). https://doi.org/10.1002/asi.24232

31. Data Protection United Kingdom Act (2018)

32. Carey, P.: Data Protection: A Practical Guide to UK and EU Law, 5th edn. Oxford University Press, United Kingdom (2018)

33. Information Commissioner Office (ICO) Information Commissioner Office. In: Inf. Comm. Off. https://ico.org.uk/action-weve-taken/enforcement/

34. Ashford, W.: Most Britons concerned about personal data sharing (2018). https://www.computerweekly.com/news/252436267/Most-Britons-concerned-about-personal-data-sharing

35. Association D& M Data & Marketing Association. In: Data Priv. What Consum. really thinks. https://dma.org.uk/research/data-privacy-what-the-consumer-really-thinks-1

36. Kokolakis, S.: Privacy attitudes and privacy behaviour: a review of current research on the privacy paradox phenomenon. Comput. Secur. **64**, 122–134 (2017). https://doi.org/10.1016/j.cose.2015.07.002

37. Williams, M., Nurse, J.R.C.: Optional data disclosure and the online privacy paradox: a UK perspective. In: Tryfonas, T. (ed.) HAS 2016. LNCS, vol. 9750, pp. 186–197. Springer, Cham (2016). https://doi.org/10.1007/978-3-319-39381-0_17

38. Addis, M., Kutar, M.: The general data protection regulation (GDPR), emerging technologies and UK organisations: Awareness, implementation and readiness. In: Implementation and Readiness. UK Academy for Information Systems Conference Proceedings (2018)

39. Sirur, S., Nurse, J.R., Webb, H.: Are we there yet? Understanding the challenges faced in complying with the general data protection regulation (GDPR). In: Proceedings of the 2nd International Workshop on Multimedia Privacy and Security, pp. 88–95 (2018)

40. Guide to data protection. https://ico.org.uk/for-organisations/guide-to-data-protection/

41. South African Government Constitution of the Republic of South Africa (1996)

42. The Parliament of the Republic of South Africa Protection of Personal Information Act (PoPIA) 4 of 2013. Cape Town (2013)

43. De Bruyn, M.: The protection of personal information (POPI) act-impact on South Africa. Int. Bus. Econ. Res. J. **13**, 1315–1340 (2014)

44. Da Veiga, A.: An information privacy culture instrument to measure consumer privacy expectations and confidence. Inf. Comput. Secur. **26**, 339–364 (2018)

45. Pelteret, M., Ophoff, J.: Organizational information privacy strategy and the impact of the PoPI act. In: 2017 Information Security for South Africa (ISSA), pp. 56–65 (2017). https://doi.org/10.1109/ISSA.2017.8251775

46. Kandeh, A.T., Botha, R.A., Futcher, L.A.: Enforcement of the protection of personal information (POPI) act: perspective of data management professionals. S. Afr. J. Inf. Manag. **20**, 1–9 (2018). https://doi.org/10.4102/sajim.v20i1.917

47. Cresswell, J.W.: Research Design - Qualitative, Quantitative, and Mixed Methods Approaches, 4th edn. SAGE Publications, Los Angeles (2014)
48. Saunders, M., Lewis, P., Thornhill, A.: Research Methods for Business Students, 7th edn. Pearson Education Limited, England (2016)
49. Prolific. https://www.prolific.co/
50. InSites Consulting South Africa. In: InSites Consult. https://insites-consulting.com/. Accessed 5 May 2020
51. Pelteret, M., Ophoff, J.: A review of information privacy and its importance to consumers and organizations. Inf. Sci.: Int. J. Emerg. Transdiscipline **19**, 277–301 (2016)

A Review of Information Security Aspects of the Emerging Covid-19 Contact Tracing Mobile Phone Applications

Georgios Magklaras[1,2(✉)] [iD] and Lucia N. López-Bojórquez[2]

[1] Norwegian Center for Molecular Medicine, University of Oslo, Oslo, Norway
[2] Steelcyber Scientific, Oslo, Norway
georgios@steelcyber.com

Abstract. This paper discusses the aspects of data reliability and user privacy for the emerging practice of mobile phone based contact tracing for the COVID-19 pandemic. Various countries and large technology companies have already used or plan to design and use mobile phone based solutions, in an effort to urgently expedite the process of identifying people who may have been exposed to the disease and limit its spread to the general population. However, serious concerns have been raised both in terms of the validity of the collected data as well as the extent to which implemented approaches can breach the privacy of the mobile phone users. This review examines the weaknesses of existing implementations and concludes with specific recommendations that can contribute towards increasing the safety of infrastructures that collect and process this kind of information, as well as the adoption and acceptance of these solutions from the public.

Keywords: COVID-19 · Contact tracing · Mobile phone · Mobile phone applications · Cybersecurity · Information security · User privacy · Differential privacy · Health records · Bluetooth · Cellular telephony

1 Introduction

On March 11th 2020, the Director General of the World Health Organization (WHO) declared the outbreak of COVID-19 a global pandemic [1]. Emergency measures have fundamentally altered the economy and society on a global scale, as health systems around the world struggled to keep up with the demand for emergency health care [2]. As part of these measures and in an attempt to quickly identify people who may have been exposed to the disease and thus limit its spread to the general population, many governments around the world have deployed mobile phone applications to make the public health process of contact tracing more efficient in a massive scale. A non exhaustive list of countries that were among the first to deploy mobile phone based contract tracing applications include Australia [3], China [4], Israel [5], Norway [6],

© IFIP International Federation for Information Processing 2020
Published by Springer Nature Switzerland AG 2020
N. Clarke and S. Furnell (Eds.): HAISA 2020, IFIP AICT 593, pp. 30–44, 2020.
https://doi.org/10.1007/978-3-030-57404-8_3

Singapore [7] and South Korea [8]. In addition, large technology companies such as Google and Apple are preparing their own infrastructure for COVID-19 contact tracing [9].

Many of the previously mentioned governments that were early adopters of the technology and made the participation of its citizens in electronic contract tracing voluntary have claimed that their applications are safe to use and prompted their citizens to download and use them. However, many technology experts have criticized the technology [10] or expressed concern about its efficacy versus its privacy implications [11]. Moreover, in certain countries, public response to the technology was lukewarm. For instance, India, Singapore and Norway have seen limited user acceptance of these solutions if one examines recently estimated application download numbers [12]. All these facts give merit to a closer examination of the problems of COVID-19 contact tracing solutions.

Before taking a closer look into the problems of contact tracing solutions, it is necessary to provide essential definitions about the concept and the technologies involved in making the transition from manual to electronic procedures.

In public health epidemiological context, contact tracing is the process of identifying persons who may have come into contact with a person whose infection has been confirmed [13]. The infected person is often referred to as the "index case" and all the people that have come into contact that meets certain criteria (proximity, type of transmission, duration) with the index case are referred to as the "contacts". The systemic collection of further information about these contacts aims to isolate them, test them for the infection and treat them where applicable. Depending on the type and expected spread of an outbreak, the process can be recursively repeated for contacts of contacts. The overall aim is to limit the spread of the infection in the general population.

Health authorities follow specific protocols that require manual contact tracing. This means that health workers evaluate the provided information, search for locating the contacts, notify the contacts (phone call) and all this depends on the accuracy of the information that the index case and his/her subsequent contacts can provide. It is thus reasonable to assume that as health infrastructures are strained for resources in a fast spreading infection, the quality as well as the accuracy of manual contact tracing procedure will suffer. This has been confirmed well before the COVID-19 outbreak. In fact, electronic contact tracing has been tested in the pre-COVID-19 world in many epidemiological emergencies, among them the Ebola virus outbreak [14]. Although this study is far from the technology implementation aspects we see in the COVID-19 mobile phone contact tracing solutions, it highlighted the power of the ubiquity of the mobile phone as a tool to aid the monitoring and spread of infectious diseases.

In a post COVID-19 world, governments and technology companies turn to various aspects of mobile and general computing infrastructures to implement contact tracing solutions. In particular, most COVID-19 contact tracing solutions make use of the following mobile phone technologies:

A) The use of Global Positioning System and Assisted GPS (A-GPS) [15] technology: Every mobile phone has an embedded GPS receiver and through to complimentary components of a 3GPP compliant [16, 17] telecommunications infrastructure, a time series of GPS coordinates of the mobile device can be recorded. Features like the Google Account Location history [18], as well as the Chinese [4], Israeli [5] and Norwegian

[6] contact tracing applications make use of the position/location data. Google has also used location data during the COVID-19 pandemic to estimate the extent of the imposed quarantine measures in various countries with the so called 'mobility reports' [19].

B) The use of the Bluetooth protocol [20]: The Bluetooth protocol is a complex wireless technology standard that encompasses different modes of transmission and functionality. The relevant bits to contact tracing concern its low energy variant called Bluetooth LE [21]. This variant is used to perform proximity sensing calculations. The calculations are used to estimate the distance between the index case and the contacts and thus play a crucial role in most COVID-19 contact tracing application implementations. Another crucial aspect that concerns the Bluetooth operation is that the technology is used to exchange data between devices. Latter paragraphs will describe that process in more detail.

C) The increase in power and data storage in mobile phones, as well as the ubiquity of reliable 3G/4G (and in the near future 5G) connections create powerful ways of constructing big data sets with different levels of anonymity and susceptibility to linkage attacks [22]. Most of the solutions claim that they take precautions to anonymize the data they exchange. Data exchange and collection can also occur in de-centralized or centralized ways. This has different implications for the privacy of the users that contribute the data in question.

Leaving the substantial variations among existing different COVID-19 contact tracing implementations to the side, in simple terms, when a user downloads a contact tracing application to a smartphone, the device will in principle perform the following actions:

A) Activate the Bluetooth LE interface and will broadcast its presence by means of transmitting an anonymous identifier. The transmission of the identifier is performed repeatedly in the form of a beacon.
B) Use the same Bluetooth LE interface to record received anonymous identifiers of other mobile phones within range.
C) For every received/intercepted anonymous Bluetooth LE identifier, the phone will attempt to estimate its proximity. This proximity sensing step is crucial to the validity of the sampled data.
D) The collected data are stored in the smartphone but are handled in different ways. An abstraction of such a record could look like the ones below:

$$r : time, date, BLE\_id, proximity\_estimation, covid19\_flag$$
OR
$$r : time, date, BLE\_id, proximity\_estimation, A\_GPS\_data, covid19\_flag$$

where BLE_ID is the anonymous identifier, proximity_estimation represents a distance (meters), A_GPS_data represent location data of the smartphone according to the data collected by its A-GPS receiver and finally covid19_flag represents whether the user of the smartphone has disclosed (voluntarily) whether he is infected with COVID-19. Different contact tracing implementations upload these records (with the user's consent) to different types of central database infrastructures for processing.

For the purposes of clarity, we need to emphasize not all mobile application implementations collect GPS data (A_GPS_data field). The collection of location data creates privacy concerns that are discussed in Sect. 3 of this paper. The A_GPS_data field can collect other forms of location data (Cell tower ID) to aid the accuracy of the proximity sensing process in various ways.

A central database will process the collected records with particular emphasis on the records that have the covid19_flag set and the proximity_estimation within a certain range (say for instance less than 2 m or less). Consequently, it is possible to message alert all users that have been within a pre-defined proximity and time exposure of a specific BLE_id whose smartphone user has declared his/her infection.

It is therefore evident that smartphones can provide time, location and proximity data that public health authorities consider valuable, in order to alert the general population [23]. This process forms the very basis of smartphone based COVID-19 contact tracing and will be used as a reference mechanism for analysis for the rest of this paper.

The following sections will focus on various implementation details of the reference mechanism. Section 2 will discuss information security aspects that concern the use of the Bluetooth LE protocol, its data accuracy, as well as its various information security weaknesses. Section 3 elaborates on the privacy aspects of storing anonymous data in central infrastructures. The fourth and final section of the paper concludes with concrete recommendations that aim to improve the security of electronic contact tracing solutions.

2 Bluetooth LE Issues and Contact Tracing

The Bluetooth protocol is a vast and complex specification [20]. Different versions and smartphone chipset implementations can result in different operational and information security aspects of its use for the purposes of contact tracing. However, in broad terms, these aspects touch on three different areas. The first is the area of user privacy. One needs to question what is the likelihood that a user can be identified as a result of the Bluetooth data exchange necessary to facilitate contact tracing. A second question relates to how accurate are the data collected by Bluetooth LE for the purposes of contact tracing. Finally, a third question to raise is what are the security implications of using it to broadcast your (in theory anonymous) presence and exchange data with devices you do not know.

Bluetooth LE allows device manufacturers to use temporary random addresses in over-the-air communication instead of their permanent address to prevent tracking, as part of the Bluetooth Core Specification version 4 [24, 25]. Earlier versions of the Bluetooth Core Specification were broadcasting the interface MAC address, a permanent identifier that is unique for every smartphone [26] and could thus be used to track an individual. While Bluetooth Core Specification version 4 addresses this issue, it also leaves gaps that could be exploited and lead, under specific circumstances, to identification of individuals.

Jameel and Dungen [27] examined Bluetooth LE beacon protocols and an array of mechanisms that facilitate localized interactions with smartphones and other Bluetooth devices via the beacon mechanisms. The advlib library [28] is a product of their work which allows software developers to easily integrate Bluetooth LE beacon advertising-based functionality into their applications, without having to embed them into the low-level protocol mechanisms. However, the practical application of this work for an adversary is that the library could be used to identify Bluetooth powered devices. While it is not possible to track a specific individual by making use of this mechanism, identifying that someone has a specific phone and a specific accessory in an area with a limited number of people could aid the process of adversarial reconnaissance aiming towards personal identification.

Becker, *et al.* [29] proceed further and demonstrate that even current Bluetooth LE anonymization measures are vulnerable to passive tracking. Their work proposes an address-carryover algorithm that exploits the asynchronous nature of the Bluetooth LE payload and achieves tracking that bypasses the attempted address randomization of a device. The worrying aspect of their study and experimental setup is that it does not use differential cryptanalysis to decrypt the content of Bluetooth LE communication. Their method works entirely by intercepting public, unencrypted Bluetooth LE advertising traffic which is necessary for steps A and B of the abstracted COVID-19 contact tracing procedure outlined in Sect. 1 of this paper. It is broad, in the sense that it is effective against all iOS, macOS and Windows 10 devices.

Another worrying aspect of the work outlined in [29] and also supported by other theoretical and experimental work [30, 31] is that despite the existence of Bluetooth MAC address randomization mechanisms to achieve anonymity, not all device manufacturers and operating system/application authors choose to employ them in the same way. There is a certain amount of flexibility in how to implement and transmit these randomized identifiers. These might include standard ways but different operating systems and applications might embed additional information as part of the Bluetooth LE public beacon payloads for the purposes of incorporating customized functionality. This additional information often leaks vital identity aspects and is dictated by software, from the operating system all the way to the application layer. Consequently, different COVID-19 contact tracing applications diverge substantially from whatever the relevant Bluetooth standards dictate and offer different levels of user privacy.

As far as the data accuracy of Bluetooth LE collected data is concerned, there are also serious doubts expressed by experts. Step C of the abstracted COVID-19 contact tracing procedure (Sect. 1 of this paper) attempts to estimate the distance of an intercepted Bluetooth LE beacon. The question here is with what accuracy can Bluetooth LE determine whether the user of another smartphone is closer than a predetermined distance (say 2 m). The best way to answer that question is to understand the mechanism employed to measure that distance.

The Bluetooth protocol uses the Received Signal Strength Indicator (RSSI) to measure distance between devices [32]. The principle is that the stronger the signal, the closer the devices are to each other, so a correlation between sensed signal strength and distance can be approximated. However, different bluetooth chipset implementations utilize the RSSI in slightly different ways. While appropriate calibration can reduce these inaccuracies, the problems do not stop there. The Bluetooth LE transmission frequency often interferes with other devices in the 2.4 GHz range, such as older WiFi routers, unshielded USB cables and microwave ovens. A Bluetooth LE device would do its best to extend the 'beacons' (advertisement of presence and availability) by keeping constant time and regulating the transmission power to overcome other sources of interference. In such a frequency congested environment, a real distance of 1.5 m could really be estimated as 2.5 m (false negative), or a real distance of 2.5 m could be estimated to under 1.5 m (false positive). Many experts, amongst them the Bluetooth inventors Jaap Haartsen and Sven Mattisson, agree that these proximity sensing inaccuracies were and remain a limiting factor [33]. As a result, the accuracy of the collected proximity data will be reduced and further post processing steps are needed, in order to allow someone to derive safe conclusions about who is in real danger to get infected due to proximity.

Finally, an often overlooked aspect of Bluetooth LE is its transmission range. While Bluetooth LE version 4 has a Line Of Sight (LOS) beacon range of 430 m, the next major version of the protocol specification (v5) extends that LOS range to 780 m [34]. At the time of writing, most mobile phones will be supporting Bluetooth LE version 5 within the next 12 months. If every smarthphone used to perform many personal and business critical things (e-banking, remote control of systems at work, email) has yet another interface that advertises the presence of an individual (apart from the 4G/5G and WiFi interfaces), this provides an advantage for an adversary and can act as a catalyst for cyberattack vectors. The fact is that bluesnarfing attacks against mobile phones have been identified from the early adoption days of the bluetooth protocol [35]. Moreover, there is good evidence that these attacks have persisted over a number of years [36] and will continue to persist with many recent notable examples that target bluetooth device firmware features [37, 38]. The conclusion derived by this body of work is that the COVID-19 contact tracing applications increase the exploitable attack footprint of the average smartphone.

3   Privacy and Security Aspects of Storing and Processing Contact Tracing Data

The COVID-19 contact tracing data collected by smartphones always require some data entry processing backend (central server or servers that operate independently). However, there are different degrees of data centralization among the various solutions. For instance, the Norwegian [6] and Singaporean [7] contact tracing implementation are some of the paradigms that require all collected data to be centralized for further processing. In direct contrast, the Temporary Contact Numbers (TCN) protocol [39] as well as the Decentralized Privacy-Preserving Proximity Tracing (DP-3T) protocol [40] constitute examples of protocols that are designed to minimize both the amount of info as well as the necessary processing in a centralized infrastructure. Google and Apple seem to follow the decentralized approach [9].

Prior discussing the relative merits of centralized versus decentralized COVID-19 contact tracing approaches and beyond the Bluetooth LE related privacy threats discussed in Sect. 2, it is useful to examine the context of what user privacy means when combined with a justified need to enhance the tools that health authorities can utilize to effectively contain the spread of a pandemic.

The European Union is among the major global players that have officially recognized the potential of smartphone and associated technological solutions to fight the

COVID-19 pandemic [41]. Part of this recognition is made amidst the presence of comprehensive regulations such as GDPR [42] that set very strict requirements for the storage and processing of personal information. Many countries have modified their national data protection laws to make urgent allowances for the data collection and processing of personal data related to the COVID-19 pandemic [43]. As an example, the Norwegian National Data Protection Authority (Datatilsynet) has explicitly permitted non anonymous location data processing for the purposes of COVID-19 smartphone contact tracing, only if it is not possible to derive safe conclusions from anonymous proximity based data [44]. These steps indicate that there is a need for balance between personal privacy and public health [45].

It is outside the scope of this paper to pass a judgement on whether amendments to national legislations should favor privacy over public health or vice versa. The goal of this review is to highlight what is in favor of the privacy of the smartphone user and thus help specialists and policy makers to implement electronic contact tracing in the least privacy intrusive manner. Achieving such a goal is not always trivial and it will require adherence to international standards. Validated international standards for smartphone based contact tracing do not exist at the time of writing. What does exist is a set of EU recommendations [46] that dictate a set of principles relevant to user privacy in the context of electronic contact tracing. In particular, the EU recommendations dictate that all smartphone based contact tracing solutions should:

A) Operate on anonymized data with the goal of alerting users that have been in close proximity to confirmed cases without revealing the identity of the index case or the contacts. Breach of anonymity and hence disclosure of the identity details of an individual
B) Not track the location of the users.
C) Be based on voluntary user participation. Any unauthorized usage of data without the knowledge or the approval of the user is strictly prohibited.
D) The entire infrastructure should be secure and effective end to end. This includes any centralized components where data are deposited for processing.
E) There need to be interoperable and scalable across a number of countries, as people travel from country to country.

Having these requirements as a guide, one of the first conclusions we can derive is that any solution that stores, sends and processes GPS and A-GPS data is not acceptable from a privacy perspective. A time series of GPS coordinates or other network assisted location data (cell tower ID) is personal information and whether deposited partly or completely in a central database server reveals too much information for a user. Research efforts that propose privacy preserving location based contact tracing exist. MIT researchers have proposed a contact tracing system based on a method that redacts, transforms and encrypts GPS coordinates to address the privacy preservation problem [47]. The contact tracing is then computed by a process known as Private Set Intersection (PSI), a technique commonly employed as part of secure multiparty computing [48], aiming to reveal only the common data values that are necessary for the computation.

However, privacy preserving contact tracing techniques that use GPS coordinates constitute best effort experimental approaches that need a reference implementation to be tested and proven. An additional practical matter is that of accuracy. GPS and A-GPS coordinates cannot at the moment provide a level of accuracy in terms of contact proximity and this is why most solutions today resort to the use of Bluetooth LE, even with the problems discussed in Sect. 2 of this paper. A last practical aspect concerns compliance to existing legislation. If the law does not provide a clear framework for the sampling of location data for health related purposes, then it is not possible to employ these techniques and thus approaches that rely on geolocating the users will be impractical and impossible to implement.

Researchers that are proponents of techniques that employ GPS coordinates [47] point out that large companies already collect user location data for operational and advertisement purposes. While this is true [18, 19], there is a distinct difference between geolocating individuals for commercial purposes and doing the same in a health context. Apart from the location info this kind of contact tracing solutions contain references to health status (infected or not infected status of an individual). Combining personal location info to health status raises the legal context and regulatory handling requirements of the collected/processed information. For instance, the European Data Protection Supervisor considers all data concerning health as a special category [49, 50] for which strict privacy preserving requirements apply when it comes to the handling and processing of the collected information.

The concentration of large amounts of (theoretically) anonymous health related information in central repositories for the purposes of centralized contact tracing solutions [6, 7] creates certain risks and operational requirements for the storage and processing of the data. Weaknesses in the anonymity protocols (such as the ones described in Sect. 2 of this paper in connection to the Bluetooth LE protocol) or in the implementation of infrastructures could place a malicious adversary in a situation to collect information that could compromise the privacy of millions of individuals. The handling of large amounts of anonymous (or desensitized) health data predates the electronic contact tracing era and can be observed in other fields of health informatics. A good example is that of genomic medicine where certain types of genomic data, even if they have been anonymised in principle, they do provide distinct probable ways to re-identify the subjects of a study [51]. For these reasons, access to these types of data requires data consumers to follow certain ethical guidelines that bind them not to use them in ways that could re-identify the anonymised study subjects and conform to strict storage and data processing requirements [52].

On the other hand, centralized processing requirements are simpler to implement in principle when compared to decentralized contact tracing solutions such as those proposed in [39] and [40]. In general terms, the aim of decentralized contract tracing solutions is to reduce the privacy and security impact of having all the necessary data in one place. They still require a minimal centralized component, especially for steps that incorporate the health status (infected or not infected contact), however the disclosure of information to central entities is minimal by design. This reduces the possibility for abuse of central data repositories. However, decentralized solutions delegate the processing of info to non trusted devices (the smartphones of the users). This increases implementation complexity. The entire concept has not been yet proven at scale, both in theory and practice. Most existing contact tracing solutions follow the centralized storage and information processing model at the time of writing.

A final consideration has to do with how the central IT infrastructure for contract tracing solutions are implemented. There seems to be certain lack of transparency on how this central part has been implemented. Taking Norway as an example, a country with good tradition on respecting the privacy of its citizens and among the first to launch a COVID-19 contact tracing application, it is evident that no tender processes have been disclosed for awarding public funds to construct the application [53], calls to open source the application in order to aid the review by security experts were denied [54] and that data that contain GPS, Bluetooth LE smartphone identifiers and health status were stored in private cloud vendors [55] with unclear status on whether the data can leave the Norwegian geographic border. As a result, the Norwegian implementation drew a lot of criticism by many IT experts around the world [56]. This is by no means unique to Norway. Other countries have faced similar criticism.

Transparency of data processing, as well as export control of health data are issues that should be taken seriously as dictated by pan European (GDPR) and other international legislation [57]. Besides compliance, choices that limit transparency make public acceptance of a technology difficult. Thus, it is evident that implementing contact tracing technology should be a process with structure and best practices that are missing at the moment. This structure and recommended practices forms the subject of the next section of this paper.

4 Conclusions and Recommendations for Implementing Electronic Contact Tracing Solutions

The previous sections of this paper have highlighted that the existing COVID-19 contact tracing applications have serious problems, both in terms of the reliability of the collected data sets, as well as in terms of preserving the end user privacy and security. Addressing these problems is not a trivial process and will require substantial efforts towards the creation of standards that oversee the development of contact tracing platforms. The existing EU recommendations [46] that were discussed in Sect. 3 of this paper can serve as a good start on a road map that will make electronic contact tracing both usable and acceptable by societies around the world.

On the issues of Bluetooth LE accuracy discussed in Sect. 2 [33], there are research and development approaches aiming to increase the proximity sensing accuracy of the protocol. Examples of such work can be found in [58, 59]. It is also possible that smartphone chipset manufacturers together with future versions of the Bluetooth LE protocol will add features that will increase the proximity sensing accuracy. However, no matter what technological measures are employed to achieve additional proximity sensing precision, the important thing is to put them to the test in a standard manner. The only reliable way to do this is to set control experiments where a group of individuals using smartphones can create verified/predetermined contacts under a variety of conditions (inside buildings with different level of RF noise environments different contact times and different number of individuals). If the subsequent analysis of the recorded data accurately represents the verified/predetermined conditions within a predetermined statistical accuracy (say less than 1% for both false positives or negatives) then this means that the data collected by a contact tracing implementation is good enough to be used for the public. Launching an application on a national scale without proving the accuracy of the sampled data and verifying it by statisticians and experts can lead to misleading results and should be avoided.

When it comes to the rest of the vulnerabilities of the Bluetooth LE protocol (range on LOS and software vulnerabilities discussed in Sect. 2 and referenced in [34–38]), there are various measures to be taken. It is prudent that the Bluetooth LE power is regulated in a standardized manner when operating a contact tracing application, so that the effective range of the protocol is reduced. Setting devices to the lowest power level to perform reliably proximity sensing will reduce the effective adversarial surveillance range [60]. In addition, smartphone manufacturers need to do a better job in addressing the firmware and mobile operating system vulnerabilities, especially for the older smartphone devices. As an example, in the Android mobile operating system, critical Bluetooth vulnerabilities such as the 'BlueFrag' CVE-2020-0022 [61] affected mainly older versions of the Android system for several months. While the vulnerability in question has been patched at the time of writing, not all Android device manufacturers have included this patch in their Android OEM versions. The result is that a substantial number of smartphone users that still operate Android version 8 are vulnerable if they use contact tracing and other Bluetooth based data exchange applications. Thus, it is our view that world wide or regional regulations should make mandatory that all smartphone vendors issue critical system updates throughout the expected life cycle of a smartphone (3–5 years).

Drawing upon the EU contact tracing implementation requirements [46], we advise against the usage of any location data (GPS, A-GPS, cell tower ID or other) in electronic contact tracing solutions. Apart from conflicts with data protection legislation discussed in Sect. 3 [49, 50], we do not see how location data can enhance the contact discovery. For the purposes of contact tracing, the Bluetooth LE proximity collected data are more relevant and accurate than any other form of satellite or network assisted location system. Incorporating location data, even when anonymised/desensitized increases the susceptibility of the collected data to differential privacy attacks [62], especially in implementations where the data is centralized and should be avoided.

We do not have enough data on existing implementations to recommend whether existing decentralized approaches should be favored over centralized approaches. As discussed in Sect. 3 of this paper there are certain advantages and disadvantages for each of these approaches. Decentralized approaches follow the principle of minimizing the amount of information necessary to perform the contact tracing, however they add implementation complexity and require information to be distributed to untrusted entities. While decentralized approaches look promising, they require further theoretical and practical implementation validation by experts, before definite conclusions are drawn. However, as both approaches require some main IT infrastructure component beyond the information gathered by smartphones, the following paragraphs discuss some concrete recommendations that can aid the security of electronic contact tracing solutions.

Section 3 discussed the paradigm of genomic medicine data [51] and its analogy to that of electronic contact tracing solutions. The common denominator is the presence of a large amount of anonymized health data. Whatever cryptographic precautions can be taken to protect the identity of the contact tracing users, this does not change the fact that a large amount of information about public health is stored in one form or another (centralized versus decentralized, different encryption standards). In our view, this should be good enough to treat this kind of anonymous data in the same way as eponymous medical data. This view is supported by existing data classification policies that form part of Information Security Management practices [63]. As an example, the University of Oslo, the largest and oldest academic institution in Norway, manages large amounts of electronic information, including sensitive eponymous data from the Oslo University Hospital. For that reason, its information security management system [64] classifies large amounts of anonymous health data at the highest level of data sensitivity [65]. This has several implications about how anonymised contract tracing information should be stored and processed.

Infrastructures that hold eponymous sensitive medical data and have approval by relevant national data protection authorities implement a lot of technical requirements to ensure that the confidentiality, integrity and availability of the sensitive data is safeguarded. Drawing from the University of Oslo's paradigm, its 'Services for Sensitive Data (TSD)' platform [66] is a practical implementation that provides these safeguards. Elements such as multi-factor authentication [67], compartmentalization of computation activities on security hardened virtual machines and storage/backup encryption are some of the techniques employed by TSD. In our view, these should be mandatory technical elements that should form a standard for every core IT infrastructure platform that handles electronic contact tracing data at national/international level. In addition, core IT infrastructures should comply to GDPR [42] and possibly the HIPAA standard [68]. Compliance to these standards can also aid the interoperability among different national contact tracing solutions across a number of countries and continents. EU requirements dictate that contact tracing solutions should be interoperable [46].

Finally, as the use of cloud computing is increasing and the pressure for healthcare systems to be more cost effective is growing [69], there are certain risks associated to placing public health data in the cloud. A principal risk is that many large private cloud providers offer a utility service without safeguarding (or even wanting to know) the criticality and importance of the data and the tasks performed in their infrastructure [70]. When private cloud providers are used for core IT contact tracing infrastructure, we recommend three concrete rules. The first is that private cloud providers should comply to the same technical requirements and regulations set of the previous paragraph. In addition and as a consequence of regulatory compliance, private cloud providers should provide IT infrastructures within the geographical territory of the country/region if laws dictate the data should be localized. A third recommendation is that an independent cost-risk analysis should be commissioned prior reaching decisions to store and process contact tracing data exclusively in private cloud providers. A better approach is to adopt hybrid cloud technologies, where a public authority can have the option of easily turning the data and compute activities back to their own infrastructure, in case they face legislation or data availability problems.

References

1. WHO announces COVID-19 outbreak a pandemic. http://www.euro.who.int/en/health-top ics/health-emergencies/coronavirus-covid-19/news/news/2020/3/who-announces-covid-19-outbreak-a-pandemic. Accessed 25 May 2020
2. Remuzzi, A., Remuzzi, G.: COVID-19 and Italy: what next? Lancet **395**(10231), 1225–1228 (2020). https://doi.org/10.1016/S0140-6736(20)30627-9
3. Australian Government Department of Health, COVIDsafe application website. https://www.health.gov.au/resources/apps-and-tools/covidsafe-app. Accessed 25 Apr 2020
4. The Chinese QR code scanning based contact tracing application (in Mandarin Chinese). https://mp.weixin.qq.com/s/amB7fBxLw8KSR9DcUsbTWg. Accessed 25 May 2020
5. Israeli Ministry of Health, HaMagen contact tracing application website. https://govextra.gov.il/ministry-of-health/hamagen-app/download-en/. Accessed 25 May 2020
6. Norwegian Government Health Portal, 'Smittestopp' contact tracing application website (in Norwegian). https://helsenorge.no/coronavirus/smittestopp. Accessed 25 May 2020
7. Government of Singapore, 'TraceTogether' contact tracing application website. https://www.tracetogether.gov.sg/. Accessed 25 May 2020
8. Baleun, S., Minji, K.: Mobile apps, websites offer real-time data on Covid-19 outbreak, Korea.net web portal (2020). http://www.korea.net/NewsFocus/Society/view?articleId=183129. Accessed 25 May 2020
9. Apple & Google Corporation proposal on Privacy-Preserving Contact Tracing. https://www.apple.com/covid19/contacttracing. Accessed 25 May 2020
10. Soltani, A., Calo, R., Bergstrom, C.: Contact-tracing apps are not a solution to the COVID-19 crisis Brookings TechStream (2020). https://www.brookings.edu/techstream/inaccurate-and-insecure-why-contact-tracing-apps-could-be-a-disaster/. Accessed 25 May 2020
11. Zastrow, M.: Coronavirus contact-tracing apps: can they slow the spread of COVID-19? Nat. Technol. Features (2020). https://doi.org/10.1038/d41586-020-01514-2
12. Findlay, S., Palma, S., Milne, R.: Coronavirus contact-tracing apps struggle to make an impact. Financial Times (2020). https://www.ft.com/content/21e438a6–32f2-43b9-b843-61b 819a427aa. Accessed 25 Apr 2020
13. Scutchfield, F.D., Keck, C.W.: Principles of Public Health Practice, 2nd edn., p. 71. Delmar Learning, Clifton Park (2003). ISBN 0-76682843-3
14. Danquah, L.O., et al.: Use of a mobile application for Ebola contact tracing and monitoring in Northern Sierra Leone: a proof-of-concept study. BMC Infect. Dis. **19**, 810 (2019). https://doi.org/10.1186/s12879-019-4354-z
15. Kaplan, E., Hegarty, C.J.: Understanding GPS/GNSS: Principles and Applications, 3rd edn. GNSS Technology and Applications Series, Artech House (2017)
16. Holma, H., Toskala, A.: LTE Advanced: 3GPP Solution for IMT-Advanced, 1st edn. Wiley, Hoboken (2012). ISBN-13: 978-1119974055
17. Frith, J.: Smartphones as locative media. Digital Media and Society Series, 1st edn. Polity Press, UK (2015). ISBN-13: 978-0745685014
18. Jonnalagada, H.: How to view your location history in Google Maps Androidcentral website (2018). https://www.androidcentral.com/how-view-your-location-history-google-maps
19. Google Corporation, COVID-19 Community Mobility Reports website. https://www.google.com/covid19/mobility/. Accessed 25 May 2020
20. Huang, A.S., Rudolph, L.: Bluetooth Essentials for Programmers. Cambridge University Press, UK (2007)
21. Townsend, K., Cuff, C., Davidson, R.: Getting Started with Bluetooth Low Energy: Tools and Techniques for Low-Power Networking. O'Reilly Press, Sebastopol (2014)

22. Menerer, M.M.: Theoretical results on de-anonymization via linkage attacks. Trans. Data Priv. **5**, 377–402 (2012)
23. Servick, K.: COVID-19 contact tracing apps are coming to a phone near you. How Will We Know Whether They Work? AAAS Science (2020). https://doi.org/10.1126/science.abc9379
24. Bluetooth Special Interest Group (SIG). Bluetooth Core Specification. v4.0. Bluetooth Special Interest Group (2010). https://www.bluetooth.com/specifications/archived-specifica tions/. Accessed 25 May 2020
25. Wooley, M.: Bluetooth Technology Protecting Your Privacy. Bluetooth website (2015). https://www.bluetooth.com/blog/bluetooth-technology-protecting-your-privacy/. Accessed 25 Apr 2020
26. Spill, D., Bittau, A.: BlueSniff: eve meets alice and bluetooth. In: WOOT 2007 Proceedings of the First USENIX Workshop on Offensive Technologies, no. 5, pp. 1–10. ACM Inc (2007)
27. Jameel, M.I., Dungen, D.: Low-power wireless advertising software library for distributed M2M and contextual IoT. In: 2015 IEE 2nd World Forum on Internet of Things (WF-IoT), pp. 597–602. Milan (2015). https://doi.org/10.1109/wf-iot.2015.7389121
28. Advlib Github Repo. https://reelyactive.github.io/advlib/. Accessed 25 May 2020
29. Becker, J.K., Li, D., Starobinski, D.: Tracking anonymized bluetooth devices. In: Proceedings on Privacy Enhancing Technologies, no. 3, pp. 50–65. Sciendo (2019). https://doi.org/10.2478/popets-2019-0036
30. Issoufaly, T., Tournoux, P.U.: BLEB: bluetooth low energy botnet for large scale individual tracking. In: 1st International Conference on Next Generation Computing Applications, NextComp, pp. 115–120. IEEE (2017)
31. Vanhoef, M., Matte, C., Cunche, M., Cardoso, L.S., Piessens, F.: Why MAC address randomization is not enough. In: Proceedings of the 11th ACM on Asia Conference on Computer and Communications Security - ASIA CCS 2016, pp. 413–424. ACM Press, New York (2016)
32. Proximity and RSSI. Bluetooth Blog. https://www.bluetooth.com/blog/proximity-and-rssi/. Accessed 25 May 2020
33. Biddle, S.: The inventors of Bluetooth say there could be problems using their tech for coronavirus contact tracing. The Intercept (2020). https://theintercept.com/2020/05/05/cor onavirus-bluetooth-contact-tracing/. Accessed 25 May 2020
34. Karvonen, H., Pomalaza-Ráez, C., Mikhaylov, K., Hämäläinen, M., Iinatti, J.: Experimental performance evaluation of BLE 4 Versus BLE 5 in indoors and outdoors scenarios. In: Fortino, G., Wang, Z. (eds.) Advances in Body Area Networks I, pp. 235–251. Springer, Cham (2019)
35. Jamaluddin, J., Zotou, N., Edwards, R., Coulton, P.: Mobile phone vulnerabilities: a new generation of malware. In: IEEE International Symposium on Consumer Electronics 2004, pp. 199–202. Reading, UK (2004). https://doi.org/10.1109/isce.2004.1375935
36. Xu, J., et al.: Pairing and authentication security technologies in low-power Bluetooth. In: 2013 IEEE International Conference on Green Computing and Communications and IEEE Internet of Things and IEEE Cyber, Physical and Social Computing, pp. 1081–1085. Beijing (2013). https://doi.org/10.1109/greencom-ithings-cpscom.2013.185
37. Sivakumaran, P., Blasco, J.: A study of the feasibility of co-located app attacks against BLE and a large-scale analysis of the current application-layer security landscape. In: Proceedings of the 28th USENIX Security Symposium, pp. 1–18. Santa Clara, CA (2019)
38. Antonioli, D., Tippenhauer, N.O., Rasmussen, K.B.: The KNOB is broken: exploiting low entropy in the encryption key negotiation of bluetooth BR/EDR. In: Proceedings of the 28th USENIX Security Symposium, pp. 1047–1061. Santa Clara, CA (2019)
39. Temporary Contact Numbers (TCN) Protocol. https://github.com/TCNCoalition/TCN/com mit/1b68b920db1fb42709c7c8eb28c3d5e10c76fc3c. Accessed 25 May 2020
40. Decentralized Privacy-Preserving Proximity Tracing Protocol. https://github.com/DP-3T/doc uments/blob/master/DP3T%20White%20Paper.pdf. Accessed 25 May 2020

41. European Commission Press Release. Coronavirus: Guidance to ensure full data protection standards of apps fighting the pandemic, April 2020. https://ec.europa.eu/commission/pressc orner/detail/en/ip_20_669. Accessed 25 May 2020

42. Voigt, P., Von Dem Bussche, A.: The EU General Data Protection Regulation (GDPR). A Practical Guide, First edn. Springer, Heidelberg (2017). https://doi.org/10.1007/978-3-319-57959-7

43. The international association of privacy professionals. DPA guidance on COVID-19. https://iapp.org/resources/article/dpa-guidance-on-covid-19/. Accessed 25 May 2020

44. Norwegian Data Protection Authority Datatilsynet, Declaration on COVID-19 and processing of personal data (in Norwegian). https://www.datatilsynet.no/personvern-pa-ulike-omrader/korona/erklaring-fra-personvernradet/?id=12303. Accessed 25 May 2020

45. Kapa, S., Halamka, J., Raskar, R.: Contact tracing to manage COVID-19 spread – balancing personal privacy and public health. Mayo Clin. Proc. (2020, in press). https://doi.org/10.1016/j.mayocp.2020.04.031

46. European commission press release. Coronavirus: An EU approach for efficient contact tracing apps to support gradual lifting of confinement measures, April 2020. https://ec.europa.eu/commission/presscorner/detail/en/ip_20_670. Accessed 25 May 2020

47. Berke, A., Bakker, M., Vepakomma, P., Larson, K., Pentland, A.: Assessing disease exposure risk with location data: a proposal for cryptographic preservation of privacy. MIT Media Lab (2020). https://arxiv.org/pdf/2003.14412

48. Zhao, C., Zhao, S., Zhao, M., Chen, Z., Gao, C., Li, H., Tan, Y.: Secure multi-party computation: theory, practice and applications. Inf. Sci. **476**, 357–372 (2019). https://doi.org/10.1016/j.ins.2018.10.024

49. European Data Protection Supervisor. The EU's independent data protection authority. https://edps.europa.eu/data-protection/our-work/subjects/health_en. Accessed 25 May 2020

50. General Data Protection Regulation GDPR. https://gdpr-info.eu/recitals/no-35/. Accessed 25 May 2020

51. Wang, S., et al.: A community effort to protect genomic data sharing, collaboration and outsourcing. npj Genomic Med **2**, 33 (2017). https://doi.org/10.1038/s41525-017-0036-1

52. Genomic Data User Code Of Conduct. National Institutes of Health (NIH). http://osp.od.nih.gov/wp-content/uploads/Genomic_Data_User_Code_of_Conduct.pdf. Accessed 25 May 2020

53. Nikel, D.: Norway: 1.4 Million People Download Coronavirus Tracking App Despite Security Concerns, Forbes (2020)

54. Digital Infection Tracking. Open source? (in Norwegian). Simula Research (2020). https://www.simula.no/news/digital-smittesporing-apen-kildekode

55. Holter, M.: Norway launches virus app to keep contagion under control. Bloomberg (2020). https://www.bloomberg.com/news/articles/2020-04-16/norway-launches-virus-app-to-keep-contagion-under-control

56. Gjøsteen, K.: Hundreds of IT experts from around the world face tracking apps like Norwegian Smittestopp, NRK.no (In Norwegian) (2020). https://www.nrk.no/norge/hundrevis-av-it-eksperter-fra-hele-verden-ut-mot-sporingsapper-som-norske-smittestopp-1.14988352. Accessed 25 May 2020

57. Mulder, T., Tudorica, M.: Privacy policies, cross-border health data and the GDPR. Inf. Commun. Technol. Law **28**(3), 261–274 (2019). https://doi.org/10.1080/13600834.2019.1644068

58. Soewito, B., Ritonga, A.Y.H., Gunawan, F.E.: Increasing accuracy of Bluetooth low energy for distance measurement applications. In: 11th International Conference on Knowledge, Information and Creativity Support Systems (KICSS), pp. 1–5. Yogyakarta (2016). https://doi.org/10.1109/kicss.2016.7951422

59. Al Qathrady, M., Helmy, A.: Improving BLE distance estimation and classification using TX power and machine learning: A comparative analysis. In: Proceedings of the 20th ACM International Conference on Modelling, Analysis and Simulation of Wireless and Mobile Systems, pp. 79–83, November 2017. https://doi.org/10.1145/3127540.3127577

60. Lonzetta, A.M., Cope, P., Campbell, J., Mohd, B.J., Hayajneh, T.: Security vulnerabilities in Bluetooth technology as used in IoT. J. Sen. Actuator Netw. **7**(3), 28 (2018). https://doi.org/10.3390/jsan7030028

61. Critical Bluetooth Vulnerability in Android (CVE-2020-0022) – BlueFrag. Insinuator (2020). https://insinuator.net/2020/02/critical-bluetooth-vulnerability-in-android-cve-2020-0022/. Accessed 25 May 2020

62. Dwork, C., Roth, A.: The algorithmic foundations of differential privacy. Found. Trends Theoret. Comput. Sci. **9**(3–4), 211–407 (2014). https://doi.org/10.1561/0400000042

63. Campbell, T.: Chapter 1: evolution of a profession. In: Practical Information Security Management: A Complete Guide to Planning and Implementation, pp. 1–14. A Press (2016)

64. Introduction to LSIS, The University of Oslo Website (2020). https://www.uio.no/english/services/it/security/lsis/introduction-to-lsis.html. Accessed 25 May 2020

65. How to classify data and information, The University of Oslo Website (2020). https://www.uio.no/english/services/it/security/lsis/data-classes.html. Accessed 25 May 2020

66. Services for sensitive data (TSD), The University of Oslo Website (2020). https://www.uio.no/english/services/it/research/sensitive-data/index.html. Accessed 25 May 2020

67. Yang, G., Wong, D., Wang, H., Deng, X.: Two-factor mutual authentication based on smart cards and passwords. J. Comput. Syst. Sci. **74**, 1160–1172 (2008). https://doi.org/10.1016/j.jcss.2008.04.002

68. Summary of the HIPAA Security Rule, US Department of Health & Human Services. https://www.hhs.gov/hipaa/for-professionals/security/laws-regulations/index.html. Accessed 25 May 2020

69. Iyengar, A., Kundu, A., Pallis, G.: Healthcare Informatics and Privacy. IEEE Internet Comput. **22**(2), 29–31 (2018). https://doi.org/10.1109/MIC.2018.022021660

70. Kuan Hon, W., Millard, C., Walden, I.: The problem of 'personal data' in cloud computing: what information is regulated? - the cloud of unknowing. Int. Data Priv. Law **1**(4), 211–228 (2011). https://doi.org/10.1093/idpl/ipr018

Awareness and Training

Towards a Cross-Cultural Education Framework for Online Safety Awareness

R. Herkanaidu[1]([⊠]) [ID], S. M. Furnell[1,2,3] [ID], and M. Papadaki[1] [ID]

[1] Centre for Security, Communications and Network Research, University of Plymouth, Plymouth, UK
{ram.herkanaidu,steven.furnell,maria.papadaki}@plymouth.ac.uk
[2] Security Research Institute, Edith Cowan University, Perth, Western Australia, Australia
[3] Centre for Research in Information and Cyber Security, Nelson Mandela University, Port Elizabeth, South Africa

Abstract. The majority of online safety awareness education programmes have been developed in advanced countries and for the needs of their own populations. In less developed countries (LDCs) not only are there fewer programmes there is also a research gap in knowing the issues that face young people in their respective country. The Young People Online Education Framework seeks to address this and provide educators, researchers and policy makers an evidence driven construct for developing education programmes that are informed by issues affecting young people in that particular country/region. This is achieved by following the steps within the framework starting first from the evidence stage, gathering the data and conducting new research if necessary. This is fed into the Young People Online Model, which looks at the environmental and social influences that shape young people's attitude and behaviour online. A novel feature of this framework is the Cultural Mask, where all topics, activities and pedagogical approaches are considered with the cultural makeup of the target audience in mind. The framework was applied in Thailand and a number of workshops were successfully carried out. More research and workshops are planned in Thailand and it is hoped other researchers will make use of the framework to extend its scope and application.

Keywords: Awareness · Education · Children · Culture · Online safety

1 Introduction

A little-explored area of online safety awareness education is the role of culture and specifically cultural differences which can lead to very different learning outcomes. Gasser, Maclay and Palfrey Jr. [5] note that:

> *"the most glaring gap in the research landscape ... [is that] most of the relevant research (with a small number of important exceptions) has focussed on safety implications of Internet usage of young people in industrialized nations, usually with emphasis on Western Europe and Northern America. Despite recent efforts*

© IFIP International Federation for Information Processing 2020
Published by Springer Nature Switzerland AG 2020
N. Clarke and S. Furnell (Eds.): HAISA 2020, IFIP AICT 593, pp. 47–57, 2020.
https://doi.org/10.1007/978-3-030-57404-8_4

... much less is known about digital safety risks to children in developing and emerging economies."

One of the reasons for this is that there is a, "lack of research and locally-relevant data ... [and] policies are developed based on assumptions or on research that may not be locally applicable" [16]. In recognising this, Livingstone, Byrne and Bulger [14] argue that, "adapting research instruments designed in the global North to Southern contexts is challenging, and requires considerable sensitivity to the local circumstances of children's lives, as well as sustained dialogue with the stakeholders who will use the research findings." This sensitivity extends to the classroom and the cultural context of learners. Hall [6] asserts that:

"each culture is not only an integrated whole but has its own rules for learning. These are reinforced by different patterns of over-all organizations. An important part of understanding a different culture is learning how things are organized and how one goes about learning them ... the reason one cannot get into another culture by applying the 'let's-fit-the-pieces-together' is the total complexity of any culture."

This paper puts forward an education framework that incorporates culture as an essential component for designing education programmes in less developed countries (LDCs); a term that will be used to represent the myriad other terms such as, 'developing', 'emerging' and 'global South'. Correspondingly, in place of, 'industrialized nations' and 'global North' this paper addresses them as 'advanced countries'. The next section discusses the background to this research and related works. Section 3 then introduces the education framework followed by how it was applied in the case study country, Thailand in Sect. 4. Finally, Sect. 5 is the conclusion and a discussion of future work.

2 Background and Related Work

The Young People Online (YPO) education framework formed the basis of a five year PhD study researching effective online safety awareness in LDCs. As stated above much of the existing research has taken place in advanced countries. One of the most influential is the Kids Online project which started as a European study to investigate and provide data for policy makers, educators and other researchers on the online experience of young people in Europe. Since its first report in 2006 it has morphed into the Global Kids Online (GKO) project which as the name suggest is a worldwide endeavour. At the time of writing there are ongoing studies in several countries including the following LDCs; Argentina, Brazil, Bulgaria, Chile, Ghana, the Philippines, South Africa and Uruguay. At their website, http://globalkidsonline.net they share project results and their research tools including survey questions.

The GKO research model has been developed over several iterations and now focuses on digital rights and well-being [15]. For the purposes of the YPO education framework it was deemed sufficient at this nascent stage to look at the risks and benefits of being online. This is the YPO model and is an integral part of the education framework as can be seen below in Fig. 1.

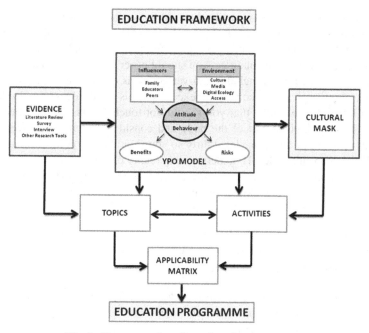

Fig. 1. Young people online education framework

Both models are influenced by Bronfenbrenner's ecological approach [7, 15]. Urie Bronfenbrenner worked in the field of developmental psychology and introduced the concept of encircling layers of influence with the child at the centre. The first layer includes the child's immediate environment with parents/guardians, family, peers, teachers. The next layer includes the interactions of institutions and the indirect influence on the child including their; school, parents' workplace, hospital and place of worship. Enveloping all this is the social and cultural layer, that is, the influence of the wider societal environment [7].

In the YPO model, Bronfenbrenner's system is represented by the **Influencers**, family, educators and peers and the **Environment**, culture, media, digital ecology and access. The Influencers have a direct affect that helps to shape the personality, attitude and behaviour of the young person. For Thailand, it was necessary to conduct original research to obtain the relevant data as there were very few existing in-country studies to draw upon and therefore a mixture of surveys (a quantitative method) and interviews (a qualitative method) were undertaken. This mixed methods approach was deemed prudent as, "both forms of data provide a better understanding of a research problem than either quantitative or qualitative data by itself" [2].

2.1 Theory of Culture

To understand better the cross-cultural nature of the education framework theories of culture were investigated. In particular, the iceberg model of culture inspired by the work of Edward T. Hall and his seminal work, 'Beyond Culture' [6]. It recognises that each country has their own set of norms and values. At the surface culture level you have the visible signs of a culture like clothes, food and music. This is the etiquette layer where you can learn the dos and don'ts of a particular culture. For example, in Thailand, as in some other South East Asian countries, you should never touch a person's head.

The shallow culture level includes non-verbal forms of communications, cues and gestures like, how to greet a person and timekeeping. This is the values or understanding layer. You know, for example, that you should not touch a person's head because in Buddhism it is the highest part of the body and considered sacred. The feet are the lowest part of the body and considered dirty so you should never point them at another person. At the deep culture level, "understanding reality of covert culture and accepting it on a gut level comes neither quickly nor easily, and it must be lived rather than read or reasoned" [6]. This is the empathy or sensitivity layer. At this point you would not even contemplate touching another person's head as it would just not feel right.

High-Context vs Low-Context. Hall distinguished between cultures where context and protocol are central with those where what is said explicitly is more important. Deng [3] as cited in Knutson et al. [13] explains that:

"individualistic, or low-context cultures indicate a preference of direct and overt communication style, confrontational and aggressive behaviors, a clear self iden-tification, and a priority of personal interest and achievement. Collectivistic, or high-context, cultures manifest a preference of indirect and covert communication style, an obedient and conforming behavior, a clear group identification, and a priority of group interest and harmony."

Hofstede's Dimensions of Culture. Geert Hofstede introduced his four dimensions of culture (later expanded to six) after analysing data from 72 countries which included 116,000 employees between the years 1967–1973 [4]. The original four are:

- **Measure of individualism:** Whether a culture leans to individualistic values or collectivistic ones.
- **Power distance:** Measures how hierarchical or unequal a society is. Stricter hierarchical structures tend to have greater adherence to authority.
- **Measure of Masculinity (and femininity):** Not to be confused with male and female. Masculine attributes include; assertiveness, toughness, competitiveness and material-ism. Feminine attributes include; modesty, tenderness and quality of life over mate-rialism. Gender roles in masculine cultures are clearly defined whereas in feminine cultures they overlap (Hofstede et al. 2010).
- **Uncertainty avoidance:** This is, "the extent to which the members of a culture feel threatened by ambiguous or unknown situations" [10]. Cultures that exhibit high uncertainty avoidance are more likely to have and adhere to rules and regulations.

By understanding and utilising Hall's high-context, low-context concept and Hof-stede's dimensions of culture a country profile can be prepared for the LDC. It should be noted that this cultural analysis can be conducted in any country. However, there are already online safety awareness education initiatives in advanced countries whereas there is a dearth of them in LDCs. It could still be a good exercise if it was applied to an education initiative aimed at a particular cultural group within an advanced country.

The next section introduces the education framework and a discussion of its component parts.

3 Young People Online Education Framework

One of the main objectives for the Young People Online study was to develop an integrative security education framework for online safety awareness in LDCs. In order to achieve this, different types of educational approaches were investigated. The framework is not solely theoretical. The Kids Online model aims to provide data for use by policy makers, researchers and educators. The YPO framework seeks to do the same and in addition offers practical solutions in the form of topics and activities that can be used by educators.

By working through the education framework the intention is to end up with an evidence based and locally relevant programme which will give it a better chance of success than just transposing one from another country.

Evidence: The first component of the framework is the evidence stage. A literature review should be undertaken to investigate the state of existing research and education programmes pertaining to the LDC. If there is insufficient data then new research should be undertaken and wherever possible with stakeholders, including; the government, education authorities, educators, NGOs and interested researchers. Depending on the LDC this process can take some time. A number of factors can influence the data collection phase including the; political climate, socio-economic considerations, the technological infrastructure and geographical considerations. Once the data is collected it is fed into the second component which is the Young People Online (YPO) model.

Young People Online Model: As noted above, the YPO model is influenced by the Kids Online model and Bronfenbrenner's ecological approach. The YPO model can take a significant amount of time and resources to accomplish. However, once the process is worked through a picture can be formed on the online attitude and behaviour of young people online including; how they access content, from where they do so, what activities are most prevalent and especially important what potentially harmful behaviour they are exposed to.

This information is then used to create a list of topics and influence the type of activities to include in an education programme or initiative.

Cultural Mask: A common definition of a mask is, "a piece of cloth or other material, which you wear over your face so that people cannot see who you are, or so that you look like someone or something else" (https://www.collinsdictionary.com/dictionary/english/mask). Within the YPO education framework the cultural mask concept can be seen in two ways.

Firstly, culture is a mask that can hide a visitor from what is really going on and this in turn can lead to misunderstandings. Hall illustrates this point with an experience he had as an American in Japan. After being at a particular hotel for several days he returned, asked for his key and went up to his room only to find that someone else's things were in there. He went back to reception and they explained that he had been moved to another room. It was not until a few years after the first incident that a Japanese friend explained the reason behind this. When you check-in at the hotel you not only become a guest but a family member. With family, rules are a little more informal and relaxed so being moved from one room to another is a sign that you have been afforded this high status. This is almost opposite to the way he thought he was being treated.

Secondly, the cultural mask within the framework can be used as a filter. When designing an education programme the teaching approach you take, the topic(s) and activities included should be seen through the lens of the cultural mask.

Topics: The online safety topics that make it into the education programme will come from the evidence stage and by working through the YPO model.

Activities: In each LDC activities should be piloted to find out its appropriateness and effectiveness. This is achieved by a combination of action research (e.g. workshops) and desktop research on effective pedagogical approaches. Table 1 gives an example of one such activity.

Table 1. Applicability matrix

Activity type	Activity	Resource/technology required	Age	Class size	Cultural context: Thailand
Digital media (audio/video)	**What is Cyber-bullying? And what can you do about it?**	Laptop/computer	12–18	Any (though smaller class sizes may lead to better discussion with more participation)	There is no direct translation of the term 'bully' in Thai even though it is very common in schools. The YPO survey also showed that Cyber-bullying is common online too with nearly 70% been upset by an online interaction.
Discussion	Students are shown a short video on Cyber-bullying followed by a discussion about its prevalence, mediation by parents/teachers and coping strategies.	Internet Connection (if video has not been downloaded)			
Whole class		Display (TV, Projector) Speakers			

Applicability Matrix: The applicability matrix is a set of readymade activities, categorised to their appropriateness in different settings. It provides educators and researchers tried and tested activities that they can add to their programme. In addition, they can add their own activities and therefore increase the choice for others as well. Table 1 gives an example activity within the applicability matrix:

4 A Case Study in Thailand

The YPO Education Framework was applied to Thailand. During the initial stage of evidence gathering it became clear that there were few research studies concerning online safety. Therefore surveys were carried out in schools in the North East of Thailand [8]. Figure 2 below shows the combined result. In total, 352 students from five schools took part in the survey. What it found is that although the students are from a semi-rural area of Thailand, 9 out of 10 owned their own smartphone and girls slightly more than boys. Facebook and Facebook Messenger is the dominant social network and chat app respectively and along with playing online games and watching videos forms the basis of their digital lives. In terms of negative experiences 7 out of 10 had been upset by an online interaction with cyber-bullying identified as the main issue with 55% reporting it. Interestingly, 41% admitted to bullying behaviour. Other significant risks were exposure to sites discussing; committing suicide, self harm, drugs, sexual content, promotion of eating disorders and hate messages aimed at particular groups and individuals. In addition 1 in 5 had sent a photo or a video to someone that they had not met offline.

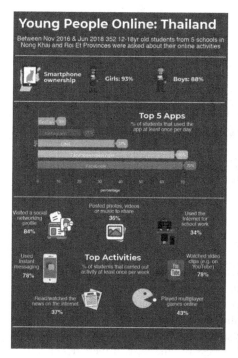
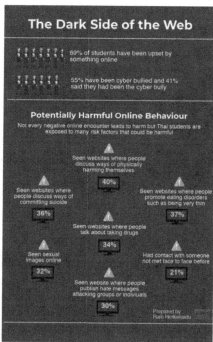

Fig. 2. Young people online survey results

4.1 Cultural Context

Thailand, as pointed out above is a high-context country. In Hofstede's cultural dimensions analysis this translates to being collectivistic on the measure of individualism. For each dimension an index of 0 to 100 was created measuring the differences between countries. Figure 3 below shows the scores for Thailand and the US, the latter an example of a low-context country. Unsurprisingly, the US scores high on individualism and masculinity In contrast, Thailand scores low in both indicating its collectivistic and feminine nature. Thailand scores higher than the US in power distance meaning it is a much more hierarchical society and also in the uncertainty avoidance index which tends towards more bureaucratic cultures with more rules and regulations. It also affects education where, "high uncertainty avoidance can also result in a preference for structured learning situations in the classroom" [4].

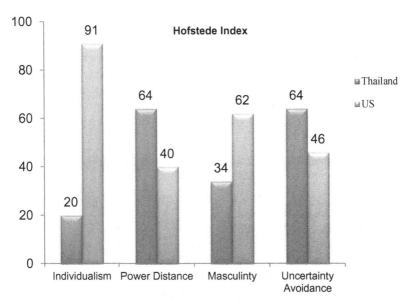

Fig. 3. Hofstede's dimensions of culture: a comparative between Thailand and the US (Data from Wilhelm & Gunawong [17])

4.2 Culture in the Classroom

A literature review was carried out on theories of culture and specifically on Thai culture and how it manifests itself within the education realm. Thailand is a hierarchal country with the king and the royal family at the top. Hierarchy is present in the classroom too with the teacher as the authority figure and the student there to receive knowledge. It is one reason why the traditional rote learning style still prevails. Thai teachers have high status but they are also responsible for the success or otherwise of their students. If a student fails in a test it is the fault of the teacher for not adequately preparing them for it. For a student to contradict or argue with a teacher would mean the latter losing face. Openly criticising a student causing them to lose face would also make everyone feel uncomfortable. This behaviour is anathema to Thai's collectivistic nature where social harmony is a core characteristic. This is in part to Thais being overwhelming Buddhists. They practice, Theravada Buddhism which, "is a philosophy, a way of life and a code of ethics that cultivate wisdom and compassion" [1].

Kainzbauer and Hunt [12] investigated foreign teachers in Thailand and found that the successful ones had adapted to the classroom culture. This is encapsulated by the approach one teacher took:

> "You never say 'you have screwed up'; you may say 'oh boy, did we screw up, didn't we? … maybe I did not show you what I really wanted, therefore you could not really give me what I wanted'. I found them quite responsive to that. You are making a joke but they understand that the joke is actually serious. But you say it with a smile, and you say it softly."

The desire for social harmony means Thais generally try to avoid conflict. Thailand is known as the land of smiles, what is less known is that Thais smile when they are happy, sad, irritated or angry. Asked a direct question they will try to choose the answer they think you are looking for. If, for example, a foreign colleague asked a Thai, "Do you want to have lunch tomorrow?" the answer is likely to be yes. Come tomorrow the Thai colleague may be nowhere to be found. In this scenario it is possible that they knew they could not make it but up until lunchtime you were happy! All is not lost however, it is better to ask indirectly, "maybe you would like to have lunch tomorrow?". This gives them a chance to say, "maybe the day after is better?" In the classroom you should never say, "do you understand?" the answer will always be yes whether the content is understood or not. Instead the teacher should find other ways to determine if understanding of the content has taken place.

Another important Thai characteristic is summed up by the phrase 'kreng jai'. There is no direct translation of it into English, it is something like not wanting to inconvenience or bother someone. In terms of online safety awareness and in particular mediation strategies this becomes an obstacle. In the interviews when students were asked what they did if they had a negative online experience invariably they would say that they did nothing and just kept silent. As one respondent replied (through an interpreter), "she said that she doesn't tell anyone if it is not important." Any online safety awareness initiative should take this into account especially on sensitive issues such as cyber-bullying.

4.3 Exploratory Workshops

With the cultural context in mind workshops were designed to test out different activities and teaching methods. As cyber-bullying was the main online safety issue it made sense to have this as the core topic. The workshops proved mostly successful [9] and were based on active learning methods like gamification. For example, one activity, the password challenge, used a password meter to show the strength, ranging from 0%–100%. Students were shown a method for creating strong passwords which they could then check on the meter [8].

While it cannot be called an education programme yet the theoretical, pedagogical and practical foundations have been laid for one to emerge. This and other aspects are discussed in the next section.

5   Conclusion and Future Work

The YPO Education Framework provides educators, researchers and policy makers a culturally relevant, evidence based construct for the effective teaching of online safety awareness. It is underpinned by sound research methodology and pedagogy with tried and tested activities that can be adapted to the needs of the target audience. The framework was applied to Thailand which resulted in a workshop series focusing on anticyberbullying [9]. Original research in the form of surveys and interviews were undertaken which sought to understand the attitude and behaviour of young people online and also the risks that could be potentially harmful.

Theories of culture were investigated and specifically how it affects teaching in Thailand. It found that Thai youth are use to the rote learning style, that what a teacher says is fact and not to be questioned. Teachers are held in high esteem but are also held responsible for the success or failure of a student. The workshops did find that students were receptive to active learning methods like gamification such as in the password challenge. The activities added to an applicability matrix which acts as a repository of tried and tested lessons. Notes on resources required and cultural context are included for the benefit of other educators and researchers. This practical aspect of the framework is in contrast to ones like the Kids Online model which focuses on data gathering and providing evidence for others.

Thus far the research has been conducted in the North East of Thailand. There is a plan to extend it to the south of the country in Songkhla province and possibly to other regions as well. By conducting further surveys, interviews and workshops it will build upon and extend the applicability of the framework. The goal will be to turn the workshops into a coherent and comprehensive education programme that can be a model for other LDCs.

References

1. Browell, S.: The land of smiles': people issues in Thailand. Hum. Resource Dev. Int. **3**(1), 109–119 (2000). https://doi.org/10.1080/136788600361975
2. Creswell, J.W.: Educational Research: Planning, Conducting, and Evaluating Quantitative and Qualitative Research, 4th edn. Pearson, Boston (2012)
3. Deng, B.C.: The influence of individualism–collectivism on conflict management style: a cross- culture comparison between Taiwanese and US business employees. Master's thesis, California State University, Sacramento (1992)
4. Eldridge, K., Cranston, N.: Managing transnational education: Does national culture really matter? J. High. Educ. Policy Manag. **31**(1), 67–79 (2009). https://doi.org/10.1080/136008 00802559286
5. Gasser, U., Maclay, C.M., Palfrey Jr., J.G.: Working towards a deeper understanding of digital safety for children and young people in developing nations: an exploratory study by the Berkman Center for Internet & Society at Harvard University, in collaboration with UNICEF.

Berkman Center Research Publication No. 2010-7; Harvard Public Law Working Paper No. 10-36 (2010). https://ssrn.com/abstract=1628276
6. Hall, E.T.: Beyond Culture. Doubleday, Garden City (1976)
7. Härkönen, U.: The Bronfenbrenner ecological systems theory of human development. Keynote presented at V International Conference Person.Color.Nature.Music, Daugavpils University, Saule. Latvia, 17–21 October 2017 (2007)
8. Herkanaidu, R., Furnell, S., Papadaki, M.: Using gamification in effective online safety awareness education. Presented at the 10th International Conference on Educational Research, ICER 2017, Faculty of Education, Khon Kaen University, Thailand, 9–10 September 2017 (2017)
9. Herkanaidu, R., Furnell, S., Papadaki, M., Khuchinda, T.: Designing an anti-cyberbullying programme in Thailand. In: Clarke, N.L., Furnell, S.M. (eds.) Proceedings of the Twelfth International Symposium on Human Aspects of Information Security & Assurance. Paper presented at HAISA 2018, Abertay University, Scotland, 29th–31st August. Plymouth, UK: Clarke Furnell (2018)
10. Hofstede, G., Hofstede, G.J., Minkov, M.: Cultures and Organizations: Software of the Mind, 3rd edn. McGraw-Hill, New York (2010)
11. Internet World Stats, 6 June 2018. Asia internet use, population data and Facebook statistics - June 2018. Internet World Stats website. http://www.internetworldstats.com/stats3.htm
12. Kainzbauer, A., Hunt, B.: Meeting the challenges of teaching in a different cultural environment – evidence from graduate management schools in Thailand. Asia Pacific J. Educ. **36**(sup1), 56–68 (2016). https://doi.org/10.1080/02188791.2014.934779
13. Knutson, T.J., Komolsevin, R., Chatiketu, P., Smith, V.R.: A cross-cultural comparison of Thai and US American rhetorical sensitivity: Implications for intercultural communication effectiveness. Int. J. Intercult. Relat. **27**, 63–78 (2003)
14. Livingstone, S., Byrne, J., Bulger, M.: Researching children's rights globally in the digital age. Report of a seminar held on 12–14 February 2015. LSE, London (2015). http://www.lse.ac.uk/media@lse/research/Research-Projects/Researching-Childrens-Rights/pdf/Researching-childrens-rights-globally-in-the-digital-age-260515-withphotos.pdf
15. Livingstone, S., Mascheroni, G., Staksrud, E.: Developing a framework for researching children's online risks and opportunities in Europe. LSE, London: EU Kids Online. (2015). http://eprints.lse.ac.uk/64470/
16. Park, J., Tan, M.: A policy review: Building digital citizenship in Asia-Pacific through safe, effective and responsible use of ICT. APEID-ICT in Education, UNESCO Asia-Pacific Regional Bureau of Education. (2016). http://unesdoc.unesco.org/images/0024/002468/246813E.pdf
17. Wilhelm, W.J., Gunawong, P.: Cultural dimensions and moral reasoning: a comparative study. Int. J. Sociol. Soc. Policy **36**(5/6). (2016). https://doi.org/10.1108/IJSSP-05-2015-0047

Towards an Heuristic Approach
to Cybersecurity and Online Safety
Pedagogy

Simon Marsden$^{(\boxtimes)}$ iD

University of Portsmouth, Portsmouth, UK
simon.marsden@port.ac.uk,
https://www.port.ac.uk

Abstract. Using a realist review approach from a qualitative and pragmatic perspective, the ultimate aim here is to develop a Cybersecurity and Online Safety (CSOS) pedagogical approach for Initial Teacher
Training. The approach here is needs based whilst societally situated. It
is primarily intended for the preparation of initial teacher trainees. However, this emerging approach could also be of interest to those developing
CSOS educational programmes. The aim here is not to outline specific
instruction for a particular online harm. Neither is it to provide further
security instruction, for example, on how to manage passwords. The aim
is to propose a theoretical approach to CSOS contexts, mechanisms and
outcomes. From this the future aim is to curate a set of appropriate
tools, or heuristics, that can be taught and utilised by lay people or
experts to address established or new CSOS issues. The work considers the current education landscape and the CSOS issues. Using Friere's
pedagogical approach, the emergent themes are situated to the needs
of the individual and society. The resulting theoretical approach should
facilitate initial CSOS dialogues between educators and learners. These
initial findings are surprising when situated alongside known pedagogies
and theories.

Keywords: Cybersecurity · Online safety · Education · Pedagogy

1 Introduction

Using a realist review approach from a qualitative and pragmatic perspective,
this papers aims to develop a Cybersecurity and Online Safety (CSOS) pedagogical approach for Initial Teacher Training. Schools prepare children for adult
life, but not just by "socializing people to function well (and without complaint)
in the hierarchical structure of the modern corporation or public office" [1, p.
ix]. Cyberspace permeates all aspects of this life and makes deviant, or socially
unacceptable content accessible to young people. As such, effective, appropriate

University of Portsmouth

© IFIP International Federation for Information Processing 2020
Published by Springer Nature Switzerland AG 2020
N. Clarke and S. Furnell (Eds.): HAISA 2020, IFIP AICT 593, pp. 58–70, 2020.
https://doi.org/10.1007/978-3-030-57404-8_5

and factual CSOS education in schools is now essential. This has been recognised in the recent "Teaching Online Safety in School" document [2]. In addition, the need to raise all teachers' awareness is apparent. "Schools also need an understanding of the risks that exist online", teaching about online safety and harms should be a **"whole school approach"** [2, p. 3, emphasis added]. This development is welcome and underpins the need for this research.

However, there is no known body of work on the preparation of trainee-teachers or their trainers to teach CSOS at this time. This work is part of a larger project to fill the gap. It aims to provide a needs based and socially situated approach to CSOS education in schools. It will start by explaining why it is unrealistic to expect that teachers, trainees or initial teacher trainers have the knowledge or skill-set to deliver the concepts and issues behind 15 pages of tabulated harms [2, pp. 3–23] without support and training. Next it will explain the methodological approach used to research and identify a suitable theoretical model for the future realist review. The findings are then presented, alongside discussion of how the approach can be utilised. Finally, the way this work will underpin future work is outlined.

2   The Need for the Approach

The teaching online safety in school document has stated that from September 2020 pupils will be taught about online safety and harms [2, p. 5]. This is to be compulsory in all United Kingdom (UK) state schools. Schools "need an understanding of the risks that exist online so they can tailor their teaching and support to the specific needs of their pupils" [2, p. 3]. Schools are also expected to safeguard children from becoming radicalised committing crime, or becoming a victim to crime [3]. The UK National Cyber Security Strategy, additionally, tells us we lack the necessary cyber skills in both the public and private sector [4, p. 22]. Yet we still do not teach the necessary skills in schools and we are only now introducing compulsory CSOS education.

This is a fast changing technological world. It is not enough to tell our children about the exploits, threats or online harms. They need tools or heuristics that they can apply to present and future problems [5]. They need to be able to understand how attacks, whether cybercrime or cyber harm, work and how to protect against them.

It could be argued that we should not show children how to carry out attacks as it could in some way weaponise them "the threat they pose is unimaginable" [6, p. 3758]. However, there are countless websites that already show you how to carry out attacks. There are many hacker groups of varying fame and there is usually a helpful video to lead you through attacks, step-by-step. It is interesting that YouTube is currently considering banning videos that show "Instructional hacking and phishing: Showing users how to bypass secure computer systems or steal user credentials and personal data" [7]. Tim Erlin, quoted by Claburn [7] saying that "Google's intention here might be laudable, but the result is likely to stifle valuable information sharing in the information security community."

Children are often not aware of the seriousness of their computer misuse [8]. Young people are the most likely to commit crimes, with peak offending occurring somewhere between the ages of 15–18, trailing off after this as they grow out of crime [9, p. 1170]. Unfortunately, this coincides with their years in education and it is clear that computer literate young people have been involved with very serious cybercrimes. It is not surprising that some would consider it dangerous to teach children about hacking techniques [6].

To enable children to avoid crime we need to teach them the techniques of crime. This is controversial [6,10], we need to be mindful of what leads young-sters to commit crime. We need to develop policies and intervention strategies for teachers. We need those with the knowledge to commit cybercrime to be channelled into more productive use [11, p. 3]. Children will not be aware if we are not discussing ethics and the law with them? Children will not develop the necessary skills if we do not have the teachers that have the knowledge and are prepared to teach them.

We can not expect to block children from accessing deviant or harmful content. For example the recent, rather ill thought out, UK age restriction plans to restrict underage access to pornography. Despite promises that a system would be in place by Summer 2019, this failed to materialise. This is not surprising. Uni-national restrictions to web-based material can be bypassed by Virtual Private Network (VPN) technology. Unregulated sites or on the Dark Web might become an alternative source that could be far more damaging to young people and additionally illegal [12,13]. Children are exposed to online harms. They are vulnerable to committing and being the victims of crime. We need them to develop a skill-set that is lacking in society. 2/3 of children aged 12 and under and almost half of 13–18 year old say they would welcome more online safety education [14, p. 87].

In just a few lines we start to touch upon the complexity of cyberspace. We can not expect trainees to come ready packaged with sufficient knowledge of this field. Therefore, schools and Initial Teacher Training (ITT) providers need guidance if teachers are to engage our young with CSOS meaningfully [14, p. 37]. Teachers and teacher trainers come to the profession from a variety of subject disciplines and a range of experiences. Many will have had little to no formal cybersecurity and online safety input. Many will have no technical background. The lack of technically qualified teachers is a continuing problem [15]. There is less empirical work on teacher CSOS knowledge, but Pusey and Sadera [16] found that teachers were not prepared to teach or model the topics. However, the proposal here is that teachers do not need to be technical experts or to have in-depth knowledge of the more deviant part of cyberspace, to understand and deliver effective CSOS. We can expect teachers and trainees to have sufficient knowledge about teaching, learning, society, law and behaviour. These are the skills and knowledge bases that we should leverage here.

Teacher education programmes are under extreme pressure of time, diversity and complexity. So trainees need accessible theoretical under-pinning rationale for the practices being promoted [17]. With only 12% of children taking a computing subject post 14 [18] it is not suitable for CSOS education to be delivered predominantly in the computing curriculum. Especially when even teachers of computing do not all feel that they have the necessary skills to teach CSOS with 65% saying that they would like training in this area [19]. Elsewhere in the curriculum we need to prevent a culture where it is acceptable to "not get technology" [20, p. 672].

We can not expect that new teachers will receive CSOS pedagogical input from their colleagues. We do not have an education workforce with skills or knowledge to teach cybersecurity skills [21, p. 103], [22, p. 7]. The lack of educational provision in universities and colleges is blamed for the huge cyber security skills gap in industry [21, p. 103] and so it is unlikely that we will be able to fulfill the needs of education. Computing teachers, themselves, are calling out for training [19].

We have a legacy of inadequate training of teachers in this area. The Ment0rs [sic] (Lloyd Blankenship) 1986 hackers' manifesto continues to make for uncomfortable and contemporary reading: incompetent teachers contributing to the development of bored young hackers who "hungered for steak but were fed baby food" [23, np]. Little has changed. Training at the time did not even meet the expectations of teachers [24], leaving them with a lack of confidence and a negative view of Information Communication Technology (ICT) [22,24–26]. This legacy created a curriculum that the 2012 education minister Gove [27] decried as boring and taught by bored teachers. This led to the change to teaching computing in 2014.

Computing can answer some CSOS issues. However, it is not the most suitable subject to engage children in understanding of social issues or deviance. CSOS is a far bigger issue and needs to have context that can only be offered as part of the wider curriculum as the DfE [2] acknowledges. Children receive little CSOS education up to the age of 14 and often none after. Only 11.9% of eligible pupils took a computing GCSE in the UK in 2017 [18,28,29]. Activities to develop useful hacking skills are reserved for elite children in schools to "encourage the best young minds" [30]. Cellan-Jones [28] states that it is hard to find anyone that is happy with the direction that computing education has gone. CSOS education is not compulsory at Further Education (FE) or university and so many will enter the workforce with no formal training or advice at all [31].

There is now a growing corpus of literature that tells us that CSOS education is needed at all levels but at the same time questions the efficacy of what we are currently doing [11,32–34]. We need to understand technology, but that understanding needs to be situated amongst our personal needs and those of society. The work suggests that in order to understand the cyberspace landscape we need: to start CSOS education earlier; to be honest and factual with children; teachers to engage in dialogue with their children.

So to sum up we find ourselves in a position where: we are asking people to teach about things they might not know about; by trying to bank information to only a proportion of our children, who might not actually care; whilst ignoring their needs and desires; out of the context of their societal situation. Perhaps another approach is needed, perhaps one where we start by considering people's attitudes, beliefs and perceptions [35].

3   Methodology

The methodological approach is a realist review. This does not "discover 'whether' an intervention works, but trades instead on its ability to discover 'why', 'when' and 'how' it might succeed" [36, p. 9]. Friere's Pedagogy of the Oppressed approach is used, a pedagogy of the cyber-oppressed if you will. Friere's work concentrated on improving literacy and general education of Brazilian peasants. He realised that a "banking approach" delivered by educated middle classes was unlikely to have impact [37]. As such he sent experts from many academic disciplines into the field to find out what the peasants needed, from their perspective. From the reports back, Friere generated themes that could be used to enter into dialogue with the peasants leading to understanding of their own problems. Problems were analysed with the learners to develop a conscious understanding of the issues, conscientisation or conscientização [37]. The parallels for this work are clear. Our teacher trainers are pedagogically aware, but might not have specific CSOS knowledge. The trainees may additionally lack the pedagogical knowledge. Neither the trainers nor trainees know every individual children's needs, beliefs or aspirations. For conscientização to occur a starting point for dialogue is needed.

The "reports back" from the experts in this work consisted of analysis and consideration of over 500 academic papers and books covering many aspects of CSOS. Relevant works were identified through a realist synthesis, zigzagging approach [38], where initial literature searching becomes increasing purposeful as more synthesis of the material is made. The process was inductive and iterative. As new works were added to the corpus new themes were identified. Themes and curated works were frequently revisited and reconsidered. The works were categorised using the commercial program Zotero resulting in over 100 initial themes (or generative words) for the purpose of this and the basis of future research. The method is outlined below.

1. **Developing generative words**
   Creating an abstract conceptual understanding of the issue. Generative words are keywords used in research about the issues under investigation.
2. **Totalising and situationalising the issue**
   Identify and situate the totality of the issue. Historical, political, geographical, sociological and criminological influences are all considered at this stage. The outcome is to produce a descriptive outline. Unfortunately, there is insufficient space to go into detail of this work here. However, the outcomes can be seen in the results and discussion section.
3. **Decoding and generating new themes**
   Themes are then developed from the constituent parts of the issues. These perspectives are normally generated with human subjects. In this case these perspectives come from analysis of a learner and trainee needs.
4. **Re-codifying the issue**
   The themes are re-framed as investigative questions to be developed between the

teacher and the learner. This leads to a theoretical framework with which to develop mutual understanding. This framework allows students and practitioners to develop their mutual understanding and to deepen their previous knowledge.

5. **Conscientisation**

This stage is part of ongoing and future research.

4 Results/Discussion

The results and discussion are run together here as the realist zigzagging approach needs explanation. Some outcomes seem simplistic if taken out of context. However, as Vygotsky reminds us, we can only understand concepts that are within our zones of proximal development [39, p. 59]. It can be argued that too often CSOS education fails because it is either of no concern to the recipient, or too far removed from what they know. As such, it is hoped that the reader appreciates that this work has the non-expert and school children at the heart of the rationale. The aim being to produce a useful framework to engage the learners in meaningful conversation about CSOS. The hope is to provide a starting point for the creation or dialogue to lead to Friere's conscientisation (conscientização) of the topic being considered [37].

The initial thematic analysis produced a bewildering and ever growing amount of over 100 themes and sub-themes associated with CSOS. This clearly illustrated the extensive and complex nature of the subject domain.

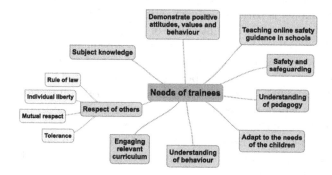

Fig. 1. The needs of the trainee to fulfil their professional role

The next stage was to consider these themes alongside the needs of the trainees. Teachers and trainees need to comply with UK teacher standards and the requirements of the government's Teaching Online Safety in school guidance. In addition, trainees need to evidence this thoroughly in order to achieve Qualified Teacher Status (QTS). The most relevant strands of the teacher standards are shown in Fig. 1. It is clear here that it is impossible to map every CSOS issue to the needs of trainees. It is also unreasonable to expect that they have the knowledge required to effectively address the issues. Following on from

Freire's pedagogical approach we need to decode and generate new themes that are relevant to the needs of the learners.

It is this rationalising of the themes that leads to simplicity and a surprise. As themes were re-codified a very familiar pattern started to emerge. The irony is not lost, as several years of work, reading and categorising over 500 sources, reduces CSOS learner needs to Maslow's Hierarchy of Needs, diagram Fig. 2. The model here is flattened and slightly modified.

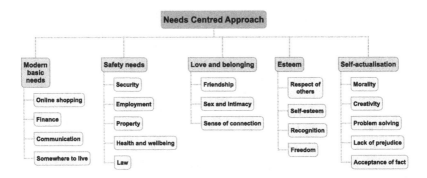

Fig. 2. CSOS needs, a deconstructed digital Maslow [40] Hierarchy of Needs

The hierarchical nature of Maslow's pyramid of needs is often critiqued (even by himself [41]) and not relevant to the usage here. Very quickly one can see how applicable the model is. Briefly, some examples might be to consider: that basic needs such as food are often bought online or in store with a card or phone; cyber security needs are self explanatory; health and well-being issues with online usage or addiction; love and belonging, where many of us find partners or like minded groups online; our self esteem needs perhaps being translated as likes or followers; respect of others online opinions or not in the case of trolling; and finally our self actualisation where we become the person we would like to be, perhaps by finding others that share our views, or sexuality, online or maybe link in with us to further our careers. Each and every CSOS issue can be considered with our personal needs or desires in a way that gives meaning to any dialogue about harms or security needs. This reduction in complexity of CSOS to Maslow's Needs should give confidence to the educator and offer a starting point for any discussion.

Much of our needs can end up turning to desires and even deviance. Like Dalal and Sharma [42] this work considers if Freud's Id, Ego and Super Ego is a suitable theory to consider when situating out needs with the needs of society. The Id being our unconscious, unchecked desires for our online pleasure seeking. The Superego parents, teachers and society with underlying moral codes, laws, ethics and customs that might not fit in with our Id desires. Our Ego or judge that helps us decide if we should fulfil our desires or not.

As shown in Fig. 1, teachers have to help pupils gain understanding for the "respect of others". This now requires us to situate our needs or Id with respect to

Table 1. Tönnies and Harris [43, p. 192] original list of Gemeinschaft and Gesellschaft

Gemeinschaft [Community]	Gesellschaft [Society]
Natural/essential will	Arbitrary/rational will
Self	Person
Possession	Wealth
Land	Money
Family law	Law of contracts

the needs of society. There are two clear theoretical contenders as starting points here. The first is what Tönnies and Harris [43] referred to as the Gemeinschaft (community) and the Gesellschaft (society) and can be seen in Table 1. The second is Ecological Theory of Bronfenbrenner [44] which can be seen in Fig. 4a. Both these ecological theories consider social change and human development. With Tönnies and Harris [43] work considered to look at societal change on a macro and historical level. Bronfenbrenner [44] being more descriptive and more focussed on considering a child's changing environment at different life stages [45].

A first attempt at trying to rationalise CSOS needs in context of Gemeinschaft and the Gesellschaft led to, the perhaps unwieldy, interpretation in diagram Fig. 3. As can be seen there is also some attempt to incorporate the Bronfenbrenner [44] Ecological Theory. The aim here was to keep the individual needs centred and situated within societal needs. Whilst also taking into consideration the knowledge and conscious cognition of what we need in order to fulfil our needs. This is a little clumsy, however. The flow of thoughts is not consecutive. The main ideas of Tönnies and Harris [43] fit well within Bronfenbrenner's and so further consideration was given to that representation.

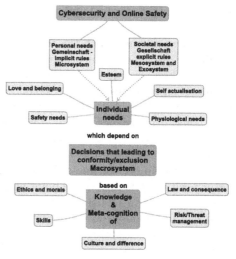

Fig. 3. Main learning centred themes of CSOS (Maslow, Bronfenbrenner and Tonnies)

In diagram Fig. 4a we can see my reproduction of a typical early representation of Bronfenbrenner's Ecological Theory. The other systems are: the microsystem or immediate environment; the mesosytem which is the connecting threads of the individuals immediate environment with the exosystem; the exosystem is the larger community that individuals and their close connections are involved with such as schools, places of work; the macrosystem is the social and cultural values that establish normal practice. This representation also has Bronfenbrenner's later addition of the Chronosystem, to reflect societal changes in time, added. Bronfenbrenner, himself declared this approach was open to interpretation and needed further refinement. One criticism, addressed here, has been the lack of focus on the individual needs and desires in the model. It is self-evident that the all pervasive nature of digital technology could now be incorporated.

This leads to diagram Fig. 4b or what has presumptively been called a "Techno-Ecological Theory". If we remember the aim here is to give an educator a tool to situate CSOS. We can not expect that educator to be a CSOS specialist, especially in the context of an ITT trainee from a non technical subject. Following Friere's approach we can not expect our learners to be interested in whatever banking approach to CSOS that we might adopt. We have to situate the topic in a manner that both can understand and that both can engage in. Topics that are within our zones of proximal development that Vygotsky tells us are necessary for understanding [39]. Topics that can be re-framed as investigative questions to be developed between the teacher and the learner. Hopefully, leading to Friere's mutual understanding [37].

The techno-ecological approach, proposed here, is intended to evolve Bronfenbrenner's representation for the current age. The centre is more obviously focussed on the individual needs. These needs might be considered first and are dependent on the learners age and stage of Piagetian development. Once personal CSOS actions are reflected upon they can be reconsidered within the scope of the other systems within the theory. The intention is to provide anchors for meaningful discussion about the issues.

Bronfenbrenner added the Chronosystem to reflect changes in time. Here this has been repurposed as the Techno-chronosystem. Historical technological changes having long been influencers on all aspects of society. In addition, factors might affect the balance of this Techno-chronosystem have been added. The balance at the bottom is to illustrate how technology changes can move our social development both forward and backward.

The words in the Techno-chronosystem are not intended to be either negative or positive. The arrows are pointing in opposite directions to illustrate this. Hacking might give us driverless cars, drones or Google Glass eyewear. All of which can be espoused for the great technological leaps forward that they are making. Someone adopting a more Luddite approach might counter that driverless cars or drones might cause accidents and, if so, who is responsible? Adoption of technology such as Google Glass might be opposed because of privacy concerns.

Online activism and passivity, cyberharm and resilience to those harms can be illustrated in similar ways. All issues can be contextualised within the scope of the other systems. This helps us to gain the "cognition" at the base of the diagram. Our conscientização that informs our decisions and realisation of needs.

Our needs might then inform actions, such as finding out how to manage passwords. Our conscientização might draw our attention to a societal wrong and this might lead to our activism. Our conscientização will help us situate

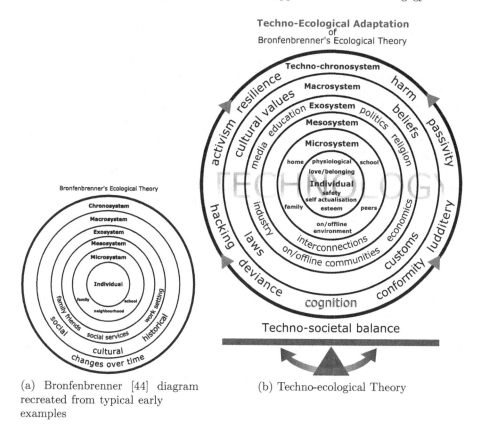

(a) Bronfenbrenner [44] diagram recreated from typical early examples

(b) Techno-ecological Theory

Fig. 4. Adaptation of Bronfenbrenner's Ecological Theory

the online safety harms outlined in the over fifteen pages of the DfE [2]. But it should do so in a way that encourages a greater understanding of technology and the place of that technology within our societal needs.

5   Conclusion

The aim of this paper is to analyse suitable and accessible theoretical approaches to support teacher trainers and trainees with context, mechanisms and outcomes of CSOS. This starting point is intended to help learners and educators of CSOS to come together on common ground and eventually develop conscientisation of the issues.

The topic areas surrounding CSOS are numerous and complex. This paper has highlighted the historical reasons why it is unlikely for teacher trainers or their trainees to be experts in the field and certainly not in all areas of the field. This paper has pointed out why it is not reasonable to expect these non-specialists to be able to deliver the requirements of the Teaching Online Safety guidance without support [2].

The approach suggested here is meant to develop understanding by prompting discussion about issues, within the context of what we know; or our zones of proximal development. According to Friere, once "conscientisation" is achieved the learner and educator can move forward together to address the issues.

The ultimate aim here is to provide a toolkit of heuristics for teachers to deliver CSOS. The theoretical position outlined above is a starting point. The next step is to use this to inform a realist review to find out what works for who, in what situations for CSOS. Not just for now but also in the future, as new CSOS issues emerge.

Early candidates are the "nudges" and "boosts" that Hertwig and Grüne-Yanoff [5] suggest. Nudges to promote good CSOS compliance, which could be as simple as a screen saver on the school computers. Boosts or heuristics that will help pupils make their own decisions in the future. An example might be Toulmin's approach to argument analysis to spot fake news [46]. Additionally, pedagogical approaches to deliver will be considered such as Papert's constructionist approach to practical computing education [47] or Bandura's theory of social learning [48].

This research adds to our knowledge by suggesting the adoption of a new approach to CSOS education. It does so by recognising that we have to avoid a banking approach to CSOS education and that Friere's pedagogy is a more suitable option. To support this approach to conscientisation, modified versions of Maslow's Needs and Bronfenbrenner's Ecological Theories have been proposed. Additionally, in order to situate individual's needs within the needs of society, Freud's theory of id, ego and superego is suggested.

References

1. Bowles, S., Gintis, H.: Schooling in Capitalist America: Educational Reform and the Contradictions of Economic Life. Routledge and Kegan Paul, Abingdon (1976)
2. DfE Teaching online safety in school. Guidance supporting schools to teach their pupils how to stay safe online, within new and existing school subjects. https://assets.publishing.service.gov.uk/government/uploads/system/uploads/attachment_data/file/811796/Teaching_online_safety_in_school.pdf
3. OFSTED Ofsted safeguarding policy (2018). https://www.gov.uk/government/publications/ofsted-safeguarding-policy/ofsted-safeguarding-policy
4. U.K. National Cyber Security Strategy (2016). https://www.gov.uk/government/uploads/system/uploads/attachment_data/file/567242/national_cyber_security_strategy_2016.pdf
5. Hertwig, R., Grüne-Yanoff, T.: Perspect. Psychol. Sci. **12**, 973–986 (2017)
6. Jamil, D., Khan, M.: Int. J. Eng. Sci. Technol. (IJEST), 0975–5462 (2011). ISSN
7. Claburn, T.: YouTube mystery ban on hacking videos has content creators puzzled (2019). https://www.theregister.co.uk/2019/07/03/youtube_bans_hacking_videos/
8. Pike, R.E.: J. Int. Technol. Inf. Manag. **22**, 67–75 (2013)
9. Newburn, T.: Criminology. Routledge, New York (2017)
10. Radziwill, N., Romano, J., Shorter, D., Benton, M.: arXiv preprint (2015) arXiv:1512.02707

11. Aiken, M., Davidson, J., Amann, P.: (2016). https://www.mdx.ac.uk/_data/assets/pdf_file/0025/245554/Pathways-White-Paper.pdf
12. Burgess, M.: Wired UK (2019). https://www.wired.co.uk/article/uk-porn-block-delayed/
13. The Guardian. The Guardian (2019). https://www.theguardian.com/commentisfree/2019/apr/18/age-verification-block-porn-ethical-sites-sex
14. Online harms team. Online harms white paper; type; her majesty's government (2019)
15. The Royal Society: After the reboot: computing education in UK schools. Roy. Soc. London (2017). https://royalsociety.org/~/media/policy/projects/computing-education/computing-education-report.pdf
16. Pusey, P., Sadera, W.A.: In: J. Digital Learn. Teacher Educ., 82 (2011)
17. Woollard, J., Wickens, C., Powell, K., Russell, T.: Technology, pedagogy and education, p. 187 (2009)
18. Kemp, P., Wong, B., Berry, M.: The roehampton computing education report: data from 2017 (2018)
19. Coleman, C.D., Reeder, E.: Three reasons for improving cybersecurity instruction and practice in schools. In: Langran, E., Borup, J. (eds.) Proceedings of Society for Information Technology & Teacher Education International Conference 2018, pp. 1020–1025. Association for the Advancement of Computing in Education (AACE), Washington, D.C., March 2018. https://www.learntechlib.org/p/182648
20. Singer, P.W., Friedman, A.: Cybersecurity and Cyberwar: What Everyone Needs to Know. Oxford University Press, Oxford (2014)
21. Cai, Y., Arney, T.: Cybersecurity should be taught top-down and case-driven, pp. 103–108. ACM Press (2017). https://doi.org/10.1145/3125659.3125687. ISBN: 978-1-4503-5100-3
22. Gipson, S.: (2003). https://dera.ioe.ac.uk/5090/1/issues-of-ict-school-reform-and-learning-centred-school-design.pdf
23. The Mentor Phrack Magazine, p. 10 (1986). http://phrack.org/issues/7/3.html
24. Barton, H.: The impact of the new opportunities fund (NOF) ICT in subject in subject teaching training programme. Ph.D. thesis, Education (2005)
25. Conlon, T.: J. In-Serv. Educ. **30**(00047), 115–140 (2004)
26. Kirkwood, M.: The new opportunities fund (NOF) ICT training for teachers programme: designing a powerful online learning environment. Paper presented at the European Conference on Educational Research, vol. 20, p. 23 (2000). http://www.leeds.ac.uk/educol/documents/00001690.htm
27. Gove, M.: Michael gove speech at the BETT show (2012). https://www.gov.uk/government/speeches/michael-gove-speech-at-the-bett-show-2012
28. Cellan-Jones, R.: Computing in schools - alarm bells over England's classes BBC News (2017). http://www.bbc.co.uk/news/technology-40322796
29. Kemp, P., Wong, B., Berry, M.: The Roehampton computing education report: data from 2015 (2016)
30. BBC News (2017). http://www.bbc.co.uk/news/technology-42016824
31. Marsden, S.: Risk UK Risk UK December 2017 - Risk UK. http://www.risk-uk.com/risk-uk-december-2017/. Accessed 03 Aug 2018
32. Choi, M., Levy, Y., Hovav, A.: The role of user computer self-efficacy, cybersecurity countermeasures awareness, and cybersecurity skills influence on computer misuse. In: Proceedings of the Pre-International Conference of Information Systems (ICIS) SIGSEC – Workshop on Information Security and Privacy (WISP) (2013)
33. Paulsen, C., McDue, E., Newhouse, W., Toth, P.: IEEE Secur. Privacy Mag., 76–79 (2012)

34. Sobiesk, E., Blair, J., Conti, G., Lanham, M., Taylor, H.: Cyber education: a multi-level, multi-discipline approach. In: SIGITE 2015 - Proceedings of the 16th Annual ACM Conference on Information Technology Education, pp. 43–47. United States Military Academy (2015). http://search.ebscohost.com/login.aspx?direct=true&db=edselc&AN=edselc.2-52.0-84960952475&site=eds-live
35. Ashenden, D.: Inf. Secur. Tech. Rep. **13**, 195–201 (2008)
36. Pawson, R.: Evidence-Based Policy: A Realist Perspective. SAGE, Thousand Oaks (2006)
37. Freire, P.: Pedagogy of the Oppressed. Bloomsbury, London (2014)
38. Cooper, C., Lhussier, M., Shucksmith, J., Carr, S.M.: BMJ Open **7**(9), e015477 (2017)
39. Aubrey, K., Riley, A.: Understanding & Using Educational Theories. SAGE, Los Angeles (2019)
40. Maslow, A.H.: Psychol. Rev. **50**, 370 (1943)
41. Maslow, A.H.: J. Humanistic Educ. Dev. **29**, 103–108 (1991)
42. Dalal, A.S., Sharma, R.: ICFAI J. Cyber Law. **6**, 34–47 (2007)
43. Tönnies, F., Harris, J.: Community and Civil Society. Cambridge Texts in the History of Political Thought. Cambridge University Press, Cambridge (2001)
44. Bronfenbrenner, U.: The Ecology of Human Development: Experiments by Nature and Design. Harvard University Press, Cambridge (1979)
45. Greenfield, P.M.: Dev. Psychol. **45**, 401–418 (2009)
46. Cummings, J., Dennis, A.R.: MIS Q. **42**, 697–717 (2018)
47. Papert, S.: Mindstorms: Children, Computers and Powerful Ideas. Basic Books, New York (1993)
48. Bandura, A.: J. Pers. Soc. Psychol. **11**, 275–279 (1969)

ContextBased MicroTraining: A Framework for Information Security Training

Joakim Kävrestad$^{(\boxtimes)}$ and Marcus Nohlberg

University of Skövde, Skövde, Sweden
{joakim.kavrestad,marcus.nohlberg}@his.se

Abstract. This paper address the emergent need for training measures designed to improve user behavior in regards to security. We do this by proposing a framework for information security training that has been developed for several years and over several projects. The result is the framework ContextBased MicroTraining (CBMT) which provides goals and guidelines for how to better implement information security training that supports the user in the situation where the user needs support. CBMT has been developed and tested for use in higher education as well as for the support of users during passwords creation. This paper presents version 1.0 of the framework with the latest refinements.

Keywords: Security training · Awareness · ContextBased MicroTraining · Information security

1 Introduction

It is well established that insecure user behavior is a major problem in information security [25]. Users are commonly referred to as the weak link in security and while there are many technical security measures that address technical security issues, there is still a need for ways to improve user behavior with regards to security [7]. Threat actors recognize this notion and are often exploiting users, making the need for measures towards secure behavior emergent [11]. Desmand [8] described a need for making users understand the consequences of insecure behavior and learn them to behave in a secure way [8].

The common suggestion for how to improve user behavior is through the use of training [24]. Further, there are many different suggestions on how to carry out security training, from the practitioner as well as the research community. Different training measures range from lectures to micro training and nudges or special purpose tools such as password strength meters. While there are research examples of individual studies where researchers provide good evidence that specific methods work, there are reports that suggests that organizations training programs are not grounded in empirical evidence of their validity [1,2]. As such, the need for further research into this area is apparent.

© IFIP International Federation for Information Processing 2020
Published by Springer Nature Switzerland AG 2020
N. Clarke and S. Furnell (Eds.): HAISA 2020, IFIP AICT 593, pp. 71–81, 2020.
https://doi.org/10.1007/978-3-030-57404-8_6

This paper reports on research in this area that has been ongoing since 2014 intending to address the following objectives:

- O1: Develop a framework of guidelines for user training that supports user awareness and security-related decision making.
- O2: Evaluate how the framework developed in O1 can assist in making users act more securely
- O3: Evaluate if the framework from O1 can be applied in higher education

As such, the paper will present and discuss the framework developed in the projects and focus on the later parts of the development where the framework is refined. Following the presentation of the research process, previously published work will be accounted for and briefly described. The paper will then discuss the final part of the research process and present the final framework developed in the research. The paper will be concluded with a discussion on the topics and directions for future work.

2   Research Process

The research has been carried out in multiple steps and the complete process is outlined in Fig. 1, below. The emphasis in this paper is on the final parts of the research process (made bold in Fig. 1) The research as a whole employs a mixed-method approach using qualitative as well as quantitative methods. The reasoning behind this approach is twofold:

- Some research steps are intended to provide input to the development of the framework, making a qualitative approach feasible, while other steps intended to measure the effects of implementations of the guidelines making a quantitative approach feasible.
- Using different methods in research around the same objective, triangulation, can increase the validity of the outcomes [21].

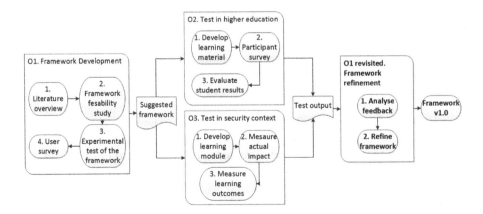

Fig. 1. Research process

While a discussion on all methodological approaches used in the research is well beyond the scope of this paper (and previously published [12,13,16–18]) the remainder of this section will introduce the methodology used in the final research steps, "Framework refinement".

During the evaluation step, quantitative data was used to evaluate implementations of the framework and qualitative data about the frameworks as well as the implementation of the framework was gathered. The data was gathered using free-text survey questions. Further, the suggested framework was presented at the 19th Seminar within the Framework of a Swedish IT Security Network for PhD students (SWITS) [13] and the following discussions were summarized and considered in the framework refinement. The gathered data was analyzed using the principles of thematic coding [5]. The following codes were established prior to the analysis:

- Strengths
- Weaknesses
- Clarification needed

The first code was used to identify the strengths of the framework. The second and third codes were used to identify areas in the framework that needed reconsideration or improvement. The coding was performed together by the authors and the results were used to refine the framework and establish the final framework as presented in this paper.

3   Previous Research Steps

This chapter briefly presents previous research in this project beginning with the developed framework, Context Based MicroTraining (CBMT). Then, the implementation and evaluation of CBMT based training will be presented.

3.1   CBMT and the Development Thereof

The development began with a literature search that intended to find what goals the framework should seek to fulfill. Fundamental problems in the domain of information security training were identified to be that users are not actively participating in information security training measures [19] and that users, while worried about cyber threats, lack awareness about the possible damage they can cause [22]. It was also evident that several sources reported that security measures must, in themselves, be easy to use, appear useful and interrupt the user's normal computer usage as little as possible [3,23,28]. Following the literature search, four requirements for what was called a "Situated Learning based defense mechanism" were established:

- Provide training that users want to make use of, instead of forcing users to participate in the training
- Include an awareness increasing mechanism

- Provide training to the user when the user is in a situation where the training is relevant
- Require no prior knowledge from the user

The first two bullets were achieved by the third bullet and the idea was that information security training should be delivered to the user when the user entered a situation where the training was of direct relevance. For instance, a training module designed to teach the user about online fraud would be presented to the user when she was in a situation where she risked being defrauded [12]. A fundamental notion in the requirements is that people need motivation in order to learn and that adults will be more likely to learn if the presented information seems meaningful, a notion based on the concept of andragogy [10, 20].

A demonstrator of a defense mechanism based on the requirements was implemented, the context was online fraud. A survey containing the demonstrator and questions about how the respondents perceived it was presented. 98 respondents answered the survey and it revealed that the respondents were, overall, positive towards the defense mechanism. The survey data did, however, stress that it was important for a defense mechanism to not be enforcing and that it should be possible to read the information presented quickly [12]. This falls well in line with what Nanolearning tries to facilitate [26]. Previous research into microlearning also shows positive results in terms of learner participation [6]. Supporting a high degree of user participation is one of the fundamental problems this research aims to address. The requirements were updated, and expressed as a small framework of goals and guidelines were the goals reflect the overall goal of the framework and the guidelines are more practical implementation guidelines. The goals were the following:

- Provide training that users want to make use of, instead of forcing users to participate in the training
- Include an awareness increasing mechanism
- Require no prior knowledge from the user
- Be short and easy to absorb

And the guidelines were:

- Delivered to users when it is relevant to their current situation.
- Delivered in short sequences
- Relevant to the users current situation
- Include a practical element
- Must be possible to opt-out

Simultaneously, an experiment where participants were asked to use the defense mechanism before rating fraudulent ads from Swedish online marketplaces was carried out. A control group rated the same ads without training. The experiment showed that the group that performed the training was better at detecting fraudulent ads than the participants in the control group. They were also better at correctly identifying legitimate ads as legitimate suggesting that the defense mechanism could be useful [16].

Next, another survey measuring how the respondents perceived using training modules developed according to the framework was performed. In this case, the respondents were asked to follow three different training modules (password creation, ransomware, and phishing) and then asked about their experience. In summary, the participants were positive towards the training modules and stressed that short sequences of training in-the-moment are preferable to training that is time consuming [18]. As such, the framework was established and the research continued to an evaluation phase. The Framework was named ContextBased MicroTraining (CBMT).

To summarize, CBMT is a teaching method that suggests that information should be presented in short sequences to the learner. It should also include a practical element and be of direct relevance to the user's current situation. A visual representation of CBMT is presented in Fig. 2, below.

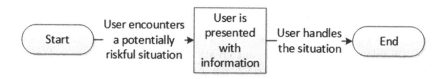

Fig. 2. CBMT overview

3.2   Evaluation of CBMT for Use in Higher Education

Following the establishment of the framework, it was evaluated in two settings. First, for use in higher education. In this evaluation, a technical undergraduate course was used and the purpose was to measure learning outcomes of CBMT based training. The course was a Cisco Network Academy course and was selected since it was very practical in nature and it teaches a standardized curriculum and is examined using a standardized test. In this particular case, the course was thought by the researchers and the use of standardized material served as a means of minimizing bias. Applying the framework to a course was selected because it allows for a relatively controlled environment where the actual learning outcomes can be compared to the learning outcomes from previous times the course has been given.

During this evaluation, several learning modules were designed according to the goals and guidelines of the framework. The students were then handed the modules as primary lecturing material. The nature of the modules was that they asked the students to listen to a short theoretical presentation and then do or follow a practical task. One module covered a small bit of theory and the time needed to consume one module was kept to a minimum. Several modules were created and combined into video lectures that covered the full curriculum. A version of the modules can be found and used freely at YouTube[1] The teaching

---

[1] www.youtube.com/playlist?list=PLEjQDf4Fr75qADv9J0UbNaiUmB8zMhw6V.

was combined with supervision that allowed the students to ask questions and discuss the content of the learning modules. The course ended with a practical and theoretical test. In terms of learning outcomes, the students that used the material developed according to the CBMT framework performed similar to, or slightly better than students from previous years where the same material was delivered as traditional lectures. The students were handed a survey that measured how they perceived the lecture material and 26/28 students reported that they preferred the CBMT learning modules over traditional lectures, when asked to pick one or the other. Further, the students reported that the CBMT learning modules motivated them in their studies and made them understand the theoretical material [17]. In terms of usage, 75% of the students reporting using 9 or 10 of the 10 available video lectures.

3.3   Evaluation of CBMT for Information Security Training

In another evaluation, CBMT was evaluated as a means of assisting users in selecting better passwords. In this case, an interactive CBMT module was created and implemented at the account creation page of a local internet service provider. The module was activated when a user clicked in the "create password" field and is showcased as a demonstrator at GitHub[2]. In essence, a window presenting basic password security tips was presented, the guidelines themselves were based on Kävrestad et al. [15]. The tip was to use passwords made up of four words or more. The user could then decide to learn more or to create a password. Upon selecting learn more, the user was presented with a series of questions that gave direct feedback and upon clicking create password, the user was taken to a password creation step.

50% of the users on the web site were assigned to use the CBMT module during account creation, the other 50% used the original account creation page. The strength of passwords created by the users was measured using the zxcvbn method by Drop box [9]. The experiment showed that users that used the CBMT module created stronger passwords than users in the control group. The effect was measured on a 4-graded scale that reflected password entropy as described by [27]. The group using the CBMT module had a median value of 3 while the other group had a median or 2, and the result was statistically significant at the 99% level.

Following the experiment, a survey was executed where participants were presented with password creation guidelines using the CBMT module, in plain text or using a link to plain text. They then received questions about the guidelines just presented to them. The survey suggested that the participants presented with the CBMT module were slightly more aware of the password guidelines than the users presented with plain text. They were significantly more aware of the guidelines compared to the users that received a link to plain text guidelines. The results of this evaluation show that CBMT can serve as a framework for the development of effective information security training that fulfilled the goals of

---

[2] https://rr222cy.github.io/SecurityAssistantWidget/.

the CBMT framework. The results of this study are accepted for publication in IFIP SEC 2020.

4   Guideline Refinement and Establishment

Following the evaluation of the CBMT in higher education and for presentation of password creation guidelines, the framework was further refined. This refinement was used in a three-step process:

1. Insights acquired by the researchers during the evaluation were considered.
2. The framework was presented and discussed at the 19th Seminar within the Swedish IT Security Network for PhD students (SWITS).
3. Free-text answers acquired from the surveys in the evaluation phase were analyzed.

During the evaluation of CBMT for use in higher education is became evident that while the framework suggests that training should be carried out in naturally occurring situations, such as when a user is browsing the Internet, this is not always possible. In some cases, the situations need to be constructed. A constructed situation includes a situation that the user is put in rather than a situation that the user encounters. A user would, for instance, encounter phishing making that encounter a natural situation. On the contrary, a constructed situation would be when the user is asked to carry out a task as part of education or training. Subsequently, when CBMT is used in a natural situation it is used in direct relation to a practical element and does not in itself include the practical element. On the other hand, it must include a practical element itself when used in a constructed situation. The guidelines in the framework were updated to support this insight.

During the discussion at SWITS, several conference participants were positive about the framework but suggested that what the framework presents must in itself be easy to follow. The original intention of the framework was to not consider the actual material presented, only the delivery thereof. However, the consensus in the discussion at SWITS led to a new guideline reflecting that the information presented must be easy to follow. That is certainly in line with the goal that states that no prior knowledge should be required by the users. The need for this addition was further made evident from the evaluation in the context of password guidelines. It is clear that many password creations guidelines are hard to use [4, 14, 29] and one can consider the meaning of a good delivery if the information itself is hard to use.

The free text answers from the surveys in two validations steps (O2 and O3) were analyzed using thematic coding. The coding was performed by the authors together simultaneously to enhance inter-coding validity. The coding revealed no negative comments about the framework and 11 comments that were positive but did not otherwise add to the development of the framework.

Several users expressed that they did not follow the guidelines in favor of their own more complex password creation guidelines. None of these users reported being negative about the learning module. This suggests that the learning module was not annoying for advanced users. Typical information security training tools, including this, is targeting all users. We argue that training presented to users that do not perceive that they need the training can be interpreted as an annoyance rather than provide value. It is therefore important that tools built using the CBMT framework are developed so that they minimize interruption and annoyance, and provide a way for users to skip the training, especially if it is repetitive.

In line with this reasoning, it is important that the presented material really highlights the most important aspects of the subject matter, a notion that was also identified in the analyzed material. While it is important that the presented material covers the essential information the users need, it is evident from the analyzed information that most users will only notice some aspect of the presented material. It is therefore important that the most crucial points in the material are, in some way, highlighted even more. One example of highlighting, which was used in the password training module, was to make the most important points bold.

Following the refinements, the final goals and guidelines of CBMT are as follows (modifications in the refinement step are in *italic*):
Goals:

- Provide training that users want to make use of, instead of forcing users to participate in the training
- Include an awareness increasing mechanism
- Require no prior knowledge from the user
- Be short and easy to absorb
- *Should minimize annoyance for all users, especially users already familiar with the subject*

Guidelines:

- Delivered to users when it is relevant to their current situation. *The situation can be constructed or natural.*
- Delivered in short sequences
- Relevant to the users current situation
- Include *or directly relate to* a practical element
- *The information presented must in itself be easy to understand*
- *The most crucial points of the information should be highlighted*
- Must be possible to opt-out *or skip*

5   Discussion

This paper reports on the latest steps of research that has been ongoing for several years and spanned several projects. The overall aim of the research has been to address the area of end-user training in information security. In this area, many suggestions for how to conduct information security and awareness training have been presented and tested, yet we are still in the situation that end-user behavior remains one of the most highlighted threats in the cyber domain.

This research began with a review of the area and initial ideas for how information security training could be conducted leveraging theories about how humans are motivated to learn. It was found feasible to train users about topics that relate to what they are doing, and present training in situations where it is of direct relevance and use to the user. At this point, a suggested framework of goals and guidelines for how to implement training mechanisms was presented.

The suggested framework was tested and analyzed in two different contexts, higher education and password creation. Higher education was chosen because it offered an opportunity to present students with reoccurring training and an ability to measure not only the direct effect but also the learning outcomes some weeks after the training was performed, in the form of exams. Password creation was chosen as the other case since it offered a good way to measure the effects of the training. In this particular case, passwords created after being presented with a password guideline training module were measured and compared with passwords that were not created using the training module and was found to be stronger. As such, the two parts of the testing process shows that the CBMT framework can yield direct results and sustained knowledge for the user.

The emphasis in this paper has been the final refinement of the framework following the testing. The refinement was based on insights drawn during the implementation of the guidelines, conference discussions and qualitative data gathered during the testing phase. The refinement phase revealed that several users were positive to the CBMT learning modules they have used and some refinements that were previously presented.

The scientific contribution of this paper is further insight into how effective information security training should be carried out. It also presents a concrete framework for information security training that we consider to be a version 1.0. It is tested in some contexts but can be developed, tested and extended further and we encourage others to continue to research around the framework that we present. The research also raises an interesting ethical point, is it ethical to continue to use the training methods that are proven not to be effective or should effort be made into developing new and better methods?

The research also brings value to the practitioner community. First, the research has resulted in implementations of CBMT that are free to use[3]. Second, the paper present a concrete and tested framework for how effective information security and awareness training can be implemented.

While this paper present a framework that we argue is ready for use, there is still room for further development and verification. Future projects could take a pedagogical angle and review the framework from a pedagogical perspective.

---

[3] Password guideline module: github.com/rr222cy/SecurityAssistantWidget, Cisco Certified Network Associate training videos: www.youtube.com/playlist?list=PLE jQDf4Fr75qADv9J0UbNaiUmB8zMhw6V.

Another area for future work is to implement CBMT in more security-related contexts and evaluate the results. This can, for instance, include phishing, online fraud and more.

References

1. Al-Daeef, M.M., Basir, N., Saudi, M.M.: Security awareness training: a review. In: Proceedings of World Congress on Engineering, vol. 1, pp. 5–7 (2017)
2. Alshaikh, M., Maynard, S.B., Ahmad, A., Chang, S.: An exploratory study of current information security training and awareness practices in organizations. In: Proceedings of the 51st Hawaii International Conference on System Sciences (2018)
3. Beckles, B., Welch, V., Basney, J.: Mechanisms for increasing the usability of grid security. Int. J. Hum Comput Stud. **63**(1–2), 74–101 (2005)
4. Biocco, P., Anwar, M.: Grid framework to address password memorability issues and offline password attacks. In: Nicholson, D. (ed.) AHFE 2017. AISC, vol. 593, pp. 52–61. Springer, Cham (2018). https://doi.org/10.1007/978-3-319-60585-2_6
5. Braun, V., Clarke, V.: Using thematic analysis in psychology. Qual. Res. Psychol. **3**(2), 77–101 (2006)
6. Bruck, P.A., Motiwalla, L., Foerster, F.: Mobile learning with micro-content: a framework and evaluation. Bled e-Conf. **25**, 527–543 (2012)
7. Bulgurcu, B., Cavusoglu, H., Benbasat, I.: Information security policy compliance: an empirical study of rationality-based beliefs and information security awareness. MIS Q. **34**(3), 523–548 (2010)
8. Desman, M.B.: The ten commandments of information security awareness training. Inf. Secur. J. A Glob. Perspect. **11**(6), 39–44 (2003)
9. Dropbox: Low-budget password strength estimation. https://github.com/dropbox/zxcvbn. Accessed 07 Oct 2019
10. Hedin, A.: Lärande på hög nivå. Uppsala universitet (2006)
11. Joinson, A., van Steen, T.: Human aspects of cyber security: behaviour or culture change? Cyber Secur. Peer-Rev. J. **1**(4), 351–360 (2018)
12. Kävrestad, J.: Defining, categorizing and defending against online fraud (2014)
13. Kävrestad, J.: Using contextbased microtraining to enforce secure behavior among computer users. In: 19th Seminar within the Framework of a Swedish IT Security Network for Ph.D. students, Karlstad (2019)
14. Kävrestad, J., Eriksson, F., Nohlberg, M.: Understanding passwords-a taxonomy of password creation strategies. Inf. Comput. Secur. **27**(3), 453–467 (2019)
15. Kävrestad, J., Lennartsson, M., Birath, M., Nohlberg, M.: Constructing secure and memorable passwords. Inf. Comput. Secur. (2020)
16. Kävrestad, J., Marcus, N.: Online fraud defence by context based micro training. In: Ninth International Symposium on Human Aspects of Information Security & Assurance (HAISA 2015), pp. 256–264 (2015)
17. Kävrestad, J., Nohlberg, M.: Using context based micro training to develop oer for the benefit of all. In: Proceedings of the 15th International Symposium on Open Collaboration, pp. 1–10 (2019)
18. Kävrestad, J., Skärgård, M., Nohlberg, M.: Users perception of using CBMT for information security training. In: Human Aspects of Information Security & Assurance (HAISA 2019) International Symposium on Human Aspects of Information Security & Assurance (HAISA 2019), Nicosia, Cyprus, pp. 122–131 (2019)

19. Kim, E.B.: Recommendations for information security awareness training for college students. Inf. Manag. Comput. Secur. **22**, 115–126 (2014)
20. Knowles, M.: Andragogy in action: applying modern principles of adult learning (1984)
21. Lincoln, Y.S., Guba, E.G.: Naturalistic inquiry (1985)
22. Marinos, L., Belmonte, A., Rekleitis, E.: Threat landscape 2013 (2013)
23. Payne, B.D., Edwards, W.K.: A brief introduction to usable security. IEEE Internet Comput. **12**(3), 13–21 (2008)
24. Puhakainen, P., Siponen, M.: Improving employees' compliance through information systems security training: an action research study. MIS Q. **34**, 757–778 (2010)
25. Safa, N.S., Von Solms, R.: An information security knowledge sharing model in organizations. Comput. Hum. Behavi. **57**, 442–451 (2016)
26. Wang, M., Xiao, J., Chen, Y., Min, W.: Mobile learning design: the LTCS model. In: 2014 International Conference on Intelligent Environments, pp. 318–325. IEEE (2014)
27. Wheeler, D.L.: zxcvbn: low-budget password strength estimation. In: 25th {USENIX} Security Symposium ({USENIX} Security 16), pp. 157–173 (2016)
28. Whitten, A., Tygar, J.D.: Why johnny can't encrypt: a usability evaluation of PGP 5.0. In: USENIX Security Symposium, vol. 348, pp. 169–184 (1999)
29. Woo, S.S., Mirkovic, J.: *GuidedPass*: helping users to create strong and memorable passwords. In: Bailey, M., Holz, T., Stamatogiannakis, M., Ioannidis, S. (eds.) RAID 2018. LNCS, vol. 11050, pp. 250–270. Springer, Cham (2018). https://doi.org/10.1007/978-3-030-00470-5_12

Social Engineering

Employees' Interest in Professional Advancement on LinkedIn Increases Susceptibility to Cyber-Social Engineering: An Empirical Test

Mohammed Khaled N. Alotaibi$^{(\boxtimes)}$

School of Computer Science and Statistics, Trinity College Dublin, Dublin, Ireland
malotaib@tcd.ie

Abstract. Social networking sites (SNS) and platforms such as LinkedIn and Indeed are perceived as trustworthy, as they are portrayed as professional, unlike multipurpose platforms, such as Facebook. In career-oriented networking sites (CSNS), aside from self-presentation of credentials, the level of engagement with peers for professional advancement to purposefully amplify one's profile, such as by connecting with someone or, sometimes unwittingly, accepting messages, e.g., for recruitment, can make them a happy hunting ground for cyber-social engineers. This study examines the impact of two variables highlighted as leading motives behind the use of LinkedIn. It presents the findings of research into the ways employees in Saudi public organisations can be susceptible to cyberthreats while accessing the most popular career-oriented social networking site, LinkedIn, while at work.

Keywords: Cyber-social engineering · LinkedIn · Susceptibility · Professional advancement · Self-presentation · Phishing

1 Introduction

This paper presents partial empirical findings of an ongoing project following an explanatory sequential design. It seeks to examine the association between employees' susceptibility to cyber-social engineering (CSE), particularly over career-oriented social networking sites (CSNS), while working in public organisations. The organisations studied offer advanced online e-government services to residents of Saudi Arabia; therefore, any internal or external weaknesses of employees that induce them to respond to malicious requests or messages could greatly jeopardize the system.

25% of the total time people spend on the internet is on SNS [1, 2]. Social engineering takes advantage of the fact that users on SNS platforms are often unaware of potential threats; they do not suspect communication from an unknown origin, or even believe they might be susceptible to manipulation by cyber-social engineering [3]. This vulnerability leaves organisations open to attack [2]. According to a report by *Sophos*, LinkedIn is among the SN platforms most affected by increased spam and malware incidents [5–7].

N. Clarke and S. Furnell (Eds.): HAISA 2020, IFIP AICT 593, pp. 85–96, 2020.
https://doi.org/10.1007/978-3-030-57404-8_7

Kim and Cha [8] suggested that there are four motivations behind the use of SNSs (Facebook, LinkedIn, Twitter):

1. Expressive information networking;
2. Entertainment, relief from boredom;
3. Professional advancement;
4. Escape through companionship.

They found that the motivations for using Facebook and LinkedIn differ. It is likely that CSE attackers will cultivate skillful influential messages to respond to these motivations, based on the context. For instance, users on LinkedIn use the site for professional advancement (sharing work-related curriculum vitae posts, networking with other professional contacts, obtaining peer support from others, etc.) and, secondly, for self-presentation (providing personal credentials, introducing or telling others about oneself). These motivations can be misused by a social engineer masquerading as an employer, a job-seeker or a colleague [9]. Several studies have looked at how users' personal information can be accessed through manipulative and persuasive tactics in the email environment [10–14].

However, SNSs have become a very attractive means of communication, and they reveal more of a user's character, as well as personal information and interactions (posts, shares, private messaging). It is easy to see how SNSs are becoming an attractive medium for CSE attacks (e.g., phishing links and impersonation) [15–17]. This type of internet crime has a financial impact on organizations infiltrated through an unsuspecting employee; in early 2016, the Internet Crime Complaint Center at the FBI reported that social engineering and associated cyber-crimes cost companies of all sizes across 108 countries more than $2bn between October 2013 and February 2016 [18].

CSE poses a serious threat to information and personal security, through its growing tendency to exploit and misuse social networks and virtual communities [19]. According to Mills [20], social networking sites are considered the new 'battleground' for cyber-attacks, since personal, employment, and other geographic and demographic information are exposed. He stresses that such sites "can be used as a means of social engineering against not only that person but any organization's information security with which this individual is affiliated" (Ibid.). For businesses that increasingly rely on remote collaboration, online channels of communication, online platforms and tools for virtual communication, CSE poses a serious threat to the security of their organizations' data centers. This is exacerbated by the growing trend towards BYOD, or 'bring your own device', which is linked by Krombholz et al. [21] with "policies and the use of online communities, communication and collaboration tools in private and business environments". Combining online tools in both private and business environments provides cyber attackers with many new opportunities for malicious operations.

Phishing attacks, or online scams, a common CSE technique, are easy to launch, since personal information can, at times, be publicly accessed from new media platforms, such as social networking sites [22]. For instance, Sivasankaran, a security architect and member of a SecureWorks research team, is quoted in [23] as stressing the increase in CSE attacks through the utilization of the user's personal social media accounts. He adds that, "In early 2017, our research team observed phishing campaigns targeting several entities in the Middle East, with a focus on Saudi Arabian organizations". Similar attacks on Reuters are reported in [24].

These attacks are not new but are becoming more frequent and sophisticated in cyberspace throughout the world.

2   Susceptibility Influenced by Self-presentation and Professional Advancement

As noted earlier, the literature has shown that the use of career-related SNS platforms usually has two basic motivations; self-presentation and professional advancement [8]. Self-presentation is a form of information disclosure that involves providing personal credentials, and introducing or telling others about oneself [8], in the course of which the user reveals his/her professional identity [25]; consequently, individuals who are self-presentation-driven are more likely to be inclined to build relationships [26].

The goal of professional advancement is to develop a professional future; it is likely to involve sharing work-related career history posts, networking with professional contacts, and obtaining peer support from others.

Motives related to career advancement can be seen as an element that could be exploited by fake recruiter scams, for example, by a social engineer posing as an employer or job seeker, or using the cloned profile of a colleague [9]. As stated by [27], "job candidates are increasingly presenting themselves in online communities to impress employers"; therefore, any active individual who engages in a high degree of professional development and self-presentation behavior exposes herself or himself to cyber social engineering.

LinkedIn members have been found to be significantly more likely than Facebook users to allow public access to their professional and educational data [28], but there is little research specifically addressing these users' attitudes and dispositions toward potential cyber risk in the context of social networking sites generally and specifically over career-oriented SNS.

These considerations lead to two main hypotheses:

H1: Users who are motivated by career advancement on LinkedIn are more susceptible to CSE victimization than those who are less motivated in this way.
H2: Users who are more motivated to present themselves and their credentials on LinkedIn are more likely than others to be susceptible to CSE attacks.

3   Methodology

To explore the association between employees' susceptibility to cyber-social engineering and their inclination for self-presentation and professional advancement, with consideration also given to demographic factors, a survey was distributed to over 460 employees. The employees were selected by purposeful sampling of those who:

- work for a major government organisation, and

- use LinkedIn, and
- use another SNS

Data were collected from employees at an organisation which has access to data provided from the Saudi National Information Centre (NIC) as this portrays the magnitude of the organisation's sensitivity in terms of state security.

After cleaning, 394 responses were considered for data analysis. Males comprise three quarters of the sample (74.9%). The majority of the respondents were aged 29–39 (66.8%), but other age groups were also represented in the sample, with at least 19 people in each. Almost 87% of respondents were Saudis. Most participants were lower-level employees, but mid-level managers and top executives are also represented (20.8% and 4.3%, respectively). Only 0.5% (2 people) of the surveyed sample reported not using any SNS and only 3.3% (13 people) did not use any career-oriented SNS, Table 1 summarizes the distribution of respondents.

Table 1. Summary of demographic data of survey respondents (n = 394)

Demographics		Count (N)	%
Gender	Female	99	25.1%
	Male	295	74.9%
Age	18–28	28	7.1%
	29–39	263	66.8%
	40–50	44	11.2%
	51–61	19	4.8%
	62 and over	40	10.2%
Nationality	Saudi Arabia	342	86.8%
	Non-Saudi (expatriate)	52	13.2%
Government organisation sector type	Social development Sector (ORGSDS2)	278	70.6%
	Labour sector (ORGLS1)	116	29.4%
Work level in organisation	Administrative officer/assistant (employee)	295	74.9%
	Department management/section supervisor or designee	85	21.6%
	Top-level management or designee	14	3.6%

The majority of respondents used social networking websites at least sometimes, with LinkedIn being by the far the most popular social networking platform. More than 90% of respondents reported that they used this career-oriented website; in the section of the survey concerning susceptibility to CSE risks, respondents were asked about their experience with LinkedIn. ANOVA and Kruskal-Wallis analyses were conducted to test for significant differences among groups of respondents, using SPSS. Logistic regression was conducted using odds ratio (OR) to interpret relationships and test the hypotheses.

3.1 Measuring Susceptibility

Previous studies in the literature have measured susceptibility by inviting users to click on spear-phishing links. This study, however, will refrain from using experimental scenarios on SNS because of the difficulties of conducting experimental attacks on a large number of participants, as well as for ethical reasons. Therefore, susceptibility measurement used a simple YES/NO question: this constitutes an indirect, non-invasive approach, addressing the binary YES/NO variable in accordance with [29, 30]. This approach was supported by expert academic reviewers in the fields of computer science, organizational psychology and human factors who were consulted on the project.

Participants were asked a binary-type self-report question; "In all the time since you have been using LinkedIn, have you ever had something bad happen (at your work or in your personal life) that you can trace back to your usage of LinkedIn?" Answers were coded (0 = No, 1 = Yes), and participants were given the option to elaborate further, in an open-ended follow-up question: "If you have answered yes to the question, could you briefly explain what happened and how you knew what you did on LinkedIn was the reason?" This question was reviewed by experts in the field of survey design and industrial and organizational psychology.

3.2 Measuring Self-presentation and Professional Advancement

Self-presentation is defined as a form of information disclosure [25]. As such, individuals who are self-presentation-driven are keen to initiate interactions and build relationships. Self-presentation involves providing personal credentials and introducing or telling others about oneself.

Because users provide credentials only once, when they create an account, two scales were created to measure and determine the correlation of self-presentation with susceptibility to CSE as discussed in the literature; one was based on profile features requested by the platform, e.g., phone number, work experience, while the other was based on user-initiated activities such as making contacts and sharing files. The first scale is binary, as shown in Table 2; the other is a frequency scale to measure professional advancement, shown in Table 3. Internal consistency was measured for both scales, reporting Cronbach's alpha of .843 and .899 respectively.

The binary scale measures how much information employees put online in relation to their self-presentation, since the more information they put online, the more information cyber social engineers can glean to create a compelling fake profile or other intervention.

Professional development motivates use of LinkedIn in several ways: it is seen as helpful for developing a professional future, sharing work-related curriculum vitae posts, networking with professional contacts, and for obtaining peer support from others. Participants were asked to rate on a scale of 1–5 (never, rarely, sometimes, often, always) how often they used LinkedIn for these purposes.

Table 2. Self-presentation on linkedIn (binary questions)

Have you put your work experience history on?
Have you put your Educational history on?
Have you put your licenses on?
Have you put your certificates on?
Have you put your work email address on?
Have you put your work telephone number on?
Have you created an about me page?
Have you put where you currently work?
Have you put your job title?
Have you put a profile picture?
Have you set your profile to public so anyone can view it?
Have you revealed or updated your current location?
Is your company logo on your profile?

Table 3. Professional advancement on linkedIn (frequency scale)

Have you connected with professionals that could help you with your professional advancement?
Have you followed other companies that you believe could increase your professional advancement?
Have you shared your work-related CV to companies which you believe could help you with your professional advancement?
Have you shared your work-related CV with professionals with whom you feel can help with your professional advancement?
Have you accepted connections from people whom you don't know but can see that they have many connections themselves?
Have you accepted network connections from people who are connected to your connections?
Have you accepted a connection request on LinkedIn because you recognized the photo?
Have you messaged your connections for support in career or work-related matters?
Have you shared documents, audio or video with connections in order to assist you with a problem?
Have you accepted documents, audio or videos from connections in relation to receiving support from them?

4 Data Analysis Findings

4.1 Susceptibility to Cyber-Social Engineering *(Dependent Variable)*

24.1% of all respondents responded that they had suffered a bad experience that they could trace to LinkedIn. According to the chi-square test results, males had more negative experiences on LinkedIn than females (28.1% of males compared to 12.1% of females, p = 0.023), while Saudis reported more such experiences than non-Saudis (26.0% vs 11.5%, p = 0.023). The results also indicate that the higher the work level of the employee in the organization – the less likely respondents were to report negative experiences (28.5% of lower-level employees, 11.8% of mid-level employees and only 7.1% of top-level managers).

No statistically significant association was found between age and susceptibility to CSE victimization; sample estimates suggest that employees aged 51+ were less suscep-tible to online attacks in CSNS, but the sample size is insufficient to claim that this effect is significant. 44 respondents explained what happened. Even though the consequences of cyberattacks differed widely (viruses, hard drive crashes, creation of fake accounts using the respondent's personal information, stealing of payment details, etc.), most sources of cyberthreat fall into one of a few categories: phishing links sent in messages (46%); phishing emails with links (13%); fake job invitations to get personal/payment information from applicants (13%); using personal information to create fake profiles (7%); paying for fake products and services online (9%); requests to upload documents containing personal information (5%) or to download files which cause problems when opened (5%).

4.2 Self-presentation *(Independent Variable)*

The binary scale of self-presentation consists of 13 yes/no items that measure how much information respondents have put online. The more information that is exposed online, the more potential there is for creating a compelling a fake profile or other undesirable cyber-intervention.

A self-presentation score (Table 5) was obtained by calculating the proportion of items put online (minimum = 0, maximum = 100) and a series of ANOVA and Kruskal-Wallis tests was conducted to test for the significance of differences among groups of respondents, based on gender, age, nationality and work level. The average self-presentation score is 44.8%. At the 5% significance level, no demographic differences were found, but at the 10% level, self-presentation is significantly higher (ANOVA p = 0.079, Kruskal-Wallis p = 0.053) for non-Saudis (M = 51.0, SD = 23.3) than for Saudis (M = 43.9, SD = 27.9). Some differences in individual items were significant at the 5% level: non-Saudis, for example, put their certificates and work telephone number on their LinkedIn page more often than Saudis see Table 4.

4.3 Professional Advancement *(Independent Variable)*

A professional advancement score was computed as the average of the 10 items and a series of ANOVA and Kruskal-Wallis tests was conducted to test for significant dif-ferences among groups of respondents, based on gender, age, nationality, and work

Table 4. Self-presentation information placed online by nationality

Items	Total	Nationality		Chi-square test of association p-value
		Saudi Arabia	Non-Saudi (Expatriate)	
company (or organisation) logo	80.2%	79.8%	82.7%	0.629
put licences on	70.1%	68.4%	80.8%	0.070
put work telephone number on	62.9%	60.8%	76.9%	0.025
put certificates on	58.6%	56.7%	71.2%	0.049
set profile to public so anyone can view it	47.7%	46.8%	53.8%	0.342
created an "About me" page	38.6%	37.4%	46.2%	0.228
put educational history on	37.6%	36.5%	44.2%	0.287
put where currently worked	35.0%	34.2%	40.4%	0.385
put a profile picture	33.8%	34.8%	26.9%	0.263
revealed or updated current location	32.5%	31.9%	36.5%	0.503
put work experience history on	28.9%	28.4%	32.7%	0.521
put work email address on	28.7%	27.8%	34.6%	0.310
put job title	27.9%	26.6%	36.5%	0.137

level. This analysis indicated that non-Saudis were significantly more actively involved (ANOVA p = 0.017, Kruskal-Wallis p = 0.019) in professional development communication on LinkedIn (M = 2.25, SD = 1.00) compared to Saudis (M = 2.61, SD = 1.03). Non-Saudis were more likely than Saudis to connect with potentially helpful professionals, follow other companies, share their CV to other companies, and both share and accept various files.

4.4 Testing the Hypotheses

Bivariate logistic regressions of susceptibility on self-presentation and professional advancement were performed and the scores are presented in Table 5. The association between self-presentation and susceptibility to bad situations on LinkedIn is insignificant (p = 0.198). However, an increase in the score characterizing behaviour associated with professional advancement (higher score meaning higher interest in professional advancement) increases the probability of having experienced cybersecurity problems over LinkedIn (OR = 1.048, p < 0.001).

The single action related to professional advancement that was most strongly associated with cybersecurity problems traceable to the use of LinkedIn was accepting connections from people who they did not know but who had many connections themselves (OR = 1.439, p < 0.001). Therefore, employees should be warned that being linked with many other people is not a sign of the contact's trustworthiness. The statistical relationship between this action and susceptibility to cyber-social engineering is shown in Table 6. Table 7 summarises the levels of support for hypotheses 1 and 2.

4.5 Limitations and Recommendations for Future Work

The findings of this study emanate from an ongoing project that attempts to examine an extended model pertaining to employees' susceptibility to cyber-social engineering

Table 5. Parameter estimates of bivariate logistic regression models (dependent variable: *susceptibility*)

Variables	B	S.E.	Wald	Sig.	Exp (B)[a]
Self-presentation score	−0.530	0.411	1.661	0.198	0.589
Constant	−0.907	0.216	17.621	0.000	0.404
Professional advancement score	0.047	0.012	15.720	0.000	1.048
Constant	−2.302	0.327	49.432	0.000	0.100

[a]Exponentiated coefficients of the logit model (Exp(B)) from the last column of regression tables) correspond to odds ratios, i.e., the number of times the odds of the bad outcome increase if the explanatory variable increases by 1 unit. Odds Ratio equals the exponentiated coefficient of the logistic regression and shows the number of times the odds of having been victimized on LinkedIn increase if the independent variable increases by 1. OR > 1 indicates that the higher the value of the independent variable, the higher the risk of victimization.

Table 6. Parameter estimates of the stepwise multivariate logistic regression model (dependent variable: *susceptibility*)

Item	B	S.E.	Wald	Sig.	Exp(B)
Accepted connections from people whom you don't know but can see that they have many connections themselves	0.364	0.085	18.346	0.000	1.439
Constant	−2.052	0.255	64.650	0.000	0.129

Table 7. Summary of hypothesis-testing results related to the effects of self-presentation and professional advancement on LinkedIn

Hypothesis		Was evidence supporting the hypothesis found?
H1:	Users who are motivated by career advancement on LinkedIn are more susceptible to CSE victimization than those who are less motivated in this way	Yes, at 1% significance level
H2:	Users who are more motivated to present themselves and their credentials on LinkedIn are more likely than others to be susceptible to CSE attacks	No

over professional networking platforms in the workplace. One limitation of the current study is that deploying a self-reporting binary question may not precisely expose real-world negative experiences and that employees may be reluctant to admit being victims of cyber-social engineering. However, conducting a scenario-based experiment can be difficult over social media platforms, particularly for legal reasons.

An overall limitation is present at this point, since future work will present findings of how personality characteristics, cognitive and dispositional factors play a role in the risks faced by employees and, consequently, their organisations. There will also be a qualitative phase to dig deeper and unearth how and to what extent these factors, including employees' desire for professional advancement, are a threat to their safe use of career-oriented social networking sites.

5 Conclusion

Cyber-social engineering has proven to be an ongoing issue, whereby cyber engineers adapt their techniques of deceptive messages, based on unsuspecting individuals' needs and behaviours. The current study has shown that top management, as the structural power in the organisation, are less susceptible to CSE attacks on LinkedIn, they do not have a significant association with professional advancement and self-presentation when examining susceptibility to CSE attack. Aspirations for career advancement are shown to be the main reason for people's readiness to share information on LinkedIn. A possible explanation is that professional advancement involves actively contacting various people on LinkedIn and disclosing sensitive information that may be valuable to actual or fake recruiters or potential business partners.

The study also shows that non-Saudis are more likely to share information than Saudis. In addition, non-Saudis show increased levels of activity in professional advancements, which makes them more susceptible to CSE attacks than Saudi employees. The current study has found that nationality is the only demographic characteristic that plays a mediating factor when examining employee's professional advancement and its susceptibility to CSE over LinkedIn. Arguably, this could be due to Saudis having greater job security than non-Saudis, who are generally employed on fixed-term contracts and consequently have an eye open for the next opportunity. Motivation for professional advancement, however, leading to a greater readiness to divulge personal information, appears to be a common factor in making susceptibility greater among lower-level employees than in management, and among expatriate employees than among Saudis.

However, a further qualitative investigation is required to substantiate this interpretation.

References

1. GlobalWebIndex GWI Social 2016 - Summary Report. GlobalWebIndex's quarterly report on the latest trends in social networking (2016). https://www.slideshare.net/globalwebindex/globalwebindex-social-q1-summary-report. Accessed 3 Feb 2019
2. Warner-Søderholm, G., et al.: Who trusts social media? Comput. Hum. Behav. **81**, 303–315 (2018). https://doi.org/10.1016/j.chb.2017.12.026
3. George, B.: Opportunities and risks in online gaming environments. University of Plymouth (2016). http://hdl.handle.net/10026.1/8083. Accessed 1 Dec 2018

4. Wilcox, H., Bhattacharya, M., Islam, R.: Social engineering through social media: an investigation on enterprise security. In: Batten, L., Li, G., Niu, W., Warren, M. (eds.) ATIS 2014. CCIS, vol. 490, pp. 243–255. Springer, Heidelberg (2014). https://doi.org/10.1007/978-3-662-45670-5_23

5. Chi, M., Wanner, R.: Reducing the risks of social media to your organization security policy and social media use GIAC (GSEC) Gold Certification Security Policy and Social Media Use', *SANS institute* (2011). https://www.sans.org/reading-room/whitepapers/policyissues/reducing-risks-social-media-organization-33749. Accessed 4 Sept 2018

6. Sophos: Malware and spam rise 70% on social networks, security report reveals (2010). https://www.sophos.com/en-us/press-office/press-releases/2010/02/security-report-2010.aspx. Accessed 4 Sept 2018

7. ITFORCE.IE. Social Media - one of the biggest threats to an organisations security - IT Force, ITFORCE (2016). https://www.itforce.ie/blog/social-media-one-of-the-biggest-threats-to-a-organisations-security. Accessed 30 Jan 2019

8. Kim, M., Cha, J.: A comparison of Facebook, Twitter, and LinkedIn: examining motivations and network externalities for the use of social networking sites. First Monday **22**(11) (2017). https://doi.org/10.5210/fm.v22i11.8066

9. Misra, S., Goswami, S.: Network routing fundamentals, applications, and emerging technologies. In: Mobile Agents in Networking and Distributed Computing, pp. 127–160 (2017) https://doi.org/10.1002/9781118135617.ch6

10. Goel, S., Williams, K., Dincelli, E.: Got phished? internet security and human vulnerability. J. Assoc. Inform. Syst. **18**(1), 22–44 (2017). https://doi.org/10.17705/1jais.00447

11. Halevi, T., Memon, N., Nov, O.: 'Spear-phishing in the wild: a real-world study of personality, phishing self-efficacy vulnerability spear-phishing attacks. SSRN Electron. J. (2015). https://doi.org/10.2139/ssrn.2544742

12. Blythe, M., Petrie, H., Clark, J.A.: F for Fake: Four Studies on How We Fall for Phish (2011). https://www-users.cs.york.ac.uk/~jac/PublishedPapers/FIsForFake.pdf. Accessed 26 Nov 2018

13. Junger, M., Montoya, L., Overink, F.J.: Priming and warnings are not effective to prevent social engineering attacks, Comput. Hum. Behav. **66**, 75–87 (2017). https://doi.org/10.1016/j.chb.2016.09.012

14. Kleitman, S., Law Id, M.K.H., Kay, J.: It's the deceiver and the receiver: Individual differences in phishing susceptibility and false positives with item profiling. PLoS ONE **13**(10), e0205089 (2018)

15. Chitrey, A., et al.: Institute of advanced engineering and science a comprehensive study of social engineering based attacks in india to develop a conceptual model. Int. J. Inform. Netw. Secur. (IJINS) **1**(2), 45–53 (2012). https://doi.org/10.11591/ijins.v1i2.426

16. Algarni, A.A.: 'The impact of source characteristics on users' susceptibility to social engineering victimization in social networks mixed method study based on facebook'. Ph.D. thesis (2016). https://eprints.qut.edu.au/95604/1/AbdullahAyedM_Algarni_Thesis.pdf. Accessed 29 Sept 2017

17. Nagy, J., Pecho, P.: Social networks security. In: 2009 Third International Conference on Emerging Security Information, Systems and Technologies, pp. 321–325. IEEE (2009) https://doi.org/10.1109/securware.2009.56

18. Scannell, K.: Cyber crime: how companies are hit by email scams (2016). https://www.ft.com/content/19ade924-d0a5-11e5-831d-09f7778e7377. Accessed 27 Nov 2017

19. Fire, M., Goldschmidt, R., Elovici, Y.: Online social networks: threats and solutions. IEEE Commun. Surv. Tutor. **16**(4), 2019–2036 (2014)

20. Mills, D.: Analysis of a social engineering threat to information security exacerbated by vulnerabilities exposed through the inherent nature of social networking websites. In: 2009 Information Security Curriculum Development Conference on – InfoSecCD 2009, p. 139 (2009). https://doi.org/10.1145/1940976.1941003
21. Krombholz, K., et al.: Advanced social engineering attacks. J. Inform. Secur. Appl. **22**, 113–122 (2015). https://doi.org/10.1016/j.jisa.2014.09.005
22. Choo, K.R., Smith, R., McCusker, R.: Future directions in technology-enabled crime. Austr. Inst. Criminol. **2007**(78), 53–54 (2007). http://www.aic.gov.au/media_library/publications/rpp/78/rpp078.pdf. Accessed 27 Nov 2017
23. Freer, E.: SecureWorks talks ransomware, cyber fraud and social engineering| Intelligent CIO Middle East (2017). http://www.intelligentcio.com/me/2017/11/01/secureworks-talks-ransomware-cyber-fraud-and-social-engineering-at-gitex/. Accessed 27 Nov 2017
24. Paul, K., Auchard, E.: Saudi agency says country targeted in cyber spying campaign| Reuters, Reuters (2017). https://www.reuters.com/article/us-saudi-cyber/saudi-agency-says-country-targeted-in-cyber-spying-campaign-idUSKBN1DK27M. Accessed 7 Feb 2019
25. Bronstein, J.: Being private in public: information disclosure behaviour of Israeli bloggers. Inform. Res. **18**(4) (2013)
26. Schwämmlein, E., Wodzicki, K.: What to tell about me? Self-presentation in online communities. J. Comput. -Mediated Commun. **17**(4), 387–407 (2012). https://doi.org/10.1111/j.1083-6101.2012.01582.x
27. Dekay, S.: 'Are business-oriented social networking web sites useful resources for locating passive jobseekers? Results recent study. Bus. Commun. Q. (2009). https://doi.org/10.1177/1080569908330378
28. Zhitomirsky-Geffet, M., Bratspiess, Y.: Professional information disclosure on social networks: the case of Facebook and LinkedIn in Israel. J. Assoc. Inform. Sci. Technol. **67**(3), 493–504 (2016)
29. Nuno, A., John, F.A.V.: How to ask sensitive questions in conservation: a review of specialized questioning techniques. Biol. Conserv. **189**, 5–15 (2014). https://doi.org/10.1016/j.biocon.2014.09.047
30. Chaudhuri, A., Christofides, T.C.: A plea for indirect questioning: stigmatizing issues of social relevance'. In: Chaudhuri, A., Christofides, T.C. (eds.) Indirect Questioning in Sample Surveys, pp. 1–7. Springer, Heidelberg (2013). https://doi.org/10.1007/978-3-642-36276-7_1

Does Ubuntu Influence Social Engineering Susceptibility?

Ntsewa B. Mokobane and Reinhardt A. Botha(✉)

Center for Research in Information and Computer Security, Nelson Mandela University,
Port Elizabeth, South Africa
reinhardta.botha@mandela.ac.za

Abstract. Ubuntu refers to living according to a set of values shared by people who believe in a certain way of life. The values of ubuntu include group solidarity, conformity, compassion, respect, human dignity, a humanistic orientation, and collective unity. Some people consciously live by ubuntu values while others do so unconsciously. Ubuntu is ingrained in human beings. The values of ubuntu in aggregate build trust, which inadvertently feeds into the social engineering approach used in information security attacks. Ubuntu appears to increase vulnerability to the success of a social engineering attack. Social engineering is a key threat to information security in many organizations. Social engineers target employees as human beings are naturally vulnerable.

This study argues that ubuntu influences the success of social engineering attacks. It views ubuntu as foundational in making humans vulnerable to social engineers. The values that ubuntu is based on lead humans to trust, conform, be compassionate and loyal, and desire to help others. Social engineers exploit these values to obtain information, which they use to breach the information security of the targeted organization. Because of ubuntu, the extensive work of building rapport and elicitation, which would otherwise have been exhausting, is already completed and ready to be exploited by the social engineer. This paper exposes the potential influence of ubuntu on social engineering attacks. It concludes that security awareness, education and training programmes must be adapted to counter these influences and safeguard information assets.

Keywords: Attitude · Subjective norms · Behaviour · Elicitation · Ubuntu · Social engineer · Social engineering

1 Introduction

Despite ever-improving technical information security measures, training, and awareness programmes, information security breaches still rage on [16, 19]. Technical measures cannot adequately protect information and ensure information security by themselves [16]. These technical measures are dependent on the users of the information asset. These users are the weakest link in information security efforts [8, 11]. Several factors

© IFIP International Federation for Information Processing 2020
Published by Springer Nature Switzerland AG 2020
N. Clarke and S. Furnell (Eds.): HAISA 2020, IFIP AICT 593, pp. 97–108, 2020.
https://doi.org/10.1007/978-3-030-57404-8_8

are responsible for the weak nature of the human in information security. Some centre around the humanness of the users [19].

Ubuntu is a Zulu word that describes "a quality that includes the essential human virtues; compassion and humanity" [24]. However, it is often used in a more philosophical sense to mean "the belief in a universal bond of sharing that connects all humanity". This paper investigates the influence of ubuntu on the success of social engineering attacks on information users. Social engineering in the context of information security is the act of manipulating people into performing actions or divulging confidential information that can be used for a malicious purpose [14]. Social engineers target the ubuntu in the user and exploit the trust that humans have by nature to obtain specific information [30]. This information enables the social engineer to breach the target's information security. A social engineer is a person who uses deception to manipulate individuals into divulging confidential or personal information in order to gain unauthorized access to information and subsequently use that information for malicious purposes [12]. The theory of planned behaviour explains possible reasons why the social engineer easily triggers the ubuntu in the user.

This paper aims to analyze ubuntu and understand how it influences social engineering susceptibility. Ubuntu disarms the victim. It creates a blind spot in evaluating the security threat, as the level of security skepticism required to protect the information is overwhelmed by the values of ubuntu in the victim. Ubuntu influences one's attitude and how one reacts to a situation requiring action. Ubuntu's analysis is performed through the application of the theory of planned behaviour, which helps predict planned human behaviour. Understanding the impact of ubuntu on users' susceptibility to social engineering attacks will enable the development of more effective information security awareness and training programmes, specifically regarding defenses against social engineering attacks [2].

2   Human Behaviour

Humans are active in nature. From time to time social and other activities require that they take action and behave in particular ways to socially fit and survive in their day-to-day lives [26]. Behaviour choices are motivated by immediate personal interest and wider social interest. The individual chooses the behaviour that is most beneficial [25]. Social evaluation of the behaviour either encourages or discourages individual behaviour [21]. There is always a balance between personal and social interests.

Ubuntu, demographics, culture, stereotypes, stigma, personality, moods, and emotions determine what an individual perceives to be the right balance between personal and social interests [5]. Human behaviour is a product of individual beliefs, how individuals evaluate the outcome of a certain behaviour, their perception of the social acceptance of the behaviour, their motivation to carry out the behaviour, and their ability to carry out the behaviour [9]. The attitude of an individual is formed by beliefs about and an evaluation of the behaviour outcome. In contrast, the perception of social acceptance of the behaviour and the motivation to implement the behaviour form the subjective norms [3].

In this paper, the theory of planned behaviour is applied to discuss and understand ubuntu and how it influences attitude as well as how the values of ubuntu influence subjective norms. Figures 1, 2, 3, 4 and 5 show our attempt at explaining the influence of ubuntu on human behaviour through the application of different elements of the theory of planned behaviour. The relationship between ubuntu, some biases, social bond theory, and personality traits and their influence on attitude and subjective norms are illustrated through Ajzen [2] 's theory of planned behaviour.

3   Ubuntu

Ubuntu is a way of life, with pillars of personhood, humanity, humaneness, and morality [21]. Group solidarity, conformity, compassion, respect, human dignity, a humanistic orientation, and collective unity have, among others, been defined as key social values of ubuntu [22]. According to Metz [21], ubuntu promotes the spirit that one should live for others. Harmony, friendliness, and community are seen as great goods. According to ubuntu, one becomes a moral person insofar as one honours communal relationships [21]. Furthermore, a human being lives a genuinely human life to the extent that he/she prizes identity and solidarity with other human beings, and an individual realizes his/her true self by respecting the value of friendship [21].

The social values of ubuntu are engrained in human existence. People have always lived in groups and used to communicate around the fire, in city markets, in pubs, or in cafés [30]. Today social media has presented instant access to millions of people and individuals have new ways of interacting and fulfilling the ubuntu life philosophy.

The status of ubuntu as a golden thread and shared set of values has also allowed judges to feel at ease with freely applying ubuntu to new areas of law [15]. Figure 1 shows how ubuntu influences the behavioural beliefs of the individual and how the individual evaluates the outcome of a specific behaviour in a given situation. Behavioural beliefs together with an evaluation of the behaviour outcome determine the individual's attitude. The attitude is one element of behaviour intention.

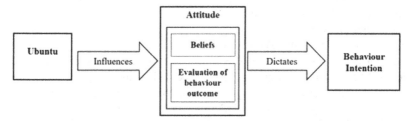

Fig. 1. Relationship between ubuntu, attitude, and behaviour intention [Author hypothesized relationship]

The values of ubuntu influence the worth of social agreement that specific reactions or behaviours are appropriate in a given situation. The individual who lives by ubuntu values always needs to comply with ubuntu values in their actions and inactions. Figure 2 shows the relationship between ubuntu values, subjective norms, and behaviour intention. Social pressure from family, friends, and others who matter to the individual urges the individual to behave and act in conformity with ubuntu values. The normative belief that an individual should comply with social expectations together with the desire to and confidence that one can live by ubuntu values form subjective norms [2].

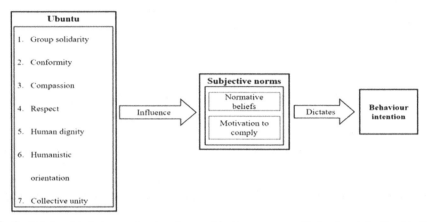

Fig. 2. Relationship between ubuntu values, subjective norms, and behaviour intention [Author hypothesized relationship]

The actual individual behaviour in a given situation is determined by factors such as predispositions, biases, traits, knowledge, ability, and skills. The values of ubuntu are some of the predispositions. Predispositions are important factors that influence an individual's emotions and behaviour [28].

Figure 3 outlines the bias ubuntu brings that influences the attitude of the individual in specific situations. Bias is a variable in the outcome evaluation and therefore sways the attitude towards, for example, the situation. Bias prevents the person from being objective [25]. Owing to the bias effect, people behave in particular ways because of how they feel rather than on a rational basis. People evaluate the outcomes of their behaviour through the frames of their bias.

Ubuntu engrains conformity, compassion, respect, human dignity, a humanistic orientation, and collective unity. These values bring the framing bias in that individuals evaluate their actions or respond to situations based on the question: "Will I still be respected if I behave in this manner or that manner?" Ubuntu brings the optimism bias in that the individual sees that behaving in a manner that is seen through the ubuntu value system confirms the humanness of the individual in the eyes of the group. It also brings the affect heuristic bias in that individuals choose how to behave based on the feelings of the group [25].

As indicated in Fig. 2, the values of ubuntu influence a person's subjective norms. Subjective norms are determined by normative beliefs and the motivation to comply with social expectation to act in a particular way. Subjective norms are regulated by social acceptance [8]. Ubuntu promotes group solidarity, conformity, compassion, and collective unity [22]. The individuals within groups are socialized and conformity is promoted through bonds such as attachment, commitment, involvement, and personal norms [16]. Social bond theory postulates that when people build upon such bonds, their urge to indulge in antisocial or anti-establishment behaviours is reduced [16]. The gain

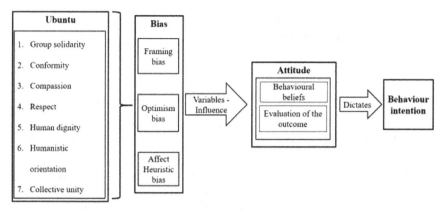

Fig. 3. Ubuntu controls attitude through bias [Author hypothesized relationship]

from behaving in the ubuntu way is that it brings praise to the individual and respect to the group. People generally have the desire to help other people and the desire to be liked by other people [11, 13]. Figure 4 shows how the influence of ubuntu on subjective norms is catalyzed by the endowment effect, trust, and the agreeable trait found in individuals.

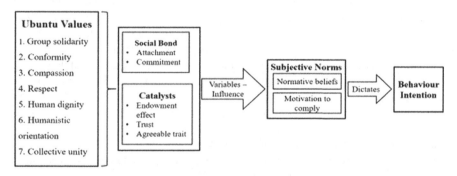

Fig. 4. Influence of ubuntu on subjective norms [Author hypothesized relationship]

Like all other human behaviour, the practicing of ubuntu values occurs when individuals believe they have control. Behavioural controls are determined by control beliefs and perceived power. Perceived behavioural control, as shown in Fig. 5, is the perception of the ease or difficulty with which a task or behaviour can be performed [28].

Individuals with apparently high self-esteem become overconfident and take high behaviour risks. The underlying belief is that they are in charge and aware of the risks relating to behaviour [19].

Tendencies such as control bias give individuals an illusion of control. They believe they can control or influence outcomes that they clearly cannot [25]. People with high self-esteem are likely to be under an illusion of control and may unconsciously suffer from confirmation bias, which makes them believe that they are in control and are capable of behaving as expected and as required by their subjective norms.

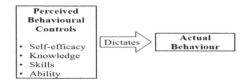

Fig. 5. Perceived behavioural control and actual behaviour [Author hypothesized relationship]

4 Social Engineering

Social engineering is increasingly becoming a way of gaining unauthorized access to information systems networks [10, 18]. Social engineering in the context of information security can be defined as the act of manipulating people into performing actions or divulging confidential information that may be used for a malicious purpose [14].

Cybercriminals are turning to social engineering as organizations continue to build enough technical security that is difficult for criminals to compromise. Social engineers target employees' psychological makeup to obtain personally identifiable information that could enable them to breach the information security of the targeted organization [4]. Employees are susceptible to social engineering tricks, as criminals apply complex ways of hacking the human in the employee [20].

Figure 6 shows the steps followed during a social engineering attack [23]. The social engineering process intends to be deceptive in nature. The social engineer who follows the steps outlined in Fig. 6 is likely to succeed in hiding his intentions. Attack formulation is the first stage, during which the goal of the attack and the target are identified. Information about the target is gathered from various sources and thoroughly assessed in the second stage. During the third stage, an attack angle is developed based on the assessment and analysis of the information. A relationship is developed during the fourth stage through communication and rapport building. In the fifth stage, the target is primed, information is elicited, and the attack is implemented. The sixth and final stage consists of aftercare and the closure of the attack assignment.

Social engineers use a variety of methods to compromise their targets. These methods may be classified as technical-based, social-based, and physical-based [1]. Technical-based attacks are conducted through the Internet via social networks and online services websites [31], while social-based attacks are performed through forming relationships with the victims in order to play on their psychology and emotions [17]. Physical-based attacks are physical actions performed by the attacker to collect information about the target [29].

5 Ubuntu and Social Engineering Vulnerability

Ubuntu is of value to persons who believe in practicing it. People can live by ubuntu values either consciously or unconsciously. Ubuntu is seen in behaviour. Behaviour is governed by attitudes, predilections, prejudices, emotions, and mental background.

In many circumstances, mental efforts must be accomplished with such rapidity that the opportunity to apply the mind does not exist [5, 8]. Ubuntu, therefore, provides a

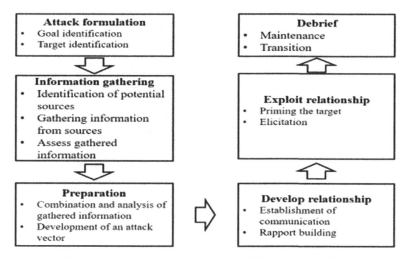

Fig. 6. Social engineering attack cycle [Mouton et al., 2016]

point of reference for human behaviour in such situations. People's behavioural beliefs and the outcome evaluation of their behaviour are directly influenced by ubuntu. Ubuntu advertently builds trust between human beings. Table 1 illustrates the authors' integration of biases, traits, and ubuntu values that may have relevance to social engineering susceptibility.

While trust between human beings is a noble thing, social engineers exploit the human element of trust to obtain or compromise information about an organization or its computer systems [10, 13, 30]. The social engineering vulnerability resides with human behaviour, human impulses, and psychological predispositions [6]. People generally have the desire to help other people as well as the desire to be liked by other people, especially strangers. Professionals want to appear well informed and intelligent. If they are praised, they will often talk more and divulge more information. Most people would not lie for the sake of lying, and most people respond kindly to those who appear concerned about them [12].

People are predisposed to trust and cooperate with other people [13]. Figure 7 shows how inherent ubuntu values expose humans as easy targets for social engineers.

Halevi et al. [13] identified five traits generally found in people. Firstly, neuroticism is a tendency to experience negative feelings, including guilt, disgust, anger, fear, and sadness. Neuroticism is likely to shape the attitude in the evaluation of the outcome of the intended behaviour (Fig. 1). People with this trait may tend to find comfort in group solidarity and collective unity, which are values of ubuntu. People with a high level of this trait are susceptible to irrational thoughts, are less able to control impulses, and do not handle stress well. This tendency increases a person's vulnerability to social engineering.

Secondly, people with a high level of the extraversion trait tend to be friendly and outgoing and enjoy interacting with people around them. Extraversion is likely to influence the intended behaviour through subjective norms, as illustrated in Fig. 2. Extraversion appears to consolidate trust, which is central to the success of a social engineering attack,

Table 1. Comparison of ubuntu values and social engineering (SE) exploitable traits

SE exploitable trait	Ubuntu values	Description of SE connection
Trust	Group solidarity Conformity Respect	Social engineers develop trust with the target and then exploit that trust to obtain authorized information Group solidarity, conformity, and respect consolidate trust between friends, associates, and families
Attachment	Group solidarity Collective unity	Group solidarity and collective unity lead to attachment, which in turn consolidates trust Social engineers exploit the trust
Commitment	Collective unity	Collective unity builds trust between individuals Social engineers exploit the trust
Agreeableness	Humanistic orientation Compassion	Humans have trust instincts. Humans trust unless proven wrong Social engineers exploit the trust
Endowment effect	Respect	Ubuntu values are held in high regard. Individuals who exhibit them are trusted Social engineers exploit the trust
Heuristic effect	Compassion Respect Humanistic orientation	Compassionate individuals are respected and trusted. Such individuals are seen as human and therefore earn trust Social engineers exploit the trust
Framing bias	Group solidarity Collective unity	Being part of a group is valued among people with ubuntu and therefore consolidates trust Collective unity is valued among people with ubuntu and therefore consolidates trust Social engineers exploit the trust
Optimism bias	Group solidarity Collective unity	Group solidarity and collective unity provide a sense of control, which in turn consolidates trust Social engineers exploit the trust

as shown in Table 1. It is ubuntu to be friendly to and interact with other people. This trait is also a vulnerability, as these people are welcoming to strangers and probably expose themselves to elicitation by social engineers.

Thirdly, people who score high on openness tend to be imaginative and intellectually curious. They also tend to be open to new and unconventional ideas and beliefs. Such people will likely fall into the trap of wanting to appear well informed and intelligent while inadvertently giving away confidential information or information required by social engineers. Openness is likely to influence the intended behaviour through attitude (Fig. 1), motivation to comply (Fig. 2), and perceived behavioural control (Fig. 5). The exploitable traits in Table 1 could facilitate this influence.

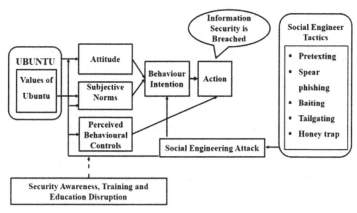

Fig. 7. Illustration of the interconnected relationship between ubuntu, the SE attack and prevention [Author hypothesized relationship]

Fourthly, highly agreeable people are co-operative, are eager to help other people, and believe in reciprocity. Agreeable people are by nature susceptible to elicitation by social engineers. Agreeable people practice the values of ubuntu, and this way of life builds exploitable trust.

Lastly, conscientious people have high levels of self-control and are very organized. They are typically purposeful and strong-minded. Their vulnerability to social engineering is likely to come from overconfidence. People with this trait who practice ubuntu are likely to overestimate their perceived behavioural control and engage in behaviours that have good ubuntu intentions but lead them into social engineering traps.

Online behaviour tends to mirror offline behaviour [7, 13, 27]. Therefore, ubuntu values lay the foundation for social engineering attacks, as trust is embedded in these values and social engineers exploit trust in human beings, as shown in Fig. 7. The social engineer just needs to be a member or be seen as a member of the real or virtual community in order to build instant rapport and benefit from a social bond (e.g. attachment or commitment) with the target [16].

6 Conclusion

This paper analyzed human behaviour, ubuntu, social engineering, and the complementary relationship between ubuntu and social engineering attacks. Ubuntu can influence intended behaviour. Ubuntu is a likely source of human weakness in social engineering attack resistance. Social engineers who deliberately target ubuntu or its values are likely to succeed in the attack.

The paper identified the balance between personal and wider social interests as a determinant of actual behaviour. Ubuntu was identified as one of the factors that inherently influences individuals in determining what they perceive as the right balance between personal and social interests.

The paper demonstrated how ubuntu influences the behavioural beliefs of the individual and how the individual evaluates the outcome of a specific behaviour in a given situation. It further demonstrated the relationship between ubuntu values, subjective norms, and behaviour intention. Bias was discussed as a variable in the evaluation of the outcome of a behaviour. Bias prevents people from being objective in evaluating the outcome of the intended behaviour. The actual behaviour was found to be dependent on the actual or perceived ability, knowledge, and skills of the individual.

This paper concludes that ubuntu builds trust and interdependence between humans, which increases the victim's susceptibility to social engineering attacks.

This paper concludes that ubuntu and social engineering have a complementary relationship. Figure 7 illustrates the relationship between ubuntu and social engineering attacks as well as a possible point of disruption through security awareness, training and education (SATE) programmes. It is, however, acknowledged that the extent of the relationship is not known and further studies need to be done in order to establish the nature and extent of this relationship. In order to mitigate the influence of ubuntu in social engineering attacks, the social engineer's exploitation of ubuntu in the victim should be disrupted. The security awareness, training and education (SATE) programme is the tool used to protect access to ubuntu from the social engineer.

Further work is still required to determine how ubuntu could be factored into security awareness, training and education programmes and to develop an effective SATE framework to counter the influence of ubuntu on people's vulnerability to social engineering attacks. The general limitation of this paper is that empirical research is required to validate the conclusions.

References

1. Abraham, S., Chengalur-Smith, I.: An overview of social engineering malware: trends, tactics, and implications. Technol. Soc. **32**(3), 183–196 (2010). https://doi.org/10.1016/j.techsoc.2010.07.001
2. Ajzen, I.: Organizational behaviour and human decision processes, pp. 179–211 (1991). https://doi.org/10.1016/0749-5978(91)90020-T
3. Ajzen, I.: Attitudes, Personality and Behavior, 2nd edn. McGraw Hill House, Maidenhead (2005)
4. Aldawood, H., Skinner, G.: Reviewing cyber security social engineering training and awareness programs: pitfalls and on-going issues. Future Internet **11**(3), 73 (2019). https://doi.org/10.3390/fi11030073
5. Wolf, W.B.: Decision processes as analysed by Chester I. Barnard. J. Manag. Hist. (Arch.) **1**(4), 1–110 (1995). https://doi.org/10.1108/13552529510102298
6. Conteh, N.Y., Schmick, P.J.: Cybersecurity: risks, vulnerabilities and countermeasures to prevent social engineering attacks. Int. J. Adv. Comput. Res. **6**(23), 31 (2016). https://doi.org/10.19101/ijacr.2016.623006
7. Campbell, C.: Solutions for counteracting human deception in social engineering attacks. Inf. Technol. People **32**, 1130–1152 (2019)
8. Donalds, C., Osei-Bryson, K.: Cybersecurity compliance behavior: exploring the influences of individual decision style and other antecedents. Int. J. Inf. Manag **51**, 102056 (2020)
9. Fishbein, M., Ajzen, I.: Predicting and Changing Behavior. Taylor and Francis Group, New York (2010)
10. Flores, W.R., Ekstedt, M.: Shaping the intention to resist social engineering through transformational leadership, information security culture and awareness. Comput. Secur. **59**, 26–44 (2016). https://doi.org/10.1016/j.cose.2016.01.004

11. Gratian, M., Bandi, S., Cukier, M., Dykstra, J., Ginther, A.: Correlating human traits and cyber security behaviour intention. Comput. Secur. **73**, 345–358 (2018). https://doi.org/10.1016/j.cose.2017.11.015

12. Hadnagy, C.: Social Engineering: The Art of Human Hacking. Wiley, Indianapolis (2011)

13. Halevi, T., Lewis, J., Memon, N.: A pilot study of cyber security and privacy related behaviour and personality traits. In: International World Wide Web Conference Committee, pp. 13–17 (2013)

14. Hatfield, J.M.: Social engineering in cybersecurity. the evolution of a concept. Comput. Secur. **73**, 102–113 (2018)

15. Himonga, C., Taylor, M., Pope, A.: Reflections on judicial views of Ubuntu (2013). https://doi.org/10.4314/pelj.v16i5.8

16. Ifinedo, P.: Information systems security policy compliance: an empirical study of the effects of socialization, influence, and cognition. Inf. Manage. **51**, 69–79 (2014). https://doi.org/10.1016/j.im.2013.10.001

17. Junger, M., Montoya, L., Overink, F.J.: Priming and warning are not effective to prevent social engineering attacks. Comput. Hum. Behav. **66**, 75–87 (2017)

18. Kaur, R., Singh, S., Kumar, H.: Rise of spam and compromised accounts in online social networks. a-state-of-the-art review of different combating approaches. J. Netw. Comput. Appl. **112**, 53–88 (2018)

19. Kearney, W.D., Kruger, H.A.: Can perceptual differences account for enigmatic information security behaviour in an organization? Comput. Secur. **61**, 46–58 (2016). https://doi.org/10.1016/j.cose.2016.05.006

20. Krombholz, K., Hobel, H., Huber, M., Weippl, E.: Advanced social engineering attacks. J. Inf. Secur. Appl. **22**, 112–122 (2015)

21. Metz, T.: Ubuntu as a moral theory and human rights in South Africa (2011). http://www.scielo.org.za/pdf/ahrlj/v11n2/11.pdf

22. Mokgoro, Y.J.: Ubuntu and the law in South Africa (1997). https://journals.assaf.org.za/per/article/view/2897

23. Mouton, F., Leenen, L., Venter, H.S.: Social engineering attack examples, templates and scenarios. Comput. Secur. **59**, 186–209 (2016). https://doi.org/10.1016/j.cose.2016.03.004

24. Oxford University Press: Ubuntu (1998). https://en.wikipedia.org/wiki/Oxford_Advanced_Learner's_Dictionary

25. Pfleeger, S.L., Caputo, D.D.: Leveraging behavioural science to mitigate cyber security risk. Comput. Secur. **31**(4), 597–611 (2012)

26. Popescu, G.: Human behavior, from psychology to a trans-disciplinary insight. Soc. Behav. Sci. **128**, 442–446 (2014)

27. Rosen, D., Stefanone, M.A., Lackaff, D.: Online and offline social networks: investigating culturally-specific behaviour and satisfaction. In: Proceedings of the 43rd Hawaii International Conference on System Sciences (2010). https://doi.org/10.1109/hicss.2010.292

28. Safa, N.S., Sookhak, M., Von Solms, R., Furnell, S., Ghani, N.A., Herawan, T.: Information security conscious care behaviour formation in organizations. Comput. Secur. **53**, 65–78 (2015)

29. Salahdine, F., Kaabouch, N.: Social engineering attacks: a survey. Future Internet **11**(4), 89 (2019). https://doi.org/10.3390/fi11040089

30. Tayouri, D.: The human factor in social media security. combining education and technology to reduce social engineering risks and damages. Procedia Manuf. **3**, 1096–1100 (2015). https://doi.org/10.1016/j.promfg.2015.07.181
31. Vishwanath, A.: Getting phished on social media. Decis. Support Syst. **103**, 70–81 (2017). https://doi.org/10.1016/j.dss.2017.09.004

Quantifying Susceptibility to Spear Phishing in a High School Environment Using Signal Detection Theory

P. Unchit[1], S. Das[1,2(✉)], A. Kim[1], and L. J. Camp[1]

[1] Indiana University Bloomington, Bloomington, USA
{punchit,sancdas,anykim,ljcamp}@iu.edu
[2] University of Denver, Denver, USA

Abstract. Spear phishing is a deceptive attack that uses social engineering to obtain confidential information through targeted victimization. It is distinguished by its use of social cues and personalized information to target specific victims. Previous work on resilience to spear phishing has focused on convenience samples, with a disproportionate focus on students. In contrast, here, we report on an evaluation of a high school community. We engaged 57 high school students and faculty members (12 high school students, 45 staff members) as participants in research utilizing signal detection theory (SDT). Through scenario-based analysis, participants tasked with distinguishing phishing emails from authentic emails. The results revealed an overconfidence bias in self-detection from the participants, regardless of their technical background. These findings are critical for evaluating the decision-making of underrepresented populations and protecting people from potential spear phishing attacks by examining human susceptibility.

Keywords: Phishing · Spear phishing · High school · User study · Usable security

1 Introduction

Phishing is used to obtain confidential information, install malware, obtain funds, or steal resources [18]. Targeted phishing is a critical component of that; for example, phishing attacks on Zoom increased four orders of magnitude between March and April 2020 and COVID-19-related phishing, including misinformation as well as attacks on the benefits for the newly unemployed. The most targeted form of phishing attack is *spear phishing* [1]. As spear phishing is a challenge essentially grounded in human behavior and decision-making [29], solutions should be informed by human subject evaluations as well.

Conversely, studies on phishing show a bias toward machine learning and purely technical solutions, with only 13.9% of published papers on phishing in

© IFIP International Federation for Information Processing 2020
Published by Springer Nature Switzerland AG 2020
N. Clarke and S. Furnell (Eds.): HAISA 2020, IFIP AICT 593, pp. 109–120, 2020.
https://doi.org/10.1007/978-3-030-57404-8_9

the ACM Digital Library utilizing human participants or user-centered methodologies [8]. Even when research does involve human subjects, it often studies convenience samples, specifically university students. Investigating high school students is particularly important, as previous research has shown that age is a critical factor in predicting susceptibility to phishing attacks [22,23,26]. Improved understanding of participants' mindsets when they click on a malicious email link can enable robust defensive and offensive techniques against spear phishing attacks. In order to contribute to this understanding, we combined phishing detection with signal detection theory (SDT) to explore how spear phishing cues impact this population [2]. SDT is often used to effectively measure and differentiate between present patterns and figuratively noisy distractions [24].

Specifically, we conducted a user study focusing on 57 high school students and staff members to explore the less-observed correlation between participant mentalities and email spear phishing attacks. Our goal was to address the following research questions:

- RQ1: How confident are participants in distinguishing between legitimate and non-legitimate spear phishing content over email?
- RQ2: How does age affect a user's ability to distinguish between legitimate and non-legitimate spear phishing content over email?

2   Related Work

The U.S. Department of Homeland Security identified the sequence of actions taken to craft a spear phishing attack: (1) identify the target, (2) meticulously craft the message with the intent of the recipient taking immediate action, and (3) deliver the message from a counterfeit email address [31]. Rajivan et al. found that phishing emails with "specific attack strategies (e.g., sending notifications, use of authoritative tone, or expressing shared interest)" were found to be more successful [32]. The use of social engineering through psychological manipulation can establish trust, and, as a result, lure in victims [20].

Previous research on phishing has focused on software- or hardware-based solutions, such as toolbars, machine learning models, and warning indicators [4]. Although significant advances in technology-based tools have emerged [30,34,35], less research has focused on end users [8]. Yet, the need for such research has long been recognized; in 2008, Friedrichs et al. argued that humans must be studied to stop web-based identity theft, including phishing attacks [15]. Such insights become even more important in light of Karakasiliotis et al.'s findings that only 36% of their study's participants could identify legitimate websites. Only 45% of participants could correctly identify malicious websites [21]. Dhamija et al. found that visual deception can fool even sophisticated users; a good phishing website fooled 90% of the participants in their study [13]. Fewer studies have focused on more vulnerable populations, such as younger students. In our background research, we did not find any studies focused on high school students or staff. Thus, we specifically selected a high school environment for our study.

In 2016, Canfield et al. performed two experiments comparing detection and performance using SDT. They found that "Greater sensitivity was positively correlated with confidence. Greater willingness to treat emails as legitimate was negatively correlated with perceived consequences from their actions and positively correlated with confidence" [2]. We implemented SDT in our research by analyzing the 'stimulus,' which triggers the decision-making in users. To evaluate the efficacy of the stimulus, we measured hits, misses, false alarms, and correct rejections (i.e., true positive, false negative, false positive, and true negative). We analyzed how users chose to click or not click links sent via electronic mail. The use of SDT enabled us to evaluate which sections of the phishing email arouse suspicion when they are present [2].

3   Methodology

To explore the relationship between the phishing susceptibility of high school students and their educators, we wanted to see what email cues both groups notice when deciding to click (or not click) on a malicious link. We conducted a non-experimental, quantitative correlation analysis by collecting data through a descriptive survey to check phishing susceptibility outcomes, age differences, and confidence levels. We primarily collected data from high school students and staff at a suburban high school in the United States. We obtained approval from the Ethical Review Board before beginning this experiment.

3.1   Recruitment

To begin, we instituted a collaboration with a suburban high school from the Midwestern part of the United States. As most high school students were under the age of 18, parental permission was required on a paper version of an informed consent document. We only allowed people to participate after their form was signed and approved by the staff and the students' parents. During the recruitment phase, we engaged with language arts classrooms to find willing research participants. English language arts classes were chosen because all students were required to enroll in these classes to graduate. The study was also advertised to every student in the building during the morning school announcements. We also distributed flyers advertising the study to 200 participants. Students who turned in the paper consent forms then received emails that contained an electronic form of the survey. To recruit teachers and faculty members, we sent out emails containing the link to the consent form and questionnaire. Because the study was announced beforehand, teachers and faculty were expecting this recruitment email. The participants received an incentive at the end of the survey by choosing to enter a drawing for Starbucks gift cards. Our power analysis showed that we required sample size of more than 50 participants. We obtained a complete response set from 57 participants in our final data set.

3.2   Survey Instrument and Study Design

The survey consisted of three parts: the informed consent information, the demographic questionnaire, and the actual phishing susceptibility assessment. We utilized Google Forms as the tool to provide the survey questionnaire because it was easily accessible to both students and teachers. The first author anonymized the data so that personally identifiable information would not be shared with anyone else, including other researchers. Participants began by opening a Google Forms link from their email and confirming their status as a student or a staff member of the high school. The staff needed to confirm their consent to the study, while students would move on to the next step due to their parents having already agreed via the consent form. Next, participants answered a set of demographic questions regarding their age group (and not their specific date of birth to reduce the risk of disclosure of identifiable information). Afterward, the participants were presented with ten questions to assess their spear phishing susceptibility through the use of images of phishing emails. We selected images instead of asking them to go through actual emails to mitigate any concern that they may respond to malicious messages. The participants classified the images as "regular email" or "phishing email". For each question, the participants rated their confidence in their decision, from least to most confident using a five-point Likert scale.

Spear Phishing Susceptibility: Based on prior phishing research, there are three main factors identified in most phishing emails: anonymous senders, suspicious URLs or installations, and a sense of urgency [14]. Figure 2 is an example that shows the present signs of a harmful phishing email such as: an anonymous sender (e.g., "is outside your organization"), a sense of urgency (e.g., "URGENT! CLICK THE LINK"), a suspicious URL (e.g., "http://baoonhd.vn/api/get.php?..."), and a risky action (e.g., clicking on "Open in Docs"). In contrast, Fig. 1 shows an authentic email from Google, as seen by the trustworthy email address, the accurate website link, and the valid email format. Non-phishing examples were adopted from personal school emails that the high school staff and students received earlier, and at least one individual reported as suspicious. This data was obtained from the high school staff and IT support, who anonymized the email samples.

Phishing examples were adopted from the Berkeley Phishing Examples Archive (PEA) [1]. The adopted phishing emails were modified to include the name of the school and actual school activities, including grades and exams. The images were edited to address the participants' real names and roles (teacher or student). Google documents addressed school-specific information to check the participants' susceptibility to spear phishing emails. The signals that were used in the phishing emails were (a) the greeting, (b) suspicious URLs with a deceptive name or IP address, (c) content that did not match the ostensible sender and subject, (d) requests for urgent action, and (e) grammatical or typograph-

---

[1] https://security.berkeley.edu/education-awareness/phishing/phishing-examples-archive.

ical errors. We selected this set of signals based on a 2016 study by canfield et al. that similarly focused on detection theory, albeit using an online survey of people aged 19–59 [2].

Fig. 1. Example of an authentic email displayed to the participants in the survey

Fig. 2. Example of a phishing email displayed to the participants in the survey

3.3 Analysis: Method

Once the data collection was complete, we analyzed the data using RStudio and SPSS Statistics. Using SDT, participants' answers were categorized as four possible outcomes: *hit, miss, false alarm, and correct rejection.* Table 1 shows the signal detection theory outcomes adjusted to become appropriate for this study. The outcomes from the phishing assessment were analyzed in a one-way analysis of variance (ANOVA) to explore the relationship between the independent variable (age group) and the dependent variables (the number of different outcomes and the average confidence levels). The one-way analysis of variance is used to determine whether there are any statistically significant differences between the means of two or more independent (unrelated) groups [17]. For ANOVA, we usually compare three or more groups. For this study, we divided the data set into seven groups.

Table 1. Modified signal detection theory implemented to evaluate spear phishing susceptibility

	Respond "regular email"	Respond "phishing email"
Phishing email	Miss	Hit
Authentic email	Correct rejection	False alarm

4   Findings and Discussions

Our data collection was done over a period of two months. We collected a complete data set of 57 subjects, who provided their consent and participated in it. Of these 57 participants, 12 were students, and 45 were staff members of the high school. Eight participants were from 12 to 17 years old; four participants were from 18 to 24 years old; 11 participants were from 25 to 34 years old; 15 participants were from 35 to 44 years old; 12 were from 45 to 54 years old; seven were from 55 to 64 years old. Thus, the participants' ages ranged from 12 to 64 years old. This study aimed to determine if there was a significant difference between the age groups (12–17, 18–24, 25–34, 35–44, 45–54, and 55–64 years old), the email outcomes (hit, miss, correct rejection, false alarm), and the confidence levels (Likert scale one through five ratings) using a ten-item test. Results of the ANOVA test are shown in Table 2. A significant difference was noted for the hit or miss email outcomes ($F(5, 51) = 2.614$, $p < .035$). The correct rejection, false alarm, and all the different confidence levels had no significant difference between the groups.

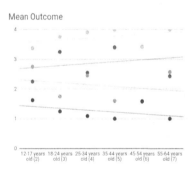

Fig. 3. SDT Mean Outcome shows the mean for the email outcomes in a linear transformation from 100% to a five point scale. It shows (from top to bottom) correct rejection in yellow, correct acceptance (hit) in blue, incorrect acceptance (miss) in red, and false alarm in green. (Color figure online)

Fig. 4. SDT Mean Outcome for Confidence Levels showing the confidence level. Misclassifying phishing email (red) is associated with the same confidence as correct rejection for 12–17 (yellow), with confidence falling with age. False alarm is shown with least confidence in ages 12–17, and increases with age. (Color figure online)

The results illustrate a significant number in the hit or miss category, but few correct rejections and false alarms across all the confidence levels. The ANOVA results of the confidence levels of the participants can be seen in Table 3. Here, we can say that age plays a significant role in responding to a stimulus, as evidenced by the participants either responding with "Authentic Email" or "Phishing Email." A potential reason for the lack of significance could be that the

Table 2. ANOVA results of the different signals (hit, miss, correct rejection, and false alarm) between and within groups (divided based on age)

		Sum of Sq	df	Mean square	F	Sig.
Hit	Between groups	13.634	5	2.727	2.614	0.035
	Within groups	53.208	51	1.043		
	Total	66.842	56			
Miss	Between groups	13.634	5	2.727	2.614	0.035
	Within groups	53.208	51	1.043		
	Total	66.842	56			
Rejection	Between groups	4.111	5	0.822	1.292	0.282
	Within groups	32.451	51	0.636		
	Total	36.561	56			
FalseAlarm	Between groups	4.111	5	0.822	1.292	0.282
	Within groups	32.451	51	0.636		
	Total	36.561	56			
HitConf	Between groups	2.156	5	0.431	0.976	0.441
	Within groups	22.079	50	0.442		
	Total	24.234	55			
MissConf	Between groups	2.954	5	0.591	1.548	0.194
	Within groups	17.554	46	0.382		
	Total	20.507	51			
CorrRejConf	Between groups	0.812	5	0.162	0.558	0.732
	Within groups	14.854	51	0.291		
	Total	15.667	56			
FalseAlarmConf	Between groups	1.457	5	0.291	0.514	0.764
	Within groups	23.818	42	0.567		
	Total	25.275	47			

confidence levels were not precisely represented and that participants' perceived confidence was subjective. One participant's response of a 5 (most confident) could be the same as another participant's 3 (average confidence). Their perceived confidence could also shift throughout the survey; a response of 1 (least confident) could be changed to a 2 (lower confidence) or 3 later on, depending on whether or not the participants believed that the questions were more or less difficult at the beginning of the survey.

Figure 3 shows correct results (yellow, blue) increase with age. Figure 4 show confidence increasing in false alarms in with age (green), with confidence about correct identification (and misidentification higher for younger age groups. Our data revealed that the highest mean for the hit outcome was from age group six (45–54 years old). The second-highest mean for the hit outcome was from age

Table 3. ANOVA descriptives for SDT confidence levels outcomes

		N	Mean	SD	SE	95% CI LB	95% CI UB	Min	Max
HitConf	2	8	3.9375	0.78142	0.27627	3.28	4.5908	3	5
	3	4	3.45	0.51171	0.25586	2.6357	4.2643	2.8	4
	4	11	3.803	0.69848	0.2106	3.338	4.2723	3	5
	5	15	3.8856	0.71328	0.18417	3.4906	4.2806	2.5	5
	6	12	3.4306	0.40644	0.11733	3.1723	3.6888	2.67	4
	7	6	3.7361	0.80003	0.32661	2.8965	4.5757	3	5
	Total	56	3.7321	0.6638	0.0887	3.5544	3.9099	2.5	5
Miss Conf	2	8	4.1354	0.42243	0.14935	3.7823	4.4886	3.67	5
	3	3	3.5	0.5	0.28868	2.2579	4.7421	3	4
	4	11	3.5606	0.57384	0.17302	3.1751	3.9461	3	4.5
	5	12	3.7708	0.66962	0.1933	3.3454	4.1963	2.5	5
	6	11	4	0.58214	0.17552	3.6089	4.3911	3	5
	7	7	3.4762	0.83571	0.31587	2.7033	4.2491	2	4.33
	Total	52	3.7756	0.63412	0.08794	3.5991	3.9522	2	5
ConRej Conf	2	8	3.7646	0.65686	0.23223	3.2154	4.3137	3	5
	3	4	3.9	0.57991	0.28996	2.9772	4.8228	3.33	4.67
	4	11	3.912	0.55523	0.16741	3.5482	4.2942	3	4.75
	5	15	4.1133	0.51564	0.13314	3.8278	4.3989	3.25	5
	6	12	3.8458	0.55674	0.16072	3.4921	4.1996	2.67	4.5
	7	7	3.9238	0.31898	0.12056	3.6288	4.2188	3.5	4.5
	Total	57	3.9327	0.52892	0.07006	3.7924	4.0731	2.67	5
False Alarm Conf	2	6	3.1944	0.62731	0.2561	2.5361	3.8528	2	3.67
	3	3	3.1667	1.04083	0.60093	0.5811	5.7522	2	4
	4	10	3.6	0.8756	0.27689	2.9736	4.2264	3	5
	5	12	3.6667	0.74874	0.21614	3.1909	4.1424	2	5
	6	11	3.4091	0.73547	0.22175	2.915	3.9032	2	4
	7	6	3.5833	0.4916	0.2069	3.0674	4.0992	3	4
	Total	48	3.4931	0.73333	0.10585	3.2801	3.706	2	5

group five (35–44 years old). Groups five and six also had the lowest mean for the miss outcome. In Fig. 3, we show the mean outcome for hit and correct rejection, which has an increasing slope, with a negative correlation with miss and false alarm. Therefore, there is strong evidence that older groups are less susceptible to spear phishing than the younger groups in a high school setting. Figure 4 shows that the other variables were not significant. This result is quite different from that hypothesized under the 'digital native' rubrics that argue for younger cohorts' lifetime exposure resulting in improved decision-making (e.g., [27]).

5   Implications

Spear phishing is an effective form of attack because attackers manipulate their targets, either through luring them in with promises of specific benefits or by coercing them with specific threats [25]. These techniques are designed to lead to impulsive or quick decision-making from the end-users. In our findings (Sect. 4), we leveraged SDT to understand participant decision-making with spear phishing stimuli. When the mean of the outcomes was graphed, the results revealed a positive slope for the hit and correct rejection outcomes, meaning that the older participants tended to be less susceptible to spear phishing. The effects of these relationships can contribute to a better understanding of how people interact with fraudulent acts online. Here we offer recommendations that our findings indicate as ways to increase resilience against spear phishing attacks.

Align Anti-Phishing Training with Self-perceived Expertise: Our work found that older participants were less susceptible to spear phishing than younger participants, as age group six had the highest average number of hits (i.e., correct detection) throughout the experiment. This is aligned with previous research from Sheng et al. [33]. One reason for this gap may be students' lack of exposure to training geared towards them. For this reason, we recommend introducing phishing training to students at a younger age and aligning it with their self-perceived expertise. Our results show both a high level of incorrect responses and a high level of confidence. This indicates that younger participants may be unaware that they have been the victim of a successful phishing attack.

Targeted Risk Communication: In addition to providing anti-phishing training, organizations should consider providing clear risk communication, especially for younger adults or children. Students may lack an understanding of the technical threats that may be present in their email inbox [19], believing that they will not be targeted. Thus, the need for context-aware risk communication [3] that has been identified as necessary for older adults [6, 7, 16] is similarly required for high school student populations.

Enable Multi-factor Authentication: To create more robust defensive techniques against spear phishing attacks, we need to reduce the risk of compromised credentials. Such compromised credentials can be used to steal sensitive information. Because of this, schools that provide laptops (or require these for online instruction) should consider adopting multi-factor authentication (MFA) for students and staff [5, 9, 28]. The introduction of these (like other training) should be aligned with user risk mental models [10–12]. The issue of over-confidence above also motivates the importance of another factor for authentication (e.g., a hardware token) in addition to their password, which would mitigate the harm of phishing.

6   Limitations and Future Work

This work, with its focus on the conference as well as correctness. Opens more questions than it answers. Other factors besides age and confidence levels should be studied to gain a holistic understanding of susceptibility to spear phishing. The suburban high school we engaged with has relatively high socio-economic homogeneity, and the study should be repeated with other high schools. To improve diversity, future work should begin with more diverse schools, and then study specific underrepresented populations, such as students with physical or learning disabilities. Interviewing the participants to collect more qualitative data and better understand user decision making is a needed expansion of this work.

7 Conclusion

With the current rise in spear phishing, especially among vulnerable populations, it is critical to developing tools and educational approaches to train users to differentiate between authentic and malicious emails. To understand spear phishing attack resilience, we studied a population in a high school environment ($N = 57$). We found that age and confidence play a critical role in the identification of spear phishing attacks. Our study concludes by providing recommendations for developing anti-phishing training tools and communicating risks and benefits.

Acknowledgement. We would like to the participants of the highschool for their valuable contribution, and Stephanie Davis for encouraging the first author throughout the entire data collection process. We would also like to thank Kevin Gingerich from Eli Lilly for their expert advice on phishing and guiding the first author. This research was supported in part by the National Science Foundation under CNS 1565375, Cisco Research Support, and the Comcast Innovation Fund. Any opinions, findings, and conclusions or recommendations expressed in this material are those of the author(s). They do not necessarily reflect the views of the U.S. Government, NSF, Cisco, Comcast, Indiana U, or the University of Denver.

References

1. APWG: Phishing Activity Trends Report (2020). https://docs.apwg.org/reports/apwg_trends_report_q1_2020.pdf. Accessed 29 June 2020
2. Canfield, C.I., Fischhoff, B., Davis, A.: Quantifying phishing susceptibility for detection and behavior decisions. Hum. Factors **58**(8), 1158–1172 (2016)
3. Das, S.: A risk-reduction-based incentivization model for human-centered multi-factor authentication. Ph.D. thesis, Indiana University (2020)
4. Das, S., Abbott, J., Gopavaram, S., Blythe, J., Camp, L.J.: User-centered risk communication for safer browsing. In: First Asia USEC-Workshop on Usable Security, in Conjunction with the Twenty-Fourth International Conference on Financial Cryptography and Data Security (2020)
5. Das, S., Dingman, A., Camp, L.J.: Why Johnny doesn't use two factor a two-phase usability study of the FIDO U2F security key. In: Meiklejohn, S., Sako, K. (eds.) FC 2018. LNCS, vol. 10957, pp. 160–179. Springer, Heidelberg (2018). https://doi.org/10.1007/978-3-662-58387-6_9
6. Das, S., Kim, A., Jelen, B., Streiff, J., Camp, L.J., Huber, L.: Towards implementing inclusive authentication technologies for older adults. Who Are You (2019)
7. Das, S., Kim, A., Jelen, B., Streiff, J., Camp, L.J., Huber, L.: Why don't older adults adopt two-factor authentication?, April 2020

8. Das, S., Kim, A., Tingle, Z., Nippert-Eng, C.: All about phishing exploring user research through a systematic literature review. In: 13th International Symposium on Human Aspects of Information Security & Assurance (2019)

9. Das, S., Russo, G., Dingman, A.C., Dev, J., Kenny, O., Camp, L.J.: A qualitative study on usability and acceptability of Yubico security key. In: 7th Workshop on Socio-Technical Aspects in Security and Trust, pp. 28–39 (2018)

10. Das, S., Wang, B., Camp, L.J.: MFA is a waste of time! Understanding negative connotation towards MFA applications via user generated content. In: 13th International Symposium on Human Aspects of Information Security & Assurance (HAISA 2019) (2019)

11. Das, S., Wang, B., Kim, A., Camp, L.J.: MFA is a necessary chore!: exploring user mental models of multi-factor authentication technologies. In: 53rd Hawaii International Conference on System Sciences (2020)

12. Das, S., Wang, B., Tingle, Z., Camp, L.J.: Evaluating user perception of multi-factor authentication: a systematic review. arXiv preprint arXiv:1908.05901 (2019)

13. Dhamija, R., Tygar, J.D., Hearst, M.: Why phishing works. In: SIGCHI Conference on Human Factors in Computing Systems, pp. 581–590 (2006)

14. Fette, I., Sadeh, N., Tomasic, A.: Learning to detect phishing emails. In: 16th International Conference on World Wide Web, pp. 649–656 (2007)

15. Friedrichs, O., Jakobsson, M., Soghoian, C.: The Threat of political phishing. In: 2nd International Symposium on Human Aspects of Information Security & Assurance (2008)

16. Garg, V., Lorenzen-Huber, L., Camp, L.J., Connelly, K.: Risk communication design for older adults. In: ISARC. Proceedings of the International Symposium on Automation and Robotics in Construction, vol. 29, p. 1. IAARC Publications (2012)

17. Girden, E.R.: ANOVA: Repeated Measures. Number 84. Sage Publications, Los Angeles (1992)

18. Hadnagy, C.: Social Engineering: The Art of Human Hacking. Wiley, Hoboken (2010)

19. Harbach, M., Hettig, M., Weber, S., Smith, M.: Using personal examples to improve risk communication for security & privacy decisions. In: SIGCHI Conference on Human Factors in Computing Systems, pp. 2647–2656 (2014)

20. Hatfield, J.M.: Social engineering in cybersecurity: the evolution of a concept. Comput. Secur. **73**, 102–113 (2018)

21. Karakasiliotis, A., Furnell, S., Papadaki, M.: Assessing end-user awareness of social engineering and phishing. In: 7th Australian Information Warfare and Security Conference, pp. 60–72. School of Computer and Information Science, Edith Cowan University, Perth (2006)

22. Kumaraguru, P., et al.: School of phish: a real-world evaluation of anti-phishing training. In: 5th Symposium on Usable Privacy and Security (SOUPS), pp. 1–12 (2009)

23. Lastdrager, E., Gallardo, I.C., Hartel, P., Junger, M.: How effective is anti-phishing training for children? In: Thirteenth Symposium on Usable Privacy and Security (SOUPS 2017), pp. 229–239 (2017)

24. Martin, J., Dubé, C., Coovert, M.D.: Signal detection theory (SDT) is effective for modeling user behavior toward phishing and spear-phishing attacks. Hum. Factors **60**(8), 1179–1191 (2018)

25. Maurer, M.-E., De Luca, A., Kempe, S.: Using data type based security alert dialogs to raise online security awareness. In: 7th Symposium on Usable Privacy and Security (SOUPS), pp. 1–13 (2011)

26. Nicholson, J., Javed, Y., Dixon, M., Coventry, L., Dele-Ajayi, O., Anderson, P.: Investigating teenagers' ability to detect phishing messages. In: EuroUSEC 2020: The 5th European Workshop on Usable Security. IEEE (2020)
27. Nikou, S., Brännback, M., Widén, G.: The impact of digitalization on literacy: digital immigrants vs. digital natives. In: 27th European Conference on Information Systems, pp. 1–15. ECIS (2019)
28. Ometov, A., Bezzateev, S., Mäkitalo, N., Andreev, S., Mikkonen, T., Koucheryavy, Y.: Multi-factor authentication: a survey. Cryptography **2**(1), 1–31 (2018)
29. Pattinson, M., Jerram, C., Parsons, K., McCormac, A., Butavicius, M.: Why do some people manage phishing e-mails better than others? Inf. Manag. Comput. Secur. **20**(1), 18–28 (2012)
30. Prakash, P., Kumar, M., Kompella, R.R., Gupta, M.: PhishNet: predictive black-listing to detect phishing attacks. In: 29th IEEE Conference on Computer Communications, pp. 1–5. IEEE (2010)
31. P.-P. A. E. Program: Phishing: don't be phooled! (2018). https://www.dhs. gov/sites/default/files/publications/2018_AEP_Vulnerabilities_of_Healthcare_IT_ Systems.pdf. Accessed 29 June 2020
32. Rajivan, P., Gonzalez, C.: Creative persuasion: a study on adversarial behaviors and strategies in phishing attacks. Front. Psychol. **9** (2018)
33. Sheng, S., Holbrook, M., Kumaraguru, P., Cranor, L.F., Downs, J.: Who falls for phish? A demographic analysis of phishing susceptibility and effectiveness of interventions. In: SIGCHI Conference on Human Factors in Computing Systems, pp. 373–382 (2010)
34. Wu, M., Miller, R.C., Garfinkel, S.L.: Do security toolbars actually prevent phishing attacks? In: SIGCHI Conference on Human Factors in Computing Systems, pp. 601–610 (2006)
35. Xiang, G., Hong, J., Rose, C.P., Cranor, L.: Cantina+ a feature-rich machine learning framework for detecting phishing web sites. ACM Trans. Inf. Syst. Secur. (TISSEC) **14**(2), 1–28 (2011)

Security Behaviour

KidsDoodlePass: An Exploratory Study of an Authentication Mechanism for Young Children

Esra Alkhamis[1,2] ⓘ, Helen Petrie[1(✉)] ⓘ, and Karen Renaud[3] ⓘ

[1] Department of Computer Science, University of York, York, UK
{ea921,helen.petrie}@york.ac.uk
[2] Department of Information Technology, King Saud University, Riyadh,
Kingdom of Saudi Arabia
[3] School of Design and Informatics, Abertay University, Dundee, UK
k.renaud@abertay.ac.uk

Abstract. Textual passwords are problematic for young children, whose cognitive, memory and linguistic capabilities are still developing. A possible alternative to using text for authentication systems for young children is drawings. In this paper, we describe an authentication system called KidsDoodlePass, which use simple drawings ("doodles") that the children themselves create. An initial evaluation of the system was undertaken with 19 children aged 6 to 9 years of age. Success of logging in with KidsDoodlePass was high, only on few occasions did a child need more than one attempt, demonstrating that the system is effective. Selection times dropped significantly on the second use of the KidsPassDoodle and were typically under 10 s per grid. Most children thought their KidsDoodlePass would be easier to remember than a text password, a significant proportion. These positive results suggest that KidsDoodlePass could be a useful mechanism for young children to use as a first experience of authentication and a useful first step toward adult authentication systems.

Keywords: Authentication systems · Usable security · KidsDoodlePass · Children

1 Introduction

Young children increasingly use electronic devices and the Internet and therefore may need to use passwords to access their devices or online accounts. UNICEF estimates that worldwide for every three adult Internet users, there is one child user [27]. In the USA, it was estimated that in 2015 60% of children aged 3 to 17 years used the Internet at home [3]. This number had increased nearly six-fold since 1997, when it was only 11%. In the UK, more than half of all children now use the Internet [21]. This means that children are probably using passwords when their cognitive, memory and linguistic capabilities are still developing, and they may not have the appropriate capability to

© IFIP International Federation for Information Processing 2020
Published by Springer Nature Switzerland AG 2020
N. Clarke and S. Furnell (Eds.): HAISA 2020, IFIP AICT 593, pp. 123–132, 2020.
https://doi.org/10.1007/978-3-030-57404-8_10

create and remember appropriately strong passwords, nor understand the importance of password best practices.

As young children's vocabulary and spelling skills are still developing, if they are asked to create their own passwords they tend to be short, simple words within the scope of their vocabulary and they may misspell passwords when trying to remember them [4, 5, 22]. In terms of cognitive development, young children are at the egocentric stage of development [13], so will be likely to create passwords which are related to themselves [17, 18] and which therefore may be very easy to break. More specifically, in terms of cognitive development, young children are in process of developing "theory of mind" or meta-cognitive processes [9, 10]. This concept refers to understanding what other people will know and understand. For example, if a child shares their password with a parent, but they are then asked to change it, until they develop a theory of mind, they will assume that the parent knows the new password. Finally, another specific aspect of cognitive development relevant to password creation and use is semantic memory and metamemory [11]. A password is a specific piece of information which needs to be remembered; children must understand the need to remember this information and have strategies for remembering it which will help them retrieve the information when it is required. Young children will not yet have developed all these skills.

A problem with asking children to undertake password practices which are beyond their linguistic and cognitive abilities is that they may teach young children poor password practices which then endure as they grow up. Graphical passwords are worth exploring as possible alternatives to text passwords for children, to begin to teach them about the importance of authentication, but using procedures which are within their skill set. There are several benefits of this alternative: using graphical information created by the child themselves is within the realm of self-related information appropriate for the egocentric stage of development; graphic information also overcomes issues of the child's stage of linguistic development, both for creation and later spelling of passwords; finally, in relation to memory development it relies on recognition rather than recall, which is cognitively far less demanding.

In this paper, we present a graphical authentication system designed specifically for young children, which is built on doodles (simple drawings) the children create themselves. We present an initial evaluation with children aged 6 to 9 years, assessing effectiveness, efficiency and satisfaction of the system.

2 Related Research

A number of studies have investigated children's understanding and use of text passwords. Read and Cassidy [22] found that 7 to 8 year old children had a basic understanding of password principles: they should be hard to guess, but simple to remember; and they should prevent other people accessing the children's devices. These researchers also asked children 6 to 10 years old to create a password. All the children created simple passwords, with younger children creating even simpler ones than older children. The children often created passwords which were easily guessable from their username and 13% misspelled their password when they came to use it. In a follow-up study, Lamichhane and Read [17] found that over half a sample of 7 to 8 year old children created self-related passwords. Coggins [2] investigated similar issues with children aged 9 to 11 years. The children in his study had some idea of how to create good passwords, as they used at least six characters and a combination of letters and digits. But only 27% of the passwords created were assessed as being "strong".

Many graphical password authentication systems have been proposed for adults, starting with the Draw-a-Secret (DAS) system proposed by Jermyn et al. [16, see 1 for a review]. Many of these systems are based on the recognition of pictures, either of human faces [6, 8] or objects [7], but some involve user-generated drawings in different ways [12, 15, 25, 27], including a system specifically for older users [23]. Some research has investigated graphical systems specifically for children. Several studies conducted in Japan investigated graphical authentication for primary school children [19, 20]. These studies used icons such as animals, flowers, and fruit. The components of the password could be remembered easily, but the children often chose them in the wrong order. Renaud [24] developed am authentication mechanism specifically for children using images the children drew called Mikons ("my icons"). Children aged 11 to 12 years were able to identify their own Mikons with ease. After three months the children had no difficulty remembering their Mikon passwords, despite the long delay. Imran [14] compared three graphical authentication mechanisms (PassTiles) using different image types: objects, images and words. These were tested with both adults and children aged 7 to 12 years. The children performed best with object PassTiles in which they recognised images of distinct objects from decoys. The word PassTiles were more difficult for children to recall. Adults and children both demonstrated a preference for graphical passwords over existing text passwords mechanisms.

Although there has been a great deal of research carried out in the graphical authentication area for adults, there has been little research on this topic for children for whom this kind of authentication system might be a useful first step to learning about authentication systems and their importance.

3 Method

The design in the study is summarized in Fig. 1. Children aged 6 to 9 were asked to use the "KidsDoodlePass" authentication system. Instead of being a textual password, their KidsDoodlePass consisted of one, two or three doodles (i.e. simple drawings), which they drew at the beginning of the study. The authentication mechanism tested their ability to correctly identify their own doodle displayed in a series of 3×3 grids with a range of distractor doodles (see Fig. 2). Each grid included another doodle from the three they had created themselves, a doodle in the same category created by another child and six other randomly selected doodles from other children participating in the study.

The study involved a pre-session and four experimental sessions, each approximately one week apart (see Fig. 1). At the pre-session, the children created three doodles. At the first experimental session, they chose one of their doodles for their KidsDoodlePass:1. They then used it to log in to an online games area. If they failed to recognize their KidsDoodlePass:1 three times, they were given a hint by the researcher. If that failed, the researcher identified their KidsDoodlePass:1 doodle (this protocol of attempts, hints and assistance was followed for all logins). The children then played an age-appropriate

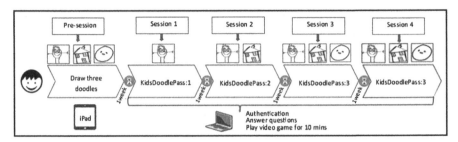

Fig. 1. Design of the study

game for 10 min, which acted as both a reward and a distractor task to allow investigation of whether they remembered the KidsDoodlePass:1 after a short time. After the play period, they were asked to log in again with KidsDoodlePass:1.

At the second session, children logged in with KidsDoodlePass:1, played a game and then logged in again with KidsDoodlePass:1. They then chose a second doodle to create their KidsDoodlePass:2 (they were told this would make their KidsDoodlePass stronger) and then logged in with that. The KidsDoodlePass:2 authentication process required them to traverse two grids of nine doodles each, correctly identifying their doodle each time.

At the third session, the procedure from the previous sessions was repeated. This time, the children started with their KidsDoodlePass:2, played a game, logged in again with KidsDoodlePass:2, then created KidsDoodlePass:3, consisting of all three doodles they had drawn. The KidsDoodlePass:3 authentication process involved traversing three grids of nine doodles each. At the fourth session, the children logged in with KidsDoodlePass:3, played a game and logged in again with KidsDoodlePass:3.

During each session, children were asked a number of questions about their use of computing devices, and their knowledge and use of passwords and authentication mechanisms.

Thus, a repeated measures design was used, with one within-participants independent variable, the number of doodles in the KidsDoodlePass. The dependent variables were: (1) the accuracy of remembering the KidsDoodlePass, to measure effectiveness and (2) the time taken to select their doodles, to measure efficiency. Satisfaction was measured by the questions asked during the sessions.

3.1 Participants

19 children took part, all were recruited from a private international school in Riyadh, Saudi Arabia. 10 boys and 9 girls. 6 were in Grade 1 (6–7 years old), 6 in Grade 2 (7–8) and 7 in Grade 3 (8–9). All children had some experience with passwords and authentication systems, either for accessing devices or online accounts. The children used a range of electronic devices, the most popular being tablet computers, used by 13 (68.4%) of the children, followed by smartphones (57.9%), game consoles (36.8%) and desktop/laptop computers (26.3%). 18 of the 19 children (94.7%) had used passwords. 8 children (42.1%) had used them for devices only, a further 8 (42.1%) used them for devices and online accounts and one child (5.3%) used them for online accounts only.

The children were offered a gift voucher worth the equivalent of USD 13 to spend at a local bookstore for participating in the study.

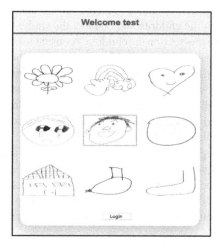

Fig. 2. Authentication grid of nine doodles for KidsDoodlePass.

3.2 Study Website and Equipment

A website was developed to present the KidsDoodlePass authentication system, to give children access to a range of age-appropriate video games and to collect data about the accuracy and timing of their responses to the KidsDoodlePass system.

The website was developed using PHP, JavaScript and XML with a MySQL database. The website consists of a username page in which the researcher enters the child's participant code, so session information is correctly stored. There is then one, two or three pages for authentication, depending on which KidsDoodlePass is being used at the time. When a doodle is selected, it is highlighted by a box (see Fig. 2), so the child can change their mind about their selection before attempting to log in. The authentication pages are programmed to record the number of attempts the child makes to log in, whether they are correct or not and how long the child spends on each page from when the page appears to when the child hits the login button.

The children drew their doodles on a 9.7 inch Apple iPad (6th Generation), running iOS 11.2.6, using a MPIO Stylus Pen with a 1.5 mm tip. The experimental sessions were all run on a 13 inch MacBook Air running MacOS High Sierra (version 10.13.4), with a 1.8 GHz Intel processor. The games used were selected from the PBS Kids website (pbskids.org).

3.3 Procedure

The study was approved by the Physical Sciences Ethics Committee of the University of York. Permission was then sought from the Head of Al Forsan International School in Riyadh who sent letters to parents of children in Grades 1 to 3. Parents replied to the Head with a physical letter of consent if they were happy for their child to participate in the study. The school gave permission for the children to take part in the study during their weekly art classes. The first author gathered all the data. She was given a quiet room at the school to meet the children and conduct the study.

At the beginning of the pre-session the children's consent to participate in the research was sought. They were asked if they would help the researcher with her work which would involve creating logging into an online account a number of times. If they did so they would be able to play video games and receive a gift voucher. They were then asked to draw three simple doodles on the iPad. They were told to draw three simple objects and that there was no need to make a perfect drawing. After each drawing, the children were asked what the doodle represented.

The doodles were categorized before the first experimental session to allow creation of KidsPassDoodle grids with appropriate combinations of doodles. Categorisation of the doodles started with the children's own descriptions and was then refined by the first author. In some cases, doodles were grouped differently if they seemed similar to other children's doodles and could easily belong to the same category. In total, 23 different categories were created.

At the beginning of each experimental session, the child was told that they could play an online game but, in order to keep the game private, they needed to have an account and that their doodles would be used as their password. At the beginning of the first session, they were asked to select one of their three doodles as their KidsDoodlePass. They were then asked to log in to the games area. If they could not identify their doodle from the 3×3 grid, or chose an incorrect doodle, a friendly error message appeared: "*Oops! Something went wrong. Please try again*". The child had three attempts at identifying their doodle, after which the researcher gave them a hint (e.g. if the doodle was a flower, the child was told the correct doodle was something natural). If the child could still not identify their KidsDoodlePass, the researcher showed them the correct one with reassurance: "*It's OK, I will help you, but you need to try to remember it for next time*".

When the child successfully logged in, there was a selection of games to play. They played for 10 min, after which the researcher asked them to log in again (they were told this was to check the game) and they were told: "*Now we need to make your KidsDoodlePass stronger so we will choose a new doodle*." In sessions 2 and 3 they were then taken to the page to choose another doodle to add to their KidsDoodlePass, and asked to log in again with the new KidsDoodlePass to test it out. They were then thanked for their participation and told there would be another session in about a week's time, if appropriate. At the end of session 4 they were thanked for their participation in the study, asked whether they had any questions about the study and given their gift voucher.

4   Results

Table 1 summarizes children's accuracy in selecting the correct doodles on each grid, the measure of the effectiveness of the authentication system. Children were in general very accurate in selecting the doodles, even on the three doodle KidsDoodlePass:3. On only a small number of occasions did children need a second attempt. Only one child needed a third attempt to recognise their doodle and only on two occasions did a child need a hint. In both the latter instances, the child repeatedly selected the same incorrect doodle from their own doodles. In addition, there was only a small drop in accuracy with increasing complexity of KidsDoodlePass, with KidsDoodlePass:3 showing slightly lower accuracy rates than KidsDoodlePass:2.

The selection times were not normally distributed (as is typical of reaction times), so medians were used to summarize the data and non-parametric statistics conducted. Figure 3 presents the median times to select the correct doodle. For KidsDoodlePass:1, there was a significant decrease in the selection time from the first to the second login (before and after playing the game) (Wilcoxon Signed Rank Test = 24.0, p = .013). None of the other differences between the selection times for the individual grids were significant.

Table 1. Summary of KidsDoodlePass accuracy (percentage of children who correctly select each doodle at first attempt, for each grid of doodles).

KidsPass Doodle	Session 1	Session 2	Session 3	Session 4
1	Login 1: 100.0 Login 2: 89.5	Login 1: 94.7 Login 2: 84.2		
2		Login 1: Grid 1: 94.7 Grid 2: 100.0	Login 1: Grid 1: 94.7 Grid 2: 100.0 Login 2: Grid 1: 94.7 Grid 2: 94.7	
3			Login 1: Grid 1: 100.0 Grid 2: 100.0 Grid 3: 94.7	Login 1: Grid 1: 94.7 Grid 2: 100.0 Grid 3: 94.7 Login 2: Grid 1: 94.7 Grid 2: 89.5 Grid 2: 94.7

In terms of satisfaction with the system in comparison to text passwords, when asked which system they preferred 12 (63.1%) children said they preferred KidsDoodlePass and 6 (31.5%) said they preferred text passwords, but this difference was not significant. (chi-square = 2, df = 2, n.s.). At the end of Session 4, after using KidsDoodlePass:2 and KidsDoodlePass:3 three times each, the children were asked whether they thought remembering the KidsDoodlePass:3 was harder than the KidsDoodlePass:2. 17 (89.4%) children thought they were equal in difficulty, the other 2 (10.5%) thought remembering KidsDoodlePass:3 was harder, a significant difference (chi-square = 11.84, df = 1, p = .0005). The children were also asked whether they thought they would be able to remember three doodles as a KidsDoodlePass for a long time. 11 children (57.8%) answered positively, 4 (21.1%) said they would not remember and 4 (21.1%) were not sure, not a significance difference (chi-square = 5.16, df = 2, n.s.).

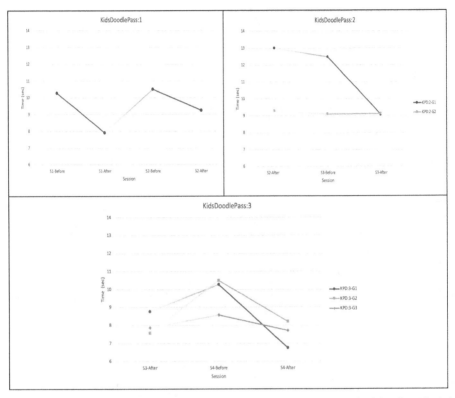

Fig. 3. Time (seconds) to select each doodle for each KidsDoodlePass grid of doodles (shaded lines show transitions between sessions, one week apart)

5   Discussion and Conclusions

Our study was an initial investigation of the effectiveness, efficiency and satisfaction of a doodle-based authentication system, KidsDoodlePass, for young children aged 6 to 9 years. In terms of effectiveness, the system worked very well, the all children successfully logged in 10 times, only once was a hint required and the researcher never had to log in for a child. In terms of efficiency, children only needed less than 10 s on average for each grid with a certain amount of practice. So, logins, even with three doodles would take less than 30 s, which seems very acceptable. Further research is needed to compare efficiency to traditional text passwords for children in this age group. This was not attempted in the present study, as we were unsure whether the doodle-based system would be effective. However, compared to Read and Cassidy's [22] results on children's ability to recall a text password, the KidsDoodlePass system is very effective. In their study, of the younger children (6 to 7 years), 23.1% failed to recall a password they had created themselves after an hour, whereas all our children recognised their KidsDoodlePass even after a week. However, this is in contrast to the results of Cole, Walsh and Pease [5] who compared performance with self-generated graphical and text passwords by children aged 6 to 12 years. The found that children had higher success rates with text passwords than with graphical passwords, both after a distraction task and two weeks later. Order of password elements was one of the difficulties children encountered, which was only a minor problem in our study. In terms of satisfaction, a significant proportion of children said the doodles for KidsDoodlePass were easier to remember than regular passwords. However, only 12 out of the 19 children said they preferred KidsDoodlePass to a text password, which was not a significant proportion, but a reasonable proportion given the small sample size

Several limitations and issues with the study need to be noted. This was a small scale evaluation with only 19 children to make an initial assessment of the effectiveness, efficiency and satisfaction of the KidsDoodlePass authentication system. Given this initial success, a larger evaluation with more children, and a comparison with passwords, is planned. In retrospect, a particular child should only ever see one of their own doodles in a grid. This design improvement might help reduce the ordering confusion, although this was only a minor problem.

We evaluated KidsDoodlePass, a graphical alternative to text password authentication for young children. We found that they were largely able to identify their own doodles appropriately, and could log in successfully using the system. Due to this successful initial experience of the children while using KidsDoodlePass, we are planning to refine the system and evaluate it with a larger group of children, extending the age range to 6 to 12 years. In addition, we will evaluate longer term memorability of KidsDoodlePass by investigating its use over a period of a month.

References

1. Biddle, R., Chiasson, S., van Oorschot, P.C.: Graphical passwords: learning from the first twelve years. ACM Comput. Surv. **44**(4), 1–41 (2012). Article 19
2. Coggins, P.E.: Implications of what children know about computer passwords. Comput. Sch. **30**(3), 282–293 (2013)
3. ChildTrend: Home computer access and internet use (2018). https://www.childtrends.org/indicators/home-computer-access. Accessed 7 Jan 2020
4. Choong, Y.-Y., Theofanos, M., Renaud, K., Prior, S.: Case study – exploring children's password knowledge and practices. In: 2009 Workshop on Usable Security (USEC), San Diego (2019)
5. Cole, J., Walsh, G., Pease, Z.: Click to enter: comparing graphical and textual passwords for children. In: 2017 Conference on Interaction Design and Children (IDC 2017), pp. 472–477. ACM, New York (2017)
6. Davis, D., Monrose, F., Reiter, M.: On user choice in graphical password schemes. In: 13th USENIX Security Symposium (2004)
7. Dhamija, R., Perrig, A.: Deja Vu: a user study using images for authentication. In: 9th USENIX Security Symposium (2000)

8. Dunphy, P., Nicholson, J., Olivier, P.: Securing passfaces for description. In: 4th ACM Symposium on Usable Privacy and Security (SOUPS) (2008)
9. Flavell, J.: Cognitive development: children's knowledge about the mind. Annu. Rev. Psychol. **50**, 21–45 (1999)
10. Frith, C., Frith, U.: Theory of mind. Curr. Biol. **15**(17), R644–R646 (2005)
11. Gathercole, S.: The development of memory. J. Child Psychol. Psychiatry **29**(1), 3–27 (1998)
12. Goldberg, J., Hagman, J., Sazawal, V.: Doodling our way to better authentication. In: Extended Abstracts on Human Factors in Computer Systems (CHI EA 2002) (2002)
13. Hurlock, E.B.: Child Development, 6th edn. McGraw Hill, New York (2017)
14. Imran, A.: A comparison of password authentication between children and adults. Ph.D. dissertation, Carleton University, Canada (2015)
15. Jebriel, S.M., Alali, H., Abuzaraida, M.A.: Investigating the usability of using doodle scan system (DSS): the case of Misurata. In: IEEE International Conference on Service Operations and Logistics and Informatics (SOLI). IEEE (2015)
16. Jermyn, I., Mayer, A., Monrose, F., Reiter, M., Rubin, A.: The design and analysis of graphical passwords. In: 8th USENIX Security Symposium (1999)
17. Lamichhane, D.R., Read, J.C.: Investigating children's passwords using a game based survey. In: 2017 Conference on Interaction Design and Children - IDC 2017, pp. 617–622 (2017)
18. Maqsood, S., Biddle, R., Maqsood, S., Chiasson, S.: An exploratory study of children's online password behaviours. In: 17th ACM Conference on Interaction Design and Children (IDC 2018). Association for Computing Machinery (2018)
19. Mendori, T., Ikenoue, N., Shimizu, A.: Password input method using icons for primary school children. In: Looi, C.-K., et al. (eds.) Towards Sustainable and Scalable Educational Innovations Informed by the Learning Sciences. IOS Press, Amsterdam (2005)
20. Mendori, T., Kubouchi, M., Okada, M., Shimizu, A.: Password input interface suitable for primary school children. In: International Conference on Computers in Education (ICCE 2002), pp. 765–766. IEEE (2002)
21. Office of communication (Ofcom): Children and parents: media use and attitudes report 2018 (2018). https://www.ofcom.org.uk/data/assets/pdf_file/0024/134907. Accessed 23 Jan 2020
22. Read, J.C., Cassidy, B.: Designing textual password systems for children. In: 11th International Conference on Interaction Design and Children (IDC 2012) (2012)
23. Renaud, K.: A visuo-biometric authentication mechanism for older users. In: McEwan, T., Gulliksen, J., Benyon, D. (eds.) People and Computers XIX—The Bigger Picture. Springer, London (2006). https://doi.org/10.1007/1-84628-249-7_11
24. Renaud, K.: Web authentication using Mikon images. In: 2009 World Congress on Privacy, Security, Trust and the Management of e-Business (CONGRESS 2009), pp. 79–88. IEEE Computer Society
25. Schwab, D., Alharbi, L., Nichols, O., Yang, L.: Picture PassDoodle: usability study. In: IEEE 4th International Conference on Big Data Computer Service and Applications. IEEE (2018)
26. United Nations Children's Fund (UNICEF): The state of the world's children 2017: children in a digital world. UNICEF (2017)
27. Varenhorst, C.: Passdoodles: a lightweight authentication method. MIT Computer Science and Artificial Intelligence Lab (2004). https://pdfs.semanticscholar.org//44ba01a9ed10db2ec3d17a56e852ac33cc78.pdf. Accessed 23 Jan 2020

Information Security Behavioural Threshold Analysis in Practice: An Implementation Framework

D. P. Snyman$^{(\boxtimes)}$ and H. A. Kruger

School of Computer Science and Information Systems, North-West University, Potchefstroom, South Africa
{dirk.snyman,hennie.kruger}@nwu.ac.za

Abstract. This paper presents the development of a framework for evaluating group behaviour in information security in practice. Information security behavioural threshold analysis is employed as the theoretical foundation for the proposed framework. The suitability of the proposed framework is evaluated based on two sets of qualitative measures (general frameworks and information security frameworks) which were identified from literature. A novel conceptual mapping of the two sets of evaluation measures is presented and used to evaluate the proposed framework. The successful evaluation of the proposed framework, guided by the identified evaluation measures, is presented in terms of positive practical applications, as well as positive peer review and publication of the underlying theory.

Keywords: Information security group behaviour · Framework development · Evaluation

1 Introduction

Many models and frameworks are used throughout information security (InfoSec) literature to determine or explain attitude that individuals exhibit towards InfoSec which is indicative of their eventual behaviour [1]. Such frameworks and models are mainly focussed on the individual's behaviour, and researchers infer that this should apply to group behaviour as well. However, this is not always the case, as there are many other influences on group behaviour, such as the lemming effect, contextual factors, influential people, etc. It is, therefore, not enough to simply expect individual behaviour to be indicative of group behaviour.

To the best of the researchers' knowledge, no framework for analysing and predicting InfoSec group behaviour is currently available in literature. In this paper, a formal framework is proposed for group behaviour in InfoSec. This proposed framework is based in part on aspects found in existing frameworks [1], i.e. norms, beliefs, attitudes, etc. The other integral part of the framework will then consist of those aspects that are specific to group behaviour, i.e. the use of a technique, such as behavioural threshold

© IFIP International Federation for Information Processing 2020
Published by Springer Nature Switzerland AG 2020
N. Clarke and S. Furnell (Eds.): HAISA 2020, IFIP AICT 593, pp. 133–143, 2020.
https://doi.org/10.1007/978-3-030-57404-8_11

analysis (BTA) that considers factors, such as the lemming effect and external contextual factors. This paper represents the culmination of an overarching study in which the use of a BTA approach was conceptualised in terms of group behaviour in InfoSec, and with the abovementioned background in mind, the aim of this study is now firstly, to *formalise a framework for evaluating information security group behaviour in practice, supported by behavioural threshold analysis as the underlying theory* thereby allowing InfoSec practitioners to utilise the approach, and secondly, to *critically evaluate the proposed framework based on qualitative measures from literature.*

The remainder of this paper is structured as follows: In Sect. 2, a brief contextualisation for applying research in practice and a theoretical view on the requirements of a successful framework are presented. In Sects. 3 and 4 the development of the resulting framework and the evaluation thereof, based on the requirements from Sect. 2 are described. A discussion on the general and specific contributions of the resulting framework is presented in Sect. 5 and the paper is concluded in Sect. 6.

2 Literature Review

2.1 Contextualisation

Translating research findings and recommendations of any nature into practice remains an elusive process [2–4]. Some of the reasons why this general disconnect exists between most types of research and the related acceptance thereof in practice include ambiguity in existing research [3, 5]; limited published reflection on implementation [5]; ongoing research is often still inconclusive [4]; decision makers lack the required information [6]; and attitudes and beliefs of individuals [3, 7] which translates to social and cultural resistance to the change associated with implementation.

This disconnect between research and practice has also been identified in the domain of InfoSec [5, 8], where it especially holds true for non-technical aspects of InfoSec such as InfoSec awareness and behaviour. Research into human behaviour (and how it relates to InfoSec behaviour and culture) is often based on, and guided by, theoretical models from the fields of sociology and social psychology. While such models can assist in uncovering the intricacies of behaviour by highlighting complexity and structuring the underlying themes, they do not necessarily provide for simple integration into actionable methods in practice.

The level of success of such an integration is, however, subject to three criteria, namely *Evidence, Context*, and *Facilitation* [4] (ECF). In terms of research pertaining to InfoSec (specifically security culture), AlHogail [8] suggests following the STOPE approach [7] to facilitate change when implementing new approaches to effect change in the culture and the eventual underlying behaviour. The dimensions to be adhered to for STOPE are *Strategy, Technology, Organisation, People*, and *Environment*.

These criteria and dimensions are therefore subsequently used to guide and evaluate the development of a framework for applying the BTA approach, in the context of InfoSec, in practice.

2.2 Framework Requirements

The qualitative criteria for evaluating frameworks in general (*Evidence, Context,* and *Facilitation*) and for frameworks for InfoSec (STOPE) will be presented here in detail and contextualised in terms of research in general versus InfoSec research. Finally, a mapping of how these two approaches align, and how they relate to this research is presented.

Evidence, Context, and Facilitation

In terms of an implementation framework, the interaction between Evidence (E), Context (C), and Facilitation (F) is said to determine the eventual Successful Implementation (SI) of the framework in practice, i.e. SI is a function of three criteria [4] so that

$$SI = f(E, C, F) \tag{1}$$

The success of the implementation is therefore dependent on the level of maturity by which each of the criteria is met. Each of the criteria and what each represents in terms of a framework is briefly described here. Where applicable, these criteria are already presented in terms of InfoSec:

Evidence - Evidence refers to the level of scrutiny that the model or approach that underpins a framework has undergone. Is there substantiated proof that the model is fit for purpose? [4]

Context - Context is concerned with the setting in which a framework is to be applied in practice. In general, this refers to the physical attributes of the environment such as buildings, people, and processes [9]. However, for the successful implementation of a framework, this view might be too narrow, since in essence context also implicitly refers to intangible qualities, such as individual and group behaviour, and the underlying (security) culture [3, 9].

Facilitation - Implementing research in practice is essentially a process whereby change of some kind is sought to be effected. Change is a process that ought to be facilitated if it is to be successful and long-lived [3]. Such facilitation refers to the under-standing of (and ultimately altering) attitudes and behaviours, specifically by leveraging the way in which "an individual is able to influence other individuals' attitudes or overt behaviour" [3, 10]. In terms of InfoSec, Snyman and Kruger [11] hypothesise that while some people may inherently be more influential [3], the behaviour of all individuals exerts influence on the eventual behaviour of a group.

STOPE

InfoSec frameworks may be evaluated by means of a critical evaluation of how well the framework addresses *Strategy, Technology, Organisation, People,* and the *Environment*. Each of these dimensions is briefly explained below, based on the work of AlHogail [8] which contextualises them in terms of InfoSec.

Strategy – Strategy refers to the suggested measures that are applied to effect change within an organisation to improve its overall levels of InfoSec. These approaches may include the implementation of formal plans of action, such as InfoSec policies and guidelines as well as the structured approach of a framework.

Technology – In this context, technological means of addressing InfoSec is referred to as technology. Frameworks should ideally provide for changes or improvements on the technical measures that are used to safeguard systems.

Organisation – The success of strategy is reliant on the underlying security culture of an organisation. This culture and eventual behaviour are often influenced by the way in which an organisation is structured. A framework should provide guidelines for how structures within an organisation will influence the application thereof and, ideally, how structures may be leveraged to achieve the goal of the framework.

People – InfoSec ultimately revolves around people. It is often people that undo security due to unwanted actions. Frameworks should seek to address the human aspect of InfoSec in terms of behaviour, culture and awareness.

Environment – Environment view refers to the greater context in which an organisation has to address InfoSec, and which should be included in the application of a framework. On a macro level, this may include concepts, such as regulatory frameworks and legislation [8], but on a smaller level can refer to the context in which an individual or group behave in terms of InfoSec [9].

Mapping STOPE to ECF

An assessment of the framework evaluation criteria as mentioned in Sects. 2.1 and 2.2 above allows for a combination of the two approaches by means of a conceptual mapping. Table 1 shows the conceptual mapping of STOPE to ECF:

Table 1. Conceptual mapping of STOPE to ECF

Evidence	Context	Facilitation
Peer review combined with resulting STOPE evaluation	O:Organisation P:People E:Environment	S:Strategy T:Technology

From Table 1, it can be seen that the individual views from STOPE could not as easily be mapped to Evidence (ECF), as all these views can contribute in some way to this criterion. It is concerned with the rigour of the underlying model on which a framework is based. It stands to reason then, that in combination with other types of measures that can confirm said rigour (e.g. peer review, or experimentation), evidence can thus be conceptualised as the resulting evaluation that is conveyed by STOPE. However, in the context of this research, Evidence will be used as a freestanding criterion, evaluated on the available peer review, case studies, and successful implementations. For the remaining criteria, the Organisation, People and Environment from STOPE [8] can be directly mapped to Context [3] from ECF. Overlapping themes include people, behaviour, culture, and physical attributes of the environment. In the final instance, Facilitation (ECF) encompasses the strategy and technology views from STOPE. The common concepts from these constructs that can be identified are the approaches for achieving positive change through organisational, technological, and human means.

3 Framework Model and Development

In order to describe the development of the suggested framework, the underlying theoretical model should first be presented. In this section, the aim is to firstly summarise the BTA model as implemented in the greater research project, followed by a description of the resulting framework and its elements.

3.1 Behavioural Threshold Analysis Model

Group behaviour is a complex phenomenon. To analyse this complexity, Granovetter [12] describes a theory called "Threshold models of collective behaviour". The model described by Granovetter is used as the underlying theoretical grounding for the framework. In short, the model takes into account the mechanisms whereby individuals influence the behaviour of each other, i.e. based on an intrinsic inclination of an individual to follow the example of existing group behaviour. This inclination to follow behaviour is conceptualised as the individual's behavioural threshold. The said threshold is expressed as a percentage of group members who perform a behaviour that will sway an individual to participate in the specific behaviour. When the (perceived) participation rate of group members exceeds the behavioural threshold of the individual, the individual will follow the group's example and also perform the behaviour. When participation in group behaviour exceeds an individual's threshold for participation, the individual might even perform group behaviour that is contrary to his/her convictions and predisposition.

Growney [13] describes how the model can be implemented in circumstances where groups of individuals congregate and how the mathematical aggregate of behavioural thresholds may be interpreted to allow for a prediction of eventual group behaviour. The model was successfully applied in InfoSec in earlier, related studies and the reader is referred to these sources for in-depth reading on the application of BTA in InfoSec [11, 14, 15].

3.2 Development of Information Security Group Behaviour Framework

In Sect. 1, reference was made to the first aim of this research, namely, to formalise a framework for the practical application of BTA in InfoSec. To address this aim, Fig. 1 shows the proposed framework for evaluating group behaviour in InfoSec and illustrates the overarching development and categorises different epochs of the framework's development. Each of the epochs is subsequently briefly described below.

1) Theoretical development – This epoch refers to the investigation into group behaviour in InfoSec. It includes a review of the related literature on the following themes: human behaviour in general and in the context of InfoSec; modelling human behaviour, e.g. the theory of planned behaviour, and its employment in security awareness and security culture; and group behaviour (threshold models of collective behaviour) and the analysis thereof (BTA). The development of the underlying theory also comprises the development of methodological and practical guidelines for experimental and practical applications.

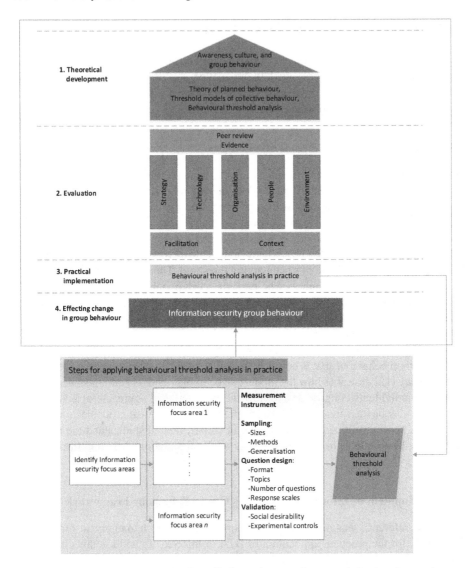

Fig. 1. Framework for the evaluation of information security group behaviour in practice

2) Evaluation – Based on the aforementioned ECF criteria and STOPE views, the evaluation epoch refers to a formal evaluation of the underlying theoretical assumptions and the framework itself. In the following section (see Sect. 4), a formal evaluation of the proposed framework is shown.
3) Practical implementation – After a successful evaluation, evidencing a well-founded theoretical basis and framework, the approach is ready for implementation. The blown-up view shows the minutia of the application of BTA in InfoSec.
4) Effecting change in group behaviour – The results of the BTA application may be interpreted to detect areas of InfoSec that need intervention to improve behaviour.

In the following segment (Sect. 4), how the combination of ECF and STOPE was employed to evaluate the proposed framework is shown.

4 Framework Evaluation

During the related research and the development of BTA as an approach for InfoSec, the requirements for ECF and STOPE were met. In this section, the extent to which peer review and practical applications contribute to the maturity of the framework is described.

4.1 Peer Review and Publication

Table 2 shows the STOPE criteria and ECF views. A critical evaluation and motivation are provided.

The applications of the approach in practice are presented in the following subsection.

4.2 Applications in Practice

Throughout the development of the approach to apply BTA in InfoSec, practical experiments were conducted to test the working of the model within this context. An initial pilot study was conducted to test the feasibility of the model [11]. After further development of the approach and the underlying theoretical foundations, such as the required methodological approach [14], two successful practical applications were conducted.

The first practical application of BTA was conducted at an Australian utility company [15]. The resulting insights and recommendations regarding employees' InfoSec behaviour were communicated in a report to the company. Feedback indicated that the insights were found to be invaluable in guiding the directions of future awareness campaigns.

The second application was in an academic context at a South African University [9]. The results from the exercise correlated with the expected and observed InfoSec behaviour of students in a university residence. The success of these practical applications, the commonalities and differences between the different contexts where the approach was applied, and the reporting publications passing peer review, verifies that this procedure for application (as presented in this framework) is effective.

5 Contributions

A twofold discussion of the successes of the framework is presented here in terms of general and specific contributions to the field of InfoSec.

Table 2. Critical evaluation of the proposed framework

	STOPE criteria	Critical evaluation and motivation	*Evidence* (peer-reviewed publications)
Context	Organisation	One of the main *contexts* with which BTA is concerned, is that of the *Organisation*. The ultimate outcome of the successful implementation of the approach is improved levels of InfoSec within any organisation where it is applied. A collection of papers, both in InfoSec journals and conference proceedings, were published that contribute to the rigour of the underlying theoretical model and approaches	Organisation forms part of all of the previous papers [9, 11, 14–18] which cannot be listed here due to space constraints. Refer to the References section for full bibliographical details
	People	BTA is based on the behaviour and interaction of people. All the previous work [9, 11, 14–18] therefore encompasses the *People* view; however one paper is highlighted here: Developing the interrelated concepts of sequential decision-making and information cascades in InfoSec, a novel view of the *context* of how InfoSec behaviour is formed was peer-reviewed, published and presented at an international conference	*Theorising on information cascades and sequential decision making for analysing security behaviour* [17]
	Environment	Given the influence of the *environment*, and its many facets on behaviour, a paper on the *contextual* factors that influence InfoSec behaviour was presented at an international conference after peer review and published in the proceedings	*External contextual factors in information security behaviour* [9]
Facilitation	Strategy	A paper that describes and validates the underlying methodology, including some practical considerations for BTA in InfoSec, was published in a peer-reviewed journal. This contributes to formalising the *strategy* to *facilitate* positive change in InfoSec	*Behavioural threshold analysis: Methodological and practical considerations for applications in information security* [14]

(continued)

Table 2. (*continued*)

STOPE criteria	Critical evaluation and motivation	*Evidence* (peer-reviewed publications)
Technology	With the aim of facilitating and partially automating BTA, a novel data collection method (optical polling) and decision support system (DSS) were developed. This *technology* can help *facilitate* the practical aspects of the model implementation. The novel data collection and the DSS was presented at an international conference and published as a peer-reviewed book chapter.	*Optical polling for behavioural threshold analysis in information security* [16]; *A management decision support system for evaluating information security behaviour* [18]

5.1 General

This research contributes to the general field of InfoSec by having 1) contributed a methodology for formalising a framework for the analysis of group behaviour in InfoSec; 2) synthesised qualitative measures to critically assess and evaluate frameworks in InfoSec by conceptually mapping methods from literature; and 3) contributed an approach to measure InfoSec group behaviour to improve the management thereof and influence change in behaviour. Supplementary to the general contributions above, certain specific contributions were made and are highlighted next.

5.2 Specific

Reflecting on the specific contributions of this research in terms of the initial research aims relating to the proposed framework, the following is pertinent: 1) BTA is identified as a mechanism to evaluate InfoSec group behaviour and expressed as a well-founded underlying theory for this framework; 2) The framework was critically evaluated in terms of the qualitative measures conceptualised from literature, and furthermore, the approach outlined in this framework was successfully applied in practice which further illustrated the suitability of the framework; 3) The framework can be construed as an instrument for appraising InfoSec awareness in organisations which allows InfoSec practitioners to effect positive change in InfoSec behaviour; 4) A methodology for identifying InfoSec focus areas was identified; and 5) An instrument was contributed that is novel in comparison to existing tools for analysing InfoSec group behaviour with respect to its sensitivity towards the influence of external stimuli, such as contextual factors and the lemming effect.

6 Conclusion

In this paper, a formal framework for the evaluation of group behaviour in InfoSec was presented. The framework is based on BTA as the central theoretical model. Two qualitative evaluation methods for frameworks were identified from literature and contextualised in terms of InfoSec group behaviour. A combination of the two evaluation methods was used to evaluate the fittingness of the proposed framework for analysing InfoSec group behaviour. Based on the resulting evaluation, grounded in scientific peer review, as well as successful applications in practice, the proposed framework was deemed to be fit for purpose.

References

1. Pham, H., Brennan, L., Richardson, J.: Review of behavioural theories in security compliance and research challenge. In: Informing Science and Information Technology Education Conference, Vietnam, pp. 65–76. Informing Science Institute (2017)
2. Grimshaw, J.M., Eccles, M.P., Lavis, J.N., Hill, S.J., Squires, J.E.: Knowledge translation of research findings. Implement. Sci. 7, 50 (2012). https://doi.org/10.1186/1748-5908-7-50
3. Kent, B.: Implementing research findings into practice: frameworks and guidance. Int. J. Evid.-Based Healthc. 17, S18–S21 (2019)
4. Kitson, A., Harvey, G., McCormack, B.: Enabling the implementation of evidence based practice: a conceptual framework. BMJ Qual. Saf. 7, 149–158 (1998)
5. Tsohou, A., Kokolakis, S., Karyda, M., Kiountouzis, E.: Investigating information security awareness: research and practice gaps. Inf. Secur. J.: Glob. Pers. 17, 207–227 (2008)
6. Haines, A., Donald, A.: Making better use of research findings. BMJ 317, 72–75 (1998)
7. Bakry, S.H.: Development of security policies for private networks. Int. J. Netw. Manag. 13, 203–210 (2003)
8. AlHogail, A.: Design and validation of information security culture framework. Comput. Hum. Behav. 49, 567–575 (2015)
9. Snyman, D.P., Kruger, H.A.: External contextual factors in information security behaviour. In: 6th International Conference on Information Systems Security and Privacy (ICISSP 2020), pp. 185–194. SCITEPRESS – Science and Technology Publications, Lda (2020)
10. Rogers, E.M.: Diffusion of Innovations. Simon and Schuster, New York (2010)
11. Snyman, D.P., Kruger, H.A.: The application of behavioural thresholds to analyse collective behaviour in information security. Inf. Comput. Secur. 25, 152–164 (2017)
12. Granovetter, M.: Threshold models of collective behavior. Am. J. Sociol. 83, 1420–1443 (1978)
13. Growney, J.S.: I Will If You Will: Individual Thresholds and Group Behavior - Applications of Algebra to Group Behavior. COMAP Inc., Bedford (1983)
14. Snyman, D.P., Kruger, H.A.: Behavioural threshold analysis: methodological and practical considerations for applications in information security. Behav. Inf. Technol. 38, 1–19 (2019)
15. Snyman, D.P., Kruger, H.A., Kearney, W.D.: I shall, we shall, and all others will: paradoxical information security behaviour. Inf. Comput. Secur. 26, 290–305 (2018)
16. Snyman, D.P., Kruger, H.A.: Optical polling for behavioural threshold analysis in information security. In: International Conference on Information and Knowledge Engineering (IKE 2017), pp. 39–45. CSREA Press (2017)

17. Snyman, D.P., Kruger, H.A.: Theorising on information cascades and sequential decision-making for analysing security behaviour. In: 5th International Conference on Information Systems Security and Privacy (ICISSP 2019), pp. 205–212. SCITEPRESS – Science and Technology Publications, Lda., Prague (2019)

18. Snyman, D., Kruger, H.: A management decision support system for evaluating information security behaviour. In: Venter, H., Loock, M., Coetzee, M., Eloff, M., Eloff, J. (eds.) ISSA 2019. CCIS, vol. 1166, pp. 15–27. Springer, Cham (2020). https://doi.org/10.1007/978-3-030-43276-8_2

Information Security Behavior: Development of a Measurement Instrument Based on the Self-determination Theory

Yotamu Gangire[1(✉)] [iD], Adéle Da Veiga[1] [iD], and Marlien Herselman[1,2] [iD]

[1] School of Computing, College of Science, Engineering and Technology, University of South Africa (UNISA), Florida Campus, Johannesburg, South Africa
ygangire@gmail.com, dveiga@unisa.ac.za, mherselman@csir.co.za
[2] Next Generation Enterprises and Institutions, CSIR, Pretoria, South Africa

Abstract. Employee information security behaviour is important in securing an organisation's information technology resources. Employees can act in a risky or secure manner. Improving employee information security behaviour is important for organisations and should follow an assessment of their behaviour. A robust measuring instrument is a necessity for effectively assessing information security behaviour. In this study, a questionnaire was developed based on the Human Aspects of Information Security Questionnaire and self-determination theory and validated statistically. Data obtained through a quantitative survey (N = 263) at a South African university was used to validate the questionnaire. The result is a questionnaire that has internally consistent items, as shown by the results of the reliability analysis. Universities can use the questionnaire to identify developmental areas to improve information security from a behaviour perspective.

Keywords: Information security · Information security behaviour · Information security policy (ISP) · Compliance · Self-determination theory (SDT)

1 Introduction

Employee information security behaviour is important in ensuring that information and other information technology (IT) resources are secure in the organisation [1, 2]. However, employees contribute significantly to the information security threats and breaches in the organisation [3, 4]. PricewaterhouseCoopers reports that insiders such as employees, suppliers, consultants and contractors, could be responsible for 30% of the reported incidents [5]. Security breaches can have unpleasant consequences, some of which are: loss of productivity, theft of information assets, system downtime, destruction of IT infrastructure, damage to the organisation's reputation, and the organisation may face lawsuits, fines and regulatory actions [6].

There is a need to understand what influences compliance with information security policies (ISPs) [7, 8]. Understanding employees' information security behaviour, is an

© IFIP International Federation for Information Processing 2020
Published by Springer Nature Switzerland AG 2020
N. Clarke and S. Furnell (Eds.): HAISA 2020, IFIP AICT 593, pp. 144–157, 2020.
https://doi.org/10.1007/978-3-030-57404-8_12

important step in the assessment and consequently the improvement of information security behaviour [9]. Hence there is a need to assess and evaluate employees' information security awareness [10].

Some studies on employee information security behaviour are based on theories for example, the study by Safa, et al. [1] was based on the protection motivation theory and the theory of planned behaviour (TPB); the study by Ifinedo [11] used the TPB, social bond theory and the social control theory and the study by Kranz and Haeussinger [12] used the TPB and the self-determination theory (SDT). These studies aimed to validate a particular theory, hence they only assessed the variables in the theory under investigation while other variables were not considered. However, employee information security behaviour is influenced by many factors besides variables from theories [13]. This study develops an instrument based on themes from the Human Aspects of Information Security Questionnaire (HAIS-Q) [13] and the information security compliant behaviour model based on the SDT (ISCBM^{SDT}) [14]. This not only contributes to the theory validation of the SDT variables, but combines these with the themes of the HAIS-Q, thereby including more variables in the assessment instrument.

The aim of this study is to develop and validate an information security behaviour questionnaire to assess the influence of perceived competence, perceived relatedness and perceived autonomy on information security behaviour. The study postulates that perceptions of competence, relatedness and autonomy influence efficacy and hence the intention to comply with ISPs. It is therefore, intended that a positive perception of competence, relatedness and autonomy will help mitigate the risk of ISP non-compliance and that developing a questionnaire can aid in measuring and determining this. It is also aimed at outlining the development of this instrument, including the validity and reliability testing of the questionnaire. The instrument could be used to assess employee information security behaviour from the perspective of the SDT. To achieve these aims, a survey was carried out at a South African university using the information security behaviour questionnaire. This paper is structured as follows: Sect. 2 gives an overview of the information security behaviour and Sect. 3 describes the research methodology. The results of the survey and statistical validation of the questionnaire are discussed in Sect. 4. This is followed by the limitations and future directions in Sect. 5 and the conclusion in Sect. 6.

2   Information Security Behaviour

Pattinson et al. [15] refer to information security behaviour as the behaviour performed by computer users, which can be either intentionally risky behaviour or intentionally secure behaviour. According to Guo [16] employee security behaviour can be desirable or undesirable. Desirable behaviour is ISP compliant whereas undesirable behaviour is not. Examples of secure behaviour include taking precautions and reporting security incidents [16]. Employees can also exhibit behaviour aimed at preventing security breaches by taking fewer risks. Other employees engage in inappropriate security behaviour, including using the default security password and relying on the computer to auto-lock when they leave their desk. Employees can also engage in behaviour that aid business continuity and recovery; these employees back up their data and inform colleagues of security issues [17]. It is argued that when employees comply with the ISPs, information security threats are reduced [18].

Alfawaz, Nelson and Mohannak [19] propose security behaviour modes as the knowing-doing mode, knowing-not doing mode, not knowing-doing mode and not knowing-not doing mode. In the not knowing-not doing mode, employees violate information security rules, because they do not know the organisation's information security rules and do not have any security knowledge [19]. In the not knowing-doing mode, employees do not know the information security rules and do not have security knowledge but still exhibit the right security behaviour. These are employees who will ask their co-workers before taking certain actions. In the knowing-not doing mode, employees know the rules and have the necessary security knowledge and skills, but still violate the rules [19]. In the knowing-doing mode, employees know the rules, have the necessary security skills and comply with the rules [19].

Ahmad, Norhashim, Song, & Hui [20] group employees into four types on the basis of whether or not they know the security rules and whether or not they comply with the information security rules. They classify them as discerning, obedient, rebel and oblivious employees. Discerning individuals conform to the information security rules because they have the necessary knowledge; some employees conform to the information security rules not because they have the knowledge but because they follow organisational rules just because they are there; some employees choose not to conform to information security rules despite having the knowledge; and other employees compromise information security because they do not have the security knowledge [20].

Alfawaz et al. [19] and Ahmad et al. [20] propose classification of employees' information security behaviour that also explain why employees fail to comply with organisational ISPs. They postulate that employees fail to comply because they are ignorant of the regulations, they choose not to or they are not competent due to lack of security knowledge. Their classifications suggest that in order for employees to comply with the ISPs, they have to be equipped with the relevant security knowledge and skills. Employees will also have to actively think about the security implications of their actions when they do their work. Therefore, security awareness, knowledge and experience are important [1]. Users must also understand their responsibilities regarding information security because an employee who lacks information security awareness is more vulnerable to information security attacks [21].

2.1 Information Security Compliant Behaviour Model

The Information Security Compliance Behavior Model (ISCBM^{SDT}) is based on the three concepts of the SDT, which are the need for competence, the need for relatedness and the need for autonomy. The three basic psychological needs are regarded as some of the sources contributing to intrinsic motivation [22, 23]. The need for autonomy is the perception that one is acting out of one's own volition and that one's behaviour is self-determined. The need for relatedness refers to the desire be attached to others. Competence is the belief of being capable and effective [22]. The ISCBM^{SDT} postulates that when perceived competence, perceived relatedness and perceived autonomy are fulfilled, the employees will comply with the ISP because it is their choice to do so

[14]. The questionnaire developed for this study is based on the ISCBM^{SDT} and the questionnaire themes/focus areas are discussed next.

2.2 Information Security Behaviour Themes

The focus areas from the HAIS-Q were mapped to the three concepts of the SDT resulting, in each focus area focusing on competence, relatedness and autonomy. The themes are as follows.

Password Management
This involves understanding how to protect information system resources by using strong and secure passwords. This includes regularly changing passwords, choosing strong passwords and not sharing passwords [17, 24, 25].

Email Usage
Employees have to understand safe email use. This includes not downloading unsafe attachments, clicking on links in email from known or unknown senders and opening attachments in emails from unknown senders [1, 15, 17, 21, 24, 26].

Internet Usage
Employees should know how to use the internet safely. This includes downloading files, accessing dubious websites and entering information online [15, 18, 26, 27].

Social Media Usage
Employees should understand safe usage of social media. This includes social media privacy settings, considering the consequences of posting information and acting responsibly regarding posting about work on social media [27].

Mobile Devices Usage
Employees should understand how to secure their mobile devices, which carry work information when working in a public area. This includes physically securing mobile devices, sending sensitive information via public Wi-Fi and guarding against shoulder surfing [27, 28].

Information Handling
Employees have to understand how to handle sensitive information. This includes disposing of sensitive print-outs, inserting removable media in work computers and leaving sensitive material on work areas [17, 27, 29].

Privacy
Employees should understand how to handle personally identifiable information. This includes non-disclosure of sensitive information [1, 17], processing client information in a lawful manner [30], processing client information for the purpose for which it was collected [30, 31], and adhering to the organisation's privacy policy [32]. When employees adhere to the privacy policy they can uphold the privacy of student data they handle. Parsons et al. [33] propose that the link between information security awareness and privacy should be investigated. Table 1 shows an extract of items in the competence, relatedness and autonomy category.

Table 1. Questionnaire items extract

Focus area	Competence	Relatedness	Autonomy
Password management	1. I have the necessary skills to use different passwords for social media and work accounts	My colleagues support me to use different passwords for social media and work accounts	I choose to use different passwords for social media and work accounts
	2. I have the necessary skills to never share my work passwords with colleagues	My colleagues support me never to share my work passwords with colleagues	I choose never to share my work passwords with my colleagues
	3. I have the necessary skills to use a combination of letters, numbers, and symbols in work passwords	My colleagues support me to use a combination of letters, numbers, and symbols in work passwords	I choose to use a combination of letters, numbers, and symbols in work passwords
Email usage	4. I have the necessary skills to click only on links in emails from people I know	My colleagues support me to click only on links in emails from people I know	I choose to click only on links in emails from people I know
	5. I have the necessary skills to avoid clicking on links in emails from people I do not know	My colleagues support me to avoid clicking on links in emails from people I do not know	I choose to avoid clicking on links in emails from people I do not know
	6. I have the necessary skills to identify when it is risky to open attachments in emails from people I do not know	My colleagues support me to identify when it is risky to open attachments in emails from people I do not know	I choose to avoid opening attachments in emails from people I do not know
Internet usage	7. I have the necessary skills to identify when it is risky to download files onto my work computer	My colleagues support me to identify when it is risky to download files onto my work computer	I choose not to download risky files onto my work computer
	8. I have the necessary skills to avoid accessing websites that could be dubious (malicious)	My colleagues support me to avoid accessing websites that could be dubious (malicious)	I choose to avoid accessing websites that could be dubious (malicious)

(continued)

Table 1. (*continued*)

Focus area	Competence	Relatedness	Autonomy
	9. I have the necessary skills to assess the safety of a website before entering information online	My colleagues support me to assess the safety of a website before entering information online	I choose to assess the safety of a website before entering information online

3 Methodology

This study adopted the positivist research paradigm with a quantitative approach. In the positivist research paradigm researchers prefer to work with observable and measurable reality. Positivists use quantitative methods in their research and the research is based on the testing of theories [34, 35]. The survey strategy was chosen and the questionnaire was used for data collection at a university in South Africa. A non-probability purposive sampling method was used. With purposive sampling the researcher deliberately selects the sample for example because they are easy to reach or are available [34]. The selection of the expert panel was done using the purposive sampling method based on the following criteria: they had all done research work in information security and had experience in information security awareness. The pilot sample was selected using convenience sampling in one of the university's departments. The survey participants were selected using purposive sampling. The survey questionnaire was sent electronically to the entire population of administrative and academic staff. Ethical clearance was obtained from the university, adhering to the research ethics policy that focuses on aspects such as anonymity, voluntary participation, confidentiality and consent for participation.

The following statistical tests were performed: ANOVA, t-test and Pearson correlation analysis. ANOVA was carried out to determine if there were significant differences among the demographical groups for age, job level, level of education and length of service groups. The t-test were performed to determine if the mean scores among the gender groups had any significant differences. The correlation analysis was carried out to determine if there was any correlation among the resulting factors from the exploratory factor analysis.

3.1 Questionnaire

A Likert scale (strongly agree, agree, unsure, disagree and strongly disagree) was used to answer the statements. The questionnaire had two sections: Sect. 1 which was for biographical information and Sect. 2 which comprised the information security behaviour questions. The final questionnaire had 75 questions: 25 questions for each of the SDT categories.

3.2 Expert Panel Reviews

A panel of experts in the research area evaluated the questionnaire. This helped to refine and improve the questionnaire [35]. The questionnaire was reviewed by a panel of six experts, four of whom were from the field of psychology (human factors scientists) who had researched the human aspects of cyber security for 11 years and had developed the HAIS-Q. The other two were an academic in information security and an IT security consultant specialising in incident response and awareness. The reviewers had 10 to 20 years of working experience. They pointed out that some of questions were not clear and others addressed two different aspects in one question. The questionnaire was updated and sent for pilot testing.

3.3 Pilot Testing

The pilot test was conducted among 12 staff members in one of the departments in the university. The questionnaire pilot test showed that some questions were not worded clearly and it was recommended that job level be added to the biographical section.

3.4 Main Study

The updated questionnaire was prepared and administered using Google Forms over the internet and participants were notified by an email invitation sent by the ICT department of the university. The email contained information on the research and the links for completing the online questionnaire. The participants were required to read the information sheet and the consent form. If they consented to participate in the study, then they proceeded to complete the online questionnaire

4   Results

Two hundred and sixty-three (263) responses were received from the online survey. The sample consisted of 54.8% females, 44.1% males and 1.1% did not disclose their gender. Those born between 1977 and 1995 were the largest group of respondents (38.40%). The highest number of survey respondents (69.08%) was from the group with postgraduate qualifications. There were more respondents from the groups with higher qualifications (i.e. the higher the qualification the higher the number of respondents). This is consistent with a university environment. Those who had worked for six to ten years were the largest group (27.38%) and most of the respondents were administrative staff (51.53%). The results of the survey are reported next.

A cut-off of 4.0 for the means was set for the information security behaviour questions [36]. A mean score of 4.0 and above indicated a positive perception, while a mean score below 4.0 indicated a neutral or potentially negative perception.

For the competence questions, the top 10 questions all had means above 4.0. This suggests that the respondents had a positive perception of the competence questions. Of the bottom 10 questions, five had means above 4.0 and five had means below 4.0, indicating areas for which further improvement is required.

For the relatedness questions, the mean values for the top statements ranged from 3.05 to 3.51 and the mean values for the bottom statements ranged from 2.68 to 3.01. These mean values for both top questions and bottom questions show that all had means below

4.0. This suggests that the participants had neutral and potentially negative perceptions of the relatedness questions, indicating areas requiring further improvement.

For the autonomy questions, the mean values for the top statements ranged from 4.41 to 4.68 and the mean values for the bottom statements ranged from 3.91 to 4.27. The top questions all had means above 4.0, suggesting that the respondents had a positive perception of the autonomy questions. For the bottom 10 questions, eight questions had means above 4.0 and two had means below 4.0. The two questions with means below 4.0 indicate areas were further improvement is required.

The results of the Pearson correlation showed that the competence and autonomy factors had a statically significant positive correlation ($r >= .287$, $n = 263$, $p < .05$), two tailed. The correlation for the competence and relatedness factors show that some factors had a positive correlation ($r >= .224$, $n = 263$, $p < .05$), two tailed and other factors did not. The correlation results for the autonomy and relatedness factors showed that some factors had a positive correlation ($r >= .134$, $n = 263$, $p < .05$), two tailed and others did not.

The results of the information security behaviour questions suggest that the respondents had a more positive perception of the competence and autonomy questions than of the relatedness questions. The Pearson correlation results show a positive correlation between competence and autonomy, suggesting that the respondents who perceive themselves to be competent also felt confident about their autonomy perception.

4.1 Validation of the Instrument

Factor Analysis

Exploratory factor analysis (EFA) was carried out to determine the underlying relationships between the variables [37], as well as the construct validity of the questionnaire [38]. O'Rourke and Hatcher [39] suggests that to achieve a sample size that is statistically adequate to carry out questionnaire validation, the responses or the collected data must be at least five times the number of questions in the questionnaire. The EFA was done for each category and new factors were determined per category. Since each category had 25 questions, a minimum of 125 responses were required per category. The recommendation of O'Rourke and Hatcher [39] and the received responses were sufficient to carry out the statistical validation of the questionnaire and the data was processed using SPSS Version 25.

Determining the Number of Factors

The Kaiser-Meyer-Olkin (KMO) test and the Bartlett sphericity tests were conducted for each of the three categories competence, relatedness and autonomy. Field [40] recommends a KMO value closer to 1 in order to produce distinct and reliable factors. For the Bartlett sphericity test, the probability should be less or equal to 0.05; this shows highly correlated variables [38]. The KMO for the competence statements was 0.915 and the Bartlett sphericity test result was statistically significant ($p = 0.000$). The KMO for the relatedness statements was 0.965 and the Bartlett sphericity test result was statistically significant ($p = 0.000$). The KMO for the autonomy statements was 0.885 and the Bartlett sphericity result was statistically significant (p = 0.000). As a result, all categories met the criteria for performing the EFA.

The factors were determined using the Eigenvalues, scree plots and cumulative percentages [41]. The item loading cut off was 0.4, as Stevens [42] suggests that item loading values should be greater than 0.4. The cumulative percentage had to be above 60% and the Eigenvalues had to be greater than 1. Competence statements resulted in four factors and these had Eigenvalues greater than 1 and a cumulative Eigenvalue of 62.38%. Relatedness statements resulted in two factors and these had Eigenvalues greater than 1 and a cumulative Eigenvalue of 70.74%. The autonomy statements resulted in six factors and these had Eigenvalues greater than 1 and a cumulative Eigenvalue of 63.68%.

Table 2 shows the resulting factors. For the competence statements, Factor 3 Statement 25 was removed as it had a factor cross-loading with a cross-loading difference of less than 0.2. Factor 4 was dropped as it had only one item, Statement 3 and factors for the competence category were reduced to 3. For the relatedness category, Questions 17 and 18 were dropped as they had cross-loading differences less than 0.2. For the autonomy category Statements 1, 2, 3, 14, 17 and 18 were dropped because they had loadings below 0.4.

Table 2. Resulting factors

Category	Factor	Statements
Competence	Factor 1	1, 10, 11, 12, 14, 15, 16, 18, 19, 20, 21
	Factor 2	4, 5, 6, 7, 8, 9, 17
	Factor 3	22, 23, 24
Relatedness	Factor 1	1, 2, 3, 4, 5, 6, 7, 8, 9, 10, 11, 12, 13, 14, 15, 16
	Factor 2	19, 20, 21, 22, 23, 24, 25
Autonomy	Factor 1	8, 9, 10
	Factor 2	4, 5, 6, 7
	Factor 3	22, 23
	Factor 4	19, 20, 21
	Factor 5	24, 25
	Factor 6	11, 12, 13, 15, 16

Naming the Factors

The factors shown in Table 2 were named to reflect the common themes of the statements grouped under that factor.

Competence

Factors in this category reflect the employee's competence/skills to carry out the information security actions. The employees are confident that they can protect the IT resources because they have necessary skills to do so. For the competence statements,

Factor 1 (11 items) was named *employee skills for data safety awareness*, Factor 2 (seven items) was named *employee skills for email and website safety* and Factor 3 (four items) was named *employee skills for privacy awareness*.

Relatedness

Factors in this category reflect the employee's need for support from colleagues to carry out information security actions. The employees perceive that they can protect the IT resources if co-workers and superiors support them. For the relatedness statements, Factor 1 (16 items) was labelled *organisational support for employee device and information protection awareness* and Factor 2 (seven items) was named *organisational support for employee information and privacy protection awareness*.

Autonomy

Factors in this category reflect the employees' need to be in control of their information security behaviour. The employees perceive that when they are in control of their information security behaviour they can protect the IT resources of their organisation. For the autonomy statements, Factor 1 (three items) was named *employee choice on privacy awareness*, Factor 2 (four items) was named *employee choice to avoid malicious emails and downloads*, Factor 3 (two items) was named *employee choice to keep privacy of student personal information*, Factor 4 (three items) was named *employee choice to report bad security behaviour*, Factor 5 (two items) was named *employee choice to adhere to information security and privacy policies* and Factor 6 (five items) was named *employee choice to keep devices and information secure*.

Two autonomy factors, *employee choice to keep privacy of student personal information* and *employee choice to adhere to information security and privacy policies*, had two statements each. They were retained because both factors had very good reliability as shown in Table 3.

4.2 Reliability Analysis

The Cronbach alpha coefficient was calculated for each of the 11 factors. Reliability refers to how consistent or dependable the measuring instrument is, and whether under similar conditions the measuring instrument produces consistent results [43]. According to Gerber and Hall [41], the Cronbach alpha coefficient can be interpreted as follows: good for values greater than 0.8, acceptable for values between 0.6 and 0.8, unacceptable for values less than 0.6. Table 3 shows the results of the Cronbach alpha values for the 11 factors. All the Cronbach alpha results were above 0.7, suggesting high reliability.

The final questionnaire had 11 revised dimensions and the individual statements were not changed. The new dimensions were a result of the factor and reliability analysis hence the new questionnaire can be considered to have good internal consistency.

5 Limitations and Future Directions

The following are some of the study's limitations:

The purposive sampling method used in this study, an accepted method of collecting data, may not produce a sample that is representative of the population. Therefore, future

Table 3. Cronbach alpha coefficient results for factors

Category	Factor	No. of items	Cronbach alpha	Comment
Competence	Employee skills for data safety awareness	11	0.906	Good
	Employee skills for email and website safety	7	0.905	Good
	Employee skills for privacy awareness	4	0.799	Good
Relatedness	Organisational support for employee device and information awareness	16	0.967	Good
	Organisational support for employee information and privacy protection awareness	7	0.945	Good
Autonomy	Employee choice on privacy awareness	3	0.775	Acceptable
	Employee choice to avoid malicious emails and downloads	4	0.836	Good
	Employee choice to keep the privacy of student personal information	2	0.904	Good
	Employee choice to report bad security behaviour	3	0.791	Acceptable
	Employee choice to adhere to information security and privacy policies	2	0.868	Good
	Employee choice to keep devices and information secure	5	0.793	Acceptable

research should consider a representative sample of the population and inclusion of more organisations. The survey questionnaire had 75 questions, which may take some time to complete hence some respondents may not complete the survey. Future work will consider reducing the number of questions.

6 Conclusion

The aim of this study was to develop and validate the information security behaviour questionnaire based on the SDT. This questionnaire can be used to investigate how the perception of competence, relatedness and autonomy influence the intention to comply with ISPs. The results of the assessment can be used to design programs to assist employees to comply with ISPs.

The questions were developed by combining the variables from the SDT and the themes from the HAIS-Q as well as privacy to come up with a new questionnaire. Through a quantitative research, data were collected using the survey method. The collected data were used to validate the questionnaire resulting in a revised questionnaire with items with high internal consistency.

Generally, the results suggest that the survey participants were more confident about their competence and autonomy regarding their information security behaviour than they were about the relatedness questions.

The Pearson correlation results indicate a positive correlation between competence and autonomy, with a partial positive correlation between competence and relatedness, as well as a partial positive correlation between relatedness and autonomy. The results suggest, for example, that improving the competence of employees could result in an increased intention to comply with ISPs. In addition, how confident employees are about their information security skills, will influence their perception of autonomy in their information security behaviour. The participants had a neutral (M = 3.08) or potentially negative perception of the relatedness questions, suggesting that area requires further development.

The practical implication of this study and this questionnaire is that it can be used by a university to assess individual employees' strengths and weaknesses in terms of their awareness of information security behaviour. The questionnaire could also be administered before and after information security awareness training to assess the effectiveness of the training.

Acknowledgment. This work is based on research supported by the University of South Africa's Women in Research Grant.

References

1. Safa, N.S., Sookhak, M., Von Solms, R., et al.: Information security conscious care behaviour formation in organizations. Comput. Secur. **53**, 65–78 (2015). https://doi.org/10.1016/j.cose.2015.05.012
2. Humaidi, N., Balakrishnan, V.: Indirect effect of management support on users' compliance behaviour towards information security policies. Heal. Inf. Manag. J. **47**, 17–27 (2017). https://doi.org/10.1177/1833358317700255
3. Pahnila, S., Karjalainen, M., Mikko, S.: Information security behavior : towards multi-stage models. In: Proceedings of the Pacific Asia Conference on Information Systems (PACIS 2013) (2013)
4. Mayer, P., Kunz, A., Volkamer, M.: Reliable behavioural factors in the information security context. In: Proceedings of the 12th International Conference on Availability, Reliability and Security - (ARES 2017), pp. 1–10 (2017)
5. PricewaterhouseCoopers. The Global State of Information Security Survey 2018: PwC (2018). https://www.pwc.com/us/en/services/consulting/cybersecurity/library/information-security-survey.html
6. Ponemon Institute: The third annual study on the state of endpoint security risk (2020). https://www.morphisec.com/hubfs/2020StateofEndpointSecurityFinal.pdf

7. Huang, H.W., Parolia, N., Cheng, K.T.: Willingness and ability to perform information security compliance behavior: psychological ownership and self-efficacy perspective. In: Proceedings of the Pacific Asia Conference on Information Systems (PACIS 2016) (2016)

8. Iriqat, Y.M., Ahlan, A.R., Nuha, N.M.A.: Information security policy perceived compliance among staff in palestine universities : an empirical pilot study. In: Proceedings of the Jordan International Joint Conference on Electrical Engineering and Information Technology (JEEIT), pp. 580–585. IEEE (2019)

9. Alaskar, M., Vodanovich, S., Shen, K.N.: Evolvement of information security research on employees' behavior: a systematic review and future direction. In: Proceedings of the 48th Hawaii International Conference on System Sciences, pp. 4241–4250. IEEE (2015)

10. Öğütçü, G., Testik, Ö.M., Chouseinoglou, O.: Analysis of personal information security behavior and awareness. Comput. Secur. **56**, 83–93 (2016). https://doi.org/10.1016/j.cose.2015.10.002

11. Ifinedo, P.: Information systems security policy compliance: an empirical study of the effects of socialization, influence, and cognition. Inf. Manag. **51**, 69–79 (2013)

12. Kranz, J.J., Haeussinger, F.J.: Why deterrence is not enough : The role of endogenous motivations on employees' information security behavior. In: Proceedings of the 35th International Conference on Information Systems, pp. 1–14. IEEE (2014)

13. Parsons, K., McCormac, A., Butavicius, M., et al.: Determining employee awareness using the Human Aspects of Information Security Questionnaire (HAIS-Q). Comput. Secur. **42**, 165–176 (2014). https://doi.org/10.1016/j.cose.2013.12.003

14. Gangire, Y., Da Veiga, A., Herselman, M.: A conceptual model of information security compliant behaviour based on the self-determination theory. In: Proceedings of the 2019 Conference on Information Communications Technology and Society, (ICTAS). IEEE (2019)

15. Pattinson, M., Butavicius, M., Parsons, K., et al.: Examining attitudes toward information security behaviour using mixed methods. In: Proceedings of the 9th International Symposium on Human Aspects of Information Security & Assurance (HAISA). pp. 57–70 (2015)

16. Guo, K.H.: Security-related behavior in using information systems in the workplace: a review and synthesis. Comput. Secur. **32**, 242–251 (2013). https://doi.org/10.1016/j.cose.2012.10.003

17. Blythe, J.M., Coventry, L., Little, L.: Unpacking security policy compliance : the motivators and barriers of employees' security behaviors. In: Proceedings of the Symposium on Usable Privacy and Security (SOUPS), Ottawa, pp. 103–122 (2015)

18. Klein, R.H., Luciano, E.M.: What influences information security behavior? A study with brazilian users. J. Inf. Syst. Technol. Manag. **13**, 479–496 (2016). https://doi.org/10.4301/S1807-17752016000300007

19. Alfawaz, S., Nelson, K., Mohannak, K.: Information security culture : a behaviour compliance conceptual framework. In: Proceedings of the 8th Australasian Information Security Conference (AISC), pp. 47–55 (2010)

20. Ahmad, Z., Norhashim, M., Song, O.T., Hui, L.T.: A typology of employees' information security behaviour. In: Proceedings of the 4th International Conference on Information and Communication Technology, pp. 3–6 (2016)

21. Alohali, M., Clarke, N., Furnell, S., Albakri, S.: Information security behavior: recognizing the influencers. In: Proceedings of the Computing Conference, pp. 844–853 (2017)

22. Ryan, M.R., Deci, L.E.: Self-determination theory and the facilitation of intrinsic motivation, social development, and well-being. Am. Psychol. **55**, 68–78 (2000)

23. Legault, L.: Self determination theory. In: Zeigler-Hill, V., Shackelford, T.K. (eds.) Encyclopedia of Personality and Individual Differences, pp. 1–9. Springer, New York (2017). https://doi.org/10.1007/978-1-4419-1005-9_1620

24. Shropshire, J., Warkentin, M., Sharma, S.: Personality, attitudes, and intentions: predicting initial adoption of information security behavior. Comput. Secur. **49**, 177–191 (2015). https://doi.org/10.1016/j.cose.2015.01.002
25. Calic, D., Pattinson, M., Parsons, K., et al.: Naïve and accidental behaviours that compromise information security : what the experts think. In: Proceedings of the 10th International Symposium on Human Aspects of Information Security & Assurance (HAISA), pp. 12–21 (2016)
26. Bélanger, F., Collignon, S., Enget, K., Negangard, E.: Determinants of early conformance with information security policies. Inf. Manag. **54**, 887–901 (2017). https://doi.org/10.1016/j.im.2017.01.003
27. Bauer, S., Bernroider, E.W.N., Chudzikowski, K.: Prevention is better than cure! Designing information security awareness programs to overcome users' non-compliance with information security policies in banks. Comput. Secur. **68**, 145–159 (2017). https://doi.org/10.1016/j.cose.2017.04.009
28. Curry, M., Marshall, B., Crossler, R.E., Correia, J.: InfoSec Process Action Model (IPAM): Systematically addressing individual security behavior. Database Adv. Inf. Syst. **49**, 49–66 (2018). https://doi.org/10.1145/3210530.3210535
29. Aurigemma, S., Mattson, T.: Deterrence and punishment experience impacts on ISP compliance attitudes. Inf. Comput. Secur. **25**, 421–436 (2017). https://doi.org/10.1108/ICS-11-2016-0089
30. Swartz, P., Da Veiga, A., Martins, N.: A conceptual privacy governance framework. In: Proceeding of the 2019 Conference on Information Communications Technology and Society (ICTAS), pp. 1–6 (2019)
31. NIST Security and privacy controls for federal information systems and organizations: National Institute of Standards and Technology (2017)
32. Dennedy, M.F., Fox, J., Finneran, T.R.: Data and privacy governance concepts. The Privacy Engineer's Manifesto, pp. 51–72. Apress, New York (2014)
33. Parsons, K., Calic, D., Pattinson, M., et al.: The human aspects of information security questionnaire (HAIS-Q): two further validation studies. Comput. Secur. **66**, 40–51 (2017). https://doi.org/10.1016/j.cose.2017.01.004
34. Oates, B.J.: Researching Information Systems and Computing. Sage, London (2006)
35. Saunders, M., Lewis, P., Thornhill, A.: Research Methods for Business Students, 7th edn. Pearson Education Limited, Essex (2016)
36. Da Veiga, A., Martins, N.: Improving the information security culture through monitoring and implementation actions illustrated through a case study. Comput. Secur. **49**, 162–176 (2015). https://doi.org/10.1016/j.cose.2014.12.006
37. Yong, A.G., Pearce, S.: A beginner's guide to factor analysis: focusing on exploratory factor analysis. Tutor. Quant. Methods Psychol. **9**, 79–94 (2013)
38. Williams, B., Onsman, A., Brown, T.: Exploratory factor analysis: a five-step guide for novices. J. Emerg. Prim. Heal. Care **8**, 1–13 (2010)
39. O'Rourke, N., Hatcher, L.: A Step-By-Step Approach to Using SAS for Factor Analysis and Structural Equation. SAS Institute, Cary (2013)
40. Field, A.: Discovering Statistics Using SPSS, 3rd edn. Sage, London (2009)
41. Gerber, H., Hall, N.: Quantitative research design. In: Data Acquisition - 1 day. HR Statistics, Pretoria (2017)
42. Stevens, J.P.: Applied Multivariate Statistics for the Social Sciences, 4th edn. Erlbaum, Hillsdale (2002)
43. Marczyk, G., Fertinger, D., DeMatteo, D.: Essentials of Research Design and Methodology. Wiley, Hoboken (2005)

Education

Addressing SME Characteristics for Designing Information Security Maturity Models

Bilge Yigit Ozkan[(✉)] [iD] and Marco Spruit [iD]

Department of Information and Computing Sciences, Utrecht University, Princetonplein 5,
3584 CC Utrecht, The Netherlands
{b.yigitozkan,m.r.spruit}@uu.nl

Abstract. This paper identifies the effects of small and medium-sized enterprises'
(SME) characteristics on the general design principles for maturity models in the
information security domain. The purpose is to guide the research on information security maturity modelling for SMEs that will fit in form and function for
their capability assessment and development purposes, and promote organizational learning and development. This study reviews the established frameworks
of general design principles for maturity models and projects the design requirements of our envisioned information security maturity model for SMEs. Maturity
models have different purposes of uses (descriptive, prescriptive and comparative)
and design principles with respect to these purposes of uses. The mapping of SME
characteristics and design principles facilitates the development of an information
security maturity model that systematically integrates the desired qualities and
components addressing SME characteristics and requirements.

Keywords: Information security · Maturity model · Assessment · Process
improvement · Organisational learning · SME

1 Introduction

Small and medium-sized enterprises (SMEs), which are the predominant form of enterprise and make up 99.8% of European enterprises in the Organisation for Economic
Co-operation and Development (OECD) area [1], are ill-prepared for cyberattacks [2].

One way of tackling the challenges of managing and implementing information security is through the use of maturity models [2]. Originating from software engineering,
maturity modelling is a method for representing domain specific knowledge in a structured way in order to provide organizations with an evolutionary process for assessment
and improvement [3, 4].

Previous research shows that maturity models promote greater levels of organisational learning [5]. Organisational capabilities are developed through organisational
learning processes [6]. From a socio-technical perspective, since information security
domain is quite complex [7], the value of maturity models is indisputable for developing the necessary information security capabilities. Addressing the characteristics and

© IFIP International Federation for Information Processing 2020
Published by Springer Nature Switzerland AG 2020
N. Clarke and S. Furnell (Eds.): HAISA 2020, IFIP AICT 593, pp. 161–174, 2020.
https://doi.org/10.1007/978-3-030-57404-8_13

the requirements of the target organisation will yield to more effective individual and organizational learning and development.

From the perspective of information security maturity models (ISMM), there is a need to facilitate SMEs with tailor-made models that are more situation aware and that can adapt to their specific needs [8]. In a recent study for adaptive information security modelling for SMEs, the authors state that utilisation of maturity models for self-assessing information security capabilities can be a remedy for SMEs [2].

There have been studies conducted on the development and design of maturity models. Mettler [9] investigated maturity models as a subject of design science. Becker et al. considering maturity models as design science artifacts, propose a procedure model that distinguishes eight phases in the development of maturity models [4]. De Bruin et al. propose a methodology to generalize the phases of developing a maturity model and outlined the main phases of generic model development [10]. Pöppelbuß and Röglinger propose a framework of general design principles for maturity models [11].

The utilisation of maturity models in different organisational structures has been another aspect that has been studied in the literature. Mettler and Rohner present a first design proposition of a situational maturity model [12]. In the information security domain, there have been several studies addressing the effect of organisational characteristics. Mijnhardt et al. investigated organisational characteristics influencing SME information security maturity [8]. In this study, they focused on four different categories of characteristics (General, in and out sourcing, IT dependency and IT complexity). These categories include 11 characteristics such as size, revenue, number of employees, time an organization can run without IT support.

Baars et al. conclude that a maturity framework should consider the differences between the characteristics of their target organizations [13]. There have also been cluster based approaches to SME information security [2, 14].

The design principles applied during the development and design of the maturity models affect their applicability in several ways. For example, designing a situational-aware maturity model enables its adaption to different organisational contexts. Being inspired by the studies investigating the maturity models as design artifacts [4, 9] and those providing guidance on the design and development of maturity models [10, 11], the research question this paper addresses is formulated as follows.

"How can SME characteristics be addressed for designing information security maturity models?"

The purpose is to support the development of SME aware ISMMs as design artifacts that will promote greater levels of individual and organisational learning.

To answer this research question, we used the SME characteristics resulting from a literature review [15]. These characteristics guided us to identify the "boundary/context" as discussed by Cronholm & Göbel in their study on guidelines supporting the formulation of design principles [16]. We discuss the effects of the SME characteristics' [15] on the general design principles [11] and propose 16 design requirements for an ISMM for SMEs.

The rest of the paper is organised as follows. First, background and related research are presented. Second, the general design principles for maturity models [11] are investigated with respect to SME characteristics and the findings are presented. Third, the associations between the SME characteristics and the design principles are presented by including the proposed design principles as a summary. Finally, conclusions are drawn.

2   Background and Related Research

2.1   Design Principles

To date, several studies have investigated the phenomenon of *"Design Principles"*. According to Hevner and Chatterjee, a principle is a clear statement of truth that guides or constrains action. A principle can also be formed as a rule or a standard of conduct [17]. Jones and Gregor state that design principles "... define the structure, organization, and functioning of the design product or design method" [18]. Chandra et al. focused on the characteristics of effective design principle formulation [19]. A recent study by Cronholm & Göbel proposed guidelines supporting the formulation of design principles [16].

2.2   Design Principles for Maturity Models

In the literature, the maturity models are distinguished by their purpose of use as descriptive, prescriptive and comparative. The maturity models for descriptive purpose of use focus on the assessment of the as-is capabilities of an organisation. The maturity models for prescriptive purpose of use provide guidance on how to proceed on the evolutionary path of the maturity levels. The maturity models for comparative purpose of use enables internal and external benchmarking through the assessment results [4, 10, 20]. De Bruin et al. argue that even though maturity model types (descriptive, prescriptive and comparative) can be seen as distinct types, they actually represent evolutionary phases of a model's lifecycle. In the final phase of this lifecycle, to be used comparatively the model must be applied in a wide range of organizations in order to attain sufficient data to enable valid comparison [10].

Pöppelbuß and Röglinger proposed general design principles (DPs) for maturity models grouped according to typical purposes of use and justified on the foundation of maturity modelling literature [11]. It is important to note that Pöppelbuß and Röglinger states that they deliberately omitted the comparative purpose of use as the fact of whether corresponding DPs can be met largely depends on external factors [11].

2.3   SME Characteristics

Several studies in the literature suggest that SMEs may be differentiated from larger companies by a number of key characteristics [15, 21, 22]. Different approaches to the phenomena of organisational characteristics were taken in the literature. Yu et al. abstract organisations as organic entities similar to humans and investigate organisational characteristics in categories theoretically rooted in psychology [23]. Mijnhardt et al. use an indicator-based approach to distinguish between a wide variety of different organizations [8].

In this paper, we focus on the characteristics present in the literature related to SME research. Cocca and Alberti conducted a literature review and analysed many papers focusing on SMEs in different fields of science [15]. Their findings were grouped into two main categories: external and internal. The factors related to external environment are typically outside the control of organisation [16]. As the implementation of maturity models (MM) is often considered as part of improvement initiatives [24], they primarily depend on the internal environment of the organisations [25].

In Internal characteristics are related to resources, structure, and management practices, we present the internal characteristics that we investigated in regard to their effects to general design principles proposed by Pöppelbuß and Röglinger [11]. To increase the readability and to enable more comprehensible referral, the third column in Internal characteristics are related to resources, structure, and management practices presents the keywords used for the corresponding internal characteristics. Internal characteristics are related to resources, structure, and management practices. The keywords were selected in a way that we consider they represent the characteristic in a recallable manner.

3   Addressing SME Characteristics for Designing Information Security Maturity Models

In order to answer the research question, we investigated each design principle proposed by Pöppeluß and Röglinger [11] and analysed the effect of the internal SME characteristics proposed by Cocca and Alberti [15] on the design principles. The authors of the paper did this analysis thus the findings need to be validated. We further elaborate on the constraints of validity in the conclusion section.

In this section, we present descriptive and prescriptive design principles proposed by Pöppelbuß and Röglinger [11] and we discuss the effect of SME characteristics, requirements and needs on these design principles. Additionally, we present our insights for the comparative type maturity models. For each design principle, we discuss the SME characteristics' effect on the design principle and we propose design requirements for an ISMM for SMEs. Table 2, Table 3 and Table 4 present basic, descriptive and prescriptive design principles respectively. To increase the readability and to enable a more comprehensible referral, the third column in these tables presents the keywords used for the corresponding design principles. The keywords were selected in a way that we consider they represent the characteristic in a recallable manner.

3.1   Basic Design Principles

The basic design principles proposed by Pöppelbuß and Röglinger [11] are given in Table 2.

For an information security model for SMEs, we elaborate on the basic design principles given in Table 2 as follows.

Regarding Information (DP1.1), the domain coverage and prerequisites for applicability of the maturity model should be provided by possibly referring SMEs to some resources. The prerequisites for applications might be confusing for SMEs who have skill shortages (Skills-IC3), lack of organisational capabilities (Capabilities-IC7) and lack of management expertise (Management-IC4). Regarding the target group, in the case of SMEs, the employees or managers who have the most experience in the information security domain should be addressed (Knowledge-IC8) but poor human resources management might make this difficult to accomplish (HRM-IC17). The results should be reported in an easily understandable way. Since SMEs have short-term vision and orientation (Short-term-IC15) and information security is a continuous initiative, it should be made clear to the target group how the ISMM would be beneficial for their business in the long term (Strategic-IC9). SMEs that are aiming at using the ISMM might not have heard of any other maturity models (Skills-IC3, Capabilities-IC7, Reactive-IC12). Therefore, the differences in the ISMM at hand from the other models available should be made clear. The differences might occur in the domain coverage, the purpose of use, target group, design process and the extent of empirical validation.

DR1 – The information on security domain coverage and prerequisites for applicability of the ISMM should be accompanied by extra resources for SMEs.

DR2 – The long-term benefits of utilising the ISMM should be made clear.

DR3 – The differences in the ISMM at hand from the other models available should be made clear.

Regarding Maturity (DP1.2), as information security is a complex domain [7], a low level of abstraction would provide more granularity and help better realisation of improvement steps to be taken by the SMEs. This design principle is related to IC14, "Learning-by-doing processes", IC16, "Incremental improvements and adjustments" and IC18 "Focus on technical aspects and production". Having these characteristics in nature, SMEs will benefit from a low-level granularity in an ISMM.

DR4 – Low-level granularity should be provided to help better realisation of improvement steps to be taken by the SMEs.

Regarding Domain (DP1.3), it is needed to provide the definitions of central constructs related to the information security domain. The utilisation of any well-known frameworks in the information security domain will increase the understandability of the maturity model [22]. Well-known standards published by Standard Developing Organisations (SDOs) in the information security domain (e.g. ISO/IEC 27002 [26]) might be a good reference to facilitate the usage of adequate language and understandability of the maturity model. This design principle is related to Skills-IC3, Resources-IC6, and Capabilities-IC7. SMEs having these internal characteristics will benefit by being provided with central constructs that are recognised and well-perceived by their stakeholders.

DR5 – The central constructs that are recognised and well-perceived by SMEs' stakeholders (i.e. standards) should be provided to facilitate the usage of adequate language and understandability of the maturity model.

Regarding Users (DP1.4), given the complexity of information security and the internal characteristics of SMEs (Skills-IC3, Capabilities-IC7, Learning-by-doing-IC14, Improvements-IC16), the documentation of the ISMM should be self-explanatory and easy to understand. Poor human resources management (HRM-IC17) should be considered here as a factor. The risk of Personal Assets (IC5) increases the importance of the ISMM for SMEs. Managing the information security risks reduces the risk of assets which is a direct positive effect for the target group. Providing SMEs with some guidance on how to estimate the cost of efforts with respect to capabilities and maturity levels should be considered (Performance-IC10).

DR6 – The documentation of the ISMM should be self-explanatory and easy to understand.
DR7 – The benefit of using the ISMM for protecting the assets should be made explicit.
DR8 – The documentation of the ISMM should include guidance on how to estimate the cost of efforts with respect to capabilities and maturity levels.

3.2   Design Principles for a Descriptive Purpose of Use

The design principles for a descriptive purpose of use are proposed by Pöppelbuß and Röglinger [11] as follows (Table 3).

Regarding Criteria (DP2.1), assessment criteria should be concise, precise and clear as defined by [11] as a general principle, specifically for information security maturity modelling for SMEs, the information source [20] for the criteria should be also be provided. The SME characteristics Skills-IC3, Capabilities-IC7, Learning-by-doing-IC14 and Improvements-IC16 are related to this principle. SMEs would benefit from well-founded assessment criteria as they rather plan for small steps of improvements (Learning-by-doing-IC14 and Improvements-IC16) and they have a lack of expertise and capabilities.

DR9 – The assessment criteria should be concise, precise and clear and the information source for the assessment criteria should be provided.

As a consequence of several SME characteristics related to lack of expertise and skills (Skills-IC3, Resources-IC6, Capabilities-IC7), SMEs might prefer to outsource the management and implementation of information security. Outsourcing information technology infrastructure is also an identifier in the decision to outsource the security of this infrastructure. Regarding Assessment (DP2.2), outsourcing decisions should be one of the parameters to consider for the applicability of assessment criteria.

DR10 – The assessment methodology should enable the configuration of the criteria according to SMEs' outsourcing decisions.

The European Digital SME Alliance has recently published a position paper on the EU Cybersecurity Act and the role of standards for SMEs [27]. In this paper, the need for distinction between different types of SMEs is emphasized. The reason of this differentiation is presented as to make sure that cybersecurity solutions and standards are tailored to them. Regarding Assessment (DP2.2), the SME categories proposed by the Digital SME Alliance can be considered to configure the assessment criteria provided by the maturity model (Knowledge-IC8).

DR11 – The assessment methodology should enable the configuration of the criteria according to different categories of SMEs' according to their role in the digital ecosystem.

The assessment methodology should be reusable to allow multiple assessments and comparisons over the time of the assessment results to present and observe the improvement [28].

3.3 Design Principles for a Prescriptive Purpose of Use

The design principles for a prescriptive purpose of use are proposed by Pöppelbuß and Röglinger [11] as follows (Table 4).

Regarding I-Measures (DP3.1), prescriptive maturity models must include improvement measures that enable the development of a road-map for improvement [10, 11]. In consideration of information security as the application domain and SMEs as the target group for maturity modelling, the improvement measures should be organised in small and achievable steps which could be facilitated by lack of bureaucracy (Structure-IC2, Learning-by-doing-IC14, Improvements-IC16).

DR12 – The improvement measures should be organised in small and achievable steps.
DR13 – The improvements required to progress to the next maturity level should be explicit.

D-Calculus (DP3.2) is related to decision alternatives and prioritization for improvement planning. Improvement objectives may stem from different sources e.g. internal (management) or external (customers). Given the limited skills, resources, capabilities and management expertise of SMEs (Skills-IC3, Management-IC4, Resources-IC6 and Capabilities-IC7), the decisions for choosing amongst different improvement road-maps is more critical and needs to be justified thus should be further supported to be clear and rational.

DR14 – Clear and rational guidelines should be provided for selecting the improvement measures.

In addition to providing a well-grounded decision for improvement, regarding D-Methodology (DP3.3), a maturity model should also provide SMEs with the tailored advice for adapting the improvement measures considering their role in the digital ecosystem [27], flexibility, control and decision-making mechanisms (Flexibility-IC1, Knowledge-IC8, Control-IC11, Decision-IC13).

DR15 – Tailored advice for adapting the improvement measures should be provided for different categories of SMEs.

3.4 Design Principles for a Comparative Purpose of Use (CPoU)

As stated earlier, our reference study for the general design principles, Pöppelbuß and Röglinger deliberately omitted the principles for the comparative purpose of use [11]. De Bruin et al. states that for a model to be used comparatively it must be applied in a wide range of organizations in order to attain sufficient data to enable valid comparison. Cholez and Girard presented a framework that allows multiple assessments and successive comparisons over the time of the assessment results in their study on information security maturity assessment in SMEs. The exemplar assessment result in this study presents a radar graphic depicting the enterprise profile [28]. We recognize that the utilisation of this kind of visuals to present the assessment results for comparative purposes can assist SMEs for better understanding and presenting their as-is and to-be positions. This will help to reduce "Misconception of performance measurement" in regards to Performance-IC19 (Table 1). As stated in Sect. 3.1, SMEs may gain strategic advantage by comparatively using the assessment results (Strategic-IC9).

DR16 – Visual presentation of the assessment results for comparative purposes should be utilized to assist SMEs to better understand and present their as-is and to-be positions.

4 Mapping of SME Characteristics and Design Principles

In this section, the mapping of internal characteristics given in Table 1 and design principles given in respective tables (Table 2, Table 3, Table 4) are presented here as a summary in Table 5. This table shows the associations between the SME characteristics and the design principles by specifying the corresponding design requirements as discussed in this paper.

5 Conclusion

In this paper, we investigated the SME characteristics [15] that may affect the general design principles of maturity models for SMEs [10, 11]. We discuss the possible effect of the SME characteristics on the general design principles and propose 16 design requirements for an ISMM for SMEs.

We present the mapping of the internal SME characteristics and the design principles by specifying the corresponding design requirements as a summary. Since the mapping of the internal SME characteristics and the design principles was done by the authors, it is important to bear in mind the possible bias in these. This limitation stimulates further research to assess the validity of the proposed design requirements by means such as evaluation by SMEs and maturity model developers. Another possibility for future research is a review of a set of existing ISMMs concerning the proposed design principles.

We believe that if the proposed design principles are taken into account from the very start of ISMM development for SMEs, one can systematically account for diverse SME characteristics profiles, thereby significantly increasing the potential usability and applicability of the resulting maturity model. This will yield a better individual and organisational learning with respect to information security.

Table 1. Internal characteristics and whether they affect the design of information security MMs for SMEs [15].

#	Internal Characteristics (IC)	Keyword
1	Flexible and adaptable to changes, innovative	Flexible
2	Loose and flat structure, lack of bureaucracy	Structure
3	Skills shortages	Skills
4	Lack of management expertise	Management
5	Risk of personal assets	Personal Assets
6	Limited resources: time, human, financial	Resources
7	Lack of organizational capabilities	Capabilities
8	Specialist and tacit knowledge	Knowledge
9	Poor strategic planning	Strategic
10	Reliance on financially based performance measures	Performance
11	Control and decision-making rest primarily with one or a few people	Control
12	Reactive, fire-fighting strategy	Reactive
13	Intuition-based decision making	Decision
14	Learning-by-doing processes	Learning-by-doing
15	Short term vision and orientation	Short-term
16	Incremental improvements and adjustments	Improvements
17	Poor human resource management	HRM
18	Focus on technical aspects and production	Technical
19	Misconception of performance measurement	Performance

Table 2. Basic design principles [11]

#	Principle	Keyword
1.1	Basic Information	Information
1.2	Definition of central constructs related to maturity and maturation	Maturity
1.3	Definition of central constructs related to the application domain	Domain
1.4	Target group-oriented documentation	Users

Table 3. DPs for a descriptive purpose of use [11]

#	Principle	Keyword
2.1	Intersubjectively verifiable criteria for each maturity level and level of granularity	Criteria
2.2	Target group-oriented assessment methodology	Assessment

Table 4. DPs for a prescriptive purpose of use [11]

#	Principle	Keyword
3.1	Improvement measures for each maturity level and level of granularity	I-Measures
3.2	Decision calculus for selecting improvement measures	D-Calculus
3.3	Target group-oriented decision methodology	D-Methodology

Table 5. Mapping of SME characteristics and design principles.

Internal characteristics	Design Principles									
	Information DP1.1	Maturity DP1.2	Domain DP1.3	Users DP1.4	Criteria DP2.1	Assessment DP2.2	I-Measures DP3.1	D-Calculus DP3.2	D-Methodology DP3.3	CPoU
Flexibility (IC1)									DR15	
Structure (IC2)							DR12, DR13			
Skills (IC3)	DR1, DR3		DR5	DR6	DR9	DR10		DR14		
Management (IC4)	DR1							DR14		
Personal Assets (IC5)				DR7						
Resources (IC6)			DR5			DR10		DR14		
Capabilities (IC7)	DR1, DR3		DR5	DR6	DR9	DR10		DR14		
Knowledge (IC8)	DR1					DR11			DR15	
Strategic (IC9)	DR2									DR16
Performance (IC10)				DR8						
Control (IC11)									DR15	
Reactive (IC12)	DR3									
Decision (IC13)									DR15	
Learning-by-doing (IC14)		DR4		DR6	DR9		DR12, DR13			

(continued)

Table 5. (*continued*)

Internal characteristics	Design Principles									
	Information DP1.1	Maturity DP1.2	Domain DP1.3	Users DP1.4	Criteria DP2.1	Assessment DP2.2	I-Measures DP3.1	D-Calculus DP3.2	D-Methodology DP3.3	CPoU
Short-term (IC15)	DR2									
Improvements (IC16)		DR4		DR6	DR9		DR12, DR13			
HRM (IC17)	DR1			DR6						
Technical (IC18)		DR4								
Performance (IC19)										DR16

References

1. Digital SME Alliance: Position paper on European cybersecurity strategy: fostering the SME ecosystem (2017). https://www.digitalsme.eu/digital/uploads/20170731-DIGITAL-SME-Cybersecurity-Position.pdf
2. Yigit Ozkan, B., Spruit, M., Wondolleck, R., Burriel Coll, V.: Modelling adaptive information security for SMEs in a cluster. JIC **21**, 235–256 (2019). https://doi.org/10.1108/JIC-05-2019-0128
3. Yigit Ozkan, B., Spruit, M.: A questionnaire model for cybersecurity maturity assessment of critical infrastructures. In: Fournaris, A.P., Lampropoulos, K., Marín Tordera, E. (eds.) IOSec 2018. LNCS, vol. 11398, pp. 49–60. Springer, Cham (2019). https://doi.org/10.1007/978-3-030-12085-6_5
4. Becker, J., Knackstedt, R., Pöppelbuß, J.: Developing maturity models for IT management. Bus. Inf. Syst. Eng. **1**, 213–222 (2009). https://doi.org/10.1007/s12599-009-0044-5
5. Bititci, U.S., Garengo, P., Ates, A., Nudurupati, S.S.: Value of maturity models in performance measurement. Int. J. Prod. Res. **53**, 3062–3085 (2015). https://doi.org/10.1080/00207543.2014.970709
6. Curado, C.: Organisational learning and organisational design. Learn. Organ. **13**, 25–48 (2006). https://doi.org/10.1108/09696470610639112
7. Tisdale, S.M.: Architecting a cybersecurity management framework: navigating and traversing complexity, ambiguity, and agility – ProQuest (2016). https://search.proquest.com/ope nview/0934ecf7a7afd537d2f2307843e1fdb3/1?cbl=18750&diss=y&pq-origsite=gscholar
8. Mijnhardt, F., Baars, T., Spruit, M.: Organizational characteristics influencing SME information security maturity. J. Comput. Inf. Syst. **56**, 106–115 (2016). https://doi.org/10.1080/088 74417.2016.1117369
9. Mettler, Tobias: A Design Science Research Perspective on Maturity Models in Information Systems-Alexandria. Institute of Information Management, Universtiy of St. Gallen, Switzerland (2009)
10. de Bruin, T., Freeze, R., Kulkarni, U., Rosemann, M.: Understanding the main phases of developing a maturity assessment model. In: ACIS 2005 Proceedings, Sydney, p. 11 (2005)
11. Pöppelbuß, J., Röglinger, M.: What makes a useful maturity model? A framework of general design principles for maturity models and its demonstration in business process management. In: ECIS (2011)
12. Mettler, T., Rohner, P.: Situational maturity models as instrumental artifacts for organizational design. In: Proceedings of the 4th International Conference on Design Science Research in Information Systems and Technology, pp. 22:1–22:9. ACM, New York (2009). https://doi.org/10.1145/1555619.1555649
13. Baars, T., Mijnhardt, F., Vlaanderen, K., Spruit, M.: An analytics approach to adaptive maturity models using organizational characteristics. Decis. Anal. **3**(1), 1–26 (2016). https://doi.org/10.1186/s40165-016-0022-1
14. Mayer, N.: A cluster approach to security improvement according to ISO/IEC 27001. In: Proceedings of the 17th European Systems & Software Process Improvement and Innovation Conference (EUROSPI 2010), Grenoble, France (2010)
15. Cocca, P., Alberti, M.: SMEs' three-step pyramid: a new performance measurement framework for SMEs. Presented at the 16th International Annual EurOMA Conference, Göteborg, Sweden (2009)
16. Cronholm, S., Göbel, H.: Guidelines supporting the formulation of design principles. In: Australasian Conference on Information Systems 2018. University of Technology, Sydney (2018). https://doi.org/10.5130/acis2018.ak

17. Hevner, A., Chatterjee, S.: A science of design for software-intensive systems. In: Hevner, A., Chatterjee, S. (eds.) Design Research in Information Systems: Theory and Practice, pp. 63–77. Springer US, Boston (2010). https://doi.org/10.1007/978-1-4419-5653-8_6

18. Jones, D., Gregor, S.: The anatomy of a design theory. J. Assoc. Inf. Syst. **8**(5), 1 (2007). https://doi.org/10.17705/1jais.00129

19. Chandra, L., Seidel, S., Gregor, S.: Prescriptive knowledge in IS research: conceptualizing design principles in terms of materiality, action, and boundary conditions. In: 2015 48th Hawaii International Conference on System Sciences. HI, USA, pp. 4039–4048. IEEE (2015). https://doi.org/10.1109/HICSS.2015.485

20. Maier, A.M., Moultrie, J., Clarkson, P.J.: Assessing organizational capabilities: reviewing and guiding the development of maturity grids. IEEE Trans. Eng. Manag. **59**, 138–159 (2012). https://doi.org/10.1109/TEM.2010.2077289

21. Storey, D.J.: Understanding the small business sector. 48 (1994)

22. Hudson, M.: Introducing integrated performance measurement into small and medium sized enterprises (2001). https://pearl.plymouth.ac.uk/handle/10026.1/400

23. Yu, D., Xiao, H., Bo, Q.: The dimensions of organizational character and its impacts on organizational performance in Chinese context. Front. Psychol. 9 (2018)

24. Helgesson, Y.Y.L., Höst, M., Weyns, K.: A review of methods for evaluation of maturity models for process improvement. J. Softw. Evol Process. **24**, 436–454 (2012). https://doi.org/10.1002/smr.560

25. Rainer, A., Hall, T.: Key success factors for implementing software process improvement: a maturity-based analysis. J. Syst. Softw. **62**, 71–84 (2002). https://doi.org/10.1016/S0164-1212(01)00122-4

26. ISO/IEC: ISO/IEC 27002:2013 - Information technology – Security techniques – Code of practice for information security controls (2013). https://www.iso.org/standard/54533.html

27. The European Digital SME Alliance: The EU Cybersecurity Act and the Role of Standards for SMEs. Brussels (2020)

28. Cholez, H., Girard, F.: Maturity assessment and process improvement for information security management in small and medium enterprises. J. Softw. Evol. Process **26**, 496–503 (2014). https://doi.org/10.1002/smr.1609

Cyber Security Education and Training Delivering Industry Relevant Education and Skills via Degree Apprenticeships

Ismini Vasileiou[1,2](✉)

[1] School of Computer Science and Informatics, De Montfort University, Leicester, UK
ismini.vasileiou@dmu.ac.uk
[2] Centre for Security, Communications and Network Research, University of Plymouth, Plymouth, UK

Abstract. The rise of Digital Transformation, global pandemics, and AI, have made Cyber skills crucial in today's world. Organisation flexibility can only be achieved when they have a strong foundation of Cyber professionals that can look after vulnerabilities and protect their systems. A multitude of evidence suggests that the economy is being held back due to a skills gap, particularly in the Cyber Security discipline. In seeking to reduce this gap, the UK government has extended a long established 'apprenticeship' programme to include degrees. Higher Education Degree Apprenticeships offer a cost-effective route for employers to upskill their staff and for apprentices to access free education (and a degree) whilst being paid. Each of the Degree Apprenticeships has an associated framework that defines core learning requirements – devised and created by a collaborative effort of industry and academia. How this framework is implemented however is very much up to individual institutions.

This paper presents an implementation of the Cyber Security Analyst degree apprenticeship undertaken at a UK Institution. Amongst the first in the UK to operationalise the standard, the approach has pragmatically dealt with a wide range of issues to create an academically rigorous yet commercially viable solution for industry. The paper presents the approach, demonstrates the academic rigor through mapping to industry-accepted standards, and discusses the collaborative role of the employer and University in providing a holistic and complete learning experience. The paper concludes by offering a critical discussion on challenges and opportunities and suggests ways employers and professional bodies can collaborate further with Higher Education in developing Degree Apprenticeships that will only be about skills, but also lifelong learning.

1 Introduction

The Cybersecurity industry is growing and developing fast. Companies, government and educational establishments have been looking into those rapid changes and to promote partnerships amongst those different stakeholders. It is calculated that 48% of the businesses have a skills gap (Pedley et al. 2020) and two thirds face issues with the cyber

© IFIP International Federation for Information Processing 2020
Published by Springer Nature Switzerland AG 2020
N. Clarke and S. Furnell (Eds.): HAISA 2020, IFIP AICT 593, pp. 175–185, 2020.
https://doi.org/10.1007/978-3-030-57404-8_14

skills gap. Over the years there has been a plethora of qualifications and certifications in the discipline. There is a growing demand across countries and governments to identify further institutional deficiencies and how to close the skills gap. The Digital Revolution and the continuous economic restructure in Europe, US and all over the world, develops new areas and skills needed and at the same time creates skills shortage. The Skills Mismatch Index (SMI) indicated that the Eurozone alone by 2020 would experience 900,000 shortage of professionals in STEM (Francis and Ginsberg 2016). The new research paper published in 2019, evidences that these figures are set to get worse and reveals that it could be 7 million under-skilled or their job requirements (Industrial Strategy Council 2019). In an attempt to address the current and forecasted skills shortage, the UK government developed the Higher Degree Apprenticeships and UK Higher Education Institutions are now introducing and offering new Bachelors degrees under this new umbrella.

The Cyber Security discipline is a relatively new profession and often organisations are not in a position to identify or recruit the specific skills they need. Although a Computer Science degree can be seen as the foundation of all IT specialisations, still within the Cyber field we need to carefully select such professionals that will bring the expertise and knowledge in the times we live.

Academia has a long-standing background on research outputs and in particular, very recently in Cyber. By developing the Cyber Degree Apprenticeship, HE institutions achieve a great milestone in bridging the gaps between research and organisational needs. In addition, employers can benefit greatly by broadening their recruitment practices and develop new upskilling and transitioning routes for their employees. Evans and Reeder (2010) identified early on that cybersecurity skills are in short supply and it can have implications on terrorism, financial crime, business insider threats and the intelligence community in general. And despite the fact this might seem like a ten-year-old and out date reference, unfortunately it is still very true and this is a long standing issue. More recent studies by Francis and Ginsberg (2016) and UK Department for Digital, Culture and Media & Sport (2020), make a cyber skills embedded across all the workforce. Globalisation not only on the job market, but also on fields such as education, gaming etc. makes it a high priority that more people get upskilled and understand the importance of cybersecurity (European Commission 2017).

The paper considers the potential of Degree Apprenticeships as a route towards supporting the need for cyber security skills. The discussion begins by presenting the pedagogical considerations that were applied whilst developing the new Degree Apprenticeships and the importance of not only embedding the skills framework, but also to initiate brand new discussions with the employers. It continues by discussing the challenges that all stakeholders faced during the implementation of such degrees, and concludes with lessons learnt and some pedagogical recommendations for a second iteration or for institutions who wish to build upon this experience.

2   The Development of Degree Apprenticeships and the Skills Framework

The patterns of academic study in the UK is continuously being explored by the government. The (NMC 2016) report offered a five-year horizon for Higher Education Institutions. The main areas the research was focused on was the use of technology but also how to improve teaching and learning and offering more opportunities within Higher Education. In particular, their research focused extensively in developing competing educational models in an attempt to assist institutions to move away from traditional courses. Having said that, the research acknowledges that such approaches could have implications on policy, leadership and practice.

Similarly, for years there has been a strong incentive to address the relationship between Higher Education and employment. In this rapidly changing world, Higher Education is called to become more responsive and enhance knowledge and skills whilst empowering the critical reflective learner. This has been widely supported by the government by producing various reports discussing the future of Higher Education such as the 2003 UK Government report, the 2008 HEFCE report, the 2011 Government White Paper (Vasileiou 2018) and the 2015 Advance HE Framework on enabling employability.

From the academic perspective, Higher Education institutions have made employability one of the key aspects of organisational commitment and vision. In traditional degrees, short work-based learning modules are offered where students are experiencing doing an academic piece of work alongside an employer (GOV.UK 2017). In addition, students go for a year long optional placement at the end of Year 2 before they enter their final year of their degree.

In addition, during the development of the degrees, the Advance HE framework was adopted on embedding employability (see Fig. 1) that can be tailored depending on the type of the degree and desirable outcomes. The host institution's familiarity with employability being a key driver in developing curriculum meant that there was significant prior experience in developing various degree models, including Fast track Degrees (Vasileiou 2018), prior to the development of the Degree Apprenticeships.

In order to develop the Degree Apprenticeship programmes four distinctive steps were followed:

1. Worked collaboratively with local 10 employers and the UK South West trailblazers group to define employability and skills needed to be addressed. Various meetings were held to discuss the triangulation between the apprenticeship standards, the skills framework and the academic expectations of the learners. Employers provided an in-depth description of the jobs and this facilitated discussions and eventually agreements of the various skills that will be addressed within the academic curriculum.
2. Considered all current policies and future institutional practices and processes and aligned the development of Degree Apprenticeships to the overall strategic vision.
3. Collaborated and shared good practices with employers who have a long-standing experience on running apprenticeships.
4. Continuously collected and assessed feedback from all stakeholders in order to inform future policies and areas of focus.

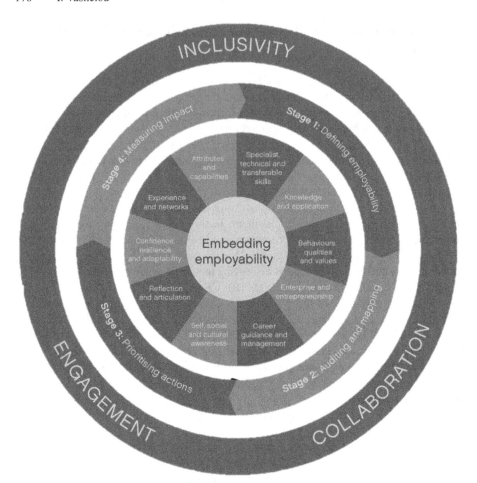

Fig. 1. The Framework for embedding employability in HE (Advance HE 2015)

The final suite of degrees was packaged into the Digital and Technology Solutions programmes Institute for Apprenticeships and Technical Education). This included Cyber Security Analyst, IT Consultant, Network Engineer and Software Engineer. All pathways had distinctive characteristics, but they all had some common modules to develop the foundations of the Computer Science field. The modules were chosen and designed carefully in collaboration with the employers in order to ensure that the Apprenticeship standard were aligned with the modules' content.

3   The Cyber Analyst Curriculum and the Professional Skills

The majority of UK Universities ensure their degrees are accredited against professional bodies. Within the Computer Science discipline and its related fields such as Cyber, it is highly important that curriculum updates regularly in order to develop employable graduates. Professional bodies such as BCS (The Chartered Institute of IT) play a key role in developing courses not only meeting the Higher Education quality assurance standards, but also to develop a relationship between HE and understand the skills-based approach. However, this can also create new problems, where professional bodies do not understand the HE context and awards and accreditations becomes a competitive behaviour rather than an informative on developing teaching excellence.

The development of the Degree Apprenticeships programmes relies heavily on the skills set needed by graduates as it was defined by the Government's analysis on the skills gap and the standards published. Such degrees combined learning with employment and the final certificate is not only a degree on understanding the discipline, but also verifies the skills set an individual has acquired. Each apprenticeship standard is a combination of a job, skills needed and the learning that needs to be undertaken. One cannot exist without the other. Traditional courses offered by the HE Institution, were already mapping their learning and skills to the professional standards with great emphasis on the SFIA framework (2018) and the CIISec Skills Framework (CIISec 2019). The professional bodies work closely with the government and inform the trailblazers and developers of the apprenticeship standards, so in that respect the development of the Cyber degrees was already very well received by students and employers. Whilst developing the academic element, a new mapping exercise was needed where an in-depth analysis of the skills acquired was needed.

Figure 2 shows the Degree Apprenticeship delivery model and how it spreads and embeds the work experience component throughout the years of study. This enables the graduates to be considered as more experienced than those from traditional degrees – even with an optional placement. This aspect was recognised by the professional body (CIISec) which was willing to grant Associate Member status to all Cyber Degree Apprenticeship graduates directly upon graduation (University Business 2018), whereas traditional degree graduates are not eligible for this level without further practical experience beyond their graduation.

	Year 1	Year 2	Year 3	Year 4
Traditional Bachelor's Degree	120 credits	120 credits	Work Experience (Optional Industry Placement)	120 credits
Degree Apprenticeship	120 credits 20% of the job	120 credits 20% of the job	120 credits 20% of the job	
	Work Experience (normal day job)			

Fig. 2. A comparison of the traditional B.Sc. with the degree apprenticeship B.Sc.

It was clear that upon completion of the first two years of the Cyber Degree Apprenticeship, that the discussions held from the outset with employers, students and the

University, the development was seen holistically and not just as an academic programme, or just a work experience. The importance embedding the academic element to the daily job - knowledge element of the apprenticeship – created clear links between the practical element of the degree and the theoretical learning. From the beginning of the apprenticeship, both the students and the employers were given clear understanding of expectations in promoting an effective learning environment. Whilst the author had similar experience with all Degree Apprenticeships pathways, extra focus and attention was placed on the Cyber pathway as it is one of the fields rapidly developing and the need to embed professional bodies' frameworks was of high importance. Such an approach enhanced the learner's effectiveness and experience and ensured that Degree Apprenticeships were developed with a holistic pedagogical approach encouraging both employers and learners to engage and meet the academic requirements. This in turn had as a result more employers to showed interest in joining the scheme, and improved attainment and retention.

4   Challenges and Opportunities

The professions have been widely challenged to look beyond standard routes into education. Universities have been developing work-based learning approaches (Advance HE 2015) for a number of years now, so they are not new in understanding the need to build a curriculum embedding professional standards. There are professions such as Healthcare, where the apprenticeship approach is the norm. However, when looking into the Cyber profession the picture is not the same. The emergence of such degrees offered professions a framework to develop partnerships whereas in the past professional bodies would not engage directly. The 'knowledge' and 'competence' frameworks are the beginning to foster practice-based academic qualifications (Lester et al. 2016). Learning becomes negotiable though, and often the professional body might focus too much on a particular skill, rather than the holistic approach to learning. During the development of the degrees, difficult discussions took place with all parties involved but it also developed the understanding of academic learning further for everyone involved. Academic learning and professional competence whilst different (Anderson et al. 2012), they became the new integrated way into and out of Higher Education. The professional bodies and their standards whilst focusing on the skills, they were now mapped against critical thinking, evaluation and reflection. Professional values within an HE degree transformed and many barriers were removed. Transdisciplinary skills reflect in academic work the generic competence a graduate needs and integration of both academic and professional standards become the core.

Patterns and processes are changing in Higher Education. With the introduction of higher fees the landscape was changing already. There has always been discussions and comparisons between apprenticeships, degrees and certifications. Students have been making those hard decisions since their early adult lives. We have seen that quite often students although competent, are not able to attend university. To date, the Higher Apprenticeships have not been offering this holistic approach to learning that Degree Apprenticeships do (Beech and Bekhradnia 2018). But despite the opportunities that arise, still the young population is struggling to either find employment that will lead them to an apprenticeship or their employer are not investing into their holistic and lifelong education. Therefore, it is of high need that when developing the Degree Apprenticeships they are not being sold as a financial investment for the employer, but in collaboration with the Government and the professional bodies, to inspire and develop the new generation (NCSC 2019).

Training and teaching learners at the same time, quite often can be problematic. By integrating a variety of pedagogical approaches, moving away from the traditional didactic approach, can enhance and empower the learner and the process in achieving a degree. Understanding just the regulatory framework often is not enough. The author spent adequate time exploring collaborations and opportunities to promote flexible learning in an attempt to promote equal opportunities and cater for diverse backgrounds. This was very well received by the employers and the student feedback was very positive. The Cyber programme was developed with careful consideration of looking into the future and how the discipline expands. Looking the now only would not be enough and upon the creation of new skills by the professional bodies it would be not achievable to reach positive results or it would lead in delays revamping the curriculum. The holistic approach benefited the employers too as they became more compliant with the skills frameworks and developed deeper understanding of the field.

5 Recommendations for Stakeholders

The table below summarises some suggestions and recommendations for each stakeholder involved in either developing or taking up a Degree Apprenticeship that derived from the current portfolios of Apprenticeships to date. In particular, the focus is placed on the Cyber pathway as it requires continuous adaptation of skills and new ones develop very quickly due to the nature of the discipline. What is noticeable is that the main recommendation is around collaboration and continuous development of the curriculum alongside the employers. Although apprenticeships have been running for a long time now, Degree Apprenticeships are moving away from just vocational study (Chapman 2018) and incorporate the academic element more strongly. From an employer's perspective, to employ staff who gain both practical experience and academic one, can prove a great advantage. What is important though is to develop those foundations on working with academia to gain the most out of the theoretical work. The table shows how each stakeholder needs to respond for the main themes when creating a Degree apprenticeship curriculum (Table 1).

Looking ahead, the above table can be used by each stakeholder involved in developing such schemes. Employers can introduce organisation wide strategies on how to identify the skills gap and either existing employers to upskill or recruit new talent. The above table can facilitate those discussions between all parties and to assist them in designing strategies to increase participation on Degree Apprenticeship schemes.

Table 1. Steps in developing a Cyber Degree Curriculum

Issue	Universities	Employers	Apprentice
Strategic	Develop an overall strategic approach to implementing Degree Apprenticeships for the Institution	Develop Degree Apprenticeships as the overall CPD strategy within the organisation	Develop strategies for self-managing work and education
Collaborative approach	Employers should play a key part from very early on	Work collaboratively with Higher Education Institutions to develop a degree that meets the organisation's needs	Develop strong collaborations with mentors, line managers and academics
Triangulation	To empower the relationship between academics and employers and identify each ones' expertise	Have a clear idea of skills shortage	Work continuously on their personal CPD, identify their own skills gap
Continuing professional development (CPD)	To re-consider and perhaps re-define/re-design the delivery approaches in an attempt that are relevant for both employers and students	Support the staff to undertake various CPD activities and where appropriate the Degree Apprenticeship route	
Outreach	Outreach activities to promote Degree Apprenticeships to schools and colleges	Welcome new talent and support them by offering Degree Apprenticeships	
Professional skills	Integrate Professional Skills within the apprentices' academic learning	Integrate Professional Skills within the apprentices' experiences and embed it in their academic learning	

6 Conclusion

The paper critically reflected on the development of the Cyber Degree Apprenticeships within a Higher Education Institution with the aim to demonstrate a new route into developing Cyber professionals. It was highlighted that such route can be valuable to employers and although the author implemented various pathways and special focus is being placed at the Cyber one. As more and more employers identify their organisations' skills gap in the Cyber field, the professional bodies such as CIISec and NCSC (2019) are accepting, promoting and recognising the Degree Apprenticeship route. This led to a rapid grow across many institutions and the Cyber pathways have become very popular. Companies such as HP and IBM, are either upskilling existing staff in this area, or investing in new talent.

Although it is felt that the strategic approach has now resulted in steady student recruitment, at the same time it was a steep learning curve for academia to enter the world of apprenticeships. What was found to be the most important factor affecting a quick growth in student numbers was aligning the development of apprenticeships with an institutional strategy, mission and values. Engaging with the employers from the start, whilst developing the curriculum is also quite important. Questioning and continuously developing a personalised degree and career development is not something that currently fits widely with the universities (Rowe et al. 2017). Teaching and learning strategies and approaches were put on the test often, and new ways of delivering the content emerged and it is still under review. Staff workloads has also been a challenge. Although there is a high need and will from all sides to deliver the same degree but in different formats to meet the employers' needs, equally it has been a great challenge to identify not only suitable staff, but also staff with capacity.

Other areas that still need to be explored are widening participation and inclusivity. HE education provides a provision for all types of learners, giving everyone an opportunity to develop as a person, as a graduate and contribute to the society. Although such educational models can inspire and remove barriers for students who are unable to get a student loan, still HE can influence less and less the student population and intakes. Employers will be providing their workforce and by embedding professional standards into the curriculum, the widening participation aspect is outsourced to all those stakeholders.

In conclusion, despite the new challenges and the changing landscape of mass Higher Education, professional bodies have, employers and the government are called to redefine what degree education means. Whilst universities are still developing and establishing a variety of Degree Apprenticeships, reflection is required on the role of employers and professional bodies (Husband 2018). The latter two, should be supporting the Higher Education establishments in developing and adapting their material (Lester et al. 2016), but not changing the nature of what HE represents and what it aims for. Currently, the implementation of such degrees does not hold the employer or the professional body responsible. With the triangulated approach the Degree Apprenticeships described in this paper followed, it recommends that here needs to be an accountability system where it will require all parties to be clear on their roles in delivering such degrees. It is important that the Government, the employers and the professional bodies, at times they need to adapt to the HE context and change their approaches and how they develop their frameworks (Mikkonen et al. 2017). If this is achieved, then the policy contexts can change, become more inclusive and align university qualifications with businesses.

The Cyber skills gap is not closing (GOV.UK 2020). On the contrary, with the rapid online developments any degree or pathway in the Computer Science discipline will need elements of embedding skills and knowledge around security and privacy. The

Cyber field can be further supported by the Degree Apprenticeships route as the learners have an ongoing exposure to the real problems and challenges of their daily job, in addition to learning the theoretical aspects. Employers are offering most of the times cutting edge technologies and as such this is offering academia the opportunity to stay current and offer the latest theoretical frameworks. Now more than ever, the need of professional bodies is high. They are the ones collecting, collating and framing the profession, offering ongoing support and guidance. Now more than ever, embedding those frameworks within the rapidly changing and growing Cyber field, can be not just a challenge for academia, but also an opportunity to reshape their offerings and produce such graduates that will come with professional and academic experience. Finally, the Degree Apprenticeships route into Cyber, alongside the embedded skills frameworks, will develop such graduates with lifelong learning characteristics which, in return, will be an asset for any organisation and the Cyber profession.

The topic of Degree Apprenticeships is still under development and both government and academia are exploring the next steps. Employers have been evaluating the effectiveness of it and of course given the sudden impact of Covid-19, it has become an interesting point of discussion. Whereas before it was mandatory there was some face to face delivery, it is now impossible due to the global pandemic. In addition, the financial difficulties it has caused to the businesses, has caused concerns of the future of Degree Apprenticeships. Nevertheless, the skills gap in Cyber is growing, and the pandemic has exposed systems even more. The author is developing a strategic approach to teaching and learning of the Degree Apprenticeships during the pandemic and this will influence the next study and outputs.

References

Advance HE: Embedding Employability in Higher Education (2015). https://www.advance-he.ac.uk/guidance/teaching-and-learning/embedding-employability

Anderson, A., Bravenboer, D., Hemsworth, D.: The role of universities in higher apprenticeship development. High. Educ. Skills Work Based Learn. Bingley 2(3), 240–255 (2012)

Beech, D., Bekhradnia, B.: Demand for higher education to 2030 HEPI report 105 (2018). www.hepi.ac.uk/wp-content/uploads/2018/03/HEPI-Demand-for-Higher-Education-to-2030-Report-105-FINAL.pdf

Billett, S.: Apprenticeship as a mode of learning and model of education. Educ. Train. Lond. 58(6), 613–628 (2016)

Chapman, B.: Apprenticeships: almost half of company managers fear government will miss target as numbers fall (2018). www.independent.co.uk/news/business/news/apprenticeship-levy-latest-government-miss-target-2020-numbers-fall-uk-cmi-survey-a8240361.html

CIISec: CIISec Skills Framework, Version 2.4, Chartered Institute of Information Security, November 2019 (2019). https://www.ciisec.org/CIISEC/Resources/Capability_Methodology/Skills_Framework/CIISEC/Resources/Skills_Framework.aspx

European Commission: A comparison of shortage and surplus occupations based on analyses of data from the European Public Employment Services and Labour Force Surveys (2017). https://www.google.com/url?sa=t&rct=j&q=&esrc=s&source=web&cd=1&cad=rja&uact=8&ved=2ahUKEwjCiprhuOjoAhVEilwKHSoDBYgQFjAAegQIAhAB&url=https%3A%2F%2Fec.europa.eu%2Fhome-affairs%2Fsites%2Fhomeaffairs%2Ffiles%2F04a_croatia_determining_labour_migration_shortages.pdf&usg=AOvVaw1GZb7wIfGu_b7DbQk1651Z

Evans, K., Reeder, F.: A Human capital crisis in Cybersecurity (2010). https://www.csis.org/ana lysis/human-capital-crisis-cybersecurity

Francis, K., Ginsberg, W.: The Federal Cybersecurity Workforce: Background and Congressional Oversight Issues for the Departments of Defense and Homeland Security (2016). https://digita lcommons.ilr.cornell.edu/key_workplace/1491/

GOV.UK: How to develop an apprenticeship standard: guide for trailblazers (2017). www.gov.uk/ government/publications/how-to-develop-an-apprenticeship-standard-guide-for-trailblazers

GOV.UK: Cyber Security skills in the UK labour market 2020 (2020). https://www.gov.uk/gov ernment/publications/cyber-security-skills-in-the-uk-labour-market-2020/cyber-security-ski lls-in-the-uk-labour-market-2020

HEFCE: When the levy breaks–facts and the future of degree apprenticeships. Knowledge Exchange and Skills, Higher Education Funding Council for England, Bristol (2016). http://blog.hefce.ac.uk/2016/03/16/when-the-levy-breaks-facts-and-the-future-of-deg ree-apprenticeships

Husband, S.: Can apprenticeships help increase diversity and address an ageing workforce? (2018). www.peoplemanagement.co.uk/voices/comment/apprenticeships-increase-div ersity-ageing-workforce

Industrial Strategy Council: UK Skills Mismatch in 2030 (2019). https://industrialstrategycouncil. org/sites/default/files/UK%20Skills%20Mismatch%202030%20-%20Research%20Paper.pdf

Lester, S., Bravenboer, D., Webb, N.: Work-Integrated Degrees: Context, Engagement, Practice and Quality, Quality Assurance Agency, Gloucester (2016)

Mikkonen, S., Pylväs, L., Rintala, H., Nokelainen, P., Postareff, L.: Guiding workplace learning in vocational education and training: a literature review. Empirical. Res. Voc. Educ. Train. **9**, 11–22 (2017)

NCSC: NCSC Degree Classification (2019). https://www.ncsc.gov.uk/information/ncsc-degree-certification-call-new-applicants-0

NMC Higher Education Institutions (2016). https://www.sconul.ac.uk/sites/default/files/docume nts/2016-nmc-horizon-report-he-EN-1.pdf

Pedley, D., et al.: Cyber security skills in the UK labour market 2020 – Findings report. Department for Digital, Culture, Media and Sport (March 2020). https://www.gov.uk/government/ publications/cyber-security-skills-in-the-uk-labour-market-2020/cyber-security-skills-in-the-uk-labour-market-2020

Rowe, L., Moss, D., Moore, N., Perrin, D.: The challenges of managing degree apprentices in the workplace: a manager's perspective. J. Work Appl. Manage. **9**(2), 185–199 (2017)

Skills Framework for the Information Age (SFIA) (2018). https://www.sfia-online.org/en

UK Department for Digital, Culture and Media & Sport: Cyber security skills in the UK Labour market 2020 (2020). https://www.gov.uk/government/publications/cyber-security-ski lls-in-the-uk-labour-market-2020/cyber-security-skills-in-the-uk-labour-market-2020

University Business: Plymouth leads way for Cyber Security Degree Apprenticeships (2018). https://universitybusiness.co.uk/Article/plymouth-leads-way-for-cyber-security-degree-apprenticeships/

Universities UK: The future growth of degree apprenticeships (2016). https://www.universitiesuk. ac.uk/policy-and-analysis/reports/downloads/FutureGrowthDegreeApprenticeships.pdf

Vasileiou, I.: An evaluation of Accelerated Learning Degrees. In: HEA STEM Conference Newcastle, UK, 31 January–1 February 2018 (2018)

Internet Self-regulation in Higher Education: A Metacognitive Approach to Internet Addiction

Dean John von Schoultz$^{(\boxtimes)}$ ⓘ, Kerry-Lynn Thomson$^{(\boxtimes)}$ ⓘ, and Johan Van Niekerk$^{(\boxtimes)}$ ⓘ

Nelson Mandela University, Port Elizabeth, South Africa
{info,s209063124,kerry-lynn.thomson}@mandela.ac.za,
johan.vanniekerk@noroff.no
https://www.mandela.ac.za/

Abstract. Etiological models of Internet Addiction (IA) have repeatedly highlighted the self-regulatory functions of an individual as an important factor in the development and maintenance of pathological use of the Internet. Moreover, neuroimaging studies have shown significant changes in the activity and structure of the prefrontal cortex in Internet Addicts. This brain region is responsible for executive functions such as impulsivity, self-regulation, self control and goal-based decision making. University students have been recognised throughout IA research as an at-risk population. Additionally, IA has recently been strongly linked to risky cybersecurity behaviour, framing students as vulnerable to cybersecurity risks. This paper presents the results of a content analysis which attempted to identify whether technological interventions have been documented within a higher educational context to assist in the prevention of IA through the promotion of self-regulatory functions of Internet use. No studies were found which met the primary objective of the analysis however, secondary objectives were achieved. Various novel findings, as well as some consistent with previous research in the field, were derived from studies that could be used towards a preventative intervention which leverages metacognitive components.

Keywords: Internet addiction · Risky cybersecurity behaviour · Prevention · Self-regulation · Meta cognition

1 Introduction

The Internet has undoubtedly had a profound impact on individuals. However, the social, psychological, educational and vocational impact of excessive use of the Internet, given its evolving nature, is difficult to track. Research into overuse of the Internet to the point of pathological behaviour and markers of addiction provides mounting evidence that frequent use of the Internet opens individuals to the possibility of Internet Addiction [27,43,47]. Moreover, undergraduate student populations appear especially vulnerable [3]. Additionally, IA has recently

© IFIP International Federation for Information Processing 2020
Published by Springer Nature Switzerland AG 2020
N. Clarke and S. Furnell (Eds.): HAISA 2020, IFIP AICT 593, pp. 186–207, 2020.
https://doi.org/10.1007/978-3-030-57404-8_15

been explicitly linked to risky cybersecurity behaviour [24], which could leave university students at higher risk for cybersecurity threats.

Various perspectives and aetiological models have been theorised and expanded on in an attempt to isolate the cognitive mechanisms which are involved in the development and maintenance of Internet Addiction. Understanding these mechanisms allows for more informed interventions to be put in place to prevent and treat this problem. One such mechanism is self-regulation [15]. Previous research by the current authors suggest that universities likely house repositories of network data, objectively revealing the student populations' Internet behaviour on campus. This could be leveraged to gather insight into students' Web usage behaviour or provide students with information about their own Web behaviour for reflection and self-regulation [56].

The present study sought to ascertain whether research has been done in line with this use of data for self-regulation or which provides insights that could inform a preventative intervention grounded in metacognition within a higher education context. Meta cognition refers to 'thinking about thinking'. It involves monitoring ones thoughts towards goal through executive control or self-regulation [17].

2   Internet Addiction, Higher Education and CyberSecurity

The conceptualisation of IA surfaced as the result of a light hearted look at pathologising common behaviours. Psychiatrist Dr. Ivan K. Goldberg posted this notion on a forum he created to remark on the rigidity of the Diagnostic and Statistical Manual of Mental Disorders (DSM-4) substance dependence criteria. However, this satirical proposal revealed a real possibility which mobilised academic inquiry [27]. The pioneer studies were conducted by psychologists Dr Mark Griffiths and Dr Kimberly Young [27,47]. However, some reviews attribute the first conceptualization and empirical research on Internet overuse to Dr Young [13,58].

There are multiple perspectives on IA and accordingly is referred to by various terms such as 'Problematic Internet Use', 'Pathological Internet Use', 'Internet Addiction' and 'Internet Dependence' [43]. Although IA has been controversially used and labelled as a misnomer as the term addiction itself is not officially recognized, it is still the most widely adopted, used as an umbrella term for describing various pathological behaviour associated with Internet use [43]. For this, reason and for linguistic brevity, the term IA will be used in this study, with the exception of studies requiring a specific model derived term for IA. Research in the field has resulted in multiple models focusing on various aspects of IA at differing granularities. For example, some depict the high level overall development [15,50], specific types of IA [12,40] and low level specific causal factors and/or relationships [9–11,29,30].

Despite the lack of consensus in the field regarding the conceptualization, clinical relevance and significance of IA, there is abundant evidence that excessive use of the Internet can lead to scenarios where individuals can experience severe negative psychological, physical, vocational and social outcomes in the same ways as substance abuse [32, 61]. One of the major models of IA, the components model has continuously asserted that addictions not involving a substance or chemical I.e. behavioural addictions, should be treated and recognized with the same authority as substance abuse. The model shows how IA can lead to negative underlying psychological and life scenarios which parallel substance addictions [22, 23].

The first formal high level model which contributed to addressing the question of what Internet users are getting addicted to, is the Cognitive-Behavioural Model of Pathological Internet Use (CBM-PIU) developed by Davis [15]. The model makes an important distinction between Generalized Pathological Internet Use (GPIU) and Specific Problematic Internet Use (SPIU). GPIU typically accounts for information searching and communication features of the Internet. Whereas, SPIU refer to specific online activities which have distinct characteristics. The most prevalent are namely, Cybersex, Online Gambling and Internet Gaming. However, certain psychological factors would be common across all forms of IA, shown by models which depict the factors shared across all instances of addictive behaviour [50]. The DSM-5 has recently acknowledged gambling as a behavioural disorder and has included Internet Gaming Disorder as a possible formal disorder warranting further research for inclusion [2].

The reality and severity of IA is evident in the IA research field and it has been repeatedly asserted that undergraduate university students are a high risk population for IA. University populations have been considered to be at-risk in early stages of IA research [28, 44] and this is found to be the case throughout the expansion of IA research and in contemporary studies [3, 33, 52]. Numerous reasons for this have been suggested. For example, students have a tendency towards Internet use given it's abundant utility, likely have unlimited free access while at university, flexible schedules and a sparsity of parental coercion. Additionally, young adults entering university are typically experiencing a time which requires the development of an identity, new relationships and self reliance [33, 58]. University students are vulnerable to loneliness and/or depression, which are well recognized precursors and co-morbidities of IA [11, 30, 59]. Moreover, the 18–25 age period has been noted as being an especially opportune period for the emergence of addiction forming behaviours [22].

In addition to this, IA has been found to be associated with cybersecurity risk factors. Hadlington [24], explored how cybersecurity attitudes, impulsivity and IA relate to risky cybersecurity behaviour. This recent study found that IA and impulsivity are a significant predictor of risky cybersecurity behaviour. The author notes that, to date, there "have been no explicit attempts to link IA to risky cybersecurity behaviours" [24]. Hadlington's study has since been replicated, presenting the same findings, adding to the robustness of the relationship [1]. To the present authors' knowledge, the mediating effect of impulsivity between IA and risky cybersecurity has not yet been studied. The full possible causal pathways between these three factors have yet to be established. It is worth noting that IA has previously been found to be associated with impulsivity and has been proposed as an impulse control disorder [7,53]. Therefore, risky cybersecurity behaviour may result from impulsivity which was originally fostered by IA. Research into the cognitive factors involved in the development and maintenance of IA has shown that deficient self-regulation is a major contributing factor. Various reviews on neuroimaging studies have shown that individuals with IA have structural and functional changes in their pre-frontal cortex, the area of the brain responsible for executive functioning. This effects the efficiency of self-regulatory cognitions such as decision making towards goals, compulsivity and self control [8,32,51]. IA is a clear candidate for compromising an individuals cybersecurity safety. Another possible way that IA could harbour increased cybersecurity risks is that IA has been linked to the use of online piracy [45] which is prone to a host of cybersecurity risks [26].

A recent and pioneer literature review on the prevention of Internet Addiction [57] explicitly asserts that there is a scarcity of literature on the prevention of IA, and research towards preventative interventions for at-risk populations should be undertaken. Moreover, a review of media multitasking and cognitive interventions [46], noted a lack of clarity in intervention studies with regards to effects on behaviour.

The present study forms part of a larger research study which is developing a framework to allow higher education institutions to use data generated from on-campus Web usage to assist students in preventing IA by providing them with useful objective views of their Web usage. The study, therefore, sought to systematically explore the literature to determine if self-regulatory focused technological interventions or preventative approaches had been formalized within a higher education institution to combat IA. The technological aspect of the larger research study is based on the assertion that self-reported use of media is typically unreliable and a more objective view would be more accurate and relevant [20,54]. For example, the use of network traffic logs or usage monitoring software. Moreover, it is premised on the self-regulatory factors described in Social Cognitive Theory [4,5] as applied in IA research [35–38] and the fundamental hypothesis established in personal informatics that monitoring ones data allows for insights on behaviour which lead to behaviour change [16].

Abstracting and leveraging Web usage data within a higher education setting can be done in countless ways. Understanding how to do this in an intervention alongside other intervention success factors, in a way that fosters engagement and desirable outcomes is important, as engagement and efficacy of productivity personal informatics software has been noted as problematic. There is then a need to consolidate research to allow for interventions to be designed for success, especially considering the importance of higher educational success, for which higher education institutions are responsible for fostering.

3   Method

The primary objective of this content analysis was to establish the existence of studies on technological facilities which are designed to support students self-regulation of their Internet behaviour. The secondary objective was to establish findings of studies considering how Internet use and self-regulatory functioning within university students can be supported and understood to inform an intervention or prevention program.

A search was conducted on seven academic databases. Namely, ACM, ERIC, Scopus, IEEE, Goggle Scholar, Science Direct and Web of Science. These databases cover disciplines of education (ERIC), information and communication technology (ACM and IEEE) and cross disciplines (Google Scholar, Scopus, Web of Science). Table 1 shows the keywords and terms used in the search.

Table 1. Keywords

Web use	["Web Usage" OR "Internet Usage" OR "Web use" OR "internet use" OR "Web behavior" OR "internet behavior" OR "Web self efficacy" OR "internet self efficacy" OR "Web self-efficacy" OR "internet self-efficacy" OR "Computer Usage" OR "Computer use" OR "Computer behavior" OR "Computer self efficacy" OR "Computer self-efficacy" OR "Web behaviour" OR "internet behaviour" OR "computer behaviour"]
Metacognitive	["self-monitor" OR "self monitor" OR "behaviour change" OR "behavior change" OR "personal informatics" OR "productivity" OR "feedback" OR "self regulation" OR "self-regulation" OR "quantified self" OR "quantified-self" OR "self-monitoring" OR "self monitoring" OR "self regulate" OR "self-regulate" OR "reflect" OR "reflection"]
Technology	["technology" OR "intervention" OR "application" OR "widget"]
Education	["education" OR "university" OR "college" OR "undergraduate" OR "student" OR "tertiary"]

The search formula was oriented as:

[Web use keyword] AND [Feedback keyword] AND [Technology keyword] AND [Education Keyword]

The initial number of results produced for each database are as follows (total n = 2258). ACM Digital Library (339), ERIC (87), IEEE (56), Google Scholar (312), Scopus (619), Web of Science (19), Science Direct (826).

A total of 2234 results were screened after duplicates were removed (n = 24). Titles and/or abstracts were screened manually for articles which may have attempted to avoid or understand Web usage behaviour that has a negative effect on a university student population. Additionally, any indication that metacognitive functioning of students was being investigated or proposed as an intervention was included. Table 2 depicts the filter criteria used. Articles which appeared to meet these criteria were collected for analysis (n = 52).

Table 2. Filter criteria

1	Paper must be peer reviewed
2	Attempting to avoid or understand Web usage behaviour that has negative effects on the population
3	Emphasis on self-regulation or metacognitive factors of behaviour
4	Undertaken in or focus on a Higher educational environment

These full text articles were manually screened for study method, population, context, objectives and results. Articles which did not meet the criteria were removed, leaving a final sample for analysis (n = 9). The final sample shown in Table 3 represents studies which either attempt to understand the relationships between self-regulation and Internet use within a higher education setting and/or suggest ways in which universities could approach reducing the negative impact of excessive Internet use in a student population. The study designs were compared and the findings were classified as either confirmatory or informative. The studies which were confirmatory contain findings which contribute to previously established trends in the field. The studies which were classified as informative contributed directly to the secondary objective of this study.

It must be noted that the primary objective of a deductive analysis could not be realized. No studies were found which used or tested a technological intervention facilitating or promoting self-regulation of university students' Internet usage. Therefore, the studies included in the final sample contribute only to the secondary objective. An inductive approach was used for the secondary objective to extract and consolidate findings which may inform such an intervention.

4   Results and Discussion

All but one study in the final sample, shown in Table 3, used a university student population to gather data for the study. The majority of the studies (n = 8) employed a survey approach.

Seven studies reported findings which were consistent with previous research. Most of these consistencies are explicitly mentioned within the study. Moreover, additional consistencies were found by the present authors. However, using informative findings was the focus of this paper and therefore, the confirmatory findings will not be detailed.

Four studies reported findings which could be used to inform an intervention [18,19,34,60]. Each of these studies are individually reviewed then discussed in terms of its applicability to the larger research study from which this study stems.

The intended manifestation of the larger study's framework is a preventative technological intervention which is scalable and calibrated based on relevant research findings. As such, although there are notable ties to other research in the field of IA and personal informatics and the reviewed studies findings, the secondary objective relates to informing this emerging framework. Therefore, in depth discussions of these ties are not prioritized. The focus is the aggregation of findings which can inform the intervention design aspect of the framework. This may be of value to other studies attempting to develop preventative measures for IA and in turn reduce risky cybersecurity behaviour.

Table 3. Final sample

Study	Size	Type	Cross Sectional	Longitudinal	Review	Testing Corellational Factors of Internet Use	Discovering Self-Regulatory Factors	Proposing Literature Derived Recommendations	Confirmatory	Informative	Regression Analysis	Structural Equation Modelling	Descriptive Statistics	Cluster Analysis
		Population		Method			Focus		Findings			Evaluation		
[50]	814	1st Year	x			x			x		x			
[49]	508	1st-4th Year		x		x			x			x		
[61]	230	1st-4th Year		x			x		x	x			x	x
[56]	380	1st-4th Year	x			x			x				x	
[18]	97	1st-4th Year	x				x		x				x	
[19]	512	1st-3rd Year	x				x		x				x	
[21]	-	-			x			x	x					
[55]	631	1st-4th Year	x			x			x		x		x	
[35]	348	1st-2nd Year	x				x		x	x			x	

Wu's study [60], the first of the four studies, investigated the degree that students are aware of their focussed attention during online learning sessions. Moreover, which self-regulatory strategies do they use, if any, and whether distinct meta-attention profiles can be derived from these. The study is based on the premise that university students typically learn and engage in academic tasks within an online environment. Moreover, the likelyhood that students will engage more actively with social media during formal and informal learning is evident in the development of pedagogical models which advocate actively using social media applications such as facebook, youtube and flickr to support and facilitate learning [14]. The result is often a learning environment in which students constantly need to control the urges to engage with other online activities available to them when undertaking online learning tasks.

These Personal Learning Environments (PLE) have many information stimuli in the form of social media notifications and the availability of task switching to any other website or search engine amongst others. Each of these stimuli require exertion of self control to maintain attention on the task at hand which may lead to reduced self control of subsequent tasks, as self control has been depicted as a finite resource [6].

The study is grounded in theories of attention, meta-attention and meta-cognition. Attention is defined as the selection of information stimuli for further processing, meta-attention then being an individuals awareness of selection of information stimuli for further processing. Meta-cognition is the reflection on ones thoughts and is central to the learning process. However, the authors argue that meta attention is a crucial part of online learning in that it initiates and maintains focus for online learning tasks, which then allows meta cognitive processes to partake in learning. Meta-attention is a less widely studied field. The authors juxtapose meta-attention and meta-cognition to operationalize meta-attention based on established work on meta-cognition. From this comparison a framework for meta-attention was derived.

The framework defines two main components. Knowledge of Attention (KA) and Regulation of Attention (RA). Applied to PLE for the study, KA refers to the acknowledgement or awareness of sustained attention or lapses of attention. RA refers to the regulatory strategies used by students to maintain focus. This framework was used to profile students based on measures of KA operationalized as Perceived Attention Discontinuity (PAD) and Social Media Notification (SMN). PAD refers to awareness of attention and engagement shifts or disruptions. SMN refers to the degree that a student is anticipating or considering social media notifications during a task.

RA, was operationalized as Behavioural Strategies (BS) and Mental Strategies (MS). BS refers to behavioural techniques employed to reduce distraction during online learning tasks, MS referring to cognitive techniques to reduce distraction.

The measurement instrument of this framework was developed through semi structured interviews and labelled the Online Learning Motivated Attention and Regulatory Strategies scale (OL-MARS) which comprised twenty 5 point lickert scale statements to which a participant indicated to what extent they agree or disagree. For example an item to measure PAD was "I often turn on the computer for studying (e.g., writing paper, learning, or searching information), but find myself always doing irrelevant things (e.g., watching YouTube, using Facebook, reading online news, or playing games)" or for SMN "I constantly watch out for the sound or pictorial signals from smartphones, Line, Facebook, or other devices and applications". An example of a BS item was "I use strategies to help myself focus on my work (e.g. unplugging, closing unrelated windows, or limiting the speed of upload/download) when using computers." and for MS "If I can focus on what I should do when using the computer (e.g. write paper, learn or search information), I will feel happy and feel a sense of achievement".

The OL-MARS was distributed to 230 university students (predominantly undergraduates) with additional measurements of cluster validation variables such as Internet Self-Efficacy, Internet use, academic achievement and online information searching strategies, which were used to test the validity of clustering of the students based on KA and RA measures as well as provide further insight into the meta-attention profiles' online learning characteristics.

Results of a K means clustering analysis revealed 5 profiles reflecting different levels of KA and RA. The measurements for each of these profiles for KA (PAD and SMN) and RA (BS and MS) is shown in Fig. 1 and further described below:

- **Motivated Strategic (MST)**
  - a low level of PAD and low level of SMN accumulatively a low level of KA.
  - a high level of BS and MS, accumulatively the highest RA score.
- **Self Disciplined (SD)**
  - a very low level of PAD and SMN accumulatively a very low level of KA.
  - a medium level of behavioural and mental strategy accumulatively a medium RA score.
- **Hanging On (HO)**
  - a high level of PAD and a medium-high level of SMN accumulatively a medium-high level of KA.
  - a medium level of behavioural and mental strategy accumulatively a medium RA score.
- **Non Responsive (NR)**
  - a high level of PAD and very high levels of SMN, accumulatively a high level of KA.
  - a very low level of behavioural and a low level mental strategy, accumulatively a low RA score.
- **Unaware (UA)**
  - a medium-low level of PAD and SMN accumulatively a low level of KA.
  - a low level of behavioural and mental strategy accumulatively a low RA score.

It is worth noting that PAD is described in the study as "perceived attention and engagement problems". This means that a low score in this may represent an absence of engagement problems or the absence of awareness of attention and engagement problems. In other words, a high score of PAD means and individual is aware of and therefore implies a presence of attention problems. However, lack of awareness of an attention problem may indicate in some profiles that there is little or no attention problem or there is an attention problem but no awareness thereof. This is not clarified in the study, however it may be safe to assume that within the groups which have low PAD measures that other variables may determine which of these instances are being observed.

The cluster validation variable values for each of these profiles can be seen in Fig. 2. Of particular interest is final grade. Given the success criteria for a PLE

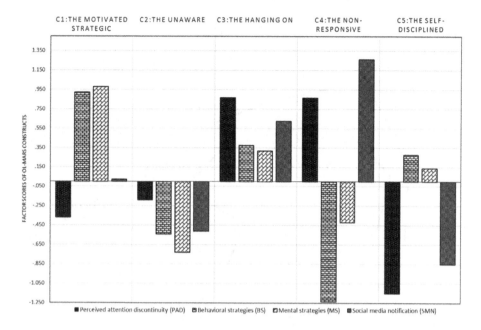

Fig. 1. OL-MARS profiles [60]

outcome is academic success for that course. Some insight can be gathered from considering the profiles in accordance to their final grades represented as zfinal in Fig. 2.

The MST had the highest final grades, followed by the SD, HO, UA and NR. RA seems to have the most impact in terms of final grades as KA scores were low for MST and SD who were both at the top of the final grade standings. The two profiles lowest in final grade scores both had low RA whereas the other profiles all had medium to high RA. The absence of RA seems to be highly impactful whereas KA does not strongly correlate. In short, the use of RA was positively associated with academic achievement.

This further indicates meaning for PAD scores. The SD scored lowest in PAD and second highest in final grades, indicating that the PAD may reflect a high percentage of that score is due to lack of awareness and not necessarily actual attention problems. Alternatively, the MS and BS may be reducing attention problems directly and therefore, there are none to observe.

Some correlations between meta-attention and cluster validation variables were considered. However, the variances in Internet use variables amongst the profiles did not implicate clear statistically significant correlations to academic success, although the profiles did have clear differences in Internet use patterns. The authors state that

"These findings suggest that regulation and knowledge of attention play a role in online learning beyond ISE and search strategies and have a unique standing in online learning."

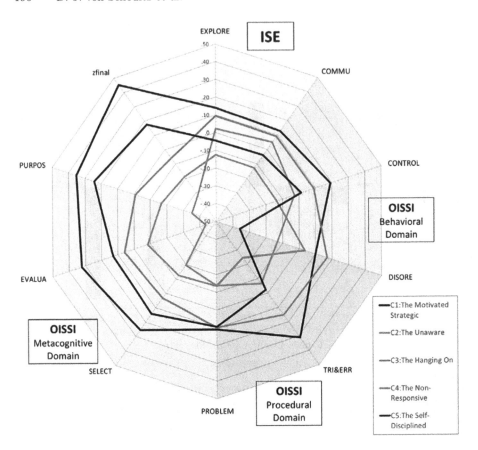

Fig. 2. OL-MARS profiles validation variable relative values [60]

Overall, the results indicate that the proposed meta-attention framework is valid and can be used to measure students KA and RA. The study findings point out that awareness of attention is not in itself enough to maintain control in online learning, RA is a key component to success.

Implications for an institutional intervention are that certain OL-MARS profiles require specific training for improvement. OL-MARS can be used to identify an individual's KA and RA to calibrate an intervention for greater effect. Specifically, increasing RA in profiles who lack MS and BS may make an intervention more effective at increasing self-regulation of Internet use.

The principle hypothesis proposed by personal informatics (gathering personal behavioural data for reflection through technology) is that insights gathered from objective views of behaviour lead to behaviour change. However, a review of PI systems [16] revealed that many studies testing PI systems indicated that the participants acknowledged correct objective views of their behaviours but did not know how or were not motivated to change their behaviour. The

Table 4. Dynamics of self-regulation model [18]

Representation	Commitment	Progress
Promotes	Highlighting of the focal goal	Balancing between all goals
Leads to	Emphasizing the focal goal at the cost of alternate goals (temptations)	Valuing alternate goals (temptations) as well as focal goal
Causing	Focal goal behaviors increase in perceived value. Alternate goal behaviors (temptations) consequently decrease in perceived value	Alternate goal behaviors (temptations) increase in perceived value. Focal goal behaviors consequently decrease in perceived value

disconnect between importance of RA versus KA found in Wu's study reflects this. However, certain MS or BS may require or benefit from objective views of Web usage behaviour. An intervention would need to provide an indication of this lack of RA and provide MS or BS suggestions or tasks for training RA. This is discussed further in the future research section.

The following two studies [18,19] together comprise a total of four studies which extend a single line of enquiry. As such they will be reviewed together as they have accumulative and cohesive findings.

Dunbar, Proeve and Robert's study [18], the second of the four studies, was based on the dual representation model of goal directed behaviour by Ayelet Fishbach and colleagues. It tested whether the presentation format of a possible action effected how an individual valued subsequent behaviours as either congruent or incongruent towards a goal. This represents insight into how an individual's self-regulatory system can be put in a state which will in turn effect the likelihood of certain actions. This approach had been used in marketing and consumer scenarios but not in clinical settings considering IA. Participants were primed to set their unconscious behavioural goals to 'reduce their Internet use to avoid IA'. They were then presented with two behavioural actions. One was congruent with avoiding IA, for example do some academic work, socialize in person with some friends. The other was not, for example do some online shopping, browse reddit. These two actions were then presented as either conflicting or harmonious. For example, you complete an online assignment **OR** browse reddit. You complete an online assignment **AND THEN** browse reddit. The first example forms a commitment self-regulatory framework, whereas the second forms a progress self-regulatory framework. Individuals in a commitment framework view subsequent congruent actions more highly than when in a progress framework. The reverse is true for individuals in a progress framework who value incongruent behaviours more highly. The differences are shown in Table 4.

Dunbar, Proeve and Robert's study [19], the third of the four studies, extended their previous study [18]. Given the studies initial findings, further aspects of Fishbach's model were explored in the same context. It comprised three studies.

Study 1 confirms that commitment and progress frameworks can be primed. Furthermore, it can be achieved through the use of basic questions. The study found that subsequent feedback about actions towards a goal elicit different value systems depending on the type of feedback, positive or negative and which framework an individual has adopted. Positive feedback prompts a different set of perceived values of congruent behaviour in a commitment framework versus a progress framework. Individuals adopting a commitment framework who are given positive feedback about goal attainment, perceive congruent behaviours with greater value and incongruent behaviours with lower value. However, when given negative feedback about goal attainment, individuals perceive incongruent behaviours with greater value and congruent behaviours with lower value. The opposite was found to be true for the progress framework. Negative feedback highlighted the gap in progress and in turn increases their perceived value of congruent behaviour. Positive feedback reinforces their progress and therefore adds to a higher perceived value of incongruent behaviour. Figure 3 shows behaviour goals applied to Internet use and academic work, a common scenario in higher education. The summarized responses to feedback are shown in Table 5.

Study 2 tested how the presentation format of feedback about behaviour towards a goal effects perceived behaviour values in individuals adopting a commitment or progress framework. The frameworks were primed in this study by promoting engagement to the overall goal of reducing personal Internet use. High engagement and commitment was achieved by exposing some individuals to additional literature on PIU which prompted a progress framework, the remaining individuals were considered to have low/uncertain engagement or commitment, which elicited a commitment framework. Feedback was presented by highlighting what has been accomplished rather than what still needs to be accomplished. I.e. to-do versus already done. Individuals exposed to feedback highlighting achievement (already done) perceived it as positive whereas feedback highlighting the need for further achievement (to-do) was perceived as negative.

Consistent with study 1, individuals adopting a commitment framework viewing positive feedback, perpetuated their higher value placement in behaviours which are in line with their goal. This type of feedback framing caused individuals adopting a progress framework to reduce their perceived value of behaviours which are congruent with their goal. The opposite was true for feedback highlighting pending progress or progress deficits. Individuals in the commitment framework lowered the perceived value of their congruent goal behaviour and progress framework individuals perpetuated value their congruent goal behaviour. This showed **how** positive and negative feedback is perceived differently depending on the framework adopted at the time of seeing the feedback.

Progress framed individuals are more interested in progress as they have no doubts about their commitment. When viewing confirmation of progress (already done), they feel accomplished and satisfied and subsequently consider other activities. Whereas, commitment framed individuals are unsure of their commitment levels and re-evaluate and bolster their commitment to the goal

Table 5. Feedback Frame Response Summary [19]

Factors that promote congruent behaviour (Goal Directed)	Factors that promote incongruent behaviour (Temptations)
Progress frame with **negative** feedback – A discrepancy is observed between actual and desired goal attainment – Congruent goal behaviour is more attractive	**Progress** frame with **positive** feedback – Balancing occurs – Enough has been done pursuing the goal for now, other behaviours seen as more attractive
Commitment frame with **positive** feedback – Highlighting occurs – Congruent goal behaviour is more attractive	**Commitment** frame with **negative** feedback – Commitment to goal is questioned, the goal is seen as less important – Other behaviours are now more attractive

because the progress indication gives them reassurance that the goal is possible, as such they continue to focus on goal related activities and do not consider others with more value. Progress framed individuals note incomplete progress as a problem and work to correct the discrepancy in progress whereas commitment framed individuals are more convinced that the goal is unattainable and their commitment wavers, goal congruent activities then have less value.

Study 3 considered whether individuals who perceived their goals as abstract/high level or as distinct/concrete actions prompt a commitment or progress framework and therefore experience alterations to their perceived value depending on the feedback provided. It was confirmed that individuals who perceived their goal as abstract triggered a commitment framework which altered the feedback effect of behaviour values as per the previous studies. Conversely, concrete goals triggered a progress framework and the associated feedback alteration effects. These studies strongly support the use of self-regulation and the ability to tailor feedback effects by priming commitment and progress frameworks in individuals. Moreover, this model holds true in and is rooted within the context of IA within a university environment.

Overall the studies by Dunbar, Proeve and Robert [18,19] show that the order and format of information presented is important as it primes internal self-regulatory systems which effect perception of feedback as well as the value of subsequent behvioural choices. Moreover, the presentation of data itself effects the activation or deactivation of these systems. This demonstrates the importance of intervention interaction feature design for effecting behaviour regulation.

In terms of how these findings can be leveraged in an intervention specifically, the initial study by Dunbar et al. [18] as well as study 1, 2 and 3 from [19] indicate that self-regulatory frameworks can be primed by presenting possible actions as complimentary or conflicting, through the use of basic questions, by the setting of abstract vs concrete goals as well as increasing engagement levels. As such, the implications for the proposed intervention are that activity options

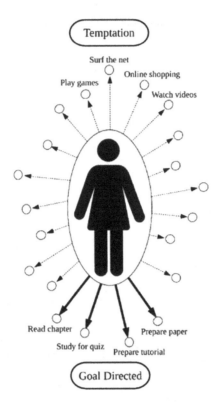

Fig. 3. Academic and Internet behaviour conflict [19]

or suggestions, questions, goal setting or engagement promoting features should be used to prompt appropriate framework. There are numerous ways this could be done depending on the intervention platform.

Of these three approaches, goal setting is the most applicable for digital interventions. Setting goals and being reminded of them are not uncommon amongst productivity management and personal informatics systems, and these designs could be calibrated to allow for abstract or concrete goal setting depending on subsequent feedback options. Moreover, goal setting has overlapping benefit with self-regulation, as goal setting has been noted as an important aspect of self-regulation [41] and is well understood. Therefore, it can be beneficial in more ways than only prompting self-regulatory frames. It is then more likely to be included in an intervention regardless of framing potential. Goal progress has also been noted as a promising feature in personal informatics studies which result in actionable behaviour change [16]. Therefore, the same benefit could be gained from re-factoring an already desirable feature instead of including features which may be cumbersome in an already possibly invasive intervention. Alternatively, engagement or commitment levels could be predetermined, which may remove the need to illicit a self-regulatory framework for certain individuals.

However, if commitment levels are low it may be too taxing for an intervention to impart high commitment or engagement, in which case the goal priming approach may be more suitable. These goal priming effects were easily done in the study and can therefore be recreated within an intervention.

Study 1 and 2 from [19] demonstrated the effects of negative vs positive feedback on subsequent value ratings of behaviours depending on the self-regulatory frame the individual is in when receiving the feedback. Kim et al. [31] tested the effects of negative and positive framed feedback on engagement in a productivity management application called TimeAware. They found that framing productive Internet use progress negatively increases engagement with the application, whereas positive productive Internet use progress framing reduced engagement significantly. This was found throughout the user sample. However, the study did not test for framework priming or subsequent behaviour valuing and can therefore not be directly compared. However, the Timeaware study did further indicate that constant negative feedback was stressful and this should be considered for the long term effect of the intervention.

Study 2 found that feedback depicted as to-do was perceived as negative regardless of framework, only the subsequent value systems are effected by self-regulatory framework state. This notion that framing progress as to-do is perceived as negative is consistent with the disengagement as a result of the positive feedback for the entire sample from the TimeAware study and engagement when negative feedback is given. Suggesting that if negative feedback improves engagement, then interventions should illicit a progress framework prior to negative feedback exposure as this will increase the perceived value of congruent behaviour. Promoting the setting of concrete goals may best serve as a precursor to negative feedback as it will illicit a progress framework and would therefore value congruent behaviours more highly.

Dunbar, Proeve and Robert's studies reveal layers of interactive effects from how information is presented and how it actually effects behaviour and should be carefully considered. Importantly the self-regulatory framing and intended overall goals should be considered before presenting feedback on behaviour and performance.

Labăr and Ţepordei [34], the last of the four studies, correlated the various possible combinations or profiles of time perspectives with multitasking during lectures using PIU as a mediating factor. Based on the time perspective assertions by Zimbardo and colleagues that individuals have subjective internal representations of time, categorized as past negative (PN), past positive (PP), present fatalistic (PF), present hedonistic (PH), and future orientation (F). PN depicts a pessimistic and unsavoury attitude towards the past and past events. PP depicts an optimistic, pleasant and auspicious view of the past. PF represents a perspective of the present as hopeless and negatively deterministic. PH represents a perspective of the present as short sighted, risky and self-indulgent. F represents a perspective of the present as long term goal oriented and forward thinking.

A significant positive relationship between PIU and multitasking was found. Individuals with high levels of PIU have high levels of multitasking traits. PN time perspective was found to be significantly positively correlated with PIU. This suggests that students who have a proclivity to highlight and remember negative events are more prone to PIU. Whereas, F time perspectives negatively correlated to PIU in a significant way. This suggests that a tendency for foresight was associated with less risk of PIU. No significant correlation was found with PIU and PP. Moreover, the intuitive positive relationship between PH and PIU was not found. Similarly, PF and PIU did not hold a correlation despite PF being strongly associated with PN. The relationship between time perspectives and multitasking are mediated to some degree by the level of PIU. PIU entirely mediated the positive relationship between PN and multitasking in class. This suggests that students who hold a pessimistic view of their past and/or have a proclivity to highlight and remember negative events are more prone to multitask, the Internet being a major expression thereof in class and likely outside of class. The expected relationship of PH positivity correlating to PIU was not found. A study looking at sensation seeking as a predictor of PIU made a similar assumption about seemingly impulsive traits and PIU. The same result occurred in that the expected relationship did not appear [39]. The notable findings from Labăr and Ţepordei's study are that a F time perspective, which has previously linked to personality trait conscientiousness, depict a desirable profile for controlling multitasking during class and low risk of PIU. Suggesting that the ability to delay gratification has some bearing on avoiding PIU, likely because of higher levels of self control associated with it. A PN time perspective was found to encompass more active multitasking during class and higher risks of PIU. This time perspective has been previously associated with anxiety, depression and likely loneliness which are recognized predictors of PIU [11,30,59]. This reiterates the importance of regulation of attention, as multitasking is often an expression of lack of focus and not parallel processing which has been wrongly associated with interpretations of millennials. Media multitasking online has also been found to be associated risky cybersecurity behaviour [25]. The study concludes that time perspective coaching could be used to alleviate PN time perspectives. However, this method requires expertise outside of typical higher education settings.

The implications of these findings for an intervention are that no clear findings can be translated directly into an intervention feature without further research into time perspective coaching. However, this does provide an additional possible avenue of inquiry which may translate well into intervention design, this is discussed further in future research. However, similar to meta-attention trait profiles in Wu's study, students can be prescreened for PN time perspectives and features of the intervention can be calibrated assist in PN time perspective coaching.

5 Limitations

Each of the seven search engines used for the analysis sample selection have unique search filtering interfaces. Therefore, the search formula used in this study needed to be calibrated based on the search engine used. This was done by testing the filtering mechanisms for consistency through spot checks and re-calibration. However, it is possible that some papers were not retrieved correctly by the search engines due to filtering logic flaws. Moreover, the searches were conducted in May 2019 and therefore will not include any published research since then. The search results were manually screened, first by title, then if flagged as possibly relevant was screened by abstract. Then if still found relevant it was read and reviewed for relevance towards the objective. As the field is still subject to terminological disparity there is of course room for human error. Therefore, the sample cannot be considered flawless. Studies using students' self reporting of Internet use may be further limited as research on IA has shown that self reported data are not completely reliable.

6 Future Research

Informative findings from this study need to be pragmatically applied to a preventative intervention prototype. Further research is needed to determine how these findings can be practically implemented, bearing in mind the availability Web usage data.

For Wu et al.'s study, establishing valid mental and behavioural strategies in the context of online learning requires further research perhaps derived from behavioural science and/or clinical psychology. Specifically, given that attention regulation has been promoted by Wu and Dunbar, Proeve and Robert and has clear importance for inclusion in interventions, understanding how these will be correctly and appropriately implemented within an engaging and useful platform in an online learning environment is necessary. Although less emphasis was placed on the reflective aspects of attention, certain mental and behavioural strategies may require or benefit from objective views of Web usage behaviour.

Labăr and Ţepordei suggestion of time perspective coaching requires that this technique be analysed for applicability within an intervention. If this coaching technique requires extensive and highly specialized long term sessions it may not be suitable. This remains to be seen. The time perspectives and subsequent behaviour traits found in their study suggest that there may be some correlation to the OL-MARS profiles from Wu's study. These correlations could be tested and merged to further refine possible prescreening functionality of an intervention as previously discussed.

These proposed features and findings can be designed and merged with research on software development design recommendations for productivity monitoring software such as [42].

7   Conclusion

Self-regulation is a fundamental trait which needs to be considered by universities if they intend to support their students in avoiding the negative effects of Internet use. This study consolidated research through useful insights into ways in which metacognition can be positively effected through carefully structured interventions, as the way in which information is presented effects different individuals' cognitions in significant and distinct ways. Moreover, certain student cognitive profiles could characterise certain students with higher risk of IA who would benefit from more specific intervention features.

Cybersecurity behaviour is a multi faceted phenomenon and metacognitive facets should be leveraged to prevent students' and universities' digital assets from being compromised. It is important that universities be more proactive in facilitating the improvement of students' metacognitive functioning and consider the repercussions of IA in order to mitigate risky cybersecurity behaviour.

References

1. Aivazpour, Z., Rao, V.S.: Impulsivity and risky cybersecurity behaviors: a replication (2018)
2. American Psychiatric Association: Diagnostic and statistical manual of mental disorders (DSM-5®). American Psychiatric Association, Washington, D.C. (2013)
3. Balhara, Y.P.S., et al.: Correlates of problematic internet use among college and university students in eight countries: an international cross-sectional study. Asian J. Psychiatry **45**, 113–120 (2019)
4. Bandura, A.: Social Foundations of Thought and Action. Englewood Cliffs, New Jersey (1986)
5. Bandura, A.: Social cognitive theory of self-regulation. Organ. Behav. Hum. Decis. Process. **50**(2), 248–287 (1991)
6. Baumeister, R.F., Bratslavsky, E., Muraven, M., Tice, D.M.: Ego depletion: is the active self a limited resource? J. Pers. Soc. Psychol. **74**(5), 1252 (1998)
7. Beard, K.W., Wolf, E.M.: Modification in the proposed diagnostic criteria for internet addiction. CyberPsychol. Behav. **4**(3), 377–383 (2001)
8. Brand, M., Young, K.S., Laier, C.: Prefrontal control and internet addiction: a theoretical model and review of neuropsychological and neuroimaging findings. Front. Hum. Neurosci. **8**, 375 (2014)
9. Caplan, S.E.: Preference for online social interaction: a theory of problematic internet use and psychosocial well-being. Commun. Res. **30**(6), 625–648 (2003)
10. Caplan, S.E.: A social skill account of problematic internet use. J. Commun. **55**(4), 721–736 (2005)
11. Caplan, S.E.: Relations among loneliness, social anxiety, and problematic internet use. CyberPsychol. Behav. **10**(2), 234–242 (2007)
12. Caplan, S.E.: Theory and measurement of generalized problematic internet use: a two-step approach. Comput. Hum. Behav. **26**(5), 1089–1097 (2010)
13. Chakraborty, K., Basu, D., Kumar, K., et al.: Internet addiction: consensus, controversies, and the way ahead. East Asian Arch. Psychiatry **20**(3), 123 (2010)
14. Dabbagh, N., Kitsantas, A.: Personal learning environments, social media, and self-regulated learning: a natural formula for connecting formal and informal learning. Internet High. Educ. **15**(1), 3–8 (2012)

15. Davis, R.A.: A cognitive-behavioral model of pathological internet use. Comput. Hum. Behav. **17**(2), 187–195 (2001)
16. Kersten-van Dijk, E.T., Westerink, J.H., Beute, F., IJsselsteijn, W.A.: Personal informatics, self-insight, and behavior change: a critical review of current literature. Hum. Comput. Interact. **32**(5), 268–296 (2017)
17. Dinsmore, D.L., Alexander, P.A., Loughlin, S.M.: Focusing the conceptual lens on metacognition, self-regulation, and self-regulated learning. Educ. Psychol. Rev. **20**(4), 391–409 (2008)
18. Dunbar, D., Proeve, M., Roberts, R.: Problematic internet usage self-regulation dilemmas: effects of presentation format on perceived value of behavior. Comput. Hum. Behav. **70**, 453–459 (2017)
19. Dunbar, D., Proeve, M., Roberts, R.: Problematic internet usage self-control dilemmas: the opposite effects of commitment and progress framing cues on perceived value of internet, academic and social behaviors. Comput. Hum. Behav. **82**, 16–33 (2018)
20. Felisoni, D.D., Godoi, A.S.: Cell phone usage and academic performance: an experiment. Comput. Educ. **117**, 175–187 (2018)
21. Flanigan, A.E., Kiewra, K.A.: What college instructors can do about student cyberslacking. Educ. Psychol. Rev. **30**(2), 585–597 (2018)
22. Griffiths, M.: The biopsychosocial approach to addiction. Psyke Logos **26**(1), 18 (2005)
23. Griffiths, M.: A 'components' model of addiction within a biopsychosocial framework. J. Subst. Use **10**(4), 191–197 (2005)
24. Hadlington, L.: Human factors in cybersecurity; examining the link between internet addiction, impulsivity, attitudes towards cybersecurity, and risky cybersecurity behaviours. Heliyon **3**(7), e00346 (2017)
25. Hadlington, L., Murphy, K.: Is media multitasking good for cybersecurity? Exploring the relationship between media multitasking and everyday cognitive failures on self-reported risky cybersecurity behaviors. Cyberpsychol. Behav. Soc. Netw. **21**(3), 168–172 (2018)
26. Association of Internet Security Professionals: Illegal Streaming and Cyber Security Risks: A Dangerous Status Quo? AISP (2014)
27. Kuss, D.J., Griffiths, M.D., Karila, L., Billieux, J.: Internet addiction: a systematic review of epidemiological research for the last decade. Curr. Pharm. Des. **20**(25), 4026–4052 (2014)
28. Kandell, J.J.: Internet addiction on campus: the vulnerability of college students. CyberPsychol. Behav. **1**(1), 11–17 (1998)
29. Kim, H.K., Davis, K.E.: Toward a comprehensive theory of problematic internet use: evaluating the role of self-esteem, anxiety, flow, and the self-rated importance of internet activities. Comput. Hum. Behav. **25**(2), 490–500 (2009)
30. Kim, J., LaRose, R., Peng, W.: Loneliness as the cause and the effect of problematic internet use: the relationship between internet use and psychological well-being. CyberPsychol. Behav **12**(4), 451–455 (2009)
31. Kim, Y.H., Jeon, J.H., Choe, E.K., Lee, B., Kim, K., Seo, J.: Timeaware: leveraging framing effects to enhance personal productivity. In: Proceedings of the 2016 CHI Conference on Human Factors in Computing Systems, pp. 272–283 (2016)
32. Kuss, D.J., Griffiths, M.D.: Internet and gaming addiction: a systematic literature review of neuroimaging studies. Brain Sci. **2**(3), 347–374 (2012)
33. Kuss, D.J., Griffiths, M.D., Binder, J.F.: Internet addiction in students: prevalence and risk factors. Comput. Hum. Behav. **29**(3), 959–966 (2013)

34. Labǎr, A.V., Ţepordei, A.M.: The interplay between time perspective, internet use and smart phone in-class multitasking: a mediation analysis. Comput. Hum. Behav. **93**, 33–39 (2019)
35. LaRose, R.: On the negative effects of e-commerce: a sociocognitive exploration of unregulated on-line buying. J. Comput. Mediat. Commun. **6**(3), JCMC631 (2001)
36. LaRose, R., Eastin, M.S.: A social cognitive theory of internet uses and gratifications: toward a new model of media attendance. J. Broadcast. Electron. Med. **48**(3), 358–377 (2004)
37. LaRose, R., Eastin, M.S., Gregg, J.: Reformulating the internet paradox: social cognitive explanations of internet use and depression. J. Online Behav. **1**(2), 1092–4790 (2001)
38. LaRose, R., Mastro, D., Eastin, M.S.: Understanding internet usage: a social-cognitive approach to uses and gratifications. Soc. Sci. Comput. Rev. **19**(4), 395–413 (2001)
39. Lavin, M., Marvin, K., Mclarney, A., Nola, V., Scott, L.: Sensation seeking and collegiate vulnerability to internet dependence. CyberPsychol. Behav. **2**(5), 425–430 (1999)
40. Lee, D., LaRose, R.: A socio-cognitive model of video game usage. J. Broadcast. Electron. Med. **51**(4), 632–650 (2007)
41. Locke, E.A., Latham, G.P.: Building a practically useful theory of goal setting and task motivation: a 35-year odyssey. Am. Psychol. **57**(9), 705 (2002)
42. Meyer, A.N., Murphy, G.C., Zimmermann, T., Fritz, T.: Design recommendations for self-monitoring in the workplace: studies in software development. Proc. ACM Hum. Comput. Interact. **1**(CSCW), 1–24 (2017)
43. Mihajlov, M., Vejmelka, L.: Internet addiction: a review of the first twenty years. Psychiatria Danubina **29**(3), 260–272 (2017)
44. Moore, D.W.: The Emperor's Virtual Clothes: The Naked Truth About Internet Culture. Algonquin Books, Chapel Hill (1995)
45. Navarro, J.N., Marcum, C.D., Higgins, G.E., Ricketts, M.L.: Addicted to pillaging in cyberspace: investigating the role of internet addiction in digital piracy. Comput. Hum. Behav. **37**, 101–106 (2014)
46. Parry, D.A., le Roux, D.B.: Media multitasking and cognitive control: a systematic review of interventions. Comput. Hum. Behav. **92**, 316–327 (2019)
47. Pontes, H.M., Kuss, D.J., Griffiths, M.D.: Clinical psychology of internet addiction: a review of its conceptualization, prevalence, neuronal processes, and implications for treatment. Neurosci. Neuroecon. **4**, 11–23 (2015)
48. Ravizza, S.M., Hambrick, D.Z., Fenn, K.M.: Non-academic internet use in the classroom is negatively related to classroom learning regardless of intellectual ability. Comput. Educ. **78**, 109–114 (2014)
49. Sebena, R., Orosova, O., Benka, J.: Are self-regulation and depressive symptoms predictors of problematic internet use among first year university students? PsychNol. J. **11**(3), 235–249 (2013)
50. Shaffer, H.J., LaPlante, D.A., LaBrie, R.A., Kidman, R.C., Donato, A.N., Stanton, M.V.: Toward a syndrome model of addiction: multiple expressions, common etiology. Harv. Rev. Psychiatry **12**(6), 367–374 (2004)
51. Sharifat, H., Rashid, A.A., Suppiah, S.: Systematic review of the utility of functional mri to investigate internet addiction disorder: recent updates on resting state and task-based fmri. Malays. J. Med. Health Sci. **14**(1), 21–33 (2018)
52. Smyth, S.J., Curran, K., Mc Kelvey, N.: Internet addiction: a modern societal problem. In: Psychological, Social, and Cultural Aspects of Internet Addiction, pp. 20–43. IGI Global (2018)

53. Spada, M.M.: An overview of problematic internet use. Addict. Behav. **39**(1), 3–6 (2014)
54. Uzun, A.M., Kilis, S.: Does persistent involvement in media and technology lead to lower academic performance? Evaluating media and technology use in relation to multitasking, self-regulation and academic performance. Comput. Hum. Behav. **90**, 196–203 (2019)
55. Varma, P., Cheasakul, U.: The influence of game addiction and internet addiction among university students on depression stress and anxiety mediated by self-regulation and social support. J. Bus. Adm. Assoc. Private Educ. Instit. Thai. **5**(2), 45–57 (2016)
56. Von Schoultz, D., Van Niekerk, J., Thomson, K.L.: Web usage mining within a south african university infrastructure: towards useful information from student web usage data. In: Proceedings of the 15th Annual Conference on World Wide Web Applications (2013)
57. Vondráčková, P., Gabrhelik, R.: Prevention of internet addiction: a systematic review. J. Behav. Addict. **5**(4), 568–579 (2016)
58. Widyanto, L., Griffiths, M.: Internet addiction: a critical review. Int. J. Ment. Health Addict. **4**(1), 31–51 (2006)
59. Wohn, D.Y., LaRose, R.: Effects of loneliness and differential usage of facebook on college adjustment of first-year students. Comput. Educ. **76**, 158–167 (2014)
60. Wu, J.Y.: University students' motivated attention and use of regulation strategies on social media. Comput. Educ. **89**, 75–90 (2015)
61. Zajac, K., Ginley, M.K., Chang, R., Petry, N.M.: Treatments for internet gaming disorder and internet addiction: a systematic review. Psychol. Addict. Behav. **31**(8), 979 (2017)

End-User Security

Bayesian Evaluation of User App Choices in the Presence of Risk Communication on Android Devices

B. Momenzadeh[1(✉)], S. Gopavaram[1], S. Das[1,2], and L. J. Camp[1]

[1] Indiana University Bloomington, Bloomington, USA
{smomenza,sgopavar,sancdas,ljcamp}@iu.edu
[2] University of Denver, Denver, USA

Abstract. In the age of ubiquitous technologies, security- and privacy-focused choices have turned out to be a significant concern for individuals and organizations. Risks of such pervasive technologies are extensive and often misaligned with user risk perception, thus failing to help users in taking privacy-aware decisions. Researchers usually try to find solutions for coherently extending trust into our often inscrutable electronic networked environment. To enable security- and privacy-focused decision-making, we mainly focused on the realm of the mobile marketplace, examining how risk indicators can help people choose more secure and privacy-preserving apps. We performed a naturalistic experiment with $N = 60$ participants, where we asked them to select applications on Android tablets with accurate real-time marketplace data. We found that, in aggregate, app selections changed to be more risk-averse in the presence of user risk-perception-aligned visual indicators. Our study design and research propose practical and usable interactions that enable more informed, risk-aware comparisons for individuals during app selections. We include an explicit argument for the role of human decision-making during app selection, beyond the current trend of using machine learning to automate privacy preferences after selection during run-time.

Keywords: Mobile app permissions · Android · Risk communication · Human-centered privacy and security · Mobile security

1 Introduction

Permissions models are an excellent initiative to inform smartphone users of the services that each application might access. However, research has shown that they have failed to consistently communicate the privacy and security risks of apps on mobile platforms [1,4,8]. Currently, many researchers are discarding permissions as futile user communication, focusing on implicit instead of explicit choices and using machine learning or agent-based permissions management after installation [13,17]. Not only does much research in this area focus on building

© IFIP International Federation for Information Processing 2020
Published by Springer Nature Switzerland AG 2020
N. Clarke and S. Furnell (Eds.): HAISA 2020, IFIP AICT 593, pp. 211–223, 2020.
https://doi.org/10.1007/978-3-030-57404-8_16

machine learning tools that regulate resources accessed by apps during runtime, but Android OS has also shifted from app permission manifests to runtime permissions. Mitigating privacy risks for apps during runtime is essential, and much of this mitigation must be automated. However, an automated system during runtime has its own limitations.

Our work motivation is to determine if a multi-level communication system can support explicit individual decision-making during app selection. In addition to supporting individual autonomy, privacy-aware decision making at the time of application election offers promise for the entire ecosystem. Supporting individual risk-aware decisions in app selection could enable app providers to differentiate themselves in the app marketplace and provide developers with an incentive to consider user privacy when building apps. In this paper, we focus on enhancing the decision-time communication of risks to the user. We built a risk-indicative warning system and tested it with an operational app store in a natural environment. This warning system is built upon the findings of previous research in usable security on mobile devices and behavioral psychology.

The essential contribution of our work is an empirical illustration of the changes in participants' decision-making when provided with simple, timely, comprehensible warnings. Instead of removing permissions interactions, an alternative approach is to improve the communication and design aspect to enable users to take privacy-aware and security-aware decisions. Specifically, we illustrate the efficacy of a multi-level system where information is immediately available and summarized, with the option of searching for additional information. As this is a recommendation for design in general practice and for warning systems specifically, this is not surprising [18]. In addition we use a Bayesian experiment design and analysis to compare the distribution of app selections from participants in our market to those in the standard app market. The purpose of using a Bayesian approach is to test the interaction in a noisy, confounded naturalistic environment and to provide a stronger confidence measure than a traditional means comparison.

2   Background Motivation

2.1   Permission Models on Mobile Phones

To develop our warning system, we leveraged the Android permissions model that was used before Android OS moved to the runtime model (which was previously only used by iOS). Instead of presenting the list of permissions immediately, we added a layer of interaction that summarizes the risk of the agreed-upon permissions by the users.

Empirical research has found a significant lack of understanding, not only about the implications of providing sensitive permissions but also about the underlying meaning of permissions [4,8]. Smartphone users are mostly unaware of the resources accessed by apps [12]. For permission manifests used in Android, repeated research has shown that people usually ignore or pay little attention to them; for example, a series of online surveys and laboratory studies conducted by

Felt et al. found that only 17% of the participants paid attention to permissions during app installation [4]. Another study conducted by Rajivan et al. four years later found that only 13% of the participants viewed the permissions by clicking on them [14].

In recognition of the fact that previous permissions models were inadequate, there has been a move to automate permissions decisions based on machine learning models of observed user behavior. Models of user preferences may be driven by background observations, possibly augmented by explicit queries about acceptable data use [13,17]. The addition of machine learning mitigates risk, but it does not enable purposeful choice. Those who value their privacy are unable to make privacy-preserving app selections, as there is a lack of adequate decision-making support at the moment of selection [2].

2.2 Visual Indicators

We based the design of our visual warning risk-indicator for aggregate privacy on previous work and chose padlocks. We decided to frame the indicator positively, so more padlocks implied a lower risk. For that reason, we refer to these ratings as *privacy ratings*. We considered the five principles proposed by Rajivan et al. [14]. First we selected *icons aligned with user mental models of security*, meaning we selected the widely-used lock icon from HTTPS. Second, given that *privacy communicating icons should be in terms of privacy offered by the app/software*, we based ratings on the permissions. Third, we made the *scale of privacy communicating icons consistent with other indicators*. Fourth, and this inherently aligns with our design, *icons should be presented early in the decision-making process, while people compare apps to choose and install*. And the fifth principle, that *privacy communication should be trustworthy*, was embedded in our use of permissions for rating the apps.

3 Methodology

The goal of the experiment is to investigate if the introduction of proposed visual indicators in an actual PlayStore would change user app selections. Thus, we built an alternate PlayStore and asked participants to select multiple apps from different categories. We then ranked the apps presented to the users based on the number of downloads they received in the experiment. We compared these rankings against the download-based rankings in the actual PlayStore. Through this study design, we aimed at answering the following research questions (RQ):

RQ1 In the absence of differing privacy options, do our participants make choices that are indistinguishable from the Android Marketplace?

RQ2 When the functionality of the apps is the same, but the privacy options differ, do our participants make choices that are indistinguishable from the Android Marketplace?

RQ3 When both functionality and privacy options vary, do our participants make choices that are indistinguishable from the Android Marketplace?

3.1   Alternate PlayStore

To answer the research questions mentioned above, we built a functional app store with real-world applications, app ratings, and download counts. The user interface for our app store resembled that of Google's PlayStore on Android Jelly Bean (Version 4.1). Unlike Google's PlayStore, our app store presented users with visual indicators for aggregate risk (privacy ratings). We derived the privacy ratings from PrivacyGrade [10, 11].[1] PrivacyGrade generated privacy grades ranging from A through D for apps on Android. We retrieved the privacy grade and converted it into a numerical rating between 1 and 5. Since we use positive framing, a privacy rating of 5 is equivalent to an A grade. The privacy rating is presented on both the *list of apps* page and the *app description* page. Figures 1 and 2 show the *list of apps* and the *app description* pages respectively alongside their counterparts from the actual PlayStore. We added a button at the top of the description page which would show permissions to the participants. We used this button to track which participants viewed the permissions.

We built the alternative PlayStore by modifying the code of *BlankScore*[2] (An open-source Google PlayStore client) and used an open-source API to query Google's servers for information. The alternative PlayStore enabled us to provide accurate user ratings, download counts, descriptions, and a list of permissions of apps. Additionally, search results for applications on the alternative PlayStore were the same as the results on the actual PlayStore, including the order of presentation of apps.

(a)   (b)   (a)   (b)

Fig. 1. (a) *List of apps* page on the alternate PlayStore with privacy ratings on the alternate PlayStore. (b) *List of apps* page with no risk score on the actual PlayStore

Fig. 2. (a) *App description* page on the alternate PlayStore with privacy ratings on the alternate PlayStore. (b) *App description* page with no risk score on the actual PlayStore

3.2   Study Design

We recruited a total of $N = 60$ participants for the experiment through our outreach at the public library and the local farmers market to obtain

---

[1] http://privacygrade.org/.

[2] https://github.com/mar-v-in/BlankStore.

socio-economically and culturally homogeneous population. A core design goal was to make the experimental interaction as close as possible to the experience of interacting with the Android PlayStore. We installed the alternate PlayStore on Nexus 7 tablets and provided those tablets to our participants. We then provided each of our participants with a list of keywords to search for on the alternate PlayStore. These keywords correspond to the app categories we chose for our experiment. Each search provided a list of up to 16 apps for a given category, and we asked the participants to select and download 4 of them. To make sure all the participants saw the same results, we ensured that each participant used the same category names. The search results for all the keywords on the alternate PlayStore were identical to the ones generated by the actual PlayStore. We did not describe the purpose of the experiment, mention security, nor describe the indicators to the participants beforehand.

3.3 Statistical Analysis Approach

We used a clinical research model with an observational study by selecting a subset of participants and exposing them to an experimental condition then comparing their outcomes with the large known set of results without the condition [15]. We compared the means of the two groups, using a posthoc Tukey pairwise comparison. We include these results for each category for the ease of comparison with other work; however, we also argue that the lack of nuance in means comparisons argues for the use of a Bayesian approach. The Kruskal-Wallis Test shows the significance of differences in weighted means of privacy ratings for the four categories, which are: 0.005 for Games; 0.53 for Flashlights; 0.02 for Photos; and 0.28 for Weather. The results of this comparison show the significance of the differences between the mean privacy rating of apps chosen by those using our experimental PlayStore and the mean privacy rating of apps chosen through the actual Android PlayStore. We calculated a region of practical equivalence (ROPE) based on a Highest Density Interval (HDI) of 95%, which means the area that contains the 95% most credible values for participants' choices have the same distribution of the users' choices in the PlayStore. The comparison is between the behavior of our experimental sample and the behavior of people using the regular Android PlayStore. The advantages of an analysis using a Bayesian approach are that it integrates historical information and that it is valid with a small sample size. Other advantages are that the Bayesian analysis requires no assumptions about normality or distribution of the data. When examining the difference of means graphs we provide in reporting our Bayesian analysis, the dotted line on zero marks the point where the distributions match. The black line underneath the bars defines the 95% HDI area. The numbers on either side of the black line to specify the start and end threshold of the 95% interval. The bars show the distribution of the Difference of Means data. We will talk about each graph individually below as we report the results for each of the four categories.

3.4   Results

Out of the 60 participants, 58% were male, and 42% were female. After completing the experiment, all the participants in the study were asked to answer questions related to their app installation behavior. One of the questions asked them about the criteria they considered when selecting an application. In response to this question, 48% of the participants stated that they prioritized an app's features over other criteria when selecting an app to install. After that, the popularity ranked second, and friends' suggestion was the third choice. The other criteria, in this case, were ads, permissions, rank, reviews, and design. The survey inquired about permissions behaviors, asking participants about how often they checked an app's permissions. To this, 22% of the participants stated that they check permissions "almost every time" or "always" when installing an app. We also asked participants if they had previously refused to continue with the installation of an app because of its permissions. 79.6% of the participants stated that they had refused to install an app because of the permissions it requested in their real life. However, in practice, there was only one instance where a participant did not continue with the installation of an app because of its permissions (or after viewing the permissions). Only 7% of the total installations preceded with a check of the app's permissions in our experiment. This discrepancy between the observed and stated behavior is consistent with previous research studies [14,19].

We also investigated if the addition of aggregate risk information was cognitively burdensome for our participants. Therefore, we used the NASA TLX instrument to measure the mental workload involved in using the alternate PlayStore to select apps [6]. The results indicate that the majority of the participants (78%) found the workload to be minimal.

3.4.1   Research Question 1: Are Participants Representative?

We chose the Flashlight category to address this research question. It is not that flashlights are particularly safe and secure; rather, such apps all have the same level of privacy in terms of permissions. Table 1 shows both participant selections, PlayStore selections, and the similar privacy ratings of all of the apps. All flashlight apps also have the same functionality. When there is no difference in the privacy indicators nor the functionality of the apps, we wanted to explore whether the selections of our participants were different from those in the PlayStore. Using Bayesian analysis we show that our participants were indistinguishable from a random sample of people selecting Android apps.

To address the frequentist results first, the weighted average privacy ratings of the flashlight apps in the PlayStore is 4.94. The weighted app ratings were 4.52 and 4.51 for the store and the experimental participants, respectively. In Fig. 3, 0 is marked with a dotted line. Zero falls near the center of the region of practical equivalence. The entire HDI is within the ROPE, so the difference is practically equivalent to the null value. In the case of the Flashlight apps, our participants were statistically indistinguishable from a random sample of the selections made in the larger PlayStore. This verifies that, in the absence of

Table 1. Flashlight category by order of downloads in the experiment: apps' rank in the PlayStore, downloads in the experiment, and privacy rating (locks)

App Name	Downloads	Locks	Exp. rank	PlayStore rank
Super-Bright LED Flashlight	38	5	1	1
Color Flashlight	34	5	2	3
Tiny Flashlight + LED	26	5	3	2
Brightest Flashlight Free	20	4	4	4
Flashlight Galaxy S7	16	5	5	10
Flashlight Galaxy	16	5	5	9
Brightest LED Flashlight	15	5	7	5
Flashlight	12	5	8	11
High-Powered Flashlight	11	5	9	6
Flashlight Widget	7	5	10	12
FlashLight	6	5	11	7
Flashlight for HTC	5	5	12	13
Flashlight	3	5	13	8

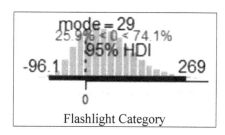

Fig. 3. Regions of Practical Equivalence for the selection of flashlight apps (RQ1). The comparison of the selections in our sample (μ_1) and the selections of our participants (μ_2). The graph shows the ROPE for the difference of means ($\mu_1 - \mu_2$), showing that our participants' selections were indistinguishable from a random sample of Android app purchasers.

differing privacy ratings, our participants' choices were indistinguishable from those of a random sample of Android users.

3.4.2 Research Question 2: Similar Functionality and Different Privacy Rating

To answer RQ2, we used the apps in the Weather category. In many cases, we expected that the individuals would trade privacy or security for some other feature-based benefit. Given the difficulty in measuring how individuals value risk avoidance, we sought a category with little functional variance and high variability in information risk. To begin with an illustrative frequentist comparison, the weighted average privacy ratings of the weather apps in the PlayStore

Table 2. Weather category by order of downloads in the experiment: apps' rank in the PlayStore, downloads in the experiment, and privacy rating (locks)

App name	Downloads	Locks	Exp. rank	PlayStore rank
Weather - The Weather Channel	40	4	1	1
AccuWeather	31	5	2	2
Yahoo Weather	27	5	3	5
MyRadar Weather Radar	27	5	3	10
Weather Underground	19	5	5	11
Weather by WeatherBug	16	3	6	6
Weather & Clock Widget Android	14	4	7	4
Transparent Clock & Weather	11	3	8	6
NOAA Weather Unofficial	7	4	9	12
Go Weather Forecast	5	4	10	3
Weather Project	5	1	10	15
Weather, Widget Forecast Radar	3	4	12	8
Weather Project	2	1	13	14
iWeather-The Weather Today	2	1	13	13
Weather	1	4	15	9

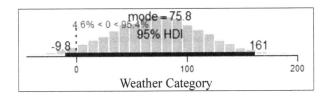

Fig. 4. Regions of Practical Equivalence, showing the difference between our participants (μ_1) and the selections in the Android marketplace (μ_2). The graph shows the ROPE for the difference of means ($\mu_1 - \mu_2$), showing less than 5% overlap with 0 region and an unskewed distribution.

were 4.26 and 4.25 for our participants. The weighted average app ratings were 4.39 for both PlayStore users and experimental participants. The Kruskal-Wallis difference in means had a p-value of 0.28. (Note that Kruskal-Wallis examines the contrast of the ways, while a Bayesian approach considers the likelihood of a distribution). The dominance of the most popular weather app, with a privacy rating of four, results in a slight skewing of the results. In many contexts, it is well-understood that people select the first choice on a list or go with defaults [7,9]. The overall difference in the means between weather apps is shown in Fig. 4. This shows little overlap between the distribution of selected weather apps between our participants and the distribution of participants in the Play-Store. That is, the likelihood that the selection of apps by our participants is an unbiased distribution resulting from a sample of the prior distribution, as shown by the PlayStore, is practically equivalent to the null value. This result indicates that the distribution is biased, and thus our warning visual risk-indicator affected our participants' choices (Table 2).

3.4.3 Research Question 3: Varying Functionality and Privacy Rating

Our other two categories, Photos and Games, were used to answer this research question. In photos, there is more variance in functionality than in weather or flashlight apps. Photo apps coordinate with different services (e.g., Instagram or Facebook), offer different filters (e.g., glitter, party hats, sepia tones),

Table 3. Games category by order of downloads in the experiment: apps' rank in the PlayStore, downloads in the experiment, and privacy rating (locks)

App Name	Downloads	Locks	Exp. rank	PlayStore rank
Fruit Ninja Free	39	5	1	2
Subway Surfers	23	5	2	1
Super Smash Jungle World	22	5	3	8
PAC-MAN	20	5	4	5
Wheel of Fortune Free Play	16	5	5	13
Color Switch	15	5	6	7
Piano Tiles 2^{TM}	15	5	6	4
slither.io	12	5	8	3
Rolling Sky	11	5	9	6
Block! Hexa Puzzle	4	1	10	9
Flip Diving	3	5	11	10
Battleships - Fleet Battle	2	5	12	17
Snakes & Ladders King	2	5	12	11
Board Games	1	5	14	13
Best Board Games	1	5	14	15
Checkers	1	5	14	12
Mancala	1	3	14	16

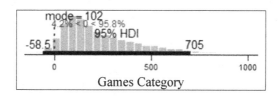

Fig. 5. ROPE for the difference of means ($\mu_1 - \mu_2$) for our participants and the Android marketplace in selection of game apps. Note the distribution of probabilities is highly skewed, decreasing confidence, while the overlap is 4.2% (RQ3)

different functionality (e.g., annotating), and different sharing modes. The weighted average privacy ratings of the game apps in the PlayStore and of the choices of participants were both 4.93. The weighted app ratings were 4.43 and 4.34 for the store and the experimental participants, respectively. The Bayesian analysis of the Games category is shown in Fig. 5. The dotted line falls into the 95% HDI. The volume of the ROPE that intersects with the likelihood of this being the practical equivalent of a random, unbiased sample of the prior known PlayStore distribution is 4.6%, approaching 5%. The initial value of the HDI (-58.5) is comparable to the distance between the zero and mode, which falls on 102. The average privacy rating of the photos apps in the PlayStore is 4.69. The weighted average privacy ratings of the choices of participants were 4.97. The weighted app ratings were 4.39 and 4.41.

In the case of photo apps, the distribution of app ratings and risk was such that individuals could mitigate risk without sacrificing any benefits. With photo applications, participants chose more secure apps over other more popular apps with more downloads, more familiarity, and more popular design. *PicsArt Photo Studio and Collage* was particularly selected by only three of our participants in our experiment for the photos category, while it was the second-ranked app in terms of the number of downloads with this search term in Google PlayStore. The results for the Photos category is quite similar to the Weather category. Zero falls at the beginning of the HDI interval. However, the distance to the start of the range is insignificant, and the distance to mode is also significant. This implies that we have influenced participants' decisions in this category as well and that participants' choices could be distinguished from options in the PlayStore. The results show that the likelihood that the parameters that characterize the distribution of the choices by our participants cannot reasonably be considered the same as the parameters that characterize the distribution of apps chosen by those in the PlayStore (Tables 3 and 4).

Table 4. Photos category by order of downloads in the experiment: apps' rank in the PlayStore, downloads in the experiment, and privacy rating (locks)

App name	Downloads	Locks	Exp. rank	PlayStore rank
Google Photos	39	5	1	1
PhotoDirector Photo Editor App	25	5	2	9
Photo Lab Picture Editor FX	24	5	3	5
Gallery	23	5	4	10
Photo Editor Pro	20	5	5	4
A+ Gallery Photos	19	5	6	12
Photo Collage Editor	17	5	7	5
PhotoGrid & Photo Collage	15	5	8	3
Toolwiz Photos - Pro Editor	13	5	9	11
Photo Editor Collage Maker Pro	9	5	10	7
PicsArt Photo Studio	3	3	11	2
Phonto - Text on Photos	1	5	12	8

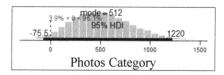

Fig. 6. Regions of Practical Equivalence for the difference of means ($\mu_1 - \mu_2$) for our participants and the Android marketplace in selection of photo apps (RQ3)

3.5 Discussion

Can we use the most common indicator of privacy on the Internet –a lock– to communicate aggregate information about mobile app privacy risk? If so, would this change the choices made by participants in the marketplace? There is no a priori answer. Information about privacy and security risks could be ignored or unwelcome. Studies in risk communication have shown that individuals find risk more acceptable if the exposure to the risk is voluntary, and when the individual exposed is capable of avoiding the risk or freely choosing it [5]. That is, shifting the nexus of control may actually increase aggregate risk-taking; the perception of control increases data sharing [16]. In privacy, this response is called the 'control dilemma' [3]. To address these questions in the context of mobile apps, we asked the research questions described above (Figure 6).

First (RQ1), can we confirm that our group of participants are indistinguishable from the Google's PlayStore users as a whole when presented with apps that had the same kind of functionality and the same privacy ratings? We used the Flashlight category for this purpose. We found that the selection of apps under this condition was indistinguishable from a random sample of app selections in the PlayStore. Our next question (RQ2) is if the participants would make different choices compared to that of Google's PlayStore users in the presence of variable ratings given the same functionality. For this question, we used the Weather category. The results from this category showed that choices in our experiment are significantly different from those made in the Google PlayStore, thus offering a high level of confidence that the ratings influenced user decision-making. Finally, we ask (in RQ3) if we can be confident that the participants' decisions are different from Google's PlayStore users when the functionality and the privacy ratings both vary. We used Games and Photos as the categories to answer this question. The Photos category indicates that the inclusion of privacy ratings, even with marginal rating differences, results in a different distribution of apps selected. In Games, we have a low level of confidence that the participants' decisions are different and can not conclude the parameters are changed.

In summary, we built a functional app store with real, accurately rated apps and added visual indicators for aggregate risk using the padlock icon. The functional app store simulation made it possible for us to compare the choices of the participants directly with those of people using Google's PlayStore. It is true that using a functional app store with real-world applications meant that we were not able to adequately control for biases, including ordering, familiarity, and reputation. However, we are confident that our participants' choices when there was no variance in privacy is indistinguishable from those of the PlayStore at large, providing confidence in the representativeness of our sample that is difficult to obtain in a traditional controlled laboratory experiment.

Acknowledgement. This research was supported in part by the National Science Foundation under CNS 1565375, Cisco Research Support, and the Comcast Innovation Fund. Any opinions, findings, and conclusions or recommendations expressed in this material are those of the author(s). They do not necessarily reflect the views of the U.S. Government, NSF, Cisco, Comcast, Indiana U, or the University of Denver.

References

1. Agarwal, Y., Hall, M.: ProtectMyPrivacy: detecting and mitigating privacy leaks on iOS devices using crowdsourcing. In: Proceeding of the 11th Annual International Conference on Mobile Systems, Applications, and Services, pp. 97–110. ACM (2013)
2. Böhme, R., Koble, S., Dresden, T.: On the viability of privacy-enhancing technologies in a self-regulated business-to-consumer market: will privacy remain a luxury good? In: 6th Workshop on the Economics of Information Security (WEIS) (2007)
3. Brandimarte, L., Acquisti, A., Loewenstein, G.: Misplaced confidences privacy and the control paradox. Soc. Psychol. Pers. Sci. **4**(3), 340–347 (2013)
4. Felt, A.P., Ha, E., Egelman, S., Haney, A., Chin, E., Wagner, D.: Android permissions: user attention, comprehension, and behavior. In: 8th Symposium on Usable Privacy and Security (SOUPS), pp. 3:1–3:14. ACM (2012)
5. Garg, V., Camp, J.: End user perception of online risk under uncertainty. In: 45th Hawaii International Conference on System Science (HICSS), pp. 3278–3287. IEEE (2012)
6. Hart, S.G., Staveland, L.E.: Development of NASA-TLX (Task Load Index): results of empirical and theoretical research. Adv. Psychol. **52**, 139–183 (1988)
7. Johnson, E.J., Bellman, S., Lohse, G.L.: Defaults, framing and privacy: why opting in-opting out. Mark. Lett. **13**(1), 5–15 (2002)
8. Kelley, P.G., Consolvo, S., Cranor, L.F., Jung, J., Sadeh, N., Wetherall, D.: A conundrum of permissions: installing applications on an Android smartphone. In: Blyth, J., Dietrich, S., Camp, L.J. (eds.) FC 2012. LNCS, vol. 7398, pp. 68–79. Springer, Heidelberg (2012). https://doi.org/10.1007/978-3-642-34638-5_6
9. Lai, Y.-L., Hui, K.-L.: Internet opt-in and opt-out: investigating the roles of frames, defaults and privacy concerns. In: 14th ACM SIGMIS CPR Conference on Computer Personnel Research: Forty Four Years of Computer Personnel Research: Achievements, Challenges & the Future, pp. 253–263. ACM (2006)
10. Lin, J., Amini, S., Hong, J.I., Sadeh, N., Lindqvist, J., Zhang, J.: Expectation and purpose: understanding users' mental models of mobile app privacy through crowdsourcing. In: 14th ACM Conference on Ubiquitous Computing, pp. 501–510. ACM (2012)
11. Lin, J., Liu, B., Sadeh, N., Hong, J.I.: Modeling users' mobile app privacy preferences: restoring usability in a sea of permission settings. In: 10th Symposium on Usable Privacy and Security (SOUPS), pp. 199–212. ACM (2014)
12. Mylonas, A., Kastania, A., Gritzalis, D.: Delegate the smartphone user? Security awareness in smartphone platforms. Comput. Secur. **34**, 47–66 (2013)

13. Olejnik, K., Dacosta, I., Machado, J.S., Huguenin, K., Khan, M.E., Hubaux, J.-P.: Smarper: context-aware and automatic runtime-permissions for mobile devices. In: 38th IEEE Symposium on Security and Privacy (SP), pp. 1058–1076. IEEE (2017)
14. Rajivan, P., Camp, J.: Influence of privacy attitude and privacy cue framing on Android app choices. In: 12th Symposium on Usable Privacy and Security (SOUPS). USENIX (2016)
15. Röhrig, B., Du Prel, J.-B., Wachtlin, D., Blettner, M.: Types of study in medical research: part 3 of a series on evaluation of scientific publications. Deutsches Arzteblatt Int. **106**(15), 262 (2009)
16. Stutzman, F., Gross, R., Acquisti, A.: Silent listeners: the evolution of privacy and disclosure on Facebook. J. Priv. Confid. **4**(2), 2 (2013)
17. Wijesekera, P., et al.: The feasibility of dynamically granted permissions: aligning mobile privacy with user preferences. In: 38th IEEE Symposium on Security and Privacy (SP), pp. 1077–1093. IEEE (2017)
18. Wogalter, M.S., DeJoy, D., Laughery, K.R.: Warnings and Risk Communication. CRC Press, Boca Raton (1999)
19. Yang, L., Boushehrinejadmoradi, N., Roy, P., Ganapathy, V., Iftode, L.: Short Paper: enhancing users' comprehension of Android permissions. In: 2nd ACM Workshop on Security and Privacy in Smartphones and Mobile Devices, pp. 21–26. ACM (2012)

Exploring Information Security
and Domestic Equality

Marcus Nohlberg and Joakim Kävrestad[(⊠)]

University of Skövde, Skövde, Sweden
{marcus.nohlberg,joakim.kavrestad}@his.se

Abstract. It is well known that men and women differ in terms of security behavior. For instance, studies report that gender plays a role in security non-compliance intentions, malware susceptibility, and security self-efficacy. While one reason for gender-based differences can be that women are vastly underrepresented in the community of security professionals, the impact that gender differences in security behavior have on equality is an underresearched area. This paper argues that cyber-inequality can impact domestic inequality and even be an enabler for domestic abuse. This paper intends to shed light on how digitalization works in households in order to problematize around equality in the digital era. It reports on a survey that measures different factors of personal information security and shows that men and women do indeed differ in personal information security behavior on a number of points such as men being more influential when it comes to ICT decisions in the household.

Keywords: Security behaviour · Gender · Equality · Domestic equality

1 Introduction

In terms of security behavior, it is well established that there are differences between men and women. For instance, Lévesque et al. (2017) [7] shows that men are more likely than women to encounter malware and Bansal et al. (2016) [4] shows that gender plays a role in information security non-compliance intention. McGill and Thompson (2018) [8] reports that men exhibit an overall stronger security behavior then women, especially for technically oriented tasks such as installing security software. However, they do not find such differences in less technical security tasks such as securing devices with passwords and using security software once it has been installed. McGill and Thompson (2018) [8] also reports that they do not find any differences in security self-efficacy, a result that conflicts with for instance Anvar et el. (2017) [3] in which differences were found, primarily in security self-efficacy, but also within experience and general computer skills. In a broader perspective, Peacock and Irons (2017) [12] reports

© IFIP International Federation for Information Processing 2020
Published by Springer Nature Switzerland AG 2020
N. Clarke and S. Furnell (Eds.): HAISA 2020, IFIP AICT 593, pp. 224–232, 2020.
https://doi.org/10.1007/978-3-030-57404-8_17

that respondents of their survey considered computer security to be a "man's job" and it is obvious that women are significantly underrepresented in the professional security community.

As described by West et al. (2019) [15], digital competences are no longer optional but required and the ability to use technology is increasingly important to a person's well-being. It is evident that skills in ICT is a necessity in order to fully participate in modern society and those who participate more enjoy advantages over those who do participate less [5]. Sey and Hafkin (2019) [13] describes that skills in security is one aspect that is needed for participation in the digital world making research into gender-based differences in personal security an important equality issue. We argue that equal, or similar participation and influence over digital matters is an important aspect of equality in a household, as well as in the workplace.

A darker aspect that is affected by security behavior is digital abuse. While physical domestic abuse is a well-known phenomenon to the wider public, the digital era brings other forms of abuse that can to a degree be tied to security behavior. Gagnier (2018) [6] described that digital abuse can for instance include identity theft, unlawful surveillance and cyberstalking, and the perpetrator is often a current or previous partner. Al-Alosi (2017) [2] reports that using different methods to get access to, and control, over the victims' digital accounts on social media, e-mail etc. is a common part of digital abuse. The ways used to get this control range from active hacking practices, such as using spyware, to asking for the passwords to said services. The extent of this phenomenon is hard to quantify, but recent studies indicate that as many as 10 % uses apps or software to spy on their current or former partners' messages, photos, phone calls etc. [1]. It is also clear that men are overrepresented as the part that monitors women. While it is hard to differentiate normal and trusting sharing of information in a relationship from sharing that can enable digital abuse, we argue that domestic digital inequality can be an enabler for digital abuse.

Gender differences in information security is an under-researched area [8] and gender differences in personal security skill and behavior is an equality matter. The aim of this paper is to look into equality factors of personal information security, such as password/account sharing and influence over decisions about digital devices and services in the household as well as perceived ICT skills. The paper intends to shed light on how digitalization works in households in order to problematize around equality in the digital era.

2   Methodology

The aim of this paper was meet using a web-based survey, built and distributed using Limesurvey, that contained Likert-style questions around the following four themes:

- [influential] How influential the respondents are when it comes to ICT-related decisions in the household.

- [sharing] To what degree the respondents share passwords to various services with their partners.
- [autonomy] To that extent the respondents install ICT devices themselves or ask for help
- [router_skill] To what degree the respondents are comfortable carrying out various tasks on their home router.

Each question theme consisted of a number of questions, each with a five-graded answer scale.

In analysing the responses, all answers were dichotomized. The answers "Fully agree" and "Mostly Agree" was converted to 1 and the other options to 0. Thus, 1 represent an agreeing answer. The dichotomized variables were used to created indexes reflecting the respondents score in each theme. For data analysis, the survey data was grouped based on the respondents reported gender. It is reasonable to assume that IT-professionals will answer differently than others [14]. Thus, all responses from respondents reporting to be IT-professionals was grouped, and all metrics reported with and without the answers from the group of IT-professionals. The Shapiro-Wilks test was used to test whether the generated data was normally distributed [10], and the means and median are reported for the indexes. Based on central tendencies observed using descriptive statistics, hypothesis testing was used to evaluate if the tendencies were significant. Because of space limitations, the results are presented in condensed form. The hypotheses were expressed as follows:

H1: There is a difference between the gender groups regarding index X
H0: There is no difference between the gender groups regarding index X

Further, Mann-Whitney U-test was used for hypothesis testing. Mann-Whitney U-test was selected in favor of T-test since no samples was normally distributed and is therefore more suitable than T-test [9]. The significance level used in this study is the conventional 95% meaning that results are significant if $p < 0.05$. SPSS was used for statistical analysis.

3   Results

The survey was distributed as an online survey and 152 respondents completed the survey. The answers were used to compute and analyze indexes for the four different themes of interest in this paper. The reminder of this chapter will describe how the indexes was calculated, and the results of the analysis.

3.1   Influential Index

Under the influential theme, the respondents were asked the following questions:

- When you are in a committed relationship, how influential are you when you decide what streaming service to use (Netflix, HBO etc)?

– When you are in a committed relationship, how influential are you when you
  decide what Internet service provider to use?
– When you are in a committed relationship, how influential are you when you
  decide what new computer/cell phone to buy for yourself?
– When you are in a committed relationship, how influential are you when you
  decide what new common use digital devices to buy together?

Each question had a five-graded answer scale labelled as follows; 1 = My
partner is much more influential than me, 3 = me and my partner are equally
influential, 5 = I am much more influential than my partner. The answers to
the questions were dichotomized so that the two most positive answer options
were represented by 1 and the three least positive answers were represented by
0. An index of all questions was computed by adding the variables together.
To exemplify, if a respondent provided positive answers to all four questions,
the index value became 4, if a respondent provided positive answers to two of
the questions, the index value became 2. Table 1, below, presents the mean and
median values for male and female respondents. The results are first presented
for the entire sample (all) and then only for respondents reporting that they are
not IT-professionals (NoIT).

Table 1. Statistics in the "influential" theme. Results are significant if $p < 0.05$

Group	Mean	Median	Mann-Whitney U-test
All Male (n = 99)	3.04	3	p = 0.000
All Female (n = 53)	2.15	2	
NoIT Male (n = 54)	2.73	3	p = 0.002
NoIT Female (n = 38)	1.84	1	

As seen in Table 1, male respondents report being more influential than
female respondent. The same tendency is seen even if respondents who report
being IT-professionals are removed from the analysis. The results of the Mann-
Whitney U-test show that the difference is significant showing that the hypothesis "There is a difference between the gender groups regarding index influential"
holds.

3.2 Sharing Index

Under the sharing theme, the respondents were asked the following questions:

– When you are in a committed relationship, how likely are you to share passwords to social networks (Facebook, Instagram etc) with your partner?
– When you are in a committed relationship, how likely are you to share passwords to your personal e-mail with your partner?

- When you are in a committed relationship, how likely are you to share passwords to work related accounts with your partner?
- When you are in a committed relationship, how likely are you to share passwords/pins to your computer with your partner?
- When you are in a committed relationship, how likely are you to share passwords/pins to your cellphone with your partner?
- When you are in a committed relationship, how likely are you to share passwords to "streaming services" (Spotify, Netflix, HBO etc) with your partner?
- When you are in a committed relationship, how likely are you to share passwords to online stores (Amazon, Steam, Ebay etc) with your partner?

Each question had a five-graded answer scale labelled as follows; 1 = very unlikely, 3 = neutral, 5 = very likely. An index was computed using the same procedure as previously, resulting in an index that ranged from 0 to 7. Table 2, below, presents the mean and median values for male and female respondents. The results are first presented for the entire sample (all) and then only for respondents reporting that they are not IT-professionals (NoIT).

Table 2. Statistics in the "sharing" theme. Results are significant if p < 0.05

Group	Mean	Median	Mann-Whitney U-test
All Male (n = 99)	3.30	3	p = 0.573
All Female (n = 53)	3.48	3	
NoIT Male (n = 54)	2.72	2	p = 0.458
NoIT Female (n = 38)	3.02	3	

As seen in Table 2, a slight tendency suggesting that female respondents are somewhat more prone to share their passwords is shown. However, the results are not significant meaning that the null hypotheses, that there is no observable difference, cannot be discarded.

3.3   Autonomy Index

Under the autonomy theme, the respondents were asked the following questions:

- When you receive a new digital device, such as an apple TV, home router or likewise. How likely is it you will install it yourself?
- When you receive a new digital device, such as an apple TV, home router or likewise. How likely is it that you will ask your partner for help installing it together with you?
- When you receive a new digital device, such as an apple TV, home router or likewise. How likely is it you will ask a friend or family member for help installing it together with you?

- When you receive a new digital device, such as an apple TV, home router or likewise. How likely is it that you will ask your partner to install it for you (you will not take part in the installation)?
- When you receive a new digital device, such as an apple TV, home router or likewise. How likely is it that you will ask a friend or family member to install it for you (you will not take part in the installation?

Each question had a five-graded answer scale labeled as follows; 1 = very unlikely, 3 = neutral, 5 = very likely. An index was computed using the same procedure as previously, except that the first question was computed as a one for answers 1 or 2. This resulted in an index that ranged from 0 to 5 that reflects how likely the respondents are to get help with the installation of new digital devices. Table 3, below, presents the mean and median values for male and female respondents. The results are first presented for the entire sample (all) and then only for respondents reporting that they are not IT-professionals (NoIT).

Table 3. Statistics in the "autonomy" theme. Results are significant if $p < 0.05$

Group	Mean	Median	Mann-Whitney U-test
All Male (n = 99)	1.20	0	$p = 0.017$
All Female (n = 53)	1.87	2	
NoIT Male (n = 54)	0.60	0	$p = 0.001$
NoIT Female (n = 38)	1.66	2	

As seen in Table 3, female respondents report being more prone to ask for help than male respondents. The same tendency is seen even if respondents who report being IT-professionals are removed from the analysis. The results of the Mann-Whitney U-test show that the difference is significant showing that the hypothesis "There is a difference between the gender groups regarding index autonomy" holds.

3.4 Router Skill Index

Under the router skill theme, the respondents were to rate the following statements about their home router using a five graded scale labeled; 1 = do not agree at all, 3 = neutral, 5 = agree fully. This short description of what a home router is was also supplied; The router is the device that that connects your home with the Internet and provides WiFi. An index was computed using the same procedure as previously, resulting in an index that ranged from 0 to 4 Table 4, below, presents the mean and median values for male and female respondents. The results are first presented for the entire sample (all) and then only for respondents reporting that they are not IT-professionals (NoIT).

– I know my WiFi password
– I know how to login to the router
– I feel comfortable changing the WiFi password
– I feel comfortable doing advanced configuration tasks

Table 4. Statistics in the "router skill" theme. Results are significant if p < 0.05

Group	Mean	Median	Mann-Whitney U-test
All Male (n = 99)	3.48	4	p = 0.001
All Female (n = 53)	2.92	3	
NoIT Male (n = 54)	3.30	4	p = 0.001
NoIT Female (n = 38)	2.56	3	

As seen in Table 4, male respondents report being more comfortable with configuring the home router than female respondents. The same tendency is seen even if respondents who report being IT-professionals are removed from the analysis. The results of the Mann-Whitney U-test show that the difference is significant showing that the hypothesis "There is a difference between the gender groups regarding index router_skill" holds.

4   Conclusions

The aim of this paper is to look into equality factors of personal information security, such as password/account sharing and influence over decisions about digital devices and services in the household as well as perceived ICT skills. The study was performed using a survey were respondents were asked about their security behavior and asked to rate their skills in relation to their home router. The answers were used to compute indexes intended to reflect:

– How influential the respondents are regarding domestic ICT decisions
– To what degree the respondents share passwords with their partners
– How autonomic the respondents are when it comes to installing new ICT devices
– How comfortable the respondents are with their home router

The results suggest that men are more influential than women when it comes to domestic ICT decisions, as well as more autonomic when it comes to installing new ICT devices and are more comfortable carrying out tasks on the home router. The results of the survey were statistically significant concerning these conclusions. The results could not find any differences in terms of password sharing even if an insignificant tendency, that females shared passwords to a greater level then males, was observed.

As with all surveys that collect self-reported data, socially desirable respond-ing (SDR) bias should be considered a risk [11]. In this particular case, it is inter-esting to consider the possible connection between SDR bias and self-efficacy. It is suggested in the literature that computer security is generally considered to be a man's job [12] and it could be interpreted as socially desirable for males to be good at security and for females to be bad at it. This aligns well with the authors' experience of teaching in the technical domain. Although not sci-entifically researched, male students we talked to report that male students are never questioned about their choice to follow a career in IT while female stu-dents very frequently have to justify their decision to family and friends. As such, the possible prevalence of an SDR bias in this context could in itself be a sign of equality problems that need to be addressed in a broad societal context. There might also be a reversed problem among males. If it is perceived to be unmanly to ask for help in technical domains, this may lead to men actually spending more time to learn about these matters, as well as helping others, pre-dominantly women, and thus actually having more knowledge. It might however also lead to under-reporting and perhaps even worse, a general false self-image of competence among males leading to ignorance related to unsafe behavior.

In this study we took, by necessity, a traditional hetero-normative approach to the concept of gender and asked about male and female; this is not a statement in itself, but a choice made due to the fact that we expected to not receive enough answers to have any relevant data to work with anything else than the two tradi-tional genders. We did take care to not assume that people were living in a het-eronormative relationship by asking for "partners" and not boyfriend/girlfriend etc. so the study is not focused on the type of relationship a person might be in, but the self-experienced gender dynamics themselves.

We do argue that this, and other research, indicates that gender has a sig-nificant impact on security behavior, and it is thus crucial to study this further in the future. Building only on this study, in which we only focused on the sub-jects' own self-reporting of their own competency, without any actual testing of knowledge. It would be interesting to measure self-image combined with actual knowledge in a larger domain to see if there is an actual difference between the genders, as well as doing interviews trying to get a deeper understanding on if, and why, these differences exit. Even if our results focus on the home environment, those values and differences might also be relevant in the work environment, and relevant to investigate further.

As this study took a binary approach to gender (male/female) it would be very interesting to extend this research into other genders, especially if a large enough dataset can be acquired.

References

1. Nearly half of americans admit to 'stalking' an ex or current partner online. NortonLifeLock, February 2020. https://investor.nortonlifelock.com/About/ Investors/press-releases/press-release-details/2020/Nearly-Half-of-Americans-Admit-to-Stalking-an-Ex-or-Current-Partner-Online/default.aspx

2. Al-Alosi, H.: Cyber-violence: digital abuse in the context of domestic violence. UNSWLJ **40**, 1573 (2017)
3. Anwar, M., He, W., Ash, I., Yuan, X., Li, L., Xu, L.: Gender difference and employees' cybersecurity behaviors. Comput. Hum. Behav. **69**, 437–443 (2017)
4. Bansal, G., Hodorff, K., Marshall, K.: Moral beliefs and organizational information security policy compliance: the role of gender. In: Proceedings of the Eleventh Midwest United States Association for Information Systems, pp. 1–6 (2016)
5. Bergström, A.: Digital equality and the uptake of digital applications among seniors of different age. Nordicom Rev. **38**(s1), 79–91 (2017)
6. Gagnier, C.M.: Cyber exploitation and perpetration of digital abuse. Family Intimate Partner Violence Q. **11**(2) (2018)
7. Lévesque, F.L., Fernandez, J.M., Batchelder, D.: Age and gender as independent risk factors for malware victimisation. In: Proceedings of the 31st British Computer Society Human Computer Interaction Conference, p. 46. BCS Learning & Development Ltd. (2017)
8. McGill, T., Thompson, N.: Gender differences in information security perceptions and behaviour. In: 29th Australasian Conference on Information Systems (2018)
9. McKnight, P.E., Najab, J.: Mann-whitney u test. In: The Corsini Encyclopedia of Psychology, p. 1 (2010)
10. Mendes, M., Pala, A.: Type I error rate and power of three normality tests. Pak. J. Inf. Technol. **2**(2), 135–139 (2003)
11. Van de Mortel, T.F., et al.: Faking it: social desirability response bias in self-report research. Aust. J. Adv. Nurs. **25**(4), 40 (2008)
12. Peacock, D., Irons, A.: Gender inequality in cybersecurity: exploring the gender gap in opportunities and progression. Int. J. Gender Sci. Technol. **9**(1), 25–44 (2017)
13. Sey, A., Hafkin, N.: Taking stock: data and evidence on gender equality in digital access, skills, and leadership. United Nations University, Tokyo (2019)
14. Siponen, M.T.: Five dimensions of information security awareness. SIGCAS Comput. Soc. **31**(2), 24–29 (2001)
15. West, M., Kraut, R., Ei Chew, H.: I'd blush if I could: closing gender divides in digital skills through education (2019)

Responding to KRACK: Wi-Fi Security Awareness in Private Households

Jan Freudenreich[1], Jake Weidman[2] (ID), and Jens Grossklags[1](✉) (ID)

[1] Technical University Munich, Munich, Germany
jan.freudenreich@tum.de, jens.grossklags@in.tum.de
[2] The Pennsylvania State University, State College, PA, USA
jakeweidman@google.com

Abstract. In this paper, we study the update and security practices of individuals in private households with an exploratory interview study. In particular, we investigate participants' awareness regarding KRACK, a patched key vulnerability in the WPA/WPA2 protocol, and similar vulnerabilities in the context of usage and management scenarios in Wi-Fi networks. We show that while most people are aware of certain dangers, they struggle to address Wi-Fi related vulnerabilities. The findings could prove to be beneficial in identifying not only the current security status of average users regarding Wi-Fi security, but also to improve update and information propagation to mitigate related threats in the future.

Keywords: WPA/Wi-Fi security · KRACK attack · Interview study

1 Introduction

Today, Wi-Fi devices are used in nearly every household with an installed base reaching 13 billion devices in 2019 [19], while Wi-Fi Protected Access (WPA and WPA2) serves as the most commonly used encryption protocol [20].

While WPA2 was widely believed to be secure against direct attacks on the protocol, Vanhoef and Piessens described a practical attack against both WPA and WPA2 networks, allowing for decryption and manipulation of data sent in these networks. The so-called Key Reinstallation Attack (KRACK) [16] was the first non-vendor-specific attack described to allow full decryption of data sent through the Wi-Fi stream.

KRACK makes use of flaws in cryptographic handshakes used to authenticate clients in wireless networks secured by WPA and WPA2. Most importantly, the 4-Way Handshake and the Group Handshake can be attacked. In an attack scenario, a victim is 'tricked' to reinstall an already used session key, severely undermining the security of the wireless network. A successful attack on the 4-Way Handshake allows for replay attacks and decryption of the data stream in

---

Jake Weidman is now with Google. The work was partially completed while being a visiting scholar at the Technical University of Munich.

© IFIP International Federation for Information Processing 2020
Published by Springer Nature Switzerland AG 2020
N. Clarke and S. Furnell (Eds.): HAISA 2020, IFIP AICT 593, pp. 233–243, 2020.
https://doi.org/10.1007/978-3-030-57404-8_18

networks secured by the TKIP and CCMP protocols. In TKIP-secured networks, the attacker is also able to forge the traffic between client and access point. The attack settings are not restricted to certain scenarios, and could, therefore, be used in private, commercial, and policy settings.

The newly developed WPA3 standard replaces the 4-Way Handshake with Simultaneous Authentication of Equals (SAE) and thereby mitigates the previously described KRACK attack vector. However, recently discovered vulnerabilities, including Denial-of-Service (DoS) and downgrade attacks, may allow an attacker to force access points to revert back to the WPA2 protocol and effectively circumvent the stronger protection of WPA3 [17]. Such vulnerabilities could possibly slow down the adoption of WPA3. Further, in early 2020, related flaws were discovered in common Wi-Fi chips, affecting an estimated number of one billion devices [4].

In addition, older devices, which are not provided with security updates anymore (or slow update behavior by users) could leave large numbers of devices unpatched even after corrective updates are introduced. This is especially true for operating systems on mobile devices - smartphones and tablets - which often have a far shorter support life cycle than desktop devices [7–9].

The main goal of this work is to analyze the awareness and security measures taken in a sample of private households concerning KRACK and, more generally, Wi-Fi security via an exploratory interview study. Our work aims to help better understand and tackle the existing problems in Wi-Fi security and to outline possible ways for improvements of update and information propagation practices in this problem domain.

2   Related Work

Relevant to our study are the update support practices by vendors, which vary substantially. Microsoft offers support for their Windows desktop products for five to ten years [9]. For Apple, the average time of support for OS X 10 variants is around 40 months [13]. Apple's iPhone products receive updates generally for a period of three to five years [11]. Updates for Android - a more open ecosystem - depend heavily on the vendor [6]. Google's Nexus and Pixel devices are supported with updates for about three years [8].

How Wi-Fi-related security vulnerabilities can create high risk scenarios for the user has been previously shown, for example, by Petters [21]. In 2012, he presented a flaw in routers manufactured by Arcadyan, including so-called Easy-Boxes distributed by Vodafone. The patents of Arcadyan revealed how the factory WPA key was calculated using the publicly broadcasted BSSID of the router. This allowed an attacker to gain complete access to a secured network by only recording the public MAC-address of the router. In 2013, Viehböck showed that through a similar flaw in the WPS algorithm it was possible to hack affected routers, even if the device password had been changed [18].

For the user perspective, a series of AOL/NCSA Online Safety Studies (see, for example, the 2004 version [1]) used an approach (partly exemplary for our study) where security perceptions of participants were directly correlated with the factual security status of the devices *in their own homes*. Poole et al. [10] further elaborated on the high need for IT support in private households and the problems arising as the result of using different providers and vendors, as well as having different sources of user knowledge.

3 Methodology and Participant Data

The research topic was approached in a qualitative way by performing exploratory semi-structured interviews in interviewees' own homes. Prior to the interview, a short questionnaire was given to the participants, which included questions about demographics and participants' Wi-Fi usage and management as well as their network topology. During the interview, more in-depth questions were provided; structurally divided in five segments. The objective of the first three segments was to provide a deepening structural tree from more broad Wi-Fi and security questions before focusing on the topic of KRACK. The questions in the fourth segment were focused on a broader understanding of security and update-related issues, aiming to find possible mitigations for challenges regarding security updates and insufficient information propagation (to learn about security problems and mitigations). The final part consisted of three questions, tracking possible behavioral changes and reactions to the interview process itself. Following the interview, an additional survey was provided to the participants, allowing us to gather information about update practices and to further evaluate participants' security assessments.

Participants were recruited (in March 2018) through snowball sampling with a focus on achieving a relatively diverse distribution of participants from different social environments and anticipated technological backgrounds to allow the gathering of insights from different perspectives. They were required to be living in a multi-person household and to have their own Wi-Fi network. The interviews were recorded, and subsequently transcribed and anonymized such that no personally identifiable information was present during the analysis process. During the design and execution of the study, we followed recommended community practices for running security usability studies [12].

The study was conducted in the Munich area, Germany. Of the 16 participants, 2 were female, and 14 were male. Nine of the participants were students from different universities and fields of study. Other occupations included a nurse, a pensioner, an unemployed and a self-employed individual. All participants had reached matriculation standard in their education. Two, additionally, had completed vocational education, one a bachelor's degree, and two held a diploma. The average age of the participants was 28.75 years (min = 20; max = 61). Laptops were present in every household; only one household did not have smartphones present. Desktop and tablet devices were used in about half of the households.

4 Results

Wi-Fi Usage and Sensitive Data. Questions about Wi-Fi usage (from the survey) allowed for gathering of information about general Wi-Fi practices and the possibility of (sensitive) data leakage. On a scale from 1 (rarely used) and 5 (always used), browing ranked highest (4.0) followed by streaming (3.8), office work (3.6), social media (2.7) and eventually gaming (2.1). Every person in our sample was using their Wi-Fi for office work and media streaming at least sometimes, whereas some people never used it to play games or to access social media platforms. All of these scenarios could possibly leak private data, which should not be publicly available.

Higher Level Encryption Not Ensured. Since the KRACK attack is performed through intercepting data in transmission, securing the transfer layer could be one possible mitigation; also for similar forms of attack. When asked whether participants pay attention to Transport Layer Security (TLS) and to the Hypertext Transfer Protocol Secure (HTTPS), the answers were rather ambiguous. The evaluation shows that there was no clear tendency in this sample group. The statement from Participant 3 is transferable to most others: "*It depends on the context. If I do some unimportant activities no, but if it is concerned with user or banking data yes.*"

The data also shows, that 10 participants (62.5%) had never used a VPN before. Only one participant used a VPN service most of the time to achieve a higher level of security. Others used the technology for work or study purposes; mostly to get access to remote file locations. We found that 13 participants (81.25%) had never used TOR, or a similar onion routing technique, before. Most of them did not recall ever hearing about this way of anonymization. Only one participant did use TOR on a regular basis.

Is Your Wi-Fi Safe? Even though every participant used their Wi-Fi on a daily basis with several devices, half of them perceived their Wi-Fi network as insecure (50.0%). In contrast, only 6 participants (37.5%) believed their Wi-Fi network to be secure, while two individuals considered their networks partly secure (12.5%). Most argued that the lack of security comes from their own actions, mostly from choosing and handling their respective Wi-Fi passwords in an insecure fashion. One example included giving the password to outside parties, like Participant 2: "*No [...] because my password is [***].*"[1] *It is really weak. Why else? Probably, because everyone in the house knows my password.*" Another reported practice was taking pictures of the factory settings and sending them using messenger apps to other individuals.

Another rather peculiar case was Participant 8 (and a flatmate), who wrote the factory password on a sheet of paper and put it on a kitchen cabinet. This alone would be problematic, because it would empower anyone having access to the kitchen to attain the password. However, their password is also visible for

---

[1] The password was given without any questioning and despite we asked the participant not to tell passwords or similar compromising information.

people outside passing by their flat, since it is hung directly beside a window: *"We have it hanging there. [...] This would be such a critical point. If you look through the window, you can see our Wi-Fi password."*

Factory Settings. Another potential vulnerability for home networks is not changing the default password and continuing using the factory setting. Indeed, many participants still use their routers with the implemented factory settings, although every manufacturer should have instructed them to change these settings. Awareness of the potential threat through an unchanged factory password differed widely across the interviewed participants. Whereas some were aware of a potential vulnerability and changed their password accordingly, like Participant 15, who when asked about why he believes his Wi-Fi network to be secure, said: *"Because of the password. Which was not the original password."* Others did not show such awareness at all (Participant 14): *"No. I trust it."* Interestingly, some participants were aware of this possible threat, and even recognized it as an attack vector, but still did not change their password.

Perceived Risks. A possible explanation for such observed behavior may be related to the perceived threat model. Most of the participants see similar hazards concerning Wi-Fi networks. A commonly stated risk was the leakage of personal or sensitive data and the possibility of someone getting access to the network and thereby allowing the attacker to use the internet under the resident's identity. The possibility of attackers gaining access to personal and private data was described, for example, by Participants 10 and 13. Such data could then also be leaked to be publicly available. Participant 10 stated: *"That everything I do is accessible to others - which websites I use."* Participant 13 mentioned: *"Getting your personal data hacked and having it presented to the whole public."* Participant 1 remarked the possibility of gaining further access to other devices and the possibility of identity theft: *"He could get in my home network, see my hard drives, and surely could get remote access to my computer - at least I could imagine. And of course he could take my identity by using my network."* Similarly, Participant 8 stated: *"Or he could do some strange internet stuff with our IP. Doing something illegal and stuff like that with our IP."*

When taking a deeper look into what participants see as sensitive data, it was firstly defined as connected to information related to financial holdings. Among these were passwords for online banking or credit card PINs. Participant 2 remarked: *"Banking information. Everything directly connected to money."* Secondly, more sophisticated and indirect attacks to gain access to privacy-concerning data were also mentioned. Indeed, several participants identified data as sensitive which would make themselves or others victims of blackmail and extortion. Participant 2 stated: *"Or pornos and stuff which would allow for blackmailing. Maybe if you Google for medical or embarrassing stuff. Or drug related things."* The listed information could pose a high risk for the victim when leaked publicly. Perceived risks could be the loss of their job, or being shamed in public or by family or friends.

Victims. Most participants were certain that they would not be the target of cyberattacks. Some argued this based on the environment they were living in, like Participant 11 who resides in a small village: "*If I would be living in a bigger city or something like that, I would be more concerned.*" Others, like Participant 8 noted: "*There are many old people in our neighborhood. They are happy if their computer is starting.*"

However, most argued that their own data or information would be irrelevant to others. As an example, Participant 14 stated: "*If I had sensitive data, I would be more concerned.*" Likewise, as participant 15 put it: "*It is exactly like your smartphone: When you type something into Google or when Google tracks you regardless whether your location is on or off. It is the same - it is as bad as if someone would get your data through such an attack.*" These sentiments represent a potential hindrance for further investments in security. Many participants had a "Not Me" mindset, meaning that they do not see themselves as possible victims. The present culture of data collection and data privacy invasions further appears to feed such mindsets as the quotes indicate [14].

Through the linking of sensitive data with money and the potential for extortion, certain other classes of possible victims were named. Among these were politicians, prominent figures and, interestingly, professors. As Participant 2 stated, when asked if he does see himself as a possible victim: "*No. Celebrities maybe or professors. People who are more important than me.*" Different to these mostly general assumptions about possible victims, Participant 14 was able to describe an example from his work-related situation: "*One of my clients is an interior architect and among other things deals with alarm systems. That's very important data. Knowing that she has designed a certain house, she explicitly could be attacked.*"

The responses show that participants were able to connect sensitive data and attack scenarios. But, interestingly, they do not see such a connection given their own situation or personal environments.

Attackers. The description of possible attackers, which could make use of flaws in Wi-Fi networks or IT vulnerabilities in general, differed between participants. Nevertheless, three basic types can be extracted from the answers given in the interviews: intelligence agencies, monetary interests and corporate and economic espionage, and miscreants.

One quote (by Participant 4), in particular, highlights the perceptions regarding information gathering or extortion and thereby gaining political power: "*There are people - spies - which are interested in what people do or say. Everyone knows that government surveillance agencies - keyword Trojan[2] - have the possibilities. And they use them, too.*" The motives of blackhat hackers are either described as being about gathering money, or like Participant 13 noted, as wanting to cause destruction: "*People who do this as some kind of hobby. They don't get anything from it, but do it solely to harm others.*" This point outlines a problem with the "Not Me" mindset: Someone without a well-defined agenda

---

[2] Participant refers to the so-called "Bundestrojaner", a controversial German state sponsored Trojan access tool used to secretly examine IT devices [3].

is not prone to economically rational modes of operations, since his benefits do not lay in gaining money or political power, but are solely hedonistic - in this case causing mayhem. Such scenarios do not offer a clear distinction between non-victims and victims and are thereby potentially dangerous for everyone.

The presented descriptions of dangers and pictorials of victims and attackers quite possible indicate the cause of participants' lack of secure behavior; especially their feelings of unimportance and the presence of a "Not Me" mindset.

Knowledge About KRACK. From all participants in this study, only two did recall hearing about KRACK beforehand (12.5%). However, most participants previously stated that they felt informed about security and technology in general - some would even try to gather specific information and news concerning IT and computer security. However, most of them did not recall the reports connected to the KRACK Attack and the underlying WPA flaws, even though the attack was covered by major German mainstream media, like the Süddeutsche Zeitung [15] and the Handelsblatt [5]. These observations clearly show a problem in information propagation.

In our sample, only 6 participants (37.5%) were concerned about attacks like KRACK. When going into detail, it became clear that again most did not see themselves among the potential victims [2]. Nearly all agreed, that the possible dangers for others could be quite high, which is consistent with findings from above: Assessing a vulnerability as problematic, but not counting themselves among the likely victims.

Security Assessment. No participant in this group reported to have checked the security status with respect to KRACK. Seven participants (43.75%) believed their devices to be safe, since they recalled doing security updates in the past few months or made use of automated update procedures. Only two participants (12.5%) believed their devices to be affected. The rest was unsure (43.75%).

Mobile Devices: We found that 37.5% of Android devices (6/16) and 62.5% of iOS devices (5/8) in this sample were still vulnerable to KRACK. It appears that the rather short overall update period for smartphones, mostly between two and four years, does not suit the longer usage period of such devices. Most vulnerable devices were indeed not eligible for security updates anymore; only two iOS devices, which could have been updated, were not updated by the user.

Desktop and Notebook Devices: No macOS (0/2) or Linux (0/7) devices were still vulnerable, and only a minority of Windows PCs (18.75%, 3/16) were still vulnerable. It should be noted that the only affected Windows PCs were either older XP models, or in one case a Windows 10 PC were the user used a registry hack to prohibit the operating system from updating. All others were running Windows 7 or 10 and had the appropriate security updates installed.

In our sample, mobile devices were far more often vulnerable to the KRACK Attack. Further, nearly all vulnerable devices were outside of the respective support time frame, which for mobile devices is usually far shorter than for desktop devices. Taken together, in this sample, 10 out of the 16 households (62.5%) had at least one vulnerable device present, and several had multiple vulnerable devices. It is important to note that the attack and also the first security updates were made available more than half a year before our study.

Further, a significant difference between the assessment of security and the actual security was observed. Interestingly, the two participants who believed their devices to be still affected had in reality no vulnerable devices present in their households. In contrast, four participants of those who noted that their devices should be in an updated and secure state, had at least one vulnerable device present in their households.

Communication. One question covered the widely discussed topic of enforcing updates without direct user consent. Most participants were clearly against this kind of enforcement. They mostly cited a loss of independence and the fear of losing functionality. Participant 9 stated, for example: *"I don't want any enforcement. They should know that an update is available, but they shouldn't be pressured."*

Therefore, a suitable way to achieve a higher level of security, and not in opposition to the participants, would be to improve the communication between users and providers. Several communication channels should be implemented simultaneously. These should be both direct channels (e.g., email) and indirect channels (e.g., newspapers, websites). Most participants want providers to inform them directly, and also seek to receive information from the media. In contrast, government, and in particular intelligence agencies seem to be suffering from a widespread lack of trust in governmental institutions. Participant 7 stated: *"I would say better by news or public media. Instead of the government, which would make me feel like my mobile phone is monitored by the government. Any message from them could mean they monitor this."*

5   Discussion and Concluding Remarks

Update Supply and Propagation. When updates are provided, participants seem to perform them on a regular basis. However, our data suggests that desktop devices are far better secured against such attacks than mobile devices. Desktop devices are usually supported with updates over a longer period of time. In opposition to that, support cycles for smartphones are far shorter. Nearly all mobile devices are highly dependent on the manufacturer of these devices. When the support period expires, a switching of operating systems is usually impossible.

The widespread usage of proprietary software and firmware - in this case contrary to open source software - extends the manufacturers' field of responsibility, since it is impossible for non-expert users, even with some technical knowledge and abilities, to control these software parts. Such software and the subordination to specific providers are prone to be problematic, since they further increase the dependence on these providers and hinder other parties from taking care of flaws or insufficient update provision.

Lack of Wi-FI Security and Wi-Fi Security Consciousness. Participants often do not engage in secure practices when using or managing their Wi-Fi infrastructure. Most prominently, many do not change factory settings, do not choose or handle passwords appropriately, and do not concern themselves with security updates for these devices (in contrast to computers and phones).

In contrast, nearly all participants seem to be generally aware that a variety of security threats and attack scenarios may exist. But they do not apply these dangers to themselves. Users often do not see themselves as potential victims, because of a perception of lack of importance of their devices and data, and an overall missing consciousness regarding data privacy.

Knowledge and Information Propagation. Judging from the presented findings, participants seem not to be informed about security flaws and vulnerabilities regarding their devices or the underlying techniques in general. The same applies for dangers associated with insecure devices or data leakages, both in personal and social settings.

How these issues could be addressed cannot be satisfactorily discussed in this short work. Nevertheless, the somewhat variable findings suggest that multiple ways should be present simultaneously. These ways include direct and indirect communication. For specific persons and vulnerability situations, a direct approach, in which households are contacted through mail or other direct communication channels, seems to be fitting. This form of information should be done by the manufacturers or providers themselves. However, this direct communication cannot fully substitute public announcements - especially in scenarios where high portions of the deployed devices are affected, like in the example of KRACK. However, the preferences for ways of informing about security flaws and dangers were very diverse necessitating a flexible approach using different ways of communication.

Update Without Consent. Users want to keep sovereignty over their owned devices, meaning that almost all of the participants in this sample did not want their devices to update without direct consent. In addition to the possible loss of functionality, most are concerned with a general loss of control over their device. However, in today's complex setting of connected devices, this desire can only be securely satisfied if people are generally able to fulfill the underlying responsibilities; likely in conjunction with adequate novel tools. On the one hand, we have the individuals' wish for sovereignty and control; on the other hand, the need for ensuring a secure collective infrastructure.

Acknowledgements. We thank the anonymous reviewers for their constructive feedback.

References

1. America Online and the National Cyber Security Alliance: AOL/NCSA online safety study (2004)
2. Bidgoli, M., Grossklags, J.: End user cybercrime reporting: what we know and what we can do to improve it. In: 2016 IEEE International Conference on Cybercrime and Computer Forensic (ICCCF), pp. 1–6 (2016)

3. Buermeyer, U.: Gutachterliche Stellungnahme zur öffentlichen Anhörung zur For-mulierungshilfe des BMJV zur Einführung von Rechtsgrundlagen für Online-Durchsuchung und Quellen-TKUe im Strafprozess - Ausschussdrucksache (2017)
4. Cermak, M., Svorencik, S., Lipovsky, R.: KR00K - CVE-2019-15126: Serious vul-nerability deep inside your Wi-Fi encryption (2020). https://www.welivesecurity.com/wp-content/uploads/2020/02/ESET_Kr00k.pdf
5. DPA: Forscher entdecken Sicherheitslücken bei WPA2 (2017). https://www.handelsblatt.com/technik/it-internet/wlan-verschluesslung-forscher-entdecken-sicherheitsluecken-bei-wpa2/20461320.html. Accessed 23 June 2020
6. Farhang, S., Kirdan, M.B., Laszka, A., Grossklags, J.: An empirical study of Android security bulletins in different vendors. In: Proceedings of the Web Con-ference (WWW), pp. 3063–3069 (2020)
7. Farhang, S., Weidman, J., Kamani, M.M., Grossklags, J., Liu, P.: Take it or leave it: a survey study on operating system upgrade practices. In: Proceedings of the 34th Annual Computer Security Applications Conference (ACSAC), pp. 490–504 (2018)
8. Google LLC: Learn when you'll get Android updates on Pixel phones & Nexus devices (2020). https://support.google.com/nexus/answer/4457705. Accessed 21 June 2020
9. Microsoft Inc.: Windows lifecycle fact sheet (2020). https://support.microsoft.com/de-de/help/13853/windows-lifecycle-fact-sheet. Accessed 21 June 2020
10. Poole, E.S., Chetty, M., Morgan, T., Grinter, R., Edwards, K.: Computer help at home: methods and motivations for informal technical support. In: SIGCHI Conference on Human Factors in Computing Systems, pp. 739–748. ACM (2009)
11. Richter, F.: How long does Apple support older iPhone models? (2019). https://www.statista.com/chart/5824/ios-iphone-compatibility/. Accessed 21 June 2020
12. Schechter, S.: Common pitfalls in writing about security and privacy human sub-jects experiments, and how to avoid them. Technical report, Microsoft, January 2013
13. SCS Computing Facilities: Operating system support lifecycle (2020). https://computing.cs.cmu.edu/desktop/os-lifecycle. Accessed 21 June 2020
14. Solove, D.: I've got nothing to hide and other misunderstandings of privacy. San Diego Law Rev. **44**, 745 (2007)
15. Tanriverdi, H.: Forscher durchlöchern Wlan-Sicherheit (2017). http://www.sueddeutsche.de/digital/it-sicherheit-krack-attack-forscher-durchloechern-globalen-wlan-standard-1.3711399. Accessed 23 June 2020
16. Vanhoef, M., Piessens, F.: Key reinstallation attacks: forcing nonce reuse in WPA2. In: ACM SIGSAC Conference on Computer and Communications Security (CCS), pp. 1313–1328 (2017)
17. Vanhoef, M., Ronen, E.: Dragonblood: analyzing the Dragonfly handshake of WPA3 and EAP-pwd. In: IEEE Symposium on Security & Privacy (S&P). IEEE (2020)
18. Viehboeck, S.: Vodafone Easybox default WPS PIN algorithm weakness (2012). https://sec-consult.com/fxdata/seccons/prod/temedia/advisories_txt/20130805-0_Vodafone_EasyBox_Default_WPS_PIN_Vulnerability_v10.txt. Accessed 23 June 2020

19. Wi-Fi Alliance: Wi-Fi in 2019 (2019). https://www.wi-fi.org/news-events/newsroom/wi-fi-in-2019. Accessed 23 June 2020
20. Wigle.net: Statistics (2020). https://wigle.net/stats. Accessed 21 June 2020
21. Wischnjak, D.: Immer Ärger mit der Easybox (2014). https://www.heise.de/security/artikel/Immer-Aerger-mit-der-EasyBox-2294914.html. Accessed 23 June 2020

Usable Security

Exploring the Meaning of "Usable Security"

Markus Lennartsson, Joakim Kävrestad$^{(\boxtimes)}$, and Marcus Nohlberg

University of Skövde, Skövde, Sweden
{markus.lennartsson,joakim.kavrestad,marcus.nohlberg}@his.se

Abstract. While there are many examples of incidents that make the need for more work around the human aspects of security apparent, the literature makes it obvious that usable security can mean many different things and usable security is a complex matter. This paper reports on a structured literature review that analyzed what the research community considers to be included in the term "usable security". Publications from the past five years were analyzed and different perceptions of usable security were gathered. The result is a listing of the different aspects that are discussed under the term "usable security" and can be used as a reference for future research of practitioners who are developing security functions with usability in mind .

Keywords: Information security · Usable · Usability

1 Introduction

A lot of attention is currently given to the human, or user, side of information security and it is widely acknowledged that user behavior is a crucial factor in information security [74]. An important topic in this area is usable security, the notion that security tools and measures have to live up to usability demands in order to function as intended [73]. Tools that are lacking in usability are likely to not be used at all or be used incorrectly. If a given tool is not used, the security value that it is supposed to add will be lost. A tool that is used incorrectly can give a false sense of security, or even have a negative impact on security [81].

While there are many papers that provide usability evaluations on various tools and techniques, there is an ambiguity in the research community as to what the concept of usable security actually encompasses. There are several examples of papers that discuss or validate usability and two examples are [79] that evaluates certain usability criteria of a phishing defense mechanism and another is [75] where usability in access control in IoT is discussed. While valuable pieces of research, none of them discuss usability in a broader sense. Further, [77] evaluates usability around the keywords "convenience, annoyance, time-consuming and tiring" and builds on the System Usability Scale (SUS) presented by [72]. While the SUS scale measures important aspects of usability, it does not factor

© IFIP International Federation for Information Processing 2020
Published by Springer Nature Switzerland AG 2020
N. Clarke and S. Furnell (Eds.): HAISA 2020, IFIP AICT 593, pp. 247–258, 2020.
https://doi.org/10.1007/978-3-030-57404-8_19

in ideas that [81] consider essential in usable security, for instance, that users should not make dangerous errors.

The existing research demonstrates that usable security is a complex area with many dimensions. However, to the best of our knowledge, there is no common definition or understanding of what the term actually includes. The aim of this paper is to address this gap by reviewing how the term is applied in recent research. The result will describe what researchers mean with usable security and can be used as a reference for future studies. Future research will build on this paper with the goal of establishing evaluation criteria for usability is security tools and measures designed to be used by end-users.

2   Methodology

The research was carried out using a structured literature review targeting research published in the past five years. The review followed the process described by [78]. The outcomes of a literature review are heavily dependent on the databases used, search terms are chosen, and the criteria applied to select relevant literature [76,80]. The databases and search terms used in this study are shown in Table 1, below.

Table 1. List of used databases and search terms

Databases	Search terms
ACM Digital library	"usable security"
IEEExplore	
Springer Link	
dblp (Digital Bibliography & Library Project)	usability AND security
ArXiv	
SCOPUS	
CSCAN HAISA	

The initial searches resulted in 378 articles, papers that were duplicates or failed to meet inclusion criteria were removed resulting in 49 papers that were selected for further analysis. Backward snowballing, as described by [82], was employed and resulted in another 21 papers, resulting in 70 papers that were included for the study. Table 2 presents the inclusion and exclusion criteria used in this study and Table 3 shows the result of the initial selection process. Table 4 shows the results of the backward snowballing.

The selected papers were analysed, using the software MAXQDA, using thematic coding as described by [71].

Table 2. Inclusion and exclusion criteria

Inclusion criteria	Exclusion criteria
IC1: Published between 2015 and 2020	EC1: Publication occurs multiple times
IC2: Published in peer-reviewed journal or conference	EC2: Fails to meet inclusion criteria
IC3: Publication is relevant to the topic	EC3: Payment required for access
IC4: Written in English, Swedish or German	EC4: Dubious description of method or results

Table 3. Initial search process

Resource	Search date	Hits	Eliminated due to:				Accepted
			EC1	EC2	EC3	EC4	
ACM Dig. Lib	20200102	12	145	159	15	10	49
IEEExplore	20200102	68					
Springer Link	20200102	14					
dblp	20200102	142					
ArXiv	20200102	20					
SCOPUS	20200111	102					
CSCAN HAISA	20200103	20					

Table 4. Snowballing process

Resource	Search date	Hits	Eliminated due to:							Accepted
			IC1	IC2	IC3	IC4	EC1	EC3	EC4	
References in publications from stage I	20200116	1641	1250	161	147	57	1	3	1	21

3   Results

Following the selection process, the included papers were analyzed using thematic coding. First, high-level aspects of usable security were identified. They were then refined into subcategories. The results are summarized in Fig. 1, below, where the high-level aspects and their subcategories are displayed. The number in parenthesis shows the number of papers connected to a given subcategory.

The remainder of this chapter will describe the discovered aspects of usable security. The papers classified in each aspect will be referenced continuously and are listed in the reference list, preceded by an asterisk (*).

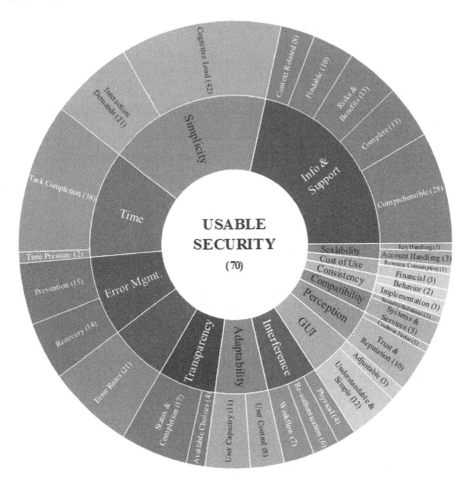

Fig. 1. Identified aspects of Usable Security. The number in parenthesis display the number of publications relation to each sub-category.

Cost of Use: This aspect addresses factors that users tend to perceive as inconvenient in terms of cost-effectiveness. *Financial* costs are mentioned repeatedly [1,25,34] and one publication [1] states that *resource consumption* (e. g. battery) might be of significance.

Consistency: Security solutions are perceived as usable when they are operating predictably. This applies to matters of *behavior* [31,34], meaning that similar tasks work identically, and *implementation* [6,55,57] factors including standardized setups, consistent phrasing, and design that allows to easily recognize requirements and conditions.

Perception: Willingness to adopt security solutions depends partially on how they are perceived by individuals. One aspect relates to *trust and reputation* [4,10–12,25,36,45,60,61,67]. Multiple studies report that users prefer solutions they feel confident with. Such beliefs arise when a solution is from reputable sources, verified by experts, or recommended. Additionally, the *coolness factor* [61] of authentication schemes might be another contributing aspect.

GUI (Graphical User Interface): This aspect is concerned with the way the GUI is constructed. First, it should be *understandable and simple* [5, 34, 40, 48, 49, 51, 54, 55, 57, 59, 66, 69]. This includes visualization of navigation options and clear menu arrangements in accordance to what users might anticipate. Also, the GUI should not require unnecessary user attention and merely display information necessary for decision making. A GUI that is *adjustable* [6, 31, 55] to the user's preferences increases usability since it improves learnability.

Scalability: Another factor is the extent to which security solutions can deal with multiple user accounts and security keys. Usable *account handling* [22, 24, 57] does not restrict the number of allowed user accounts and allows to operate multiple accounts with mutual keys. Concerning *key handling* [12], a scalable solution should be able to install and control multiple keys without complicating usage.

Compatibility: Security solutions should be compatible with commonly used *systems and services* [1, 20, 22, 24, 57] to be perceived as usable. The trend of developing new security solutions with separate and fragmented user bases is a hinder to usability. Compatibility with other *security solutions* [1] is crucial since users will presumably reject overly incompatible products such as communication tools that only allow conversations with other instances of themselves.

Adaptability: How well a security solution can be adapted to the specific needs of individuals represents an important factor according to 19 publications. The first subcategory deal with the amount of allowed *user control* [20, 22, 28, 31, 40, 49, 55, 69]. Enabling users to customize configurations to their preferences increases convenience. Facilitating memorability by allowing users to choose their own passwords is also advantageous. Regarding *user capacity* [5, 12, 18, 27, 28, 34, 38, 49, 51, 55, 70], security solutions should be adaptable to various expertise levels and be able to, preferably intelligently, adapt to individual abilities and disabilities.

Interference: Usability is reduced when users' primary tasks are disturbed. The first subcategory addresses *workflow* [20, 26, 27, 30, 49, 53, 63] interference. Necessary security actions should be arranged in ways that minimize interruptions. Even *re-authentication* [3, 6, 14, 24, 27, 39] requests are described as disruptive and inconvenient . They can be perceived as wasted time and cause increased complexity. Also, compelling users to remember passwords repeatedly interrupts other tasks since enforced context switches may cause confusion. Finally, there is a *physical* [15, 56, 57, 61] category to this aspect. Users are anxious to lack immediate access to a token when needed, fear of loss or theft are common.

Error Rate: [3, 4, 17, 20, 21, 26, 33–40, 53, 57, 58, 63, 66, 68, 70] To which extent a security solution enables users to conduct their primary task without having to deal with annoying completion failures is a prominent usability precondition.

Increasing error rates cause substantial inconvenience since users are forced to repeat actions. Solutions become ineffective since they are unable to complete tasks as intended. In this context, it is secondary if errors are caused directly by the system or indirectly via users. When security solutions are error-prone, users may choose to circumvent them to preserve usability.

Error Management: Effective means of *prevention* [4,6,20,28,31,33,34,48, 49,54,55,57,59,67,69] are required to reduce error rates. Users should be provided with clear and simple instructions that help to prevent frequent errors. Incorrect operations can be prevented by automatic means such as input validity checks. Before errors occur, easy-to-understand warning messages should be communicated clearly and point out problem causes. Making users aware of their actions' negative consequences beforehand is beneficial. If such hints go unheeded, execution should be rejected. If errors cannot be prevented, proper means of error *recovery* [4,8,12,14,20,22,29,34,40,40,49,54,55,57] should exist to maintain usability. One way to recover is to allow users to cancel or revert their actions. Laborious recovery procedures are harmful to usability. Giving simple hints about causes and recommended actions are preferable. Users should be empowered to address most errors without external help, but help should still be available if needed.

Simplicity: A great quantity of studies report that users become overwhelmed by overly complex systems. Lots of papers stress that the *cognitive load* [2,3,5–7,9–15,19,21,22,24,26,28,30,30,33,34,36,39–42,44,45,49,51–55,57,60,62–64,66,67] put on users needs to be minimized to preserve usability. Reducing the amount of required knowledge , things a user has to recall , or the number of available choices and necessary decisions are important in this context. This also applies for frequent task switching demands. Also, default configurations should be appropriate and safe to use. Twenty-one publications find that high amounts of *interaction demands* [1,3,4,6,10,12,16,20,22,24,25,30,37, 42,46,58,60–62,64,67] affect usability negatively since users generally favor solutions that don't require significant effort. Necessary interaction should be simple. Integrating security solutions into existing well-known systems reduces required efforts. So does centralized authentication.

Info and Support: This aspect is addressed by the second largest amount of studies. It covers how information should be presented to users. Firstly, it should be highly *comprehensible* [1,2,4–6,9,12,15,20,22,27,28,31,33,34,40, 41,49,51,55,57–59,66,67,69,70] in both formulation and amount. Low abstraction levels facilitate understanding by non-experts. Reasonable amounts prevent overexertion of users. Furthermore, information needs to be *findable* [1,15,20–22,28,41,49,55,59,67], meaning that users should not have to conduct taxing searches, especially external ones. Information should also be *complete* [4–6,9,12,14,27,31,34,43,55,57,59] enough to sufficiently address potential problems regarding all functionalities. Explaining *risks & benefits* [9,11,12,21–23,26,28,51,55,59,60,70] of security solutions and particular user decisions reduces usability issues and increases trust. Making users aware of threats and consequences helps increasing acceptance of security requirements and enables better system understanding and utilization. *Context related* [6, 21, 22, 28, 55, 59, 62, 65] information corresponds directly to executed tasks and allows to exhibit specifically required actions without the need to interrupt said tasks. This reduces perceived complexity and strain.

Transparency: Systems should be transparent regarding *status and completion* [11, 22, 27, 36, 42, 46, 48–50, 54, 55, 57, 58, 61, 62, 67]. Feedback should be provided about underlying mechanisms, the progress of security actions, the system's status, and task completion. This approach facilitates trust and reduces error rates. Providing knowledge about *available choices* [11, 28, 33, 65] when users need to make important decisions helps them to react properly and reduces error rates.

Time: Secondary only to cognitive load, invested time until successful *task completion* [4, 7, 11, 14, 16–20, 24, 28, 30–35, 37–40, 42, 44, 46, 47, 49, 51, 53, 54, 56, 58, 59, 61, 64–66, 68, 70] is one of the most prominent usability aspects. Inefficient time utilization due to delays can impair users' primary objectives and thereby reduce usability significantly. Periods of delay and idle waiting should be minimized. Additionally, putting users under *time pressure* [56, 68] by time-out settings increases error rates and stress levels and reduces perceived usability.

4   Conclusions

This paper aimed to summarize the meaning of usable security by analyzing recently published research to identify the dimensions that encompass the term usable security. Using a structured literature review, this research identified 70 papers from the past five years that discussed the topic of usable security. Using thematic coding, 14 aspects were created from analyzing the included papers, the aspects were then refined into 31 subcategories that describe usability factors for security measures. The most discussed subcategories dictate that the time needed to complete security tasks, the cognitive load added by security tasks and the ease of completing security tasks. While this research does not attempt to weight the different identified aspects, this aligns well with the common understanding of a need for time-efficient and easy-to-use security functions.

The results of this paper is a summary of current research that can help researchers as well as practitioners to better understand the topic of usable security, a necessity in implementing user-centred security measures and applications. It also provides a better understanding of the users roles and challenges in security and can be used as a reference model when developing security functions, applications and procedures. While this research employs measures such as backwards snowballing to be as complete as possible, a given limitation is that it relies on previous research. A possible impact on that is that no previously unknown usability factors has been discovered.

An apparent direction for future work would be to research the identified usability factors from a user-centred standpoint. Such a project could aim to include users in an attempt to weight the different factors according to the users perception. Another direction for future work would be to continue the research by developing concrete guidelines for implementation of user-centered security. Such a project would include practitioners as well as researchers and users.

References

1. * Abu-Salma, R., Sasse, M.A., Bonneau, J., Danilova, A., Naiakshina, A., Smith, M.: Obstacles to the adoption of secure communication tools. In: 2017 IEEE Symposium on Security and Privacy, pp. 137–153 (2017)
2. * Acar, Y., Fahl, S., Mazurek, M.L.: You are not your developer, either: a research agenda for usable security and privacy research beyond end users. In: 2016 IEEE SecDev, pp. 3–8 (2016)
3. * Al Abdulwahid, A., Clarke, N., Stengel, I., Furnell, S, Reich, C.: Security, privacy and usability – a survey of users' perceptions and attitudes. In: Fischer-Hübner, Simone, Lambrinoudakis, Costas, Lopez, Javier (eds.) TrustBus 2015. LNCS, vol. 9264, pp. 153–168. Springer, Cham (2015). https://doi.org/10.1007/978-3-319-22906-5_12
4. * Al-Sarayreh, K.T., Hasan, L.A., Almakadmeh, K.: A trade-off model of software requirements for balancing between security and usability issues. Int. Rev. Comput. Softw. **10**(12), 1157–1168 (2015)
5. * Alarifi, A., Alsaleh, M., Alomar, N.: A model for evaluating the security and usability of e-banking platforms. Computing **99**(5), 519–535 (2017)
6. * Almutairi, E., Al-Megren, S.: Usability and security analysis of the keepkey wallet. In: 2019 IEEE ICBC, pp. 149–153 (2019)
7. * Alshamsi, A., Williams, N., Andras, P.: The trade-off between usability and security in the context of egovernment: a mapping study. Proc. BCS-HCI **30**, 1–13 (2016)
8. * Alshanketi, F., Traore, I., Ahmed, A.A.: Improving performance and usability in mobile keystroke dynamic biometric authentication. In: 2016 IEEE SPW, pp. 66–73. IEEE (2016)
9. * Andriotis, P., Oikonomou, G.C., Mylonas, A., Tryfonas, T.: A study on usability and security features of the android pattern lock screen. Inf. Comput. Secur. **24**(1), 53–72 (2016)
10. * Atwater, E., Bocovich, C., Hengartner, U., Lank, E., Goldberg, I.: Leading Johnny to water: designing for usability and trust. In: SOUPS 2015 (2015)
11. * Bai, W., Kim, D., Namara, M., Qian, Y., Kelley, P.G., Mazurek, M.L.: Balancing security and usability in encrypted email. IEEE Internet Comput. **21**(3), 30–38 (2017)
12. * Bai, W., Namara, M., Qian, Y., Kelley, P.G., Mazurek, M.L., Kim, D.: An inconvenient trust: user attitudes toward security and usability tradeoffs for key-directory encryption systems. In: SOUPS 2016, pp. 113–130 (2016)
13. * Belk, M., Pamboris, A., Fidas, C., Katsini, C., Avouris, N., Samaras, G.: Sweet-spotting security and usability for intelligent graphical authentication mechanisms. In: WIMS, vol. 17, pp. 252–259 (2017)
14. * Benenson, Z., Lenzini, G., Oliveira, D., Parkin, S., Uebelacker, S.: Maybe poor Johnny really cannot encrypt: the case for a complexity theory for usable security. In: NSPW 2015, pp. 85–99 (2015)
15. * Bhagavatula, R., Ur, B., Iacovino, K., Kywe, S.M., Cranor, L.F., Savvides, M.: Biometric authentication on iphone and android: usability, perceptions, and influences on adoption. In: USEC. Citeseer (2015)

16. * Bindu, C.S.: Secure usable authentication using strong pass text passwords. In: IJCNIS (2015)

17. * Bošnjak, L., Brumen, B.: Examining security and usability aspects of knowledge-based authentication methods. In: 2019 MIPRO, pp. 1181–1186 (2019)

18. * Caputo, D.D., Pfleeger, S.L., Sasse, M.A., Ammann, P., Offutt, J., Deng, L.: Barriers to usable security? Three organizational case studies. IEEE Secur. Priv. **14**(5), 22–32 (2016)

19. * Carbone, R., Ranise, S., Sciarretta, G.: Design and security assessment of usable multi-factor authentication and single sign-on solutions for mobile applications. In: Kosta, E., Pierson, J., Slamanig, D., Fischer-Hübner, S., Krenn, S. (eds.) Privacy and Identity 2018. IAICT, vol. 547, pp. 51–66. Springer, Cham (2019). https://doi.org/10.1007/978-3-030-16744-8_4

20. * Colnago, J., Devlin, S., Oates, M., Swoopes, C., Bauer, L., Cranor, L.F., Christin, N.: "it's not actually that horrible": exploring adoption of two-factor authentication at a university. In: CHI 2018 (2018)

21. * Das, S., Dingman, A., Camp, L.J.: Why Johnny doesn't use two factor a two-phase usability study of the FIDO U2F security key. In: Meiklejohn, Sarah, Sako, Kazue (eds.) FC 2018. LNCS, vol. 10957, pp. 160–179. Springer, Heidelberg (2018). https://doi.org/10.1007/978-3-662-58387-6_9

22. * Das, S., Russo, G., Dingman, A.C., Dev, J., Kenny, O., Camp, L.J.: A qualitative study on usability and acceptability of yubico security key. In: STAST 2017, pp. 28–39. ACM (2018)

23. * Das, S., Wang, B., Tingle, Z., Camp, L.J.: Evaluating user perception of multi-factor authentication: a systematic review. arXiv preprint arXiv:1908.05901 (2019)

24. * Ebert, A., Marouane, C., Rott, B., Werner, M.: KeyPocket - improving security and usability for provider independent login architectures with mobile devices. In: Thuraisingham, Bhavani, Wang, XiaoFeng, Yegneswaran, Vinod (eds.) SecureComm 2015. LNICST, vol. 164, pp. 41–57. Springer, Cham (2015). https://doi.org/10.1007/978-3-319-28865-9_3

25. * Fagan, M., Khan, M.M.H.: Why do they do what they do?: A study of what motivates users to (not) follow computer security advice. In: SOUPS 2016, pp. 59–75 (2016)

26. * Feth, D.: User-centric security: optimization of the security-usability trade-off. In: ESEC/FSE 2015, pp. 1034–1037 (2015)

27. * Tryfonas, T., (ed.): HAS 2017. LNCS, vol. 10292. Springer, Cham (2017). https://doi.org/10.1007/978-3-319-58460-7

28. * Feth, D., Polst, S.: Heuristics and models for evaluating the usability of security measures. In: MUC 2019, pp. 275–285 (2019)

29. * Fukumitsu, M., Hasegawa, S., Iwazaki, J., Sakai, M., Takahashi, D.: A proposal of a password manager satisfying security and usability by using the secret sharing and a personal server. In: AINA 2016, pp. 661–668 (2016)

30. * Glass, B., Jenkinson, G., Liu, Y., Sasse, M.A., Stajano, F.: The usability canary in the security coal mine: a cognitive framework for evaluation and design of usable authentication solutions. arXiv preprint arXiv:1607.03417 (2016)

31. * Gordieiev, O., Kharchenko, V.S., Vereshchak, K.: Usable security versus secure usability: an assessment of attributes interaction. In: ICTERI (2017)

32. * Goudalo, W., Kolski, C.: Towards advanced enterprise information systems engineering. In: ICEIS 2016, pp. 400–411 (2016)

33. * Green, M., Smith, M.: Developers are not the enemy!: The need for usable security apis. IEEE Secur. Priv. **14**(5), 40–46 (2016)

34. * Hasan, L.A., Al-Sarayreh, K.T.: An integrated measurement model for evaluating usability attributes. In: IPAC 2015. ACM (2015)
35. * Hausawi, Y.M., Allen, W.H.: Usable-security evaluation. In: HAS 2015 (2015)
36. * İşler, D., Küpçü, A., Coskun, A.: User perceptions of security and usability of mobile-based single password authentication and two-factor authentication. In: Pérez-Solà, Cristina, Navarro-Arribas, Guillermo, Biryukov, Alex, Garcia-Alfaro, Joaquin (eds.) DPM/CBT -2019. LNCS, vol. 11737, pp. 99–117. Springer, Cham (2019). https://doi.org/10.1007/978-3-030-31500-9_7
37. * Karapanos, N., Marforio, C., Soriente, C., Capkun, S.: Sound-proof: Usable two-factor authentication based on ambient sound. In: USENIX 2015 (2015)
38. * Katsini, C., Belk, M., Fidas, C., Avouris, N., Samaras, G.: Security and usability in knowledge-based user authentication: a review. PCI **16**, 1–6 (2016)
39. * Khan, H., Hengartner, U., Vogel, D.: Usability and security perceptions of implicit authentication: convenient, secure, sometimes annoying. In: SOUPS 2015, pp. 225–239 (2015)
40. * Khodadadi, T., Islam, A.K.M.M., Baharun, S., Komaki, S.: Evaluation of recognition-based graphical password schemes in terms of usability and security attributes. Int. J. Electr. Comput. Eng. **6**(6), 2939–2948 (2016)
41. * Krombholz, K., Mayer, W., Schmiedecker, M., Weippl, E.: " i have no idea what i'm doing"-on the usability of deploying {HTTPS}. In: USENIX 2017, pp. 1339–1356 (2017)
42. * Lerner, A., Zeng, E., Roesner, F.: Confidante: usable encrypted email: a case study with lawyers and journalists. In: EuroS&P 2017, pp. 385–400 (2017)
43. * Ling, Z., Borgeest, M., Sano, C., Lin, S., Fadl, M., Yu, W., Fu, X., Zhao, W.: A case study of usable security: usability testing of android privacy enhancing keyboard. In: Ma, L., Khreishah, A., Zhang, Y., Yan, M. (eds.) WASA 2017. LNCS, vol. 10251, pp. 716–728. Springer, Cham (2017). https://doi.org/10.1007/978-3-319-60033-8_61
44. * Mayron, L.M.: Biometric authentication on mobile devices. IEEE Secur. Priv. **13**, 70–73 (2015)
45. * McGregor, S.E., Charters, P., Holliday, T., Roesner, F.: Investigating the computer security practices and needs of journalists. In: USENIX 2015, pp. 399–414 (2015)
46. * Melicher, W., Kurilova, D., Segreti, S.M., Kalvani, P., Shay, R., Ur, B., Bauer, L., Christin, N., Cranor, L.F., Mazurek, M.L.: Usability and security of text passwords on mobile devices. In: CHI 2016, pp. 527–539 (2016)
47. * Meng, W., Liu, Z.: TMGMap: designing touch movement-based geographical password authentication on smartphones. In: Su, C., Kikuchi, H. (eds.) ISPEC 2018. LNCS, vol. 11125, pp. 373–390. Springer, Cham (2018). https://doi.org/10.1007/978-3-319-99807-7_23
48. * Merdanoğlum, N., Onay Durdu, P.: A systematic mapping study of usability vs security. In: CEIT 2018. pp. 1–6 (2018)
49. * Napoli, D.: Developing accessible and usable security (accus) heuristics. In: Extended Abstracts of the CHI 2018, pp. 1–6 (2018)
50. * Naqvi, B., Seffah, A.: Interdependencies, Conflicts and trade-offs between security and usability: why and how should we engineer them? In: Moallem, A. (ed.) HCII 2019. LNCS, vol. 11594, pp. 314–324. Springer, Cham (2019). https://doi.org/10.1007/978-3-030-22351-9_21
51. * Nwokedi, U.O., Onyimbo, B.A., Rad, B.B.: Usability and security in user interface design: a systematic literature review. Int. J. Inf. Technol. Comput. Sci. **8**, 72–80 (2016)

52. * Oluwafemi, A.J., Feng, J.H.: Usability and security: a case study of emergency communication system authentication. In: Stephanidis, C. (ed.) HCII 2019. CCIS, vol. 1032, pp. 205–210. Springer, Cham (2019). https://doi.org/10.1007/978-3-030-23522-2_26

53. * Patil, A.D., De Meer, H.: Usability of it-security in smart grids. In: e-Energy 2018, pp. 393–395. ACM (2018)

54. * Qin, L., Lapets, A., Jansen, F., Flockhart, P., Albab, K.D., Globus-Harris, I., Roberts, S., Varia, M.: From usability to secure computing and back again. In: SOUPS 2019 (2019)

55. * Realpe, P.C., Collazos, C.A., Hurtado, J., Granollers, A.: A set of heuristics for usable security and user authentication. In: Interacción 2016, pp. 1–8. ACM (2016)

56. * Reese, K., Smith, T., Dutson, J., Armknecht, J., Cameron, J., Seamons, K.: A usability study of five two-factor authentication methods. In: SOUPS 2019 (2019)

57. * Reynolds, J., Smith, T., Reese, K., Dickinson, L., Ruoti, S., Seamons, K.: A tale of two studies: the best and worst of yubikey usability. In: 2018 IEEE Symposium on Security and Privacy, pp. 872–888 (2018)

58. * Ruoti, S., Andersen, J., Heidbrink, S., O'Neill, M., Vaziripour, E., Wu, J., Zappala, D., Seamons, K.E.: "we're on the same page": a usability study of secure email using pairs of novice users. In: CHI 2016 (2016)

59. * Ruoti, S., Andersen, J., Hendershot, T., Zappala, D., Seamons, K.E.: Private webmail 2.0: simple and easy-to-use secure email. In: UIST 2016 (2016)

60. * Ruoti, S., Andersen, J., Monson, T., Zappala, D., Seamons, K.: A comparative usability study of key management in secure email. In: SOUPS 2018, pp. 375–394 (2018)

61. * Ruoti, S., Roberts, B., Seamons, K.E.: Authentication melee: a usability analysis of seven web authentication systems. In: WWW 2015 (2015)

62. * Ruoti, S., Seamons, K.E.: Johnny's journey toward usable secure email. IEEE Secur. Priv. **17**(6), 72–76 (2019)

63. * Sasse, A.: Scaring and bullying people into security won't work. IEEE Secur. Priv. **13**(3), 80–83 (2015)

64. * Schwab, D., ALharbi, L., Nichols, O., Yang, L.: Picture passdoodle: usability study. In: IEEE Big Data Service 2018, pp. 293–298 (2018)

65. * Shay, R., et al.: A spoonful of sugar?: the impact of guidance and feedback on password-creation behavior. In: CHI 2015, pp. 2903–2912. ACM (2015)

66. * Shirvanian, M., Saxena, N.: On the security and usability of crypto phones. In: ACSAC 2015, pp. 21–30 (2015)

67. * Vaziripour, E., Wu, J., O'Neill, M., Whitehead, J., Heidbrink, S., Seamons, K.E., Zappala, D.: Is that you, alice? A usability study of the authentication ceremony of secure messaging applications. In: SOUPS 2017 (2017)

68. * Wang, T., Ge, H., Chowdhury, O., Maji, H.K., Li, N.: On the security and usability of segment-based visual cryptographic authentication protocols. In: CCS 2016, pp. 603–615 (2016)

69. * Weber, S., Harbach, M., Smith, M.: Participatory design for security-related user interfaces. In: USEC 2015, p. 15 (2015)

70. * Wolf, F., Kuber, R., Aviv, A.J.: "pretty close to a must-have" balancing usability desire and security concern in biometric adoption. In: CHI 2019, pp. 1–12 (2019)

71. Braun, V., Clarke, V.: Using thematic analysis in psychology. Qual. Res. Psychol. **3**(2), 77–101 (2006)

72. Brooke, J.: Sus-a quick and dirty usability scale. Usability Eval. Ind. **189**(194), 4–7 (1996)

73. Das, S., Dingman, A., Camp, L.J.: Why Johnny doesn't use two factor a two-phase usability study of the FIDO U2F security key. In: FC 2018 (2018)
74. Furnell, S., Esmael, R., Yang, W., Li, N.: Enhancing security behaviour by supporting the user. Comput. Secur. **75**, 1–9 (2018)
75. He, W., Golla, M., Padhi, R., Ofek, J., Dürmuth, M., Fernandes, E., Ur, B.: Rethinking access control and authentication for the home internet of things (IoT). In: USENIX 2018, pp. 255–272 (2018)
76. Jesson, J., Matheson, L., Lacey, F.M.: Doing Your Literature Review: Traditional and Systematic Techniques. Sage, London (2011)
77. Khan, H., Hengartner, U., Vogel, D.: Usability and security perceptions of implicit authentication: convenient, secure, sometimes annoying. In: SOUPS 2015, pp. 225–239 (2015)
78. Kitchenham, B.: Procedures for performing systematic reviews. Keele, UK, Keele University **33**, 1–26 (2004)
79. Marchal, S., Armano, G., Gröndahl, T., Saari, K., Singh, N., Asokan, N.: Off-the-hook: an efficient and usable client-side phishing prevention application. IEEE Trans. Comput. **66**(10), 1717–1733 (2017)
80. Meline, T.: Selecting studies for systematic review: Inclusion and exclusion criteria. Contemporary issues in communication science and disorders **33**(21–27) (2006)
81. Whitten, A., Tygar, J.D.: Why Johnny can't encrypt: a usability evaluation of PGP 5.0. In: USENIX 1999, vol. 348, pp. 169–184 (1999)
82. Wohlin, C.: Guidelines for snowballing in systematic literature studies and a replication in software engineering. In: EASE 2014. Citeseer (2014)

Dyslexia and Password Usage: Accessibility in Authentication Design

Karen Renaud[1,2(✉)], Graham Johnson[1], and Jacques Ophoff[1]

[1] School of Design and Informatics, Abertay University, Dundee, UK
{k.renaud,g.johnson,j.ophoff}@abertay.ac.uk
[2] Rhodes University, Grahamstown, South Africa

Abstract. Governments and businesses are moving online with alacrity, driven by potential cost savings, changing consumer and citizen expectations, and the momentum towards general digital provision. Services are legally required to be inclusive and accessible. Now consider that almost every online service, where people have to identify themselves, requires a password. Passwords seem to be accessible, until one considers specific disabilities, one of which can lead to many challenges: dyslexia being a case in point. Dyslexia is associated with word processing and retention difficulties, and passwords are essentially words, phrases or alphanumeric combinations. We report on a literature review conducted to identify extant research into the impact of dyslexia on password usage, as well as any ameliorations that have been proposed. We discovered a relatively neglected field. We conclude with recommendations for future research into the needs of a large population of dyslexics who seem to struggle with passwords, in a world where avoiding passwords has become almost impossible. The main contribution of this paper is to highlight the difficulties dyslexics face with passwords, and to suggest some avenues for future research in this area.

Keywords: Passwords · Dyslexia · Authentication · Accessibility

1 Introduction

The ability to create, retain and enter passwords requires a number of cognitive skills. These include literacy, the ability to focus, creativity, problem-solving, decision making, attentional abilities, and the ability to keep secrets [34]. When someone enters a password, they subsequently have to be able to remember it, including the exact spelling, or order, of the password symbols. Having done so, they have to type the password, mentally tracking the position of the character typed, and advancing to the next character as they type. For many, this is straightforward. However, consider how one specific disability, dyslexia, affects this process. Dyslexia has been defined [20] as: "...*a specific learning disability that is neurobiological in origin. It is characterized by difficulties with accurate and/or fluent word recognition and by poor spelling and decoding abilities... Secondary consequences may include problems in reading comprehension and reduced reading experience that can impede growth of vocabulary and background knowledge.*"

© IFIP International Federation for Information Processing 2020
Published by Springer Nature Switzerland AG 2020
N. Clarke and S. Furnell (Eds.): HAISA 2020, IFIP AICT 593, pp. 259–268, 2020.
https://doi.org/10.1007/978-3-030-57404-8_20

Powell et al. [33] consider dyslexia as something of a mismatch between overall cognitive and language ability. They state that this mismatch and extent of disability varies from person to person. Dyslexics generally have poor handwriting, spelling and reading. They sometimes have poor short-term memory abilities and can organise themselves inadequately. On the other hand, many are particularly strong at visualisation, spatial awareness, creativity, and lateral thinking [52].

The research literature into dyslexia, which spans many years, is extensive and occasionally contradictory, with continued debates, especially in the domains of definition and diagnosis. As Kirby [23] points out: "*it is useful to think of dyslexia as a both an ongoing psychological diagnosis and a social construct, with all that entails*" (p.59).

Whatever its nature, the difficulties experienced by dyslexics are clear. One particular difficulty lies in processing sequenced symbolic information [33]. Morris et al. [30] explored the impact of dyslexia on web searching, given the need to be able to spell and read efficaciously, and recommend enhancing readability into search interfaces to help dyslexics. Powell et al. [33] suggest a number of guidelines for the design of websites to accommodate those with dyslexia; however, these are not necessarily applicable to authentication design where passwords are the dependency. De Santana et al. [11] also derived a number of guidelines to inform the design of accessible websites for dyslexics.

However, creating, remembering and entering passwords also requires skills that many dyslexics tend to struggle with [37]. Helkala [19] explores the dimensions of these difficulties. Spelling is particularly challenging for dyslexics [15]. Spelling of words is unstable, with many dyslexics spelling the same word differently on different days, with frequent confusion of letter ordering within words. Figure 1 demonstrates the difficulties dyslexics experience in reading, via the example of relatively simple words. Figure 2 demonstrates how a password such as "Belladonna!" could be altered due to dyslexia.

Fig. 1. This image demonstrates how dyslexics might see words [25] (p.5).

Fig. 2. This image demonstrates how dyslexics might enter a password

Some estimates suggest that up to 20% of English speakers suffer from dyslexia [30]. Given the fact that, at least in the European Union, websites are required to ensure accessibility, and as the W3C advises [49], we cannot ignore the fact that passwords and dyslexia might well be a problematical combination. There is evidence that some dyslexics make use of spelling checkers to alleviate or correct the errors they might make in other web uses [2]. On the other hand, spell-checkers are an inappropriate tool to alleviate password-related issues, nor are electronic readers useful in this respect [37].

Other opportunities to explore authentication options, for example in the recent design of ATM (Automated Teller Machine) interface to accommodate dyslexics [44], have not focused upon this aspect of PIN authentication. Alternatives such as biometrics [8, 38] or alternative visual approaches (e.g. [9, 10]) have also been proposed. Shih et al. [43] have attempted to address the core elements of the interaction design in terms of fonts, ordering, colours and contrast, and so forth, as do, for instance, UX Movement [47]. We wanted to find guidelines that applied specifically to authentication design, and to the most widely used authentication mechanism, the password. As a relative of the password, the verification and confirmation codes, and on-time passwords, which continue to proliferate, will require attention we assume. The next section outlines how we went about doing this.

2 Literature Review

We searched the literature to exhaustively to find out what the research had to teach us about how dyslexics cope with passwords, the challenges they experience, and the solutions proposed to help them. We used the search term: ("dyslexia" or "dyslexic") and "passwords". Papers were included if they reported on dyslexics using passwords. In terms of criteria, if dyslexia was only mentioned in passing, or the paper was not considering passwords, then this was excluded from our comprehensive search results. As recommended by Lowry [27], we searched Academic Search Premier, SCOPUS, Social Science Citation Index, Science Citation Index, ACM Digital Library, IEEE Xplore, Springer, JSTOR, ProQuest, PsychInfo and ERIC.

Our simplified and truncated review meant that peer reviewed papers and chapters were included, as were postgraduate theses and related papers, although all patents were deliberately excluded. We attempted a thorough search, and adapted our criteria for inclusion as we encountered several challenges finding relevant literature in this specific area of conjunction. In many respects, we have noted a HCI (Human-Computer Interaction) bias within many of the resulting finds. Figure 3 depicts the range of research that we identified as touching on dyslexia that emerged from our literature search. It highlights the sparse attention paid to passwords across all these papers and visualises the relationship between many of the key areas.

Our main results are illustrated in Table 1, wherein the more salient papers are grouped together within their associated topic and category. This categorisation was developed bottom-up, taking a pragmatic approach, to the drawing out these five main themes in order to develop our understanding of previous research as reflected by the literature within the domain.

Only three prior studies relate to our topic of interest. The work of Subashini and Sumitra [45], addressing disabilities and passwords, examined the use of One-Time Passwords (OTPs) and multimodal approaches in the context of banking-like authentication. Dyslexic users were studied alongside people with visual disabilities, as they advocated for approaches encompassing more than one modality. Similarly, Helkala [19] looked at some of the inherent issues in recall, delay and misspelling. The password alternative explored by Gibson et al. [16] used musical clips instead of alphanumeric strings. People chose "their" secret clip from successive challenge sets, in order to authenticate. The paper alludes to the benefits of such a scheme in improving authentication accessibility for dyslexics.

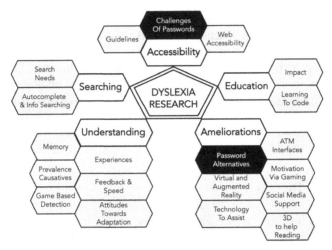

Fig. 3. Range of dyslexia related research (Password Topics Highlighted)

3 Reflections on the Literature and Emerging Trends

The literature demonstrates a growing use and application of augmented environments and approaches, perhaps as a function of advancement of technology. In line with the development of assistive technologies, designed to support those with a myriad of challenges, we predict increasing deployment of mixed reality technologies in this respect.

For many services offered online, or at least accessed after online authentication, there is a growth of hybrid and multi-step approaches. Whilst improving overall security, these are likely to negatively affect those with dyslexia. The expectation of further handling and use of passwords and extra steps being required is inherent in this approach. The OTP (one-time password) approach is similar in many regards, often requiring entry of a meaningless alphanumeric string. The way in which those with dyslexia encounter these scenarios, where ability to replicate a string perfectly is required is, thus far, relatively neglected. The research by Fuglerud and Dale [13] being a notable exception, their work tackling identity management and passwords for the elderly and those with disability.

As we are often reminded, password strength is generally encouraged, in order to improve access, and thus system security (e.g. [32]). However, it is likely that, from the viewpoint of a dyslexic user, this will worsen matters, making the task of remembering and entering the password correctly even more challenging. There are open research questions related to how dyslexics currently cope with increasing password strength requirements. Which strategies are adopted and how do these impact security and usability?

The competing constructs and requirements of security and usability have been noted as a balancing act of sorts (e.g. [18]). Our investigation highlights a third construct that cannot be ignored: that of accessibility. The Web Accessibility Initiative explains that

Table 1. Main categories of dyslexia-related research.

Understanding	
Experiences of living with dyslexia	[14, 26, 48]
Understanding prevalence and causatives and assessment	[41, 42, 46, 51]
Memory and dyslexic information interaction	[7]
Feedback and speed in digital tasks	[22]
Game-based detection of dyslexia	[37]
Attitudes among dyslexics towards adaptation	[4]
Education	
Impact of dyslexia on education	[29, 31, 39, 40]
Impact of dyslexia on learning to code	[33]
Accessibility	
Accessibility guidelines for dyslexia	[33]
Accessibility challenges of passwords	[19, 45]
Web Accessibility and approaches	[11, 28, 37]
Searching	
Search needs and behaviour	[7, 12, 30]
Autocomplete and information-searching	[3]
Ameliorations	
Password alternatives	[16]
ATM interfaces for dyslexics	[43]
Social Media support	[53]
Motivation via gaming	[17]
Multisensory three-dimensional environments to aid reading	[5]
Virtual and augmented reality environments	[21, 35]
Technology to assist learners	[6, 36]

accessibility *"addresses discriminatory aspects related to equivalent user experience for people with disabilities"* [50].

We have had over two decades to try to resolve the tension between security and usability identified by Adams and Sasse [1]. The addition of accessibility as an extra dimension undeniably adds complexity to the design process. The tensions between these three needs potentially compete with one another in the designer's mind.

Accessibility needs cannot be ignored. The UK's Disability Discrimination Act[1] of 1995 requires websites to ensure equality in access to people with all kinds of disabilities. The European Union also has an accessibility act[2] which requires those delivering

---

[1] http://www.legislation.gov.uk/ukpga/1995/50/contents.

[2] https://ec.europa.eu/social/main.jsp?catId=1202&langId=en.

products and services to accommodate the disabled. Finally, the United Nations Convention on the Rights of Persons with Disabilities[3], adopted on the 13 December 2006, is the first international, *legally binding* instrument that sets minimum standards for the rights of people with disabilities. Accessibility is clearly a legal mandate and there is no reason to believe that password authentication is excluded.

A number of researchers have highlighted existing accessibility issues that impact people with different kinds of disabilities e.g. blindness [44], age-related infirmities [47] and general accessibility failures of e-government websites [24]. It is clear that authentication design also needs to ensure accessibility to accommodate the needs of dyslexics and people with other disabilities, in addition to paying attention to security and usability design considerations.

Limitation of our investigation into dyslexia and password usage, reported here, include our focus solely on English language literature, excluding all literature in other languages. In addition, we adopted a narrow, security-focus, in our review and examination of this condition, as opposed to a addressing much broader social and psychological perspective.

4   Discussion and Recommendations for Future Research

In summary, from our practical review of the literature, and the discovery of this largely neglected topic of dyslexia in the context of password usage, we propose several recommendations for future research. These are:

1) *Real-world coping strategies and behaviours* – given the dearth of studies in the area of dyslexia and password usage, research is needed to study how dyslexic users of systems approach password creation, retention and everyday use. It is likely that coping strategies are, to a certain extent, common across this group, and may lead to suggestions as to how we may design more accessible and dyslexic-friendly authentication approaches.

2) *Password managers and their adoption* – in what ways can we refine and adapt approaches to strong and yet centralised passwords to enable a more convenient usage experience for those experiencing dyslexia challenges. How can this be implemented effectively across multiple devices and platforms, e.g. mobile devices.

3) *Multi-factor authentication* – where some tokens are to be remembered, or indeed, where OTPs have to be entered, are clearly going to negatively impact dyslexics. How can these mechanisms be made more accommodating of, or designed for, the needs of dyslexic users? A growing number of services demand multi-stage authentication, and this may prove increasingly problematic.

4) *Alternative authentication mechanisms* – as we look to more inclusive perspectives to authentication, and as more essential services mandate passwords, can we consider a greater diversity of technologies, processes and opportunities to meet the needs of those for whom alphanumeric passwords are challenging [10, 16]. What additional accessibility issues may such alternatives introduce?

---

[3] https://ec.europa.eu/social/main.jsp?catId=1138&langId=en.

5) *Understanding dyslexia in the security context* – there is a growing body of literature in the area of pupils, students and learning (for those with dyslexia and similar challenges). The demands of particular technology-mediated tasks warrants serious consideration in order to ensure that we design security for all.

6) *Carrying out studies with dyslexics* – for ethical purposes it is important for truly informed consent to be obtained. For dyslexics, this means ensuring that the consent form is clear, unambiguous and uses simple language. Online survey pre-screening could assist in providing access to participants, but is dependent on them self-identifying as such. Moreover, it might be best to conduct verbal interviews rather than asking dyslexics to complete online surveys.

In summary, dedicated research in this area should seek to answer at least the following research questions:

1) In which contexts do dyslexics struggle with passwords, and to what extent?
2) What strategies do dyslexics employ, if any, to cope with the demands of passwords?
3) How could we help dyslexics to cope with the passwords and equivalent authentication steps, in their lives?
4) How should organizations go about making their websites and services more accessible to dyslexics if they use passwords as an authentication mechanism?

5   Conclusion

In this paper, we highlight the fact that dyslexics are likely to struggle with passwords and make the argument for accessibility, and this specific area, to join security and usability as essential dimensions of the authentication design process. Until some other authentication mechanism supplants the password in everyday life, accessibility of authentication needs to be given the prominence it deserves. It is proposed that people-based rigorous research is required to gain a deeper understanding of dyslexia and its impact. We suggest some directions for essential research in this area.

Acknowledgements. We are grateful to the School of Design and Informatics, Abertay University, for funding this research. Also, we thank our colleagues and students in the Division of Cyber Security for their keen input into discussions and deliberations.

References

1. Adams, A., Sasse, M.A.: Users are not the enemy. Commun. ACM **42**(12), 40–46 (1999)
2. Baeza-Yates, R., Rello, L.: Estimating dyslexia in the web. In: Proceedings of the International Cross-Disciplinary Conference on Web Accessibility, pp. 1–4 (2011)
3. Berget, G., Sandnes, F.E.: Do autocomplete functions reduce the impact of dyslexia on information-searching behavior? The case of Google. J. Assoc. Inf. Sci. Technol. **67**(10), 2320–2328 (2016)
4. Berget, G., Fagernes, S.: "I'm not Stupid" - attitudes towards adaptation among people with dyslexia. In: Kurosu, M. (ed.) HCI 2018. LNCS, vol. 10901, pp. 237–247. Springer, Cham (2018). https://doi.org/10.1007/978-3-319-91238-7_20

5. Broadhead, M., Daylamani-Zad, D., Mackinnon, L., Bacon, L.: A multisensory 3D environment as intervention to aid reading in dyslexia: a proposed framework. In: Proceedings of the 10th International Conference on Virtual Worlds and Games for Serious Applications, pp. 1–4. IEEE (2018)
6. Chai, J.Y., Chen, C.J.: A research review: how technology helps to improve the learning process of learners with dyslexia. J. Cogn. Sci. Hum. Dev. **2**(2), 26–43 (2017)
7. Cole, L., MacFarlane, A., Makri, S.: More than words: the impact of memory on how undergraduates with dyslexia interact with information. In: Proceedings of CHIIR 2020, Vancouver, Canada, pp. 1–5 (2020)
8. Coventry, L., De Angeli, A., Johnson, G.I.: Usability and biometric verification at the ATM interface. In: Proceedings of the SIGCHI Conference on Human Factors in Computing Systems, pp. 153–160. Association for Computing Machinery (ACM) (2003)
9. De Angeli, A., Coutts, M., Coventry, L., Johnson, G.I., Cameron, D., Fischer, M.H.: VIP: a visual approach to user authentication. In: De Marsico, M., Levialdi, S., Panizzi, E. (eds.) Proceedings of the Working Conference on Advanced Visual Interfaces, AVI 2002, pp. 316–323. Association for Computing Machinery (ACM), New York (2002)
10. De Angeli, A., Coventry, L., Johnson, G.I., Renaud, K.: Is a picture really worth a thousand words? Exploring the feasibility of graphical authentication systems. Int. J. Hum. Comput. Stud. **63**(1–2), 128–152 (2005)
11. De Santana, V.F., de Oliveira, R., Almeida, L.D.A. Baranauskas, M.C.C.: Web accessibility and people with dyslexia: a survey on techniques and guidelines. In: Proceedings of the International Cross-Disciplinary Conference on Web Accessibility, pp. 1–9 (2012)
12. Fourney, A., Morris, M.R., Ali, A., Vonessen, L.: Assessing the readability of web search results for searchers with dyslexia. In: The 41st International ACM SIGIR Conference on Research & Development in Information Retrieval, pp. 1069–1072 (2018)
13. Fuglerud, K., Dale, O.: Secure and inclusive authentication with a talking mobile one-time-password client. IEEE Secur. Priv. **9**(2), 27–34 (2011)
14. Garcia, J.M.: The lived experience of adolescents with dyslexia. Master of Science in Communication Sciences and Disorders. University of New Hampshire (2007)
15. Ghisi, M., Bottesi, G., Re, A.M., Cerea, S., Mammarella, I.C.: Socioemotional features and resilience in Italian university students with and without dyslexia. Front. Psychol. **7**, 478 (2016)
16. Gibson, M., Renaud, K., Conrad, M., Maple, C.: Play that funky password!: recent advances in authentication with music. In: Handbook of Research on Emerging Developments in Data Privacy, pp. 101–132. IGI Global (2015)
17. Gooch, D., Vasalou, A., Benton, L., Khaled, R.: Using gamification to motivate students with dyslexia. In: Proceedings of the 2016 CHI Conference on Human Factors in Computing Systems, pp. 969–980 (2016)
18. Gutmann, P., Grigg, I.: Security usability. IEEE Secur. Priv. **3**(4), 56–58 (2005)
19. Helkala, K.: Disabilities and authentication methods: usability and security. In: 2012 Seventh International Conference on Availability, Reliability and Security, pp. 327–334. IEEE (2012)
20. International Dyslexia Organization. https://dyslexiaida.org/definition-of-dyslexia/. Accessed 8 Mar 2019
21. Kalyvioti, K., Mikropoulos, T.A.: Virtual environments and dyslexia: a literature review. In: 5th International Conference on Software Development and Technologies for Enhancing Accessibility and Fighting Info-exclusion, DSAI 2013, Procedia Computer Science, vol. 27, pp. 138–147 (2014)
22. Kazakou, M.N., Soulis, S.: Feedback and the speed of answer of pupils with dyslexia in digital activities. In: 6th International Conference on Software Development and Technologies for Enhancing Accessibility and Fighting Infoexclusion, DSAI 2015, Procedia Computer Science, vol. 67, pp. 204–212 (2015)

23. Kirby, P.: A brief history of dyslexia. Psychol. BPS **31**, 56–59 (2018)
24. Kuzma, J.M.: Accessibility design issues with UK e-government sites. Gov. Inf. Q. **27**(2), 141–146 (2010)
25. Kwarteng-Amaning, E., Michaels, F., Maher, C.: Dyslexia awareness workshop. https://www.wandsworthccg.nhs.uk/newsAndPublications/Publications/PPI/Dyslexia%20Awareness%20Workshop%2003.07.pdf. Accessed 10 Mar 2020
26. Leitão, S., et al.: Exploring the impact of living with dyslexia: the perspectives of children and their parents. Int. J. Speech-Lang. Pathol. **19**(3), 322–334 (2017)
27. Lowry, P.B.: An emerging scholar's guide to the leading international information systems and business analytics research resources and publication outlets (2002). https://papers.ssrn.com/sol3/papers.cfm?abstract_id=3252222
28. McCarthy, J.E., Swierenga, S.J.: What we know about dyslexia and web accessibility: a research review. Univ. Access Inf. Soc. **9**, 47–152 (2010). https://doi.org/10.1007/s10209-009-0160-5
29. Michail, K.: Dyslexia: the experiences of university students with dyslexia. Doctoral dissertation, University of Birmingham (2010)
30. Morris, M.R., Fourney, A., Ali, A., Vonessen, L.: Understanding the needs of searchers with dyslexia. In: Proceedings of the CHI Conference on Human Factors in Computing Systems, pp. 1–12 (2018)
31. Naz, A., Nasreen, A., Liaquat, S., Shoukat, H.: An investigative study of learning disabilities in students studying computer. J. Secondary Educ. Res. **1**(1), 35–43 (undated)
32. Ophoff, J., Dietz, F.: Using gamification to improve information security behavior: a password strength experiment. In: 12th IFIP World Conference on Information Security Education (WISE), June 2019, Lisbon, Portugal, pp. 157–169 (2019)
33. Powell, N., Moore, D., Gray, J., Finlay, J., Reaney, J.: Dyslexia and learning computer programming. Innov. Teach. Learn. Inf. Comput. Sci. **3**(2), 1–12 (2004)
34. Prior, S., Renaud, K.: Age-appropriate password "Best Practice" ontologies for early educators and parents. Early Child. Educ. J. **23–24**, 100169 (2020)
35. Rega, A., Mennitto, A.: Augmented reality as an educational and rehabilitation support for developmental dyslexia. In: Proceedings of ICERI 2017 Conference, 16th–18th November, Seville, Spain, pp. 6969–6972 (2017)
36. Rello, L., Baeza-Yates, R., Saggion, H., Bayarri, C., Barbosa, S.D.: An iOS reader for people with dyslexia. In: Proceedings of the 15th International ACM SIGACCESS Conference on Computers and Accessibility, pp. 1–2 (2013)
37. Rello, L., Ballesteros, M., Bigham, J.P.: A spellchecker for dyslexia. In: Proceedings of the 17th International ACM SIGACCESS Conference on Computers & Accessibility, pp. 39–47 (2015)
38. Riley, C., Buckner, K., Johnson, G., Benyon, D.: Culture & biometrics: regional differences in the perception of biometric authentication technologies. AI Soc. **24**(3), 295–306 (2009). https://doi.org/10.1007/s00146-009-0218-1
39. Robson, L.: Additional help, additional problem – issues for supported dyslexic students. In: HEA STEM Annual Conference, 30 April - 01 May 2014, University of Edinburgh, Scotland (2014)
40. Rontou, M., Provision for students with dyslexia in EFL: an ethnographic case study. Doctoral dissertation, University of Birmingham (2010)
41. Shaywitz, S.E.: Dyslexia. N. Engl. J. Med. **338**(5), 307–312 (1998)
42. Shaywitz, S.E., Shaywitz, B.A.: Dyslexia (specific reading disability). Biol. Psychiat. **57**(11), 1301–1309 (2005)
43. Shih, M-S., Chang, J-C., Cheng, T.Y.: The design guideline for dyslexics-friendly Chinese ATM interface. In: IC4E 2019: Proceedings of the 10th International Conference on E-Education, E-Business, E-Management and E-Learning, pp. 416–420 (2019)

44. Stanford, B.: Barriers at the ballot box: the (In) accessibility of UK polling stations. Coventry Law J. **24**(1), 87–92 (2019)

45. Subashini, K., Sumithra, G.: Secure multimodal mobile authentication using one time password. In: Second International Conference on Current Trends in Engineering and Technology ICCTET, pp. 151–155. IEEE (2014)

46. Tadros, K., Fiset, D., Gosselin, F., Arguin, M.: A medium spatial frequency trough causes letter-by-letter dyslexia in normal readers. J. Vis. **9**(8), 822 (2009)

47. Vitman-Schorr, A., Ayalon, L., Khalaila, R.: Perceived accessibility to services and sites among Israeli older adults. J. Appl. Gerontol. **38**(1), 112–136 (2019)

48. UX Movement.: 6 Surprising Bad Practices That Hurt Dyslexic Users. https://uxmovement.com/content/6-surprising-bad-practices-that-hurt-dyslexic-users/. Accessed 10 Mar 2020

49. W3C – Web Accessibility Initiative: Web Content Accessibility Guidelines (WCAG) 2 requirements and techniques. https://www.w3.org/WAI/WCAG21/quickref/?versions=2.0. Accessed Mar 2020

50. W3C – Web Accessibility Initiative. Accessibility, Usability, and Inclusion. https://www.w3.org/WAI/fundamentals/accessibility-usability-inclusion/. Accessed Mar 2020

51. Warrington, E.K., Shallice, T.I.M.: Word-form dyslexia. Brain: J. Neurol. **103**(1), 99–112 (1980)

52. Wilson, P.: Dyslexics, know your brain. https://senmagazine.co.uk/articles/1096-how-your-brain-works-differently-as-a-dyslexic.html. Accessed Jan 2020

53. Wu, S., Reynolds, L., Li, X., Guzmán, F.: Design and evaluation of a social media writing support tool for people with dyslexia. In: Proceedings of CHI 2019, 4–9 May, Glasgow, Scotland, UK, pp. 1–14. ACM (2019)

Securing User eXperience: A Review for the End-Users' Software Robustness

Panagiotis Zagouras and Christos Kalloniatis[(✉)] [iD]

Privacy Engineering and Social Informatics Laboratory, Department of Cultural Technology and Communication, University of the Aegean, 81100 Mytilene, Lesvos Island, Greece
{ctd16015,chkallon}@aegean.gr

Abstract. Millions of users all over the world nowadays spend many hours daily using social networks on a range of devices (desktop, tablet, mobile), in many languages and countries, under very different systems of governance, and in wide-ranging social, religious, cultural and political environments. But the same software (System Services, Operating Systems "OSes", Hypervisors, Applications and Utilities) is still called upon to function in contexts defined by these vast differences in terms of quality, reliability, efficiency and security. All domestic appliances, contemporary cars and almost everything powered by electricity is now equipped with at least a rudimentary interface and ready-to-run software. Electronic transactions are now routine and there is a huge need for online security and privacy. Bring your own device (BYOD) is a trend that is appearing even in SMBs (Small and Midsize Business) with aspects, policy considerations, security models and traps. The success off all the above depends on User eXperience where the user intersects with the product (software). In this paper, we analyse the different approaches taken under the concept of User eXperience (UX) in tandem with the development of contemporary software, and examine their ramifications for the level of security and privacy. We will show that UX is a different concept from usability, examine the different academic approaches and their underlying viewpoints, and show how the tasks in question relate to security. We believe that the interface between UX and security is a demanding area which requires research in multiple dimensions. The need for designing and developing contemporary software which is smart, user-friendly, adaptive, secure and capable of protecting every type of user is immense.

Keywords: User eXperience · Usability · Security

1 Introduction

It is absolutely obvious that the concept of computing today has changed completely. Technology is ubiquitous in industrialized countries (Weiser 2002). Everyday procedures are not conducted as they once were and computers no longer interface with humans — "they interact" (Cooper 2012). "Smart shoes, appliances and phones are already here, but the practice of User eXperience (UX) design for ubiquitous computing is still

© IFIP International Federation for Information Processing 2020
Published by Springer Nature Switzerland AG 2020
N. Clarke and S. Furnell (Eds.): HAISA 2020, IFIP AICT 593, pp. 269–285, 2020.
https://doi.org/10.1007/978-3-030-57404-8_21

relatively new" (Kuniavsky and Founder 2010). Mobile communications are probably the fastest-evolving area within the ubiquitous computing sector (Hartson and Andre 2001) and are one of the areas featuring the most intense work on designing a quality User eXperience (UX). UX is an entire scientific field with extensions 'Beyond Usability' (Zimmermann and Eth 2012) while additionally different purposes for the usability and User eXperience (UX) evaluation methods (Bevan 2009) are introduced continuously. Various standards introduce different concepts for user experience like ISO 9241-11 which includes the concepts of effectiveness, efficiency, satisfaction, and content of use, while ISO 13407 provides guidance on designing usability with reference to ISO 9241-11. While the aforementioned efforts provide a sufficient map of concepts for dealing with user experience during system development security is still not clearly related with the specific concept during the development process (Jokela et al. 2003). While it is clear that usability differs from user experience the relationship with security and their interrelation is not sufficiently addressed.

In our modern and networked society people provide personal information in various online services over insecure networks and without having a satisfactory degree of awareness in using these services in a secure way. One of the major issues related to security is the way that these services alert and interact with the user and the degree of user's experience in dealing with these issues accordingly. Considering the fact that new GDPR legislation demands a higher degree of interaction with Internet users for various types of approvals/consents developing methods and tools that consider user experience as an important aspect of enhancing system's security and user's protection is immense.

The terms "look" and "feel" while using a modern and secure software, are now more than ever very important. In every daily interaction (work applications, finance transactions, social media responses) it's already reasonable and acceptable that "End Users play a critical role in computer security" (Minge & Thüring 2018) and we must research about the "interplay between usability and visual aesthetics" and focus seriously in "halo effects". Further difficulties also present themselves when we try to create 'relationships' between the UX and Security. There is now a pressing need to develop frameworks and methodologies capable of combining more specialized UX extensions with cutting-edge technologies for designing, developing, installing and monitoring secure IT systems. The new software that results will have to be user-friendly while combining ease of use with results in terms of security and privacy in whatever natural environment the device interacts with.

Given the aforementioned concerns the specific paper examines the role of security in connection with User eXperience. More specifically, it presents a review of all existing frameworks dealing with user experience along with their basic characteristics. Additionally, every framework is examined regarding its security extensions. Finally, the basic UX characteristics of these frameworks are examined and matched with the three basic security principles (Confidentiality, Integrity and Availability) in order to identify how every UX characteristic impacts security.

More specifically the paper is structured as follows. In Sect. 2 the relationship between security and user experience is presented. In Sect. 3 a review of the current User experience frameworks is presented along with the presentation of their characteristics and their relationship with basic security principles. Finally Sect. 4 concludes the paper by providing discussion on the studied works and raises issues for future research on the respective field.

2 User eXperience (UX) and Security

Recent years have witnessed vast changes in the field of design encompassing product design, semantics and emotional response in line with social change, the conservation of resources and energy, emerging environmental problems, and customer-oriented trends.

Products have a range of technical, practical and semantic functions. Monö in (Demirbilek & Sener 2003) defines four semantic functions for products. By allowing the designer to communicate 'cleanly' with the system, these functions create the conditions that govern what can and cannot be achieved in terms of communication with the product. The proposed semantic functions are: (a) *To Describing*: The product gestalt describes facts (e.g. its purpose is to define the task), mode of use, handling. (b) *To Expressing*: The product gestalt expresses the product's values and qualities. (c) *To Signalling*: The product gestalt urges the user to react in a specific way—for example, to be careful and precise in his/her work. (d) *To Identifying*: The product gestalt identifies the origin, nature and area of the product, its connection to the system, family, product range etc., and the function and placement of individual parts. The specific semantic functions thus seem to define the desired boundaries of the product in every situation in which it interacts with the user. The above approach is more technocratic and understandable to designers with IT knowledge.

Another approach which focuses more on the user, proposes a model of software design based on emotional flow (Demirbilek & Sener 2003). Authors believe that the emotional response or reaction to meaning triggered by a product varies between people from different backgrounds, social classes, levels of education, religion etc. The same authors have identified six different types of affective programs which involve 'happy' feelings, joy, or the evocation of dreams. The different types are: senses, fun, cuteness, familiarity, metonymy and colour. The above factors allow the user to use the software correctly and for the purpose for which it was designed for. Mistakes made while using the software can have irreparable consequences. Social structures (which have a direct bearing on human life), military installations and every simple, everyday item must be secure and 'respectful' of the human aspect of their use.

The beginning of security analysis in IT environments was set by using formal methods and the basis of those methods were discrete maths and logic. The progress took place by introducing business dynamics methodology (Sterman 2000) and the socio—technical systems. However, during the last years, security research and analysis has been oriented towards human behaviour. Nowadays, Information Security lies in various and different aspects and fields like: Philosophical, Behavioural, Technical, Managerial. It deals with prevention and detection of intrusions, as well as more specific fields of today, such as socio philosophical fields and socio organizational fields (Zagouras et al. 2017).

We appreciate that the field of User eXperience (UX) has not been recently researched in combination with the development cycle for contemporary, secure software while similar efforts from the field of Usability Engineering and HCI have addressed similar issues (Kainda et al. 2010; Yee 2004). There is thus a need to create methodologies and tools which will provide assistance to software engineers involved in the modern software industry.

This paper will bring together research projects which have taken a wide range of different approaches to the subject-matter, creating a reference point of our own which we believe warrants thorough exploration through the combination of different research approaches. The extensions of User eXperience (UX) in our contemporary software-dominated reality are vast and bring together different fields which may not have been associated before. Below, we will present research conducted in the field in question, looking at how the different strands can be combined and parameterized, and anything else that might be of service to the software creation industry.

3   Related Works

We now know that the concept of User eXperience (UX) is a different field of research from usability and contains issues that go beyond satisfaction. It is a highly demanding field, because it involves a set of entirely different and complex factors (parameters) and combines methodologies and fields which have not been applied together in this context. A target approach for UX mentions exemplary: "UX is not only about the times when people are using our products, but also about the times when they are not. In the era of ever-vibrating smartphones and increasingly demanding apps, there is no better user experience than peace of mind"[1].

Our research focused on the search for User eXperience frameworks while also exploring their security extensions. In relation to UX Frameworks in general, Blythe (Law et al. 2007) proposed five bipolar dimensions to characterize UX frameworks as shown in Table 1. These dimensions were used for comparing the UX frameworks as shown below.

Table 1. Dimensions to characterize UX Frameworks.

Aspect	Content Dimension
Theory	Reductive—Holistic
Purpose	Evaluation—Development
Method	Quantitative—Qualitative
Domain	Work Based –Leisure based
Application	Personal—Social

A review paper from (Zarour and Alharbi 2017) explains each element of the UX in detail. Specifically, the article compares the frameworks that have been created for UX, parametrized them with its own approach before ultimately presenting the authors' preferred framework.

---

[1] https://uxdesign.cc/designing-for-less-98d64259f770.

The framework in question categorizes UX disciplines, dimensions, aspects, categories and descriptions, illustrates the dimensions, presents the different measurement methods for UX, illustrates them with dimensions, and analyzes one by one the various proposed UX Frameworks currently dealt with in the literature. At the end, it outlines a proposed framework for UX which includes dimensions, aspects categories and measurement methods. Specifically the suggested UX dimensions are: (a) *Value*: This is related to the studies that have been focused on the gained value. (b) *User Needs Experience (NX)*: This is related to the studies that have been focused on user needs and gained qualities. (c) *Brand Experience (BX)*: This is related to the studies that have focused on the organization's brand image. (d) *Technology Experience (TX)*: This is related to the studies that have focused on the technology that has been used to deliver the product or the service. (e) *Context*: This is related to the studies that have focused on the context of use and the interaction between the previous dimensions.

The identified UX frameworks are shown in Table 2. Specifically Mahlke (Sascha & Aus Berlin 2008) presents in detail for UX the influencing factors, the instrumental and no instrumental quality perceptions, the emotional user reactions and the consequences of UX. (Vyas et al. 2012) "deals" with the affordances in interaction. It proposes two broad classes of affordances: Affordance in information and affordance in articulation and the notion of affordance should be treated at two levels: at the 'artefact level' and at the 'practice level'. The third framework proposed by Jetter and Gerken (2007) basic concepts are the 'product', the 'user' and the 'organization' and emphasizes in traditional Human – Computer Interaction that is different with the Extended Human – Computer Interaction. Authors in (Möller et al. 2009) taxonomies the quality of service and quality of experience that they carry following a multimodal human-machine interaction. Katrin Schulze and Heidi Krömker in (Schulze & Krömker 2010) saw that the motivation – emotion – reflection are basic components for the UX by mentioning basic human needs and product qualities. In (Chen & Zhu, 2011) authors put forward four dimensional assessment system of mobile application user eXperience: User characteristic, app properties, app system supports and context parameters. Gegner et al. in (2012) discuss the managing of UX components between value – benefit- attribute following the Means End theory. In (Fuchsberger et al. 2012) authors consider the Values In Action (ViA). The approach ViA consider Usability (U), User eXperience (UX) and User Acceptance (UA) a priori as equally important. In (Gross & Bongartz 2012) authors make an experiment with three different mobile applications and present a regression analysis with important results. In (Pc & Prabhu 2012) authors focus on requirements engineering (RE) and user experience design (UXD) and how these values effect the entire scientific field (UX). Tan et al. (2013) taxonomies usability and UX attributes using a well – known Goal Question Metric (GQM) approach. Gao et al. (2013) construct an evaluation index system of user experience and a user experience quality evaluation. In (Kujala et al. 2012) authors proposed quality dimensions that are related to no-instrumental qualities. Kremer et al. (2017) present the ExodUX approach about the application methodologies, the factor representation sheets (FRS) and the general process documentation (GPD). Finally, in (Zarour and Alharbi 2017) authors present a retrospective user experience evaluation method called "UX Curve" revealing long—term aspects of user experience.

In Table 2 the aforementioned frameworks along with their basic characteristics and a brief description are shown.

Table 2. UX Frameworks published on the research community.

Authors of the Framework	Basic UX Components	Small Description
Mahlke	Perception of instrumental qualities, emotional user reactions and perception of non-instrumental qualities	"Non-instrumental quality perceptions and emotional user reactions are considered as distinct aspects of user experience and complement the perception of instrumental quality"
Vyas and van der Veer	Affordance in Information and affordance in Articulation	Affordance in information refers to users' understanding of a technology based on their semantic and syntactic interpretation; and affordance in articulation refers to users' interpretations about the use of the technology
Hans-Christian Jetter and Jens Gerken	User, product, organization	The traditional or extended human—computer interactions have different user and organizational values
Sebastian Möller et al.	Quality of Service (QoS) and Quality of Experience (QoE)	"The taxonomy consists of three layers, two of them addressing QoS and one addressing QoE". (1) QOS-INFLUENCING FACTORS, (2) QOS INTERACTION PERFORMANCE ASPECTS, (3) QOE ASPECTS
Katrin Schulze and Heidi Krömker	Basic human needs, Product qualities, Motivation, Emotion, Reflection	The specific approach defined UX as "the degree of positive or negative emotions that can be experienced by a specific user in a specific context during and after product use and that motivates for further usage"
Zhi Chen and Shangshang Zhu	User characteristics, App properties, App system supports and context parameters	The specific approach "study mobile application User eXperience (UX) and quantitative assessment through Analytic Hierarchy Process"

(continued)

Table 2. (*continued*)

Authors of the Framework	Basic UX Components	Small Description
Lutz Gegner et al.	Strategy—ladder, Studio—ladder, Life—ladder, Value, Benefits (Consequences), Attribute	The framework follows the Means-End Theory proposed by Gutman and the elements of the framework have links between them in order Value — > Benefits — > Attribute
Verena Fuchsberger et al.	Usability (U), User Experience (UX), User Acceptance (UA)	The values: Interpersonal, Emotional, Social, Functional, Conditional, Epistemic encapsulates the ViA (Values in Action) Usability, UX and UA
Alice Gross and Sara Bongartz	Aesthetics, Fun, SUS (System Usability Scale), SAM (SELF-ASSESSMENT MANIKIN), Overall judgment	This approach consists of an experiment with three different mobile applications with a specific device and specific operating system. The Regression analysis of UX components have bring important results
Anitha PC and Beena Prabhu	Requirements engineering (RE) and user experience design (UXD)	The framework has "several synchronization points where RE and UXD professionals should collaborate"
Jia Tan et al.	A taxonomy for usability and UX attributes and generic questions and measures for developing measurements instruments	The framework evaluation have done in a small telecom company and the results can lead better decisions to improve the usability and the UX of the mobile industry products
Gao Changyuan et al.	Instinct reflection layer, interaction layer, depth perception layer	This approach "constructs the evaluation index system of user experience and also does the user experience's quality evaluation"
Sari Kujala et al.	Hedonic product quality. Quality dimensions that are related to no-instrumental qualities such us aesthetics, innovativeness and originality	The retrospective user experience evaluation method "UX Curve" is a "promising method to reveal long—term aspects of user experience"

(*continued*)

Table 2. (*continued*)

Authors of the Framework	Basic UX Components	Small Description
Simon Kremer et al.	Setting, aesthetics, interaction, cognitive processes, technology	The application methodologies, the factor representation sheets (FRS) and the general process documentation (GPD) create a three—part framework to improve the flows of the proposed framework
Mohammad Zarour and Mubarak Alharbi	UX Dimensions, aspects categories, aspect, measurements methods	This framework proposes the relation between value and UX Dimension : Value, user need experience (NX), brand experience (BX), technology experience (TX)

Studying in detail the aforementioned frameworks, we have focused on the information analysis that reports security extensions. We can see that an approach reports security references in system factors and context factors. Other approaches focus on security references when it comes to basic human needs and psychological needs. More technical approaches report: security features or attributes like safety etc. Table 3 below presents more clear a list of the referenced UX frameworks proposed in literature in association with security and privacy issues they propose.

Table 3 shows that the 'connection' between UX και Security is "weak" and there is a gap between presentation and studying. Specifically the UX field needs to be linked with all the security extensions provided by contemporary software. None of the proposed frameworks comes with a detailed presentation and exploration of the available security. Recent bibliography has resulted in 3 basic areas based on (Mishra & Harris 2006) for creating secure information systems: technical, formal and informal systems. However, the term "Information Systems" has gotten different connotations from different researchers.

Various and varied studies and approaches have been developed on the basis of theories and frameworks from other academic fields to explore contingent factors of the end user's security behaviours. As stated in (Hu et al. 2011) "The rational decision-making process will be subject to a variety of individual and situational factors". We must focus to "those information security misbehaviours that are intentionally performed by insiders without malicious intent" state the authors in (Dang-Pham et al. 2017).

For better understanding how the aforementioned UX frameworks are related with the basic security principles in order to safeguard the basic security principles (C.I.A) we have initially identifies all UX characteristics presented in all fifteen frameworks and matched then with the respective security principles. More specifically we created a group of categories which include the specific attributes (from all the frameworks) in accordance with the approach taken by (Arhippainen & Tähti 2003). We then categorized the components for the UX: user, social factors, culture factors, context of use, product

Table 3. UX Frameworks in association with security and privacy issues.

	UX Framework	Security (References–Components)
1.	Mahlke	–
2.	Vyas and Van Der Veer	–
3.	Jetter and Gerken	–
4.	Moller et al.	System factors (security- critical systems), Context factors (privacy and security issues)
5.	Schulze and Krömker	Basic human needs: security. Feel secure, feel not being watched, build trust, hand over responsibility, have data control
6.	Chen and Zhu	–
7.	Gegner et al.	The life ladder: UX is primarily a result of the satisfaction of psychological needs such as security (calmness, order, routines, relaxation)
8.	Fuchsberger, Moser, and Tscheligi	–
9.	Gross and Bongartz	–
10.	Anitha and Prabhu	Myth2#: RE and UXD Can be Done by Architects or Domain Professionals: "Architect came up with an excellent security feature…" Myth4#: User Experience = Usability: Visceral processing help users make rapid decisions about what is good, bad, safe, or dangerous
11.	Tan, Ronkko and Gencel	Taxonomy for Usability and UX Attributes Attributes Safety. Sub—attributes Security
12.	GAO Changyuan et al.	Rational judgment: Security Depth perception layer: Safety of operation
13.	Kujala et al.	–
14.	Kremer et al.	–
15.	Zarour and Alharbi	UX Aspects: Trustworthiness, privacy

(system in our approach) in line with the UX aspects proposed by (Hiltunen et al. 2002) which are user, task space, physical context, social context, technological context, device and connection.

It should be noted that the tables below have been compiled in line with a user-oriented approach to each attribute. Our research sought to analyze the security approaches from the user's point of view. Thus, the tables list all the attributes taking a consistently user-oriented approach (Tables 4, 5 and 6).

For the user (U) we can see that attributes Confidentiality (C) and Integrity (I) have very strong presentation compared to availability. For the system (S) we can see that the C.I.A. attributes have a huge dissemination in all attributes. It is very important

Table 4. UX attributes User and System in association with security C.I.A. issues

User (U)				System (S)			
Attributes	C	I	A	Attributes	C	I	A
Age	✔	✔		Acceptability	✔	✔	✔
Assessment (every user)	✔	✔		Acceptance	✔	✔	✔
Attention	✔	✔		Accessibility			
Autonomy	✔	✔		Access restrictions	✔	✔	✔
Beautiful of colour, text, graphics				Acoustic	✔		
Behavioural tendencies	✔	✔		Adaptivity	✔	✔	✔
Brand loyalty	✔	✔		Aesthetics	✔		
Choise of alternatives	✔	✔		Ambiguity	✔	✔	✔
Cognitive appraisals	✔	✔		Appeal	✔	✔	
Competencies	✔	✔		Appearance	✔	✔	
Computer anxiety	✔	✔		Appropriation-Enactment	✔	✔	✔
Consistent layout	✔	✔	✔	Attractiveness	✔	✔	
Consumer experience	✔	✔		Authenticity	✔	✔	
Coolness	✔	✔		Balance (Interaction)	✔	✔	✔
Cultural background	✔	✔		Beauty	✔		
Cultural differences	✔	✔		Challenge	✔		✔
Curiosity	✔	✔		Clarity of navigation	✔		✔
Decision	✔	✔	✔	Clear	✔	✔	
Emotional status	✔	✔	✔	Closely (View)	✔	✔	
Emotions	✔	✔		Communicative symbolics	✔	✔	
Enjoyment	✔	✔		Compatibility of users knowledge	✔	✔	
Fun	✔	✔		Completeness	✔	✔	
Gender				Compliance	✔	✔	
Generalizability	✔	✔		Consistency	✔		
General SAM	✔			Content rich	✔		
Haptic quality	✔	✔	✔	Controllable	✔	✔	✔
Hedonic	✔	✔	✔	Convenience	✔	✔	
Image	✔		✔	Correlation of search results	✔	✔	
Influence	✔	✔		Credibility	✔	✔	✔
Instincts	✔	✔		Desirability	✔	✔	
Knowledge	✔	✔		Dialog acts	✔	✔	✔

(*continued*)

Table 4. (*continued*)

User (U)				System (S)			
Attributes	C	I	A	Attributes	C	I	A
Learning	✔			Dialogue	✔	✔	✔
Likeability	✔			Ease of use	✔	✔	
Logic between interfaces	✔	✔	✔	Effectiveness			✔
Memories	✔	✔		Effective of link	✔	✔	
Motivation	✔	✔		Emotional value	✔	✔	✔
Motor expressions	✔	✔		Epistemic value	✔	✔	
Native language	✔	✔		Everyday operations	✔	✔	
Needs				Exciting	✔	✔	
Novelty	✔	✔		Extensibility	✔		
Overall judgments	✔	✔		Fault tolerance	✔	✔	✔
Perceptions	✔	✔		Flexibility	✔	✔	✔
Personality	✔	✔		Fluidity	✔		✔
Physiological reactions	✔	✔		Functionality	✔	✔	✔
Pleasure	✔	✔		Functional value	✔	✔	
Popularity	✔	✔		General SUS	✔	✔	✔
Predispositions	✔	✔		Gesture	✔	✔	
Preference	✔	✔		Goals	✔	✔	
Product use	✔	✔		Hedonic quality	✔	✔	✔
Readability	✔	✔		Helpfulness	✔	✔	
Relatedness	✔	✔	✔	Highlight important info	✔	✔	
Relevance	✔			Identification	✔	✔	✔
Safety	✔	✔	✔	Impressive	✔	✔	
Satisfaction	✔	✔	✔	Inter-behavioural	✔	✔	
Security	✔	✔	✔	Interesting	✔	✔	
Sensory (Sensitivity)	✔	✔	✔	Learnability	✔		✔
Sexiness	✔	✔		Memorability	✔	✔	
Skills	✔	✔	✔	Motivational aspects	✔	✔	
Stimulation	✔	✔		Navigability	✔	✔	✔
Simplicity	✔	✔		Operability	✔		
Subjective feelings	✔	✔	✔	Operation	✔		

(*continued*)

Table 4. (*continued*)

User (U)				System (S)			
Attributes	C	I	A	Attributes	C	I	A
Surprise	✔	✔		Response time		✔	
Time	✔	✔	✔	Personality system	✔	✔	
Trustworthiness	✔	✔	✔	Platform stability	✔	✔	✔
Uncertainty	✔	✔	✔	Presentation	✔		
Usage behaviour	✔	✔	✔	Productivity	✔		
Usage mode	✔	✔	✔	Reliability	✔	✔	✔
User Performance			✔	Safety of operation	✔	✔	✔
User's knowledge	✔	✔	✔	Speech	✔	✔	
Verbal ability	✔	✔	✔	Supporting	✔	✔	
Visual aesthetics	✔	✔	✔	Symbolic aspects	✔	✔	
				Understandability	✔	✔	
				Usability	✔	✔	
				Useful	✔	✔	
				Utility	✔	✔	
				Visual attraction	✔		
				Vocabulary	✔	✔	

therefore to include these aspects in the system development lifecycle and especially during system design.

Again in Table 5 we see that all attributes belonging to physical Context play a critical role for the security of a system as well as Task Space attributes. It should be noted that Task space is very critical from a user point of view since it is the area were the user interacts with the system and any type of misunderstanding or misbehavior may potentially harm system security or user's privacy.

Finally, in Table 6 we see the same pattern as in the previous tables. In both the technological context and the device attributes all three security aspects have a connection with the UX elements. Except from the retail experience and usage volume all other elements have an impact on systems confidentiality, Integrity and Availability.

The above tables allow us to conclude, first off, that the group consisting of Physical Context (PHC), Task space (TS), Technological Context (TC), and Device (D) includes attributes whose C.I.A. attributes are very close to 100%. This is logical, given that the attributes in this group–the physical context in which the user employs the software, the attributes of the tasks, the technological context and the devices users employ–are all directly linked to the actual system use. There are differences between the user and system groups in terms of their C.I.A. attributes, but we can still see a significant dovetailing of values for the C.I.A. attributes, meaning that the security extensions have

Table 5. UX attributes Physical Context and Task space in association with security C.I.A. issues.

Physical Context (PHC)				Task space (TS)			
Attributes	C	I	A	Attributes	C	I	A
Accuracy	✔	✔	✔	Number of available tasks	✔	✔	✔
Activities	✔	✔	✔	Task consequences	✔	✔	✔
Appropriateness	✔	✔	✔	Task frequency	✔	✔	✔
Availability	✔	✔	✔	Tasks complexity	✔	✔	✔
Conditional value	✔	✔	✔	Time behaviour	✔	✔	✔
Environment (Accuracy)	✔	✔	✔	Type of tasks	✔	✔	✔
Home environment	✔	✔	✔				
Lighting condition	✔	✔	✔				
Mobile environment	✔	✔	✔				
Office environment	✔	✔	✔				
Potential parallel activities	✔	✔	✔				
Precision	✔	✔	✔				
Public usage	✔	✔	✔				
Resulting costs	✔	✔					
Space (condition)	✔	✔	✔				
Transmission channels also sensory	✔	✔	✔				

Table 6. UX attributes technological context and device in association with security C.I.A. issues

Technological Context (TC)				Device (D)			
Attributes	C	I	A	Attributes	C	I	A
Controllability	✔	✔	✔	Brand	✔	✔	✔
Efficacy	✔	✔	✔	Business communications	✔	✔	✔
Efficiency	✔	✔	✔	Marketing	✔	✔	✔
Infrastructure	✔	✔	✔	Retail experience			
Platform technology	✔	✔	✔	Strategy (Brand)	✔	✔	✔
Service response time	✔	✔	✔	Usage volumes			✔

a significant impact on the UX. The extent to which the C.I.A. attributes are influenced by UX components is clear.

From the above we can safely conclude that these approaches provide a huge amount of knowledge and lay the foundations for creating contemporary, smart, adaptive software for every user. However, the problem remains on how to create a secure and user-friendly environment to house every aspect of the average user's everyday experience using smart and adaptive software.

Developments in desktops, tablets, smartphones have been huge in recent years. Millions of users around the world now use smartphone apps for every sort of everyday procedure. Frequently, their functionality "relies on, and produces, sensitive and personal data" (Gerber et al. 2017). All values are stored on the device, including usage data, location and biometrics. There have been numerous instances of unintended live sessions on Instagram and of personal moments being shared live due to software being set up and used incorrectly.

The "privacy paradox" is also frequently observed, following the development of social networks: "The privacy paradox explained as a temporally discounted balance between concerns and rewards" (Hallam & Zanella 2017) presents the way in which contemporary users behave. "The privacy paradox has significant implications for e-commerce, e-government, online social networking, as well as for government privacy regulation" (Kokolakis 2017).

We understand the importance of the phenomenon in question and how important security and privacy now are. Thus, the need to "develop products capable of automatically adapting to any given environment or user" (Zagouras, n.d.) is huge, and requires the incorporation of concepts such as understanding, concerns, awareness, attitudes and feelings into the software and its users.

Our study has shown us that psychological needs are a very important aspect of this research. Features like autonomy, competence, relatedness, self-actualization, security, popularity, money/luxury, physical/bodily, self-esteem, stimulation, and keeping it meaningful must be taken into account at every stage in the software creation process, and especially in those aspects relating to user interaction.

An interest work about the psychological needs as motivators for security and privacy actions on smartphones is presented from Kraus et al. (2017) with details about the behaviour for security and privacy action in smartphones. The need is growing every day. However, the users must acquire knowledge both via the distributors and the software itself. We must also do our utmost to ensure, given the speed of the technological advances and the human needs for privacy, that data is not lost.

4   Discussion and Conclusion

This paper has analyzed the field of User Experience (UX) across the whole spectrum of academic research from the last quarter century. We have presented the changing meanings ascribed to the concept of a software product in recent years and the changing reality that has taken shape in the procedures pertaining to the everyday use and experience of software. We have separated the concept of 'usability' from the concept of 'user experience', focusing on usability as a non-emotional aspect and UX being felt internally by the user. We have looked at the different academic fields involved in the latter, which include human computer interaction (HCI), psychology, design approaches, marketing and philosophy. The theories on which the examined approaches are based are well-known and have produced important scientific results.

The approaches that have been taken to the combination of security and User eXperience are numerous, but it seems that the research is still overly-generalized and needs to develop approaches and frameworks which take a more specialized look at software development. It is obvious that data leaks via social media and other organizations made deliberately and for gain must be stopped, not at the level of policy decisions within the company but at the level of the software being used to protect data privacy. The software must be equipped with the technology and the 'judgment' required to deny the possibility even to its creator of using data of this kind for purposes other than those for which it was provided, or to transfer it elsewhere.

There is a need to create contemporary smart software using the best software development techniques, artificial intelligence — and always in full awareness of the security and privacy issues — which emphasizes and empathizes with the future user population. We believe that the field of UX with security (and privacy) extensions requires more research and has to connect the psychological needs of the users with UX approaches under the prism of security and privacy, to minimize the software's entropy. This area is still in its infancy. Methodologies of this sort will help the users to use — and the manufacturers to create — contemporary, smart and safe (for the user) software globally. The key conclusion from the aforementioned analysis is that UX elements presented in various studies have a huge impact on all three aspects of Information Security which means that designers and software analysts should consider UX as a key design factor when eliciting security (and privacy) requirements for the system to be. Providing a holistic approach for assisting analysts in this direction will be one important extension for both Usability Engineering and Security Engineering domains.

References

Arhippainen, L., Tähti, M.: Empirical evaluation of user experience in two adaptive mobile application prototypes. In: Proceedings of the 2nd International Conference, pp. 27–34 (2003). http://www.ep.liu.se/ecp/011/007/ecp011007.pdf

Bevan, N.: What is the difference between the purpose of usability and user experience evaluation methods? (2009). https://www.researchgate.net/publication/238775905

Chen, Z., Zhu, S.: The research of mobile application user experience and assessment model. In: Proceedings of 2011 International Conference on Computer Science and Network Technology, ICCSNT 2011, vol. 4, pp. 2832–2835 (2011). https://doi.org/10.1109/ICCSNT.2011.6182553

Cooper, A.: The Inmates are Running the Asylum (2012). https://doi.org/10.1007/978-3-322-99786-9_1

Dang-Pham, D., Pittayachawan, S., Bruno, V.: Exploring behavioral information security networks in an organizational context: An empirical case study. J. Inf. Secur. Appl. **34**, 46–62 (2017). https://doi.org/10.1016/j.jisa.2016.06.002

Demirbilek, O., Sener, B.: Product design, semantics and emotional response. Ergonomics **46**(13–14), 1346–1360 (2003). https://doi.org/10.1080/00140130310001610874

Fuchsberger, V., Moser, C., Tscheligi, M.: Values in action (ViA): combining usability, user experience and user acceptance. In: Proceedings of the 2012 ACM Annual Conference Extended Abstracts on Human Factors in Computing Systems Extended Abstracts, pp. 1793–1798. ACM, New York (2012). ISSN: 978-1-4503-1016-1

Gao, C., Wang, S., Zhong, C.: Research on user experience evaluation system of information platform based on web environment. In: Proceedings of 2013 2nd International Conference on Measurement, Information and Control, ICMIC 2013 (2013). https://doi.org/10.1109/MIC.2013.6758026

Gegner, L., Runonen, M., Keinonen, T.: Oscillating Between Extremes: A Framework for Mapping Differing Views on User eXperience (2012)

Gerber, P., Volkamer, M., Renaud, K.: The simpler, the better? Presenting the COPING Android permission-granting interface for better privacy-related decisions. J. Inf. Secur. Appl. **34**(March), 8–26 (2017). https://doi.org/10.1016/j.jisa.2016.10.003

Gross, A., Bongartz, S.: Why do I like it? Investigating the product-specificity of user experience (2012)

Hallam, C., Zanella, G.: Online self-disclosure: The privacy paradox explained as a temporally discounted balance between concerns and rewards. Comput. Hum. Behav. **68**, 217–227 (2017). https://doi.org/10.1016/j.chb.2016.11.033

Hartson, H.R., Andre, T.S., Williges, R.C.: Usability evaluation methods (2001)

Hiltunen, M., Laukka, M., Luomala, J.: Mobile User Experience. IT Press, Finland (2002)

Hu, Q., Xu, Z., Dinev, T., Ling, H.: Does deterrence work in reducing information security policy abuse by employees? Commun. ACM **54**(6), 54–60 (2011). https://doi.org/10.1145/1953122.1953142

Jetter, H.-C., Gerken, J.: A simplified model of user experience for practical application (2007). http://nbn-resolving.de/urn:nbn:de:bsz:352-opus-31516

Jokela, T., Iivari, N., Matero, J., Karukka, M.: The standard of user-centered design and the standard definition of usability: Analyzing ISO 13407 against ISO 9241-11. Design **46**, 53–60 (2003). https://doi.org/10.1145/944519.944525

Kainda, R., Fléchais, I., Roscoe, A.W.: Security and usability: analysis and evaluation. In: International Conference on Availability, Reliability and Security, Krakow, 2010, pp. 275–282 (2010). doi:https://doi.org/10.1109/ARES.2010.77

Kokolakis, S.: Privacy attitudes and privacy behaviour: A review of current research on the privacy paradox phenomenon. Comput. Secur. **64**, 122–134 (2017). https://doi.org/10.1016/j.cose.2015.07.002

Kraus, L., Wechsung, I., Möller, S.: Psychological needs as motivators for security and privacy actions on smartphones. J. Inf. Secur. Appl. **34**, 34–45 (2017). https://doi.org/10.1016/j.jisa.2016.10.002

Kremer, S., Schlimm, A., Lindemann, U.: The ExodUX framework: Supporting comprehensive user experience design. In: PICMET 2017 - Portland International Conference on Management of Engineering and Technology: Technology Management for the Interconnected World, Proceedings (2017). https://doi.org/10.23919/PICMET.2017.8125371

Kujala, S., Roto, V., Väänänen-Vainio-Mattila, K., Sinnelä, A.: Identifying hedonic factors in long-term user experience (2012). https://doi.org/10.1145/2347504.2347523

Kuniavsky, M., Founder, T.M.: Smart Things Ubiquitous Computing User Experience Design. Morgan Kaufmann Publishers Inc, San Francisco (2010). https://doi.org/10.1016/C2009-0-20057-2

Law, E., Vermeeren, A., Hassenzahl, M., Blythe, M.: An analysis framework for user experience (ux) studies: A green paper. In: International Conference HCI 2007, September 2007

Minge, M., Thüring, M.: Hedonic and pragmatic halo effects at early stages of user eXperience. Int. J. Hum. Comput. Stud. **109**, 13–25 (2018). https://doi.org/10.1016/j.ijhcs.2017.07.007

Mishra, S., Harris, M.A.: Human behavioral aspects in information systems security literature review (2006)

Möller, S., Engelbrecht, K.-P., Kühnel, C., Wechsung, I., Weiss, B.: A taxonomy of quality of service and quality of experience of multimodal human-machine interaction. In: International Workshop on Quality of Multimedia Experience, San Diego, CA, pp. 7–12 (2009). https://doi.org/10.1109/QOMEX.2009.5246986

Pc, A., Prabhu, B.: Integrating requirements engineering and user experience design in product life cycle management. In: First International Workshop on Usability and Accessibility Focused Requirements Engineering (UsARE), Zurich, pp. 12–17 (2012). https://doi.org/10.1109/UsARE.2012.6226784

Sascha, D.-P., Aus Berlin, M.: User experience of interaction with technical systems (2008)

Schulze, K., Krömker, H.: A framework to measure user experience of interactive online products (2010)

Sterman, J.D.: Business Dynamics. McGraw Hill, Boston (2000)

Tan, J., Rönkkö, K., Gencel, C.: A framework for software usability & user experience measurement in mobile industry. In: Proceedings - Joint Conference of the 23rd International Workshop on Software Measurement and the 8th International Conference on Software Process and Product Measurement, IWSM-MENSURA 2013 (2013). https://doi.org/10.1109/IWSM-Mensura.2013.31

Vyas, D., Chisalita, C.M., van der Veer, G.C.: Affordance in interaction (2012). https://doi.org/10.1145/1274892.1274907

Weiser, M.: The computer for the 21st Century. IEEE Pervasive Comput. 1(1), 19–25 (2002). https://doi.org/10.1109/MPRV.2002.993141

Yee, K.-P.: Aligning security and usability. IEEE Secur. Priv. 2(5), 48–55 (2004). https://doi.org/10.1109/msp.2004.64

Zagouras, P., Kalloniatis, C., Gritzalis, S.: Managing user experience: Usability and security in a new era of software supremacy. In: Tryfonas, T. (ed.) HAS 2017. LNCS, vol. 10292, pp. 174–188. Springer, Cham (2017). https://doi.org/10.1007/978-3-319-58460-7_12

Zarour, M., Alharbi, M.: User experience framework that combines aspects, dimensions, and measurement methods. Cogent Eng. 4(1), 1–25 (2017). https://doi.org/10.1080/23311916.2017.1421006

Zimmermann, P.G., Eth, D.N.: Beyond usability – measuring aspects of user experience thesis June 2008 (2012)

Security Policy

SMEs' Confidentiality Concerns for Security Information Sharing

Alireza Shojaifar[1,2](✉) and Samuel A. Fricker[1,3]

[1] FHNW, IIT, 5210 Windisch, Switzerland
{alireza.shojaifar,samuel.fricker}@fhnw.ch, a.shojaifar@uu.nl,
samuel.fricker@bth.se
[2] Department of Information and Computing Sciences, Utrecht University, Utrecht,
The Netherlands
[3] Blekinge Institute of Technology, SERL-Sweden, 37179 Karlskrona, Sweden

Abstract. Small and medium-sized enterprises (SME) are considered an essential part of the EU economy; however, highly vulnerable to cyber-attacks. SMEs have specific characteristics which separate them from large companies and influence their adoption of good cybersecurity practices. To mitigate the SMEs' cybersecurity adoption issues and raise their awareness of cyber threats, we have designed a self-paced security assessment and capability improvement method, CYSEC. CYSEC is a security awareness and training method that utilises self-reporting questionnaires to collect companies' information about cybersecurity awareness, practices, and vulnerabilities to generate automated recommendations for counselling. However, confidentiality concerns about cybersecurity information have an impact on companies' willingness to share their information. Security information sharing decreases the risk of incidents and increases users' self-efficacy in security awareness programs. This paper presents the results of semi-structured interviews with seven chief information security officers (CISOs) of SMEs to evaluate the impact of online consent communication on motivation for information sharing. The results were analysed in respect of the Self-Determination Theory (SDT). The findings demonstrate that online consent with multiple options for indicating a suitable level of agreement improved motivation for information sharing. This allows many SMEs to participate in security information sharing activities and supports security experts to have a better overview of common vulnerabilities.

Keywords: Cybersecurity · Small and medium-sized enterprises · Online consent · Confidentiality concerns · Information sharing

1 Introduction

Small and medium-sized enterprises (SMEs) have a considerable diversity and form the backbone of the EU's economy [12]. However, although they need to deal with a similar level of cybersecurity risk as large companies, information security is not always a priority [17, 24]. Moreover, the lack of written security policy, financial resources, and

© IFIP International Federation for Information Processing 2020
Published by Springer Nature Switzerland AG 2020
N. Clarke and S. Furnell (Eds.): HAISA 2020, IFIP AICT 593, pp. 289–299, 2020.
https://doi.org/10.1007/978-3-030-57404-8_22

security expertise are other operational constraints and make SMEs more vulnerable [11, 13]. To having an effective understanding of security policy and fostering a security culture, providing appropriate training and awareness tools specifically for small enterprises is necessary [11].

Training and awareness programs are the most commonly suggested approaches in the literature for security policy compliance, and they can alleviate employees' limited knowledge of cybersecurity [20]. Systematic training programs are a good means of facilitating continuous information security communication in organisations. Information security training should apply content and approaches that enable and motivate learners to systematic cognitive processing of information they receive in training [20].

CYSEC is a self-paced SME-specific training and awareness method that provides training by automating the elements of security communication between employees and a security expert [2]. Since there is a resistance to changing cybersecurity behaviour and adopting security tools by employees [16], the method implements the motivational constructs—namely, the needs for autonomy, competence, and relatedness—in the self-determination theory (SDT) [4, 29] to motivate learners to adopt advice. CYSEC provides training, recommendations, and relevant hands-on skills based on SMEs' answers to the self-assessment questions to enable them to become more self-determined.

Security information sharing is a challenge for companies, and they are reluctant to share their information and report their incidents [9, 15, 30]. Fear of negative publicity and competitive disadvantage, believing that the chance of a successful prosecution is not high, believing that the cyber incident was not severe enough to be reported, and a lack of motivation and trust are some of the major hindrance to information sharing activities [15, 30]. However, security information sharing is a significant measure to reduce the risks of similar incidents and develop a better understanding of the risks facing a community [21, 30]. The European Network and Information Security Agency (ENISA) [21] explains that the nature of cyber incidents and attacks is borderless. To support the management of threats and vulnerabilities in the community of cybersecurity, the exchange of data and cross-border cooperation is necessary [21]. ENISA indicates that trust is the critical element to enhance security information sharing. Therefore, the actual usage of CYSEC requires further investigation.

The current study aims to evaluate the impact of online consent communicating on SME's chief information security officers (CISOs) motivation for security information sharing. Taking approaches that motivate users to adopt security recommendations can support the effectiveness of cybersecurity communication [1]. The semi-structured interview method was selected for data collection about behavioural motivation. The data was qualitatively analysed based on a proposed theoretical model by Yoon and Rolland [26] for explaining knowledge-sharing behaviours in virtual communities. The model studies the effect of basic psychological needs in SDT (autonomy, competence, and relatedness) and two antecedents of the basic needs: familiarity and anonymity. Familiarity refers to an individual's understanding of the environment and increases the trust of other people [8]. Anonymity refers to the inability of others to identify an individual or for others to identify one's self [6] and may influence individuals' knowledge sharing behaviour in a virtual community [26].

Our study results indicate that SDT and two antecedents (familiarity and anonymity) account for motivation for security information-sharing behaviour, and online consent has a positive impact on CISOs' motivation. The online consent increased users' trust and provided value for SMEs to make choices and decisions about the suitable level of relatedness for sharing information.

The remainder of the paper is organised as follows. Section 2 presents the research background, the theoretical model, and the research prototype. Section 3 describes the design of our study. Section 4 presents the analysis approach and the answer to the research question. Section 5 discusses the significance of the results and the threats to validity. Section 6 summarises and concludes.

2   Research Background

Security information sharing has been identified to increase end-users' self-efficacy in security awareness programs [9, 19]. Security information sharing means *the exchange of network and information security-related information such as risks, vulnerabilities, threats, internal security issues, and good practice* [21]. Security information should be shared to understand the risks facing the community and any related significant information infrastructure and reduce the risk of incidents.

Confidentiality concerns and the lack of incentives prevent companies to share security information [9, 30]. Geer et al. [30] state *individual companies might have some rudimentary understanding of their own information security health, but we have no aggregate basis for public policy because organisations do not share their data.* The companies' confidentiality concerns include worries about reputation, losing customers, fears of misuse of the information, and strong emotional relatedness to the organisational data. These concerns exist even if security information is anonymised.

Trust influences a user's willingness to share knowledge [26, 28] and security information [21]. Hosmer [25] defines trust as *the expectation by one person, group, or firm of ethically justifiable behaviour on the part of the other person, group, or firm in a joint endeavour or economic exchange.* Some arrangements could mitigate confidentiality concerns relevant to trust issues. The arrangements include to (1) give control of information to the company which shared it, (2) agree about how to use and protect shared information, (3) preserve data anonymity, and (4) develop standard terms for communicating information [9]. Deci et al. [5] explain that also autonomy support, including the offering of choice and relevant information, impacts trust.

The Self-Determination Theory (SDT) has been proposed as a theoretical framework to study humans' motivational dynamics and consequent behaviours [4, 5, 29]. People have different levels and orientations of motivation. Self-determination in SDT is defined as: *the capacity to choose and to have those choices, rather than reinforcement contingencies, drives, or any other forces or pressures, to be the determinants of one's actions. But self-determination is more than capacity. It is also a need.* Deci and Ryan [7] have hypothesised a basic, innate aptitude to be self-determining that leads humans and organisations to engage in desirable behaviours.

SDT assumes that the satisfaction of humans' basic psychological needs - autonomy, competence, and relatedness – leads to self-motivation and positive outcomes [27].

Autonomy refers to a desire to engage in activities with a choice of freedom. Competence implies that individuals have a desire to interact effectively with the environment for producing desired outcomes and preventing undesired events. Relatedness reflects a sense of belongingness and connectedness to others or a social environment.

To explain knowledge-sharing behaviours, Yoon and Rolland [26] extended SDT with two antecedents, familiarity and anonymity. Familiarity refers to an individual's understanding of an environment based on the prior experience and learning of the what, who, how, and when of what is happening [8]. Familiarity may improve perceived competence, the feeling of relatedness [26]. Anonymity refers to the inability of others to identify a person or for others to identify one's self [6]. It can reduce social barriers and allow group members to contribute their opinions [26]. Anonymity may impact on autonomy and the feeling of relatedness. Figure 1 shows the complete model.

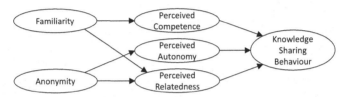

Fig. 1. Research model (Yoon and Rolland [26])

We applied Yoon and Rolland [26] model to evaluate the impact of the motivational factors in online consent on the security information-sharing activities of SME CISOs. We asked SMEs to use self-assessment questionnaires to collect security information and share with a community of security experts and other SMEs. The consent provides choices and the opportunity for CISOs to exert control over information sharing. Through the choices, CISOs can define their relatedness to the tool and the community. Each choice gives information and explains how and where the shared information will be used to increase users' familiarity with the data usage environment. The consent emphasises that the shared information will be used anonymously.

The consent form included three choices based on three levels of relatedness and agreement. (1) disagreement to share security information. (2) agreement to automated processing of security information for recommendations of cybersecurity improvements in their company. (3) agreement to share security information for cybersecurity research. The form includes the choice of anonymity. It supports familiarity by elaborating on the usage of security information to reduce the complexity for new users and enhance the users' competence. Figure 2 shows the consent form

3   Method

This study aims at finding out the impact of online consent communicating on SME's CISOs motivation for sensitive information sharing behaviour. Semi-structured interviews [10] were applied to conduct the empirical part of this study. The interview is one of the most frequently used methods and the most significant sources of data in empirical

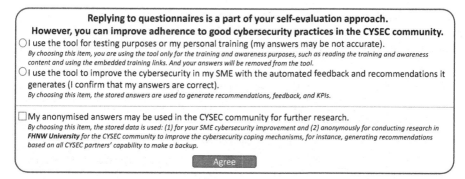

Fig. 2. Screenshot of the Online Consent prototype

studies in software engineering. Interviews provide researchers with important insights into the quality and usability of artefacts since much of the knowledge that is of interest is only available in the minds of users [14]. The same method (interview with CISOs, and key informants who are Network and Information Security experts) has already been used in the context of cybersecurity [22] and security information sharing [9].

A theoretical model based on SDT (Fig. 1) was chosen to analyse the CISOs' information-sharing motivation and whether online consent can motivate them. When we have a developed theory as a template, the model of generalisation is the analytic generalisation [10]. The study seeks answers to this research question: *Do the choice of anonymity and the elaboration of how shared information will be used motivate CISOs of SMEs to share security information?* Security information sharing is a necessary measure in the context of cybersecurity [18, 21] and for SMEs [3, 23]. We are studying how motivational constructs, controlling over data through choices, online agreement, and familiarity with the usage of shared information, can impact information-sharing behaviour. Recorded interviews were analysed based on content analysis (interviewees' argumentations) and theoretical cause-effect relationships [10].

At first, a pilot study, including three interviews with three SMEs' CISOs (project partners), has been conducted—the pilot study allowed to identify and resolve initial problems in the interview questions and the online consent design. The selection of the subjects was based on the availability of the SMEs. There were twelve SMEs (four project partners and eight open call partners), and seven of them participated in the interviews. The participating SMEs came from five EU countries, and all were active in the IT industry. All of them implemented some security controls, including password management, basic approaches for privacy protection, using firewalls, two-factor authentication, cloud security features, and anti-virus installation. One person from each SME was interviewed. The people interviewed were chosen because they all were CISOs or senior managers, and all have been involved in cybersecurity tasks within their companies. All were college graduates and had several years of experience in security. One of the interviewed people was a cybersecurity expert and provided a more in-depth perspective on the importance of security information sharing, the necessity for an agreement, and anonymity. Table 1 presents the SMEs' demographics. In the European Union, companies are considered to be SMEs if they have fewer than 250 employees and an annual turnover of less than € 50 million [31].

Table 1. SMEs' Demographics

ID	Org. size	Offices	Maturity	Structure
1	Small	2	Some controls implemented	CEO, security team, employees
2	Small	1	Some controls implemented	Professors, manager, security team, users
3	Medium	3	Some controls implemented	CEO, security team, employees
4	Small	2	Some controls implemented	CEO, security manager, employees, behavioural scientist
5	Small	2	Some controls implemented	CEO, employees
6	Small	1	Some controls implemented	CEO, employees
7	Small	2	Some controls implemented	CEO, security team, employees

Interviews were conducted face-to-face when possible. For four SMEs, a request for the online interview has been sent. All interviewees had the possibility to find a suitable time. In the online interviews, the screen of the interviewer's computer was shared, and the interviewees were able to see and read the content and had enough time to think about the answers. All the interviews were conducted without distraction. Each interview started with an explanation of the study. Then we presented each interviewee with a screenshot of the online consent and asked them about their understanding of it. All interviewees understood the idea and content. To collecting honest responses, the researcher emphasised that the collected data would be applied anonymously for academic purposes and then obtained the subjects' consent. In the end, a summary of the key findings and answers presented to the interviewees. All interviews were recorded and transcribed.

4   Analysis of the Interview Results

For answering the research question, we studied the impact of anonymity choice and elaboration of data use on SME CISOs' motivation for security information sharing. The interview transcripts showed that both design elements of the online consent form affected the CISOs' motivation for security information sharing. They supported relatedness, autonomy, and competence, and enhanced the CISOs' trust perception. The study participants were motivated to share security information when they perceived that they had control of the communication, and the information was securely stored.

Security Information Sharing Behaviour. Through the interviews, it became clear that the agreement form encouraged the CISOs' information sharing with the tool. ID7 emphasised that the agreement was not only useful but also legally necessary. ID3 and ID7 stated that the agreement positively affected their trust. ID3: *"it has a positive effect on trust because it shows that you take care of the data process and make it clear."* ID7: *"the online consent impacts on trust and shows me that there are thoughts, conditions, and efforts to provide different options and approaches for disclosure."* ID1: *"with this agreement, I feel safer."*

Role of Autonomy Through Choice The analysis of the study participants' arguments showed that the autonomy offered by the choice of sharing security information influenced their information-sharing intention. ID7: *"providing options show me that these people know what they are asking for and give you options."* All interviewees recognised the importance of security information sharing for receiving better advice; however, some of them selected the third choice (sharing information for research). ID1: *"I may change my answer later."* ID7: *"I need to check with my boss. Do I still have the ability to edit my selection? I can decide and let you use the answers, but until the end of the duration of the project."* The respondents were asked whether they wanted to add a new option to the online consent, but no new option was suggested.

Role of Familiarity Through Elaboration of Security Information Use. Improving the CISOs' familiarity with how security information would be used positively affected competence and relatedness. All except ID6 wanted to have a clear description of how their information would be used. ID6 stated: *"the text is clear and understandable, and it improves my awareness."* IDs 1, 3, 4, 7 emphasised that the agreement has not provided sufficient information. When asked why, ID1 stated: *"I do not know how my company information is stored; also, it should be stated if we can change our answer later."* ID3: *"I assumed that after generating recommendations, the data should be destroyed."* ID7: *"it should be clearly stated if the data will be used in the future and after the project."* ID4 also wanted to know more about the security information recipient "FHNW" indicated on the consent form. The interviewees were also asked to state if they wanted to know how the information is processed. Most interviewees stated that their organisations only wanted to have the results of the analysis, i.e. the tool's recommendations. ID2: *"I do not care how and when my data will be used for the research. I just want to have the results."* ID5 and ID6 wanted to know, however, how their information would be processed.

The content of the agreement was perceived to be confusing for some of the subjects. Some of the interviewees suggested modifications to the content. ID2: *"the second option should be rephrased: [try to answer the questionnaires to the best of your knowledge to help us give you more accurate recommendations]."* *"Options should be re-arranged: Options #2 and #3 should be separated from option #1."* *"Option #3 should be rephrased, something like [if you allow us to collect your answer, we will be able to improve the tool, provide you better analysis, and better help you in the future. (Yes or No)]?"* ID4: *"rephrasing can clarify the message because I do not know if I select option #1, I will receive a recommendation."* ID7: *"I think giving an option to SMEs that indicates my answer may or may not be accurate can demote the whole."*

Role of Anonymity Through Security Information Anonymisation. Anonymising the security information could influence perceived relatedness and autonomy and, in

turn, encourage security information sharing. The analysis of the interviewees' arguments showed that all believed that anonymity would reduce the risks of sharing information. They felt more secure when the tool support anonymity. ID2: *"if my data is anonymised, I don't care how my data will be used."* ID1: *"anonymised data sharing shows that it is safe."* ID7: *"I presume that when you put stress on anonymity in the third option, it can imply that the second option is not anonymised. I assume that even for other usages (KPI, recommendations), SMEs should not be recognisable."*
The interviewees would not share security information that would expose details about their organisation, hence would break their anonymity. ID3: *"consent cannot change my opinion; I am not answering the textbox questions."* ID7: *"I know that Yes/No or multi-choice questions can be used for the statistical analysis; however, any question that refers more to deterministic answers, I don't want to answer."*

5 Discussion

5.1 Security Information Sharing

Security information sharing is widely acknowledged [9, 21, 30]; however, confidentiality worries, lack of incentives, and lack of trust lead the companies to avoid sharing information and reporting vulnerabilities [9, 30]. To motivating companies to share their security information, attention to arrangements such as giving control of information to the company which shared information, having an agreement, and preserving data anonymity is necessary [9].

In this study, based on a theoretical model for knowledge-sharing behaviour in virtual communities [26], we have evaluated the impact of online consent communicating on SME CISOs' motivation for information sharing. The model [26] extended the self-determination theory and included two antecedents (familiarity and anonymity) on basic psychological needs (perceived autonomy, perceived competence, and perceived relatedness). Yoon and Rolland [26] study indicates that perceived autonomy does not influence knowledge-sharing behaviours in virtual communities since a virtual community is a voluntary environment that is not controlled by anyone else. However, our findings show that in the context of security information sharing, users' perception of controlling over information sharing increased their motivation, and providing choices enabled users to have selective permission controls. This finding is consistent with the previous study [9]. Moreover, Yoon and Rolland [26] study shows that anonymity has a negative impact on knowledge-sharing activities since the anonymity in a virtual community can be used to attack the opinions of other people, and *in a highly anonymous environment, individuals may think about other people's reactions to their opinion.* In our study, users emphasised that preserving anonymity is essential. Although our study is based only on qualitative findings and a small sample, we can explain the anonymity based on the perception of altruism [28] and the risk of information misuse [3].

In CYSEC, the self-assessment questionnaires are used to collect security information (including cybersecurity awareness, practices, and vulnerabilities) and share with a community of security experts and other SMEs. The results demonstrated that online consent with the choice of anonymity and the elaboration of how shared information is used motivated CISOs of the SMEs to share their information. Also, we discovered that CISOs would not share security information that would expose details. For future research, the other legal and economic incentives [18] should be considered, and not only CISOs opinions but also employees' viewpoints should be studied.

5.2 Study Limitation

This study has some limitations. One criterion influencing the sufficiency of the interviews was saturation. The saturation point is reached when no new information is gathered, or the subjects' viewpoints are repeated [14]. Due to the small sample size, we could not reliably validate saturation and implement a statistical analysis in our study. The study is based on seven interviewed persons from seven SMEs that were active in the IT industry, which limits generalizability. Further research with a larger sample and a diversity of SMEs could reveal more robust results and provide more insights into the influence of the industry type on the SME engagement in security information sharing. Second, since the study is based on the CISOs and senior managers' viewpoints of security information sharing, our study lacks the view of SMEs' employees. To having a wider perspective, the views of SMEs' employees are needed.

6   Summary Conclusions

The paper has evaluated the impact of online consent communicating on motivating CISOs of SMEs for security information sharing. This study followed a deductive approach and tested constructs drawn on the Self-Determination Theory (SDT) as well as two antecedents of SDT constructs (familiarity and anonymity) to evaluate the impact of the online consent on the security information sharing motivation. We applied semi-structured interviews with seven CISOs from seven SMEs for data collection. The study results indicate that online consent increased CISOs' trust and had a positive impact on security information sharing intention. The consent supports familiarity with the environment through the elaboration of security information usage. Moreover, online consent considers the role of anonymity and autonomy through security information anonymisation and the choice of sharing information.

Acknowledgments. This work has received funding from the European Union's Horizon 2020 research and innovation programme under grant agreements No. 740787 (SMESEC), No. 883588 (GEIGER), and the Swiss State Secretariat for Education, Research and Innovation (SERI) under contract number 17.00067. The opinions expressed and arguments employed herein do not necessarily reflect the official views of these funding bodies.

References

1. Cranor, L.F.: A framework for reasoning about the human in the loop. In: 1st Conference on Usability, Psychology and Security. San Francisco, CA, USA (2008)
2. Shojaifar, A., Fricker, S., Gwerder, M.: Elicitation of SME requirements for cybersecurity solutions by studying adherence to recommendations. In: REFSQ Workshops (2018)

3. Lewis, R., Louvieris, P., Abbott, P., Clewley, N., Jones, K.: Cybersecurity information sharing: a framework for sustainable information security management in UK SME supply chains. In: Proceedings of the European Conference on Information Systems (ECIS) (2014)

4. Ryan, R.M., Deci, E.L.: Self-determination theory and the facilitation of intrinsic motivation, social development, and well-being. Am. Psychol. **55**(1), 68–78 (2000)

5. Deci, E.L., Connell, J.P., Ryan, R.M.: Self-determination in a work organisation. J. Appl. Psychol. **74**(4), 580–590 (1989)

6. Christopherson, K.M.: The positive and negative implications of anonymity in Internet social interactions: "On the Internet, Nobody Knows You're a Dog". Comput. Hum. Behav. **23**(6), 3038–3056 (2007)

7. Deci, E.L., Ryan, R.M.: Intrinsic Motivation and Self-determination in Human Behaviour. Plenum Publishing Co, New York (1985)

8. Gefen, D.: E-Commerce: The role of familiarity and trust. Omega **28**(6), 725–737 (2000)

9. Robinson, N., Disley, E.: Incentives and challenges for information sharing in the context of network and information security. In: European Network and Information Security Agency (ENISA) (2010)

10. Yin, R.K.: Case Study Research: Design and Methods. Sage, Thousand Oaks, CA (2009)

11. Furnell, S.M., Gennatou, M., Dowland, P.S.: A prototype tool for information security awareness and training. Log. Inf. Manag. **15**(5/6), 352–357 (2002)

12. Muller, P., Julius, J., Herr, D., Koch, L., Peycheva, V., McKiernan, S.: Annual report on European SMEs 2016/2017: Focus on self-employment. European Commission (2017)

13. Gupta, A., Hammond, R.: Information systems security issues and decisions for small businesses. Inf. Manag. Comput. Secur. **13**(4), 297–310 (2005)

14. Runeson, P., Höst, M., Rainer, A., Regnell, B.: Case Study Research in Software Engineering - Guidelines and Examples. Wiley, Hoboken (2012)

15. Choo, K.-K.R.: The cyber threat landscape: Challenges and future research directions. Comput. Secur. **30**(8), 719–731 (2011)

16. West, R.: The psychology of security. CACM **51**(4), 34–40 (2008)

17. Kurpjuhn, T.: The SME security challenge. Comput. Fraud Secur. **2015**(3), 5–7 (2015)

18. Gal-Or, E., Chose, A.: The economic incentives for sharing security information. Inf. Syst. Res. **16**(2), 186–208 (2005)

19. Rhee, H., Kim, C., Ryu, Y.: Self-efficacy in information security: It's influence on end users' information security practice behavior. Comput. Secur. **28**(8), 816–826 (2009)

20. Puhakainen, P., Siponen, M.: Improving employees' compliance through information systems security training: an action research study. MIS Q. **34**(4), 757–778 (2010)

21. Bedrijfsrevisoren, D., Muynck, J.D., Portesi, S.: Cyber security information sharing: An overview of regulatory and non-regulatory approaches. In: The European Union Agency for Network and Information Security (ENISA) (2015)

22. Beebe, N.L., Rao, V.S.: Examination of organizational information security strategy: A pilot study. In: Americas Conference on Information Systems (AMCIS), USA (2009)

23. Birkás, B., Bourgue, R.: EISAS-european information sharing and alerting system. In: European Union Agency for Network and Information Security (2013)

24. Osborn, E.: Business versus technology: Sources of the perceived lack of cyber security in SMEs. In: The 1st International Conference on Cyber Security for Sustainable Society (2014)

25. Hosmer, L.T.: Trust: The connecting link between organisational theory and philosophical ethics. Acad. Manag. Rev. **20**(2), 379–403 (1995)

26. Yoon, C., Rolland, E.: Knowledge-sharing in virtual communities: familiarity, anonymity and self-determination theory. Behav. Inf. Tech. **31**(11), 1133–1143 (2012)

27. Vallerand, R.J.: Toward a hierarchical model of intrinsic and extrinsic motivation. Adv. Exp. Soc. Psychol. **29**, 271–360 (1997)

28. Chang, H.H., Chuang, S.: Social capital and individual motivations on knowledge sharing: Participant involvement as a moderator. Inf. Manag. **48**(1), 9–18 (2011)
29. Deci, E.L., Ryan, R.M.: The General Causality Orientations Scale: Self-determination in personality. J. Res. Pers. **19**(2), 109–134 (1985)
30. Geer Jr., D., Hoo, K.S., Jaquith, A.: Information security: Why the future belongs to the quants. IEEE Secur. Priv. **1**(4), 24–32 (2003)
31. European Commission. What is an SME? https://ec.europa.eu/growth/smes/business-fri endly-environment/sme-definition_en

Validation of an Information Privacy Perception Instrument at a Zimbabwean University

Kudakwashe Maguraushe[(✉)] [ID], Adéle Da Veiga[ID], and Nico Martins[ID]

School of Computing, College of Science, Engineering and Technology,
University of South Africa (UNISA), Florida Campus, Johannesburg, South Africa
kmagraushe@gmail.com, {dveiga,martin}@unisa.ac.za

Abstract. Privacy issues extend to students as universities acquire and use their personal information for various reasons. This research study was aimed at determining the awareness, expectations and confidence levels of students when the university processes their personal information. The research was also aimed at validating the Information Privacy Perception Survey (IPPS) instrument. The instrument was designed based on the Fair Information Practice Principles, incorporating privacy principles and guidelines from the Organisation for Economic Cooperation and Development's Protection of Privacy and Transborder Flows of Personal Data document, the General Data Protection Regulation and the Zimbabwe Data Protection Act bill. A survey research strategy was used following a quantitative research design where data were collected from 287 students at a selected university using a convenience sampling method. The IPPS instrument was validated using exploratory factor analysis. Seven factors resulted; university confidence, privacy expectations, individual awareness, external awareness, privacy education, practice confidence and correctness expectations. The IPPS can be used by universities to establish the level of awareness and confidence students have regarding how their privacy is upheld by the university. The results show the areas of improvement in the university's privacy practices to create an environment that instils and favours upholding the privacy of students' personal information. Aspects for improvement can be integrated in the university's awareness programmes or policies.

Keywords: Privacy · Personal information · Expectations · Awareness · Confidence · Questionnaire

1 Introduction

Privacy of personal information differs from country to country and many nations now have privacy laws aligned to the international privacy principles [1]. This research focuses on privacy expectations, student privacy awareness and confidence levels of students in universities' capability to uphold privacy values. The protection of privacy within the Zimbabwean context is partly enshrined in the constitution, although there is no prescription on how it will be executed and enforced [2]. This led to the drafting of the

© IFIP International Federation for Information Processing 2020
Published by Springer Nature Switzerland AG 2020
N. Clarke and S. Furnell (Eds.): HAISA 2020, IFIP AICT 593, pp. 300–314, 2020.
https://doi.org/10.1007/978-3-030-57404-8_23

Zimbabwe Data Protection Act (ZDPA) bill with the objective of guiding and protecting the privacy of personal information of individuals/people and organisations/institutions [3, 4].

Many studies have been carried out on privacy, privacy breaches and concerns, privacy compliances, privacy culture, privacy practices, privacy and trust, privacy when online, privacy in eLearning environments, and all this was done in industries, the health sector, for consumers and for employees of organisations [5–9]. According to [10], it is not easy and clear as yet within the Zimbabwean context to comprehend the privacy expectations of students, their privacy awareness levels and their confidence in the university's ability to uphold the privacy of their personal information.

The objectives of this research were to determine the awareness, expectations and confidence levels of students when the university processes their personal information and to validate the Information Privacy Perception Survey (IPPS) instrument using factor and item analysis.

2 Background

Privacy has been defined [11] in terms of the confined mentality of individuals that it is always limited to the ability to access personal data and the impact of self-disclosure, especially on the internet. This is in line with the privacy definition that privacy is "the ability of an individual to control the terms under which their personal information is acquired and used" [12]. Privacy of students personal information at universities is now equally important, especially in the digital context where information can be collected anytime from anywhere [13]. According to research [10], it is important that a university has measures that help in improving students' personal information protection after grasping their awareness, expectations and confidence levels in privacy-related issues.

2.1 Privacy Awareness

Students' awareness of their privacy rights, university privacy policies and university awareness programmes is prudent. Awareness provides a perception about a situation, similar to notice, which is one of the fundamental Fair Information Practice Principles (FIPPs) for information privacy [14]. The awareness is normally concealed through privacy notices by the university [14]. So it follows that students, as users, also need to be aware of the importance of awareness about their privacy rights and university privacy policies, especially when using electronic means [15]. University compliance with the privacy policies, as alluded to by [16] and [17], goes hand in hand with awareness because a lack of awareness means that a user is not privy to the finer details needed to comply, which may result in non-compliance with privacy issues even by the student. Research [18] has shown that awareness of privacy can also be used in creating an atmosphere where all students are knowledgeable about all privacy-related issues, which also assists in their participation in university-related tasks. This must be initiated by universities through the use of privacy policies and other awareness means. As acclaimed by [17], institutions are indebted in making sure that students are aware of the legal, moral and ethical expectations when they share their personal information and one way of accomplishing that is through countless and timeous awareness campaigns.

Awareness is typically conducted within organisations (universities) through privacy notices [14]. Research results [19] indicated students' lack of knowledge in appreciating privacy awareness within universities. Awareness is deemed a precondition for achieving compliance, as indicated by [20]. Results [21] also indicated that compliance to laws, privacy policies and privacy concerns are an end product of appropriate awareness line-ups in organisations. Universities need to stimulate privacy awareness, which permits students to consent, particularly when handling personal information [22]. The Zimbabwean constitution declares that it is the prerogative of the data controller (university, in this case) to propagate and publicise knowledge, and hence awareness, to students [8].

2.2 Privacy Expectations

FIPPs claim that individuals (students) expect privacy of their personal information [23]. There is an expectation that the collection of personal information will be as minimal as possible and relevant to the purpose of collection, even when there is a requirement that the organisation (university) acquire personal information and process it [23]. Research results [6] point to the fact that consumers regard organisations (institutions) with expectations of privacy when they process their personal information. In the event that the consumers (students) start to perceive the organisation (university) as having shortfalls in meeting their privacy expectations, they tend to become impassioned and consequently and might reject personal information sharing with the data collector (university) [24].

2.3 Privacy Confidence

It was proved that sometimes students do not have a need to seek documentation related to privacy from the university because they have full confidence in their institutions upholding privacy [7]. According to [25], a sense of trust that implants confidence is strengthened if universities make privacy pledges which will eventually create a privacy culture that saturates the whole university as an institution. Research [26] corroborated by [27] indicated that trust is an element of confidence, which is to be tested within this research to validate its relevance for students' expectations and awareness. This implies that if privacy regulations and protection are improved and prioritised, the confidence levels of the users (students) will increase proportionally [28]. The lack of trust in using personal information can have negative implications like low confidence levels of students in the university [26, 29]. This was also emphasized by [27], which indicated that it would have undesirable retrogressive consequences. Low confidence levels in the business (university) by customers (students) can be a result of data and privacy breaches [30]. In the end, it is the mandate of the university to come up with privacy policies and make the students knowledgeable about it in a bid to increase confidence and compliance with the privacy policies [31]. The implementation of an information privacy culture within institutions inspires trust and hence confidence as attested by [29].

3 Methods

This research study was conducted using a survey research strategy in a deductive app-roach of a quantitative research design. The questionnaire survey was used as a research method to gather information on students' perceptions and behaviour [32]. In terms of ethics [33], surveys tend to have the advantage of not exposing participants as it can be anonymous. The online distribution of a questionnaire is fast, inexpensive, with moder-ately faster turnaround time, easier administration and easy follow-ups, which all help to increase the reliability of the instrument since many responses reveal more detail [34]. Furthermore, most quantitative research adopts the survey design, as posited by [35]. Online surveys were chosen and according to [35], surveys are efficient and effective when the respondents are all information technology literate and have access to the internet, like in the case of students in this research.

3.1 Questionnaire

The quantitative IPPS instrument was developed with a set of 54 items based on a the-oretical framework [10], all perceived to be of similar value, to which the respondents responded by agreeing or disagreeing with each item or statement. A five-point Likert scale was used with options being strongly disagree, disagree, do not disagree or agree, agree and strongly agree. After using theories from the literature to design the statements, the statements were subjected to a process of expert panel review. The experts assisted by undertaking a focused and comprehensive review of the questions, structure of the questionnaire and its suitability, and provided feedback or made recommendations [35], [36]. The expert review panel consisted of four people with experience in privacy con-sultancy, data protection, privacy compliance and privacy advisory services. The experts recommended the restructuring of some questions for clarity and some statements which were deemed inessential were adjusted.

After the expert review, the instrument was used with a total of 15 students in a pilot study. The purpose was to make sure that the statements were clear, easily understood and comprehensive. A pilot study helps in assessing if the questions are comprehensible to the targeted audience, ensuring that the instrument used in the study is reliable and valid measures of the constructs of interest (i.e. face and construct validity) [37]. After the pilot study, the time was reduced from 20 to 15 min. Also, clarity was added to reduce the notion that some questions were repeated, since each statement was assessed from the three dimensions of awareness, expectations and confidence. A statement was consequently added to the instrument to this effect.

In the design of the IPPS, an introduction with a preface and some privacy definitions used in the research study were included in the front section. The research instrument was divided into two sections that would assist in achieving the stated purpose of the study: Sect. 1: Biographical Information and Sect. 2: Personal information privacy – Awareness, expectations and confidence questions. Section 1 required personal information such as the age, gender, nationality, learning mode, year of study and programme. Section 2 contained nine components of the questionnaire. Each was measured in terms of the three dimensions (i.e. awareness, expectations and confidence). The nine components used the FIPPs as the baseline and were underpinned in the OECD's Protection of Privacy and Transborder Flows of Personal Data document of 2013, the General Data Protection Regulation and the Zimbabwe Data Protection Act [10].

3.2 Sampling

Students at a university in Zimbabwe were selected as the sample by virtue of them being registered students. The sample size was derived using the rule of thumb suggested by [32], multiplying the five-point scale with the number of items in the questionnaire in order to have enough responses to statistically validate the questionnaire. This gives the minimum number of responses expected from the respondents in the research. For the sample size, 270 was the minimum number of students required to participate. A non-probability sampling technique was used for the survey. The researchers chose purposive sampling for the selection of experts to participate in the expert panel research on the survey questions. The experts were recruited based on their expertise in the field of information privacy. The researchers also chose convenience sampling for the pilot study participants because it allows for a quicker way of obtaining the data since the researcher picks "whomever is convenient as a participant in the study" [38]. For the final survey, the convenience sampling method was considered the most appropriate [35, 39]. Two hundred and seventy eight students participated in the survey, which was an adequate sample. The researcher recruited the participants by means of a presentation to the students highlighting the purpose of the research and also seeking their participation. Participation in the research was voluntary, anonymous and confidential.

3.3 Questionnaire Administration

In this research study, an invitation with a hyperlink to the html questionnaire was sent to the respondents through email as the primary method for sending out the survey. Hard-copy questionnaires were provided to some students who indicated their unavailability on the internet. The estimated completion time for the questionnaire was approximately 15 min and the collection period was five weeks. The electronic/online IPPS was administered using the Survey Tracker software [40]. There was a "Yes" and a "No" button to the questionnaire where the students could click on "Yes" if they consented to continue to participating and move to the next page or "No" if they no longer wanted to participate and it would move to the last page.

3.4 Data Analysis

The data analysis was done using SPSS version 25 for the descriptive statistics per subscale (such as the means and standard deviations) and for the questionnaire validation using the Kaiser-Meyer-Olkin (KMO) measure and Bartlett's Test of Sphericity (BTS), factor analysis and Cronbach alpha analysis.

4 Results

The results of the responses per age band are shown in Table 1.

Table 1. Survey responses

Response	Frequency	Percentage
1996–2019	67	23.3
1977–1995	177	61.7
1965–1976	41	14.3
1946–1964	1	0.3
Born 1945 or earlier	1	0.3
No response	0	0.0

Of the 287 responses, 143 were female and 140 male respondents with four who selected the "Other" option. 284 were Zimbabweans and three were from other African countries.

4.1 Validation of Measurement Instrument

The collected data was first subjected to the KMO to measure the sampling adequacy and the BTS to ascertain the presence of correlations and significance among the variables [41]. The BTS is considered significant at the level of $p < 0.05$ [41] (Table 2).

Table 2. Test for sample adequacy and significance

Kaiser-Meyer-Olkin measure of sampling adequacy		0.647
Bartlett's test of sphericity	Approx. Chi-Square	231.517
	df	6.000
	Sig.	0.000

Table 3. Cronbach alpha values for the new factors

Factor/Dimension	Number of items	Cronbach alpha
Factor 1: University confidence (UC)	8	0.922
Factor 2: Privacy expectations (PE)	7	0.789
Factor 3: Individual awareness (IA)	5	0.820
Factor 4: External awareness (EA)	3	0.807
Factor 5: Privacy education (PE)	4	0.737
Factor 6 (eliminated factor)	2	0.225
Factor 7: Practice confidence (PC)	8	0.917
Factor 8: Correctness expectations (CE)	6	0.781
Total	**43**	

Table 4. Questionnaire statements extract for the new factors

New factor	Statement	Component examined
University confidence	I am confident that the university has reasonable justification (e.g. consent, a contract, legal requirement) for processing my personal information	Use limitation
	I am confident that the university's privacy notice is easy to understand	Notice/openness
Privacy expectations	I expect my personal information not to be disclosed, made available or used, unless it is in line with the law	Use limitation
	I expect the privacy policy to be easily understood	Privacy policy
Individual awareness	I am aware that I should be able to request copies of the records of my personal information from the university	Individual participation
	I am aware that the university should have a process whereby I can request whatever personal information the university has collected about me	Individual participation
External awareness	I am aware that the university should specify the purpose of collecting my personal information	Purpose specification
	I am aware that the purpose should be specified no later than at the point of collection	Purpose specification
Privacy education	I am aware that the university should, as part of best practice, conduct privacy training for students	Privacy education
	I expect the university to conduct privacy training for students	Privacy education
Practice confidence	I am confident that the university conducts privacy training for students	Privacy education
	I am confident that the privacy policy is easily understood	Privacy policy
Expect correctness	I expect the university to take reasonable steps to ensure that my personal information processed by them is correct (e.g. accurate, up to date, complete and relevant) for the purpose of collection	Information quality
	I expect the university to specify the purpose of collecting my personal information	Purpose specification

Table 5. Mean and standard deviation values for the final seven factors

Descriptive statistics					
Factor	N	Min	Max	Mean	Std deviation
University confidence	287	1.25	5.00	3.5740	0.90282
Privacy expectations	287	2.86	5.00	4.5610	0.41050
Individual awareness	287	1.80	5.00	4.0774	0.75485
External awareness	287	1.67	5.00	4.1429	0.77054
Privacy education	287	1.75	5.00	4.1254	0.73406
Practice confidence	287	1.63	5.00	3.4194	0.88332
Correction expectation	287	2.33	5.00	4.5296	0.45205
Valid N (listwise)	287				

In this research, a KMO value of 0.647 was obtained – greater than the threshold value of 0.60 postulated by [41, 42], implying that there was a strong correlation structure. The BTS was significant at $p < 0.00$ for overall significance for the awareness, expectations and confidence concepts, adding further evidence of sampling validity and the conduct of exploratory factor analysis (EFA). The value showed that a meaningful factor analysis could be conducted, as attested to by [43].

4.2 Factor Analysis

The IPPS was subjected to the EFA using the principal axis factoring with Oblimin rotation with Kaiser normalisation. The rotated pattern matrix for the 54-item instrument is shown in Table 6 in Appendix A.

In research, items with factor loadings that are less than the agreed threshold (≤ 0.40) [43] and those with cross loadings that are high (with < 0.20 difference) in a single factor are eliminated. In this research, items with lower factor loadings but above the cut-off loading included items 11, 23, 26, 27, 36, 38, 39, 45, 58 and 59. They were all retained except item 59, which had a cross loading together with item 41 which were excluded. Factor 6 had two items and therefore it was excluded. Furthermore, the Cronbach alpha of factor 6 was very low (0.225), which falls outside the cut-off Cronbach value (≥ 0.7).

The new factors were labelled based on the items in the respective factors. The Cronbach alpha measures the internal consistency of a scale [43]. The Cronbach alpha values for the new factors, number of items and the Cronbach alpha are shown in Table 3 below.

The final seven factors had Cronbach alpha coefficient values that were higher than 0.7, which indicated that there was a strong item covariance [32], [35] of between 0.7 and 0.9, rendering the values adequate as posited by [34]. This resulted in the Cronbach alpha values being considered suitable and adequate for the purpose of this study. The Cronbach alpha values for factor 6 (eliminated factor) was very low, with a loading of 0.225, and thus it was removed. An extract of the questionnaire statements per factor is shown in Table 4.

4.3 Means and Standard Deviations of the Factors Interpretation

Research conducted by [44] used an average of 4.0 as a threshold for distinguishing between positive and potential negative perceptions given the importance of privacy and information security together with the legal requirements for privacy, and this was used as a baseline for this research. Table 5 shows the mean and the standard deviation values for the final seven factors.

Using the cut-off value adopted from [44] as the baseline, the following were observed:

- A mean value of 4.56 was recorded for the privacy expectations (factor 2), which is more than the cut-off value of 4.0 prescribed. It shows that students had positive perceptions about how the university handled and used their personal information.
- Correction expectation (factor 8) showed a mean value of 4.53, which was also considered to be highly positive in terms of students' perceptions.
- External awareness (factor 4) recorded a mean value of 4.14. This also shows positive perceptions.
- Privacy education (factor 5) recorded a mean value of 4.13, which is also above the cut-off value. This also shows positive perceptions of students.
- Individual awareness (factor 3) recorded a mean value of 4.08, showing slightly positive perceptions of students.
- University confidence (factor 1) scored 3.57, which is lower than the cut-off mean value. This shows that the perceptions of confidence and the confidence in the university could be improved.
- The lowest mean value was recorded under practice confidence (factor 7) with a value of 3.43. This represents the most negative dimension, for which improvement was required.

From the results, it can be drawn that privacy expectations and correction expectation are meaningful factors which are pivotal for the development of personal information privacy for a university, resulting in students developing confidence with the university in upholding the privacy of their personal information.

5 Discussion

The results show that the students had both positive and negative perceptions about how the university handled and used their personal information. Based on the research instrument used, the students had positive perceptions and expectations of privacy components like the use limitation, privacy policy, collection limitation, consent and notice/openness privacy components. These included the expectation and awareness that the university would justify the need for information collection and processing, confidence to be given, the provision to review collected personal information, confidence in the existence of the publishing privacy notices and privacy policy, and that these would be easy to comprehend.

The students had positive perceptions on the correction expectations. This focused on students' expectations of the university, on how the university had to come up with privacy policies and notices that were easily understandable, that the university would only use students' personal information for extreme scenarios like legal requirements and that this would be done with the students' consent. They expected the university to justify the collection and processing of their personal information, the information should not be just disclosed. Students also seemed to be aware of what they needed to do individually to uphold the privacy of their personal information. Individual awareness recorded positive perceptions by students in terms of consent, use limitation and individual participation. These included being aware of when to opt in for the use of their personal information, their rights to opt out in case they no longer chose to share their personal information and being aware that they had the right to decide who to share their personal information with. The university can focus on increasing the students' individual awareness levels by engaging in privacy training sessions, sending short message service (sms) or emails, letters and other notices.

External awareness also showed positive perceptions. This revealed perceptions about students' awareness levels in specifying the purpose of collection and the limitations of information use thereof. Students seemed to be aware and expected the university to remind them continuously of privacy-related issues through privacy newsletters, magazines, notices and so on as part of privacy best practices. Students were aware and expected the university to conduct privacy training to increase their privacy awareness.

The results showed that practice confidence was an area needing improvement, especially in terms of how to handle consent, privacy education, individual participation and privacy policy. Another area of improvement could be the university's privacy practices in creating an environment that favours the upholding of privacy of personal information. The university has to improve and create an environment that instils student confidence in the university regarding privacy.

The contribution is the identification of the factors and validation of the questionnaire. Further more the questionnaire can aid univeristies to identify how to further improve student awareness about privacy to be in line with their expectations. This will ultemately aid in better protection of student personal information also aiding in addressing concerns for information privacy amongst students.

6   Limitations and Future Research

This research was conducted on one institution. In future, research will aim to extend the study to wider sample of universities. There is also need to validate the conceptual framework using structural equation modelling (SEM).

7   Conclusion

An IPPS questionnaire was developed for this research to measure the expectations, awareness and confidence of students in the university upholding the privacy of their personal information. After the questionnaire was used at a university in Zimbabwe, the data obtained was used to validate it by means of the EFA. The results from the validated instrument led to the formulation of seven new factors. The questionnaire can be used by other universities to measure and improve the privacy awareness and confidence based on the expectations of students thereby aiding to improve the protection of personal information.

Acknowledgement. The researchers are grateful to Organisational Diagnostics for hosting the survey and Liezel Korf Associates for assisting in the statistical analysis. This research paper is wholly supported by Unisa's Master's and Doctoral Research Bursary funding.

Appendix A

Table 6. Rotated pattern matrix for the eight-factor model

Item number	Factor							
	1	**2**	**3**	**4**	**5**	**6**	**7**	**8**
q30	0.77							
q19	0.76							
q18	0.73							
q24	0.62							
q31	0.62							
q13	0.60							
q25	0.60							
q12	0.56							
q28		0.63						
q29		0.60						
q46		0.59						
q47		0.58						
q34		0.54						
Item Number	**1**	**2**	**3**	**4**	**5**	**6**	**7**	**8**
q58		0.44						
q11		0.42						
q56			-0.89					
q57			-0.87					
q27			-0.46					
q38			-0.45					
q39			-0.44					
q20				-0.80				
q21				-0.68				
q26				-0.47				
q59			-0.40	0.47				
q51					0.70			
q50					0.70			
q52					0.58			
q53					0.56			
q41		0.46				0.61		
q40						0.56		
q36						0.40		
q61							-0.84	
q54							-0.81	
q60							-0.80	

(*continued*)

Table 6. (*continued*)

q55							-0.74	
q43							-0.65	
q49							-0.58	
q48							-0.54	
q42							-0.53	
q16								-0.75
q22								-0.63
q17								-0.58
q14								-0.53
q23								-0.48
q45								-0.45

Extraction method: Principal axis factoring
Rotation method: Oblimin with Kaiser normalization
a. Rotation converged in 25 iterations

References

1. Piper, D.L.A.: Data protection laws of the world, Attorney Advertising (2020). https://www.dlapiperdataprotection.com/index.html
2. Republic of Zimbabwe: Constitution of the Republic of Zimbabwe 2013 (2013)
3. Chetty, P.: Presentation on Zimbabwe Data Protection Bill, Harmon. ICT Policies, Sub-Sahara Africa (2013)
4. Zimbabwe Data Protection Act Bill: The Zimbabwe Data Protection Act Bill, Harare, Zimbabwe, pp. 1–47 (2013)
5. Ivanova, M., Grosseck, G., Holotescu, C.: Researching data privacy in eLearning. In: 2015 International Conference on Information Technology-Based Higher Education and Training (ITHET), pp. 1–6 (2015)
6. Da Veiga, A.: An information privacy culture instrument to measure consumer privacy expectations and confidence. Inf. Comput. Secur. **26**(3), 338–364 (2018)
7. Stange, C.: Privacy Concern and Student Engagement in the Virtual Classroom, pp. 1–73. University of Victoria, Canada (2011)
8. Chua, H.N., Herbland, A., Wong, S.F., Chang, Y.: Compliance to personal data protection principles: a study of how organizations frame privacy policy notices. Telemat. Inform. **34**(4), 157–170 (2017)
9. Katurura, M., Cilliers, L.: The extent to which the POPI Act makes provision for patient privacy in mobile personal health record systems. In: Conference, IST-Africa 2015, pp. 1–8 (2016)
10. Maguraushe, K., Da Veiga, A., Martins, N.: A conceptual framework for a student personal information privacy culture at universities in Zimbabwe. In: Proceedings of 4th International Conference on the Internet, Cyber Security and Information Systems 2019, vol. 12, pp. 143–156. Kalpa Publications in Computing (2019)
11. Miltgen, C.L.: Online consumer privacy concerns and willingness to provide personal data on the internet. Int. J. Netw. Virtual Organ. **6**(6), 574 (2009)

12. Schwaig, S.K., Kane, G.C., Storey, V.C.: Compliance to the fair information practices: How are the Fortune 500 handling online privacy disclosures? Inf. Manag. **43**(7), 805–820 (2006)

13. Kokolakis, S.: Privacy attitudes and privacy behaviour: a review of current research on the privacy paradox phenomenon. Comput. Secur. **64**, 122–134 (2017)

14. Vail, M.W., Earp, J.B., Antón, A.L.: An empirical study of consumer perceptions and comprehension of web site privacy policies. IEEE Trans. Eng. Manag. **55**(3), 442–454 (2008)

15. Kyobe, M.: Knowledge management using information technology: ethical and legal issues in a university. In: 2010 International Conference on Information Society, pp. 592–597 (2010)

16. Botha, J.G., Eloff, M.M., Swart, I.: The effects of the POPI Act on small and medium enterprises in South Africa. In: Proceedings of the 2015 Information Security for South Africa (ISSA 2015) Conference (2015)

17. Kyobe, M.: Towards a framework to guide compliance with IS security policies and regulations in a university. In: Proceedings of the 2010 Information Security for South Africa Conference ISSA, pp. 1–6 (2010)

18. Fink, C.: Privacy and confidentiality in the virtual classroom : instructor perceptions, knowledge and strategies (2012)

19. Chen, L.F., Ismail, R.: Information technology program students' awareness and perceptions towards personal data protection and privacy. In: International Conference on Research and Innovation in Information Systems (ICRIIS), vol. 2013, pp. 434–438 (2013)

20. Aghasian, E., Garg, S., Gao, L., Yu, S., Montgomery, J.: Scoring users' privacy disclosure across multiple online social networks. IEEE Access **5**, 13118–13130 (2017)

21. Nwaeze, A.C., Zavarsky, P., Ruhl, R.: Compliance evaluation of information privacy protection in e-government systems in Anglophone West Africa using ISO/IEC 29100:2011. In: 2017 12th International Conference on Digital Information Management, ICDIM 2017, vol. 2018–Janua, no. Icdim, pp. 98–102 (2018)

22. Isabwe, G.M.N., Reichert, F.: Revisiting students' privacy in computer supported learning systems. In: International Conference on Information Society (i-Society), pp. 256–262 (2013)

23. Cate, F.: The failure of fair information practice principles. In: Conference on Consumer Protection in the Age of the Information Economy, pp. 341–378 (2006)

24. Morton, A., Sasse, A.M.: Desperately seeking assurances: segmenting users by their information-seeking preferences A Q methodology study of users' ranking of privacy, security & trust cues. In: PST 2014 International Conference on Privacy, Security and Trust Proceedings, April, pp. 1–10. IEEE (2014)

25. Alnatheer, M., Chan, T., Nelson, K.: Understanding and measuring information security culture. In: Pacific Asia Conference on Information Systems (PACIS), vol. 144, no. 12, pp. 1–15 (2012)

26. Dwyer, N., Marsh, S.: How students regard trust in an elearning context. In: 14th Annual Conference on Privacy, Security and Trust, PST, pp. 682–685 (2016)

27. OECD: Recommendation of the Council Concerning Guidelines Governing the Protection of Privacy and Transborder Flows of Personal Data, no. C(2013)79, pp. 11–37 (2013)

28. BSA: BSA Privacy Framework, pp. 1–2. The Software Alliance (2018)

29. OAIC: Privacy Management Framework, pp. 1–4. Office of the Australian Information Commissioner (2015)

30. Bush, D.: How data breaches lead to fraud. Netw. Secur. **2016**(7), 11–13 (2016)

31. Kurkovsky, S., Syta, E.: Monitoring of electronic communications at universities: policies and perceptions of privacy. In: Proceedings of the 44th Annual Hawaii International Conference on System Sciences, 2011, pp. 1–10 (2011)

32. Gerber, H., Hall, R.: Quantitative research design, pp. 1–64. HR Statistics, Pretoria (2017)

33. Mathers, N., Fox, N., Hunn, A.: Implementing adminstrative surveys and questionnaires (2009)

34. Creswell, J.W., Creswell, J.D.: Research Design: Qualitative, Quantitative and Mixed Methods Approaches, 5th edn. Sage Publications, Los Angels, USA (2018)
35. Saunders, M., Lewis, P., Thornhill, A.: Research Methods for Business Students, 7th edn. Pearson, Essex, England (2016)
36. Kumar, R.: Research Methodology: A Step-By-Step Guide for Beginners, 3rd edn. Sage Publications, London (2011)
37. Bhattacherjee, A.: Introduction to research, social science research: principles, methods, and practices (2012)
38. Jackson, S.L.: Research Methods and Statistics: A Critical Thinking Approach (2009)
39. Salkind, N.J.: Exploring Research, 9th edn. Pearson Education Limited, Essex, England (2017)
40. Scantron: Online & paper survey management – SurveyTracker. https://www.scantron.com/assessment-solutions/surveys/online-paper-survey-management-survey-tracker-plus/#surveytracker-plus. Accessed: 15 Apr 2020
41. Gie, A., Pearce, S.: A beginner's guide to factor analysis: focusing on exploratory factor analysis (2012)
42. O'Rourke, N., Hatcher, A.: A step-by-step approach to using SAS for factor analysis and structural equation modelling. Cary, NC (2013)
43. Hair, J.F., Black, W.C., Babbin, B.J., Anderson, R.E.: Univariate Data Analysis, 7th edn. Pearson Education Limited, Essex, England (2014)
44. Da Veiga, A., Martins, N.: Information security culture: a comparative analysis of four assessments. In: Proceedings of the 8th European Conference on IS Management and Evaluation, vol. 8, no. 2014, pp. 49–57 (2014)

Are We Really Informed on the Rights GDPR Guarantees?

Maria Sideri[1](✉) ⓘ and Stefanos Gritzalis[2] ⓘ

[1] Privacy Engineering and Social Informatics Laboratory, Department of Cultural Technology and Communication, University of the Aegean, 81100 Lesvos, Greece
msid@aegean.gr
[2] Laboratory of Systems Security, Department of Digital Systems, University of Piraeus, 18534 Piraeus, Greece
sgritz@unipi.gr

Abstract. Enhancing data subjects' rights in order to increase control over personal data is doubtless GDPR's priority. Though, the protection of personal data and human rights does not rely only on the legal framework, but also on data subjects' knowledge regarding their right to data protection. This paper building upon a research having explored a group of Greek data subjects' extent of knowledge about the rights GDPR guarantees which revealed that there is not sufficient knowledge for all the rights investigated, aims to explore factors that affect the extent of rights knowledge focusing on information sources and demographic variables. The results show that rights knowledge extent is not that much affected by respondents' demographic characteristics, while on the contrary the sources of information on GDPR impact more. This generates the need for more awareness programs, national campaigns and educational interventions on GDPR targeted to the public, in order to prevent the emergence of a new form of inequality between data subjects as a result of rights' knowledge gap.

Keywords: General data protection regulation (GDPR) · Data subjects' rights awareness · Informative sources · Demographic characteristics

1 Introduction

In a data-driven economy, personal data are daily collected, processed, interlinked, transmitted and exchanged between different actors, agencies and states worldwide becoming a tradeable asset. Thus a high-risk reality emerges for social subjects and severe threats come up regarding the protection of personal data and human rights.

Despite the several legal documents for personal data protection produced in Europe since 1980 s and the implementation of Directive 95/46 in all member-states of European Union (EU), countries differentiated in their legal culture and practice [1–3]. In this frame, the General Data Protection Regulation (GDPR) is expected to further harmonize data protection legislation ensuring a "coherent and uniform application of the rules on the protection of fundamental rights and of the freedoms of natural persons with regard

© IFIP International Federation for Information Processing 2020
Published by Springer Nature Switzerland AG 2020
N. Clarke and S. Furnell (Eds.): HAISA 2020, IFIP AICT 593, pp. 315–326, 2020.
https://doi.org/10.1007/978-3-030-57404-8_24

to the processing of personal data" (recital 10) [4]. Without departing from previously established principles, GDPR aims at enhancing data subjects' rights introducing also new ones in order to increase data subjects' control over their data. Simultaneously, it sets a stricter framework regarding data controllers' and processors' obligations emphasizing on regulatory compliance monitoring measures too.

Although the strengthening of data protection legislation is considered over time very important, data subjects' knowledge about their rights is equally significant, considering that data protection and privacy preservation presuppose individual and collective responsibility, while their infringement seriously affects both persons and societies. In this context, an exploratory research [5] took place in spring 2019 aiming to investigate a group of Greek adult data subjects' knowledge about their rights as set in GDPR. This paper building upon that research aims to explore the impact of information sources (e.g. mass media, Internet) and socio-demographic characteristics on data subjects rights' knowledge. The paper is organized as follows. Section 2 provides a brief overview of the framework and the main findings of the research, while presenting the statement of interest for this paper. Section 3 records the findings regarding the impact of demographic variables and information sources on the extent of rights' knowledge. Section 4 discusses the findings and concludes the paper.

2 Research on Data Subjects' Knowledge Regarding GDPR Rights

2.1 Research Framework

Data subjects often think they can control the data they share, ignoring that these are now possessed and controlled by others [6, 7]. Despite concerns increase about data protection, in several cases data subjects do not adopt protective behavior [8]. This situation becomes more complicated when data subjects are unaware of data protection laws and/or believe that others protect their data (e.g. governments or service providers) [7, 9, 10]. On the contrary, data subjects' knowledge of technical aspects and data collection practices used by organizations and service providers, knowledge about legislation, legal aspects of data protection and protection policies and strategies can help data subjects to make informed decisions to control their data [11, 12].

Data subjects' knowledge about data protection legislation, their rights and the role of public Authorities has been studied before the implementation of GDPR [11, 13, 14]. However, to the best of our knowledge there was no relevant research in Greece or EU exploring data subjects' awareness of the rights GDPR guarantees up to the date our research began. Special Eurobarometer 487a is the first official survey published in June 2019 [15] exploring awareness of the rights to access, correct and have personal data deleted, object to receive direct marketing, have a say to automated decisions and data portability right. Our exploratory research, based on Trepte et al. [11] and Park [12] arguments, aimed to investigate a group of Greek data subjects' extent of knowledge regarding their GDPR rights, while also exploring other issues related to data protection. Comparing to Eurobarometer 2019, our research included several items addressing to data subjects' right to be informed and data subjects' consent. The right to information fits in the first stage of processing timeline and it is linked to consent which is valid only if it is informed [16], while consent is the very first decision that data subjects make.

A four-section questionnaire[1] was used for the research carried out from March 18 to April 18, 2019.

2.2 Main Findings

In order for the readers to have an overview of the research findings, these are briefly presented below. Out of the 101 people that voluntarily participated in the research, 49 are men and 51 women (one didn't respond). Half of them (49.5%) are 36–45 years old. Among respondents, 36.6% are public sector employees, 31.7% private sector employees, 42.6% hold a master and 38.6% a graduate degree (section D).

Most participants were informed on GDPR by Internet (44.6%), 13.9% by mass media, 16.8% by someone else, while 24.8% stated personal interest/engagement with the topic. Only 5% of the respondents stated that GDPR addresses to "data subjects' rights strengthening", while 17.8% selected the "stricter delimitation of data collection and processing procedures" reply (section A).

Participants were asked to self-assess the extent of their knowledge regarding GDPR rights (section B) using a 5-point scale (questions 1–12) and to declare the conditions for exercising the right to be forgotten and the right to data processing restriction having the option of multiple responses (questions 13–14). The results showed that respondents were more aware of the right to be informed about data processing and less of that to be informed about data transmission or data breach. They also knew very well that consent is required for data processing, but were less aware of their ability to withdraw consent. Data portability right knowledge was rather low. Almost 1/5 of the sample didn't know the conditions for exercising the right to be forgotten and 29.7% the conditions for exercise the data processing restriction right.

Although respondents showed high level of concerns and acknowledged risks (security issues and data usage for fraud) when providing personal data, only 6.9% read the whole privacy policy text. Moreover, 24.8% was unsure if providing their consent explicitly, approximately 21% stated not doing this, while 5.9% didn't know if they had information on the conditions for data processing when providing data and 10.9% stated "never". Participants' views regarding their responsibility, the role of providers, Regulatory Authorities and governments for data protection showed that 61.4% do not agree that governments protect their data, 52.4% do not trust service providers to protect their data and only 26.7% stated aware of data protection legislation to protect themselves (section C).

2.3 Exploring Factors that Affect Data Subjects' Extent of Rights Knowledge. Statement of Interest

The first results of our research revealed fluctuations regarding data subjects' extent of knowledge about their rights. In order to detect what affects these fluctuations, this paper seeks to identify possible relationships between rights knowledge extent and the demographic characteristics of the sample. Furthermore, assuming that the extent of

---

[1] https://drive.google.com/file/d/1BXlxqMMxqOUc3gindABJf2cqNYflCY9b/view?usp=sharing.

knowledge may be related to some kind of expertise or the sources of information on GDPR[2], the relationship between knowledge extent and information sources is also explored. Beyond the differentiations observed between EU countries regarding their legal culture and practice [1–3], differences have been also recorded "in the intensity and scope of information campaigns, media attention, and public debate" regarding data protection [3] (p. 234). This argument supports our assumption that information sources may impact on data subjects' knowledge on GDPR and the rights it sets.

In order to explore the impact of the variables mentioned above on data subjects' extent of knowledge, inferential statistics are employed using SPSS v.21. Transformations in variables values are necessary in order for the statistic tests to be better applied. Firstly, the values of age, educational level and employment are re-codified in order for more coherent clusters within variables considering the small number of respondents in some clusters. Thus, regarding i) "age", the cluster "18–25 years old" (n = 6) is included in the following (26–35), while the cluster ">56 years old" (n = 3) in the preceding (46–55), ii) "educational level", the cluster of those holding a PhD (n = 3) is included in that of those holding a M.Sc., iii) "employment", teachers (n = 2) are included in the cluster of public sector employees, freelancers (n = 18) in the cluster of private sector employees, while students (n = 9) and other (n = 3) constitute one cluster. Secondly, in order for all questions in section B to be measured in the same scale, the results of questions 13–14 (nominal scale) are transformed into ordinal scale. Consequently, we assume that those having chosen i) all four replies in B.14 have accomplished a score of 5, ii) three replies a score of 4, iii) two a score of 3 and iv) one a score of 2. In question B.13, a 4-point scale is used. Thus participants who have chosen i) all three replies achieve a score of 4, ii) two a score of 3 and iii) one a score of 2. The "don't know" answer is equivalent to "not at all" (score 1) for both questions.

3   Results

Having reformed the results of questions B.13–14, Table 1 presents data subjects' self-assessment regarding the extent of rights knowledge.

To identify possible relationship between gender and rights knowledge, Mann-Whitney test was used revealing statistically significant difference (Tables 2 and 3) between men and women regarding the form of consent [U(49,51) = 883.00, p = .009] with women having a higher mean (3.88) than men (3.28). The opposite was shown for the right to data processing restriction [U(49,51) = 959.00, p = .040] where men had a higher mean (2.91) than women (2.33).

Spearman rho was used to explore the correlation between age and educational level variables with rights knowledge extent. The results showed that age was negatively related at low degree to the extent of knowledge regarding the right to be forgotten (rho = −.269, p = .007), revealing that as age increases the knowledge regarding all or most of the conditions for the exercise of the right decreases. In other words, younger people are more familiar with all the conditions for the exercise of this right. Educational level was shown to be positively related at a low degree also to consent withdraw (rho

---

[2] In Eurobarometer 2019 survey [15], participants were asked to declare if they had heard (or not) each of the six rights explored and not to state the information source.

Table 1. Data subjects' extent of knowledge per right

		Not at all (1)	Little (2)	Moderate (3)	Well (4)	Very well (5)
Right to be informed	for data processing and subject's rights (B.1)	9.9	10.9	23.8	28.7	25.7
	for data used for profiling and consequences (B.7)	14.9	19.8	19.8	29.7	14.9
	for data transmission to third party (B.8)	18.8	19.8	17.8	20.8	21.8
	for high-risk personal data breach, consequences, measures taken (B.9)	18.8	20.8	19.8	18.8	21.8
Consent	required for data use (B.3)	5.0	9.9	9.9	27.7	46.5
	form (free, specific…) (B.4)	7.9	7.9	23.8	36.6	23.8
	withdraw (B.5)	18.8	11.9	21.8	17.8	26.7
	not required for service usage (unless necessary for service provision) (B.6)	16.8	16.8	28.7	20.8	15.8
Right to oppose	to data processing (incl. profiling) (B.10)	13.9	25.7	21.8	23.8	13.9
	(not to be subjected) to automated decision (B.11)	17.8	28.7	25.7	15.8	10.9

(*continued*)

Table 1. (*continued*)

	Not at all (1)	Little (2)	Moderate (3)	Well (4)	Very well (5)
Right to data rectification (B.2)	10.9	10.9	30.7	26.7	18.8
Right to data portability (B.12)	29.7	23.8	14.9	22.8	7.9
Right to be forgotten (B.13)	22.8	29.7	32.7	14.9	
Right to data processing restriction (B.14)	29.7	19.8	21.8	18.8	9.9

Table 2. Gender differences regarding knowledge about the form of consent

Gender	N	Mean rank	Median	Range	Mean
Man	49	43,02	3,0000	4,00	3,2857
Woman	51	57,69	4,0000	4,00	3,8824

Table 3. Gender differences regarding knowledge about data processing restriction right

Gender	N	Mean rank	Median	Range	Mean
Man	49	56,43	3,0000	4,00	2,9184
Woman	51	44,80	2,0000	4,00	2,3333

$= .229$, $p = .023$) and the right to data processing restriction (rho $= .217$, $p = .029$). Specifically, those holding a M.Sc./Ph.D. have a higher extent of knowledge for these rights. Regarding employment, Kruskal-Wallis test showed that employment affects the extent of knowledge regarding the form of consent only [$H(2) = 7.071$, $p = .029$] (Table 4).

Table 4. Employment differences regarding knowledge about the form of consent

Employment	N	Mean rank	Median	Range	Mean
Public sector employee/teacher	39	53,74	4,0000	4,00	3,6923
Private sector employee/freelancer	50	44,82	4,0000	4,00	3,3800
Students/other	12	67,83	4,5000	3,00	4,2500

Up to this point it can be concluded that demographic variables do not generally affect the extent of knowledge regarding data subjects' rights or their consent. Table 5 presents the results of the impact of information sources on knowledge extent for each right (non-parametric Kruskal-Wallis was used in this case too).

Table 5. Effect of information source on the extent of knowledge rights

Rights		Information sources					
			N	Mean rank	Mean	Median	Range
B.1	H(3) = 10.543, p = .014	MM[a]	14	42,18	3,0714	3,5000	4,00
		Int	45	54,16	3,6889	4,0000	4,00
		PIn	25	59,58	3,8800	4,0000	4,00
		InSb	16	33,31	2,7500	3,0000	4,00
B.7	H(3) = 10.425, p = .015	MM	14	42,11	2,7143	2,5000	4,00
		Int	44	51,92	3,1591	3,0000	4,00
		PIn	25	62,60	3,6800	4,0000	3,00
		InSb	17	35,94	2,4118	2,0000	3,00
B.8	H(3) = 4.116 ns	No statistically significant differences found					
B.9	H(3) = 7.484 ns	No statistically significant differences found					
B.3	H(3) = 8.206, p = .042	MM	14	41,46	3,7143	4,0000	4,00
		Int	44	52,89	4,1364	4,5000	4,00
		PIn	25	59,66	4,4000	5,0000	3,00
		InSb	17	38,29	3,4118	4,0000	4,00
B.4	H(3) = 7.083 ns	No statistically significant differences found					
B.5	H(3) = 4.581 ns	No statistically significant differences found					
B.6	H(3) = 16.360, p = .001	MM	14	35,64	2,3571	2,5000	3,00
		Int	44	53,40	3,1591	3,0000	4,00
		PIn	25	64,82	3,6800	4,0000	4,00
		InSb	17	34,18	2,2353	2,0000	4,00
B.10	H(3) = 8.845, p = .031	MM	14	40,07	2,5000	2,5000	4,00
		Int	45	48,54	2,8889	3,0000	4,00
		PIn	24	64,58	3,6250	4,0000	3,00
		InSb	17	44,38	2,7059	3,0000	4,00
B.11	H(3) = 10.285, p = .016	MM	14	42,21	2,3571	2,0000	4,00
		Int	45	49,07	2,6667	2,0000	4,00
		PIn	24	65,38	3,4167	3,5000	4,00
		InSb	17	40,12	2,2353	2,0000	3,00

(continued)

Table 5. (*continued*)

Rights			N	Mean rank	Mean	Median	Range
				Information sources			
B.2	H(3) = 16.075, p = .001	MM	14	32,93	2,5000	3,0000	4,00
		Int	44	52,41	3,4545	3,0000	4,00
		PIn	25	64,20	3,9200	4,0000	4,00
		InSb	16	36,13	2,7500	3,0000	4,00
B.12	H(3) = 11.156, p = .011	MM	13	37,19	1,9231	2,0000	4,00
		Int	45	49,70	2,5111	2,0000	4,00
		PIn	25	64,90	3,2400	3,0000	4,00
		InSb	17	41,62	2,1176	2,0000	3,00
B.13	H(3) = 11.312, p = .010	MM	14	36,50	1,8571	1,5000	2,00
		Int	45	50,34	2,3778	2,0000	3,00
		PInt	25	65,28	2,9200	3,0000	3,00
		InSb	17	43,68	2,1176	2,0000	2,00
B.14	H(3) = 12.698, p = .005	MM	14	43,82	2,2857	2,0000	4,00
		Int	45	54,73	2,7556	3,0000	4,00
		PInt	25	61,38	3,1200	3,0000	4,00
		InSb	17	31,76	1,7059	1,0000	3,00

[a]MM (Mass Media), Int (Internet), Pin (Personal Interest), InSb (Informed by Somebody)

According to Table 5, those personally interested or engaged with GDPR showed unsurprisingly higher extent of knowledge regarding their rights, followed in all cases by those informed by Internet. The ones informed by mass media are in the 3rd mean rank with the exception of B.10 (right to object to data processing), B.2 (right to data rectification), B.12 (right to data portability) and B.13 (right to have data deleted) where those informed by someone else precede. No statistically significant relationships were shown in the cases of consent form (B.4), consent withdraw (B.5), right to be informed for data transmission to third party (B.8) and for high-risk personal data breach (B.9). It can be thus concluded that those informed by mass media or someone else lag regarding the extent of rights knowledge.

Considering that a) mass media as an information source were stated more by women (71.4%), more by those aged 36–45 years old (71.4%), equally by university graduates and M.Sc/Ph.D. (42.9% each) and more by private sector employees and freelancers (50%) and b) information by someone else was stated more by women (58.8%), more by those over 46 years old (41.2%), equally by primary/secondary education graduates and M.Sc/Ph.D. graduates (35.3% each) and equally by public and private sector employees (41.2% each), a generalized need is recorded for more targeted and systematic information in order for data subjects to have better insight to the provisions of GDPR and their rights and be able to make informed decisions to protect their data.

4 Discussion and Conclusions

The results above reveal that the source of information on GDPR is related to rights knowledge supporting thus that some kind of expertise or acquaintance with GDPR contributes positively to rights knowledge extent. Consequently, those informed on GDPR due to personal interest were better informed than others. This is valid also for those informed by Internet though in lower degree and it can be explained considering that they had probably read websites information regarding the new GDPR compliance policy. Obviously there are other factors that contribute to the extent of rights knowledge. For example, educational level had a positive effect on knowledge regarding both consent withdraw and data processing restriction right, while age was negatively related to knowledge extent regarding the right to be forgotten.

Evaluating the results regarding the extent of data subjects' rights knowledge (Table 1) it is clear that awareness increase is required for several rights in order for data subjects to make informed decisions to optimize control over their data and ultimately to be protected. For instance, half of the respondents have little or no knowledge at all regarding the rights to data portability, to have their data deleted or to data processing restriction. These control rights are very important. Data portability right constitutes a first step towards "preselected ownership" of personal data [17], while the right to have data deleted effectively eliminates the possibility of uncontrolled digital reproduction of personal data [16]. Data processing restriction right is also of significance especially in cases when the right to be forgotten can't be applied for legal reasons. Even in the cases where data subjects showed high extent of knowledge (e.g. for the form of consent) differentiations were recorded that need to be eliminated.

Since GDPR implementation, emphasis has been given to organizations to become GDPR compliant. In this frame, data protection awareness training programs are addressed to their staff [18]. But what about data subjects awareness increase?

In Greece, the Hellenic Data Protection Authority provides in its website[3] useful information on data protection legislation, including specific information about data subjects' GDPR rights both in textual and audiovisual form and guidelines on submitting complaints. Moreover, the European Data Protection Board[4] website has useful content for data subjects' rights, while there are also other websites with relevant information (e.g. European Commission). So theoretically, data subjects have a range of sources to be informed on their rights. Considering, though, that some individuals may not be able to find this information or ignore it exists, national information campaigns and information via mass media are very important. To the best of our knowledge, there was no national information campaign on GDPR in Greece previously to its implementation. Regarding information on GDPR via mass media and specifically newspapers, during the period from March 2018 to March 2019, approximately 20 articles referring to GDPR were published to seven newspapers with high circulation at national level. Only four articles refer exclusively to data subjects' rights, while the rest focus on the obligations of data controllers, organizations' necessary changes to their processing activities, country's readiness to implement GDPR or fines imposed (e.g. Google). This reveals that national

---

[3] http://www.dpa.gr/.

[4] https://edpb.europa.eu/.

media paid less attention to data subjects' rights which obviously impacts on information availability.

Considering that digital literacy is a basic life-skill, measures that "directly aim to strengthen users' awareness about the extent of their knowledge" should be taken [19] (p. 218). In this frame, public informational campaigns have been shown to improve users' knowledge and to provide skills to combat cyber threats [20], while educational programs and interventions involving knowledge about data collection and processing procedures, data usage and data accessibility by others are also crucial [21]. These awareness measures should obviously include information regarding current legislation [22] in an understandable way using, for instance, examples and icons for the rights GDPR guarantees as well as instructions for the exercise of these rights.

Although the results of this research can't be generalized due to the small sample and the sampling method, they reveal the need for a more thorough investigation of data subjects' awareness regarding each right GDPR guarantees and the factors affecting awareness, considering that "just because respondents in a country have a high level of awareness of GDPR and what it is does, it does not automatically follow they have heard of all the rights GDPR guarantees" [15] (p. 27). Researches should not focus only on demographic characteristics (e.g. gender, education, employment) but also explore how information provision by governmental agencies, Data Protection Authorities, mass media and social media, as well as data subjects' access to information sources, social inequalities or digital illiteracy impact on the extent of rights' knowledge. In this frame, researches in EU member states such as Netherlands, Sweden, Bulgaria and Malta, which were shown to have different level of awareness for the rights explored [15] would be helpful for decision makers to take the appropriate actions in order to increase European citizens awareness on the rights GDPR sets.

GDPR aims to empower individuals in order to have more control over personal data and its implementation involves equally people, organizations and processes. The actual protection of personal data and data subjects' freedoms doesn't depend only on the legal framework, the procedures it sets and the organizations that have the obligation to become GDPR compliant and protect personal data, but also on data subjects' rights knowledge highlighting thus the individual responsibility for personal data protection. In this frame, data subjects need to be better informed, to become more aware of their rights and understand them fully. If this doesn't happen, it is rather probable that Custers et al. [3] forecast that -despite GDPR's aim to harmonize law and practice- differences may continue to exist between EU countries, will be verified on an individual (data subjects) level, as some will know and exert their rights to data protection and others not, leading thus to a reality of data protection rights inequality between EU citizens.

References

1. Mitrou, L.: Law in the Information Society. Sakkoulas Publ, Athens (2002). (in Greek)
2. Sobolewski, M., Mazur, J., Paliński, M.: GDPR: a step towards a user-centric internet? Intereconomics **52**(4), 207–213 (2017). https://doi.org/10.1007/s10272-017-0676-5
3. Custers, B., Dechesne, F., Sears, A.M., Tani, T., van der Hof, S.: A comparison of data protection legislation and policies across the EU. Comput. Law Secur. Rev. **34**(2), 234–243 (2018)
4. European Council: Regulation (EU) 2016/679 of the European Parliament and of the Council of 27 April 2016 on the protection of natural persons with regard to the processing of personal data and on the free movement of such data, and repealing Directive 95/46/EC (General Data Protection Regulation) (2016)
5. Sideri, M., Fontaras, A., Gritzalis, S.: What do we know about our rights to data protection? A Greek case study. In: Katsikas, S., Zorkadis, V. (eds.) e-Democracy 2019. CCIS, vol. 1111, pp. 18–33. Springer, Cham (2020). https://doi.org/10.1007/978-3-030-37545-4_2
6. Conger, S., Pratt, J.H., Loch, K.D.: Personal information privacy and emerging technologies. Inf. Syst. J. **23**(5), 401–417 (2013)
7. Mantelero, A.: The future of consumer data protection in the EU Re-thinking the "notice and consent" paradigm in the new era of predictive analytics. Comput. Law Secur. Rev. **30**(6), 643–660 (2014)
8. Baek, Y.M.: Solving the privacy paradox: a counter-argument experimental approach. Comput. Hum. Behav. **38**, 33–42 (2014)
9. Surveillance Project: The Globalization of Personal Data Project: An International Survey on Privacy and Surveillance, Summary of Findings. Queen's University, Kingston. https://qspace.library.queensu.ca/bitstream/handle/1974/7660/2008_Surveillance_Project_International_Survey_Findings_Summary.pdf?sequence=1&isAllowed=y (2008). Accessed 21 Apr 2020
10. Kelley, P.G., Cranor, L.F., Sadeh, N.: Privacy as part of the app decision-making process. In: Proceedings of the SIGCHI Conference on Human Factors in Computing Systems, pp. 3393–3402. ACM, Paris (2013)
11. Trepte, S., Teutsch, D., Masur, P.K., Eicher, C., Fischer, M., Hennhöfer, A., Lind, F.: Do people know about privacy and data protection strategies? Towards the "Online Privacy Literacy Scale" (OPLIS). In: Gutwirth, S., Leenes, R., de Hert, P. (eds.) Reforming European Data Protection Law. LGTS, vol. 20, pp. 333–365. Springer, Dordrecht (2015). https://doi.org/10.1007/978-94-017-9385-8_14
12. Park, Y.J.: Digital literacy and privacy behavior online. Commun. Res. **40**(2), 215–236 (2011)
13. Miltgen, C.L., Peyrat-Guillard, D.: Cultural and generational influences on privacy concerns: a qualitative study in seven European countries. Eur. J. Inf. Syst. **23**, 103–125 (2014)
14. European Commission: Special Eurobarometer 431. Data Protection Report. http://ec.europa.eu/commfrontoffice/publicopinion/archives/ebs/ebs_431_en.pdf (2015). Accessed 25 Apr 2020
15. European Commission: Special Eurobarometer 487a. The GDPR. Report. https://www.privacy-web.nl/cms/files/2019-06/ebs487a-en.pdf (2019). Accessed 25 Apr 2020
16. van Ooijen, I., Vrabec, H.U.: Does the GDPR enhance consumers' control over personal data? An analysis from a behavioral perspective. J. Consum. Policy **42**, 91–107 (2019)
17. De Hert, P., Papakonstantinou, V., Malgieri, G., Beslay, L., Sanchez, I.: The right to data portability in the GDPR: towards user-centric interoperability of digital services. Comput. Law Secur. Rev. **34**(2), 193–203 (2018)
18. Perry, R.: GDPR-project or permanent reality? Comput. Fraud Secur. **1**, 9–11 (2019)

19. Moll, R., Pieschl, S., Bromme, R.: Competent or clueless? Users' knowledge and misconceptions about their online privacy management. Comput. Hum. Behav. **41**, 212–219 (2014)
20. Marcolin, B.L., Compeau, D.R., Munro, M.C., Huff, S.L.: Assessing user competence: conceptualization and measurement. Inf. Syst. Res. **11**(1), 37–60 (2000)
21. Lawler, J.P., Molluzzo, J.C.: A study of the perceptions of students on privacy and security on social networking sites (SNS), on the internet. J. Inf. Syst. Appl. Res. **3**(12), 3–18 (2010)
22. Sideri, M., Kitsiou, A., Tzortzaki, E., Kalloniatis, C., Gritzalis, S.: Enhancing University students' privacy literacy through an educational intervention. A Greek case-study. Int. J. Electron. Gov. **11**(3/4), 333–360 (2019)

Attitudes and Perceptions

"Most Companies Share Whatever They Can to Make Money!": Comparing User's Perceptions with the Data Practices of IoT Devices

Mahdi Nasrullah Al-Ameen[1(✉)], Apoorva Chauhan[2], M. A. Manazir Ahsan[1], and Huzeyfe Kocabas[1]

[1] Utah State University, Logan, USA
mahdi.al-ameen@usu.edu, {manazir.ahsan,huzeyfe.kocabas}@aggiemail.usu.edu
[2] University of Waterloo, Waterloo, Canada
apoorva.chauhan@uwaterloo.ca

Abstract. With the rapid deployment of Internet of Things (IoT) technologies, it has been essential to address the security and privacy issues through maintaining transparency in data practices, and designing new tools for data protection. To address these challenges, the prior research focused on identifying user's privacy preferences in different contexts of IoT usage, user's mental model of security threats, and their privacy practices for a specific type of IoT device (e.g., smart speaker). However, there is a dearth in existing literature to understand the mismatch between user's perceptions and the actual data practices of IoT devices. Such mismatches could lead users unknowingly sharing their private information, exposing themselves to unanticipated privacy risks. To address these issues, we conducted a lab study with 42 participants, where we compared the data practices stated in the privacy policy of 28 IoT devices with the participants' perceptions of data collection, sharing, and protection. Our findings provide insights into the mismatched privacy perceptions of users, which lead to our recommendations on designing simplified privacy notice by highlighting the unexpected data practices.

Keywords: IoT · User study · Mismatched privacy perceptions

1   Introduction and Background

The Internet of Things (IoT) is a system of interrelated devices provided with unique identifiers and the ability to transfer data over a network without requiring human intervention [9]. The IoT devices are becoming increasingly popular in day-to-day lives, with nearly two-thirds of Americans owning at least one IoT connected device [3]. Despite the increasing popularity and immense potential of IoT devices, security and privacy issues remain as major concerns [2,12].

© IFIP International Federation for Information Processing 2020
Published by Springer Nature Switzerland AG 2020
N. Clarke and S. Furnell (Eds.): HAISA 2020, IFIP AICT 593, pp. 329–340, 2020.
https://doi.org/10.1007/978-3-030-57404-8_25

The study of Naeini et al. [7] explored the privacy preferences of users in different contexts of IoT usage, where participants reported to be less comfortable with data collection in private places as compared to public settings. The limited technical understanding of people often contributes to their incorrect mental model of security threats in an IoT environment [12]. A recent study by Malkin et al. [5] reported that almost half of their participants who were users of Amazon and Google smart speakers, did not know that their recordings were being permanently stored by the devices. Due to such unawareness, only a quarter of their participants reviewed their recorded interactions, where very few had ever deleted any recordings [5]. A separate study [4] on smart speakers identified that users trade privacy for convenience with different levels of deliberation and privacy resignation.

People reported their interest to be notified about the data practices of IoT device [7]. However, the privacy notice often fails to help users with making an informed decision to protect their privacy preferences while purchasing or using an IoT device [2]. The study of Page et al. [8] unpacked the relation between people's perceptions and adoption of IoT technology. The authors [8] divided the IoT users into two categories: "user-centric", who think that the IoT devices are to be controlled by users; and "agentic", who think that the control of IoT devices are to be negotiated between the machine and human. The study highlighted privacy concerns for the people coming from a user-centric perspective given that consumer-oriented IoT is currently moving towards the agentic view [8]. The findings from these studies call for an investigation to identify the gaps between people's perceptions and the actual data practices of IoT devices. We addressed this challenge in our work, which is guided by the following research enquiries:

- What are users' perceptions of information collection by IoT devices? How do their perceptions vary from the actual data practices?
- What are users' perceptions of information sharing (with third-party entities) by IoT devices? How do their perceptions vary from the actual data practices?
- What are users' perceptions of data protection strategies adopted by IoT devices? How do their perceptions vary from the actual data practices?

To address these research questions, we selected 28 IoT devices from different categories, including health & exercise, entertainment, smart homes, toys & games, and pets, and reviewed their privacy policies. We then conducted a lab study with 42 participants, where they reported their perceptions of data collection, sharing, and protection by IoT devices. Our analysis identifies the gaps between participants' perceptions and the actual data practices of IoT device. The findings from this study would contribute towards the design of simplified and usable privacy notice by highlighting the unexpected data practices of users.

2   Methodology

We conduced individual study session with each participant in a lab setting. We recruited participants by sharing our study information through email and online social media. A total of 42 participants (16 females, 25 males, and 1 other), who live in Logan, Utah, took part in this study. The age-range of our participants varied between 18 and 64, where most (35, 83.3%) of them belonged to the age group 18–34. Among our participants, 26 (61.9%) identified as White, followed by Asian (16, 33.3%), Hispanic/Latino (1, 2.4%), and Other (1, 2.4%). A majority (26, 61.9%) of participants were students. None of our participants had any academic or professional background in cybersecurity. Our study was approved by the Institutional Review Board (IRB) at Utah State University.

Selection of IoT Devices. We selected 28 devices for our study (see Table 4 in Appendix) from the list of IoT devices compiled by Mozilla Foundation[1], where the devices are divided into different categories (e.g., health & exercise, entertainment, smart homes, toys & games, and pets) based on their core service and functionality. We conducted a series of focus-group discussion among researchers in this project and with our colleagues to finalize our device selection.

Types of Information. In light of prior work [10] and the privacy policy of selected devices, we identified nine categories of information that are generally collected by a device or service provider, where each type of information is divided into sub-categories. For example, name, gender, and date of birth of a user are collected as 'personal information'. The other types of information considered in our study include: *Contact* (email address, postal address, and phone number), *Financial* (bank account details, and credit or debit card number), *Health* (height, weight, and work out details), *Location* (current location: city level or more precise), and *Media* (audio, and video). We also considered the information about IoT device usage, and the information an IoT device may collect from a connected device (e.g., contact list from a smartphone) and from an online social media (e.g., friend list from Facebook).

Procedure. We conducted the study in a lab environment, where participants completed the survey hosted on Qualtrics[2] after they had read and agreed to informed consent document. Each participant was presented with four IoT devices, selected in a semi-random process from our list of 28 devices (each IoT device was presented to six participants). For each IoT device, the participant was presented with a visual description about its functionality. Participants could take as much time as they needed to familiarize themselves with the functionality of the device. Thereafter, they reported their perceptions of information collection and sharing by that device, where we presented them with each type of information (see the above paragraph for further details). Participants were also asked about their perceptions of the reasons behind information collection and sharing. Then, participants reported their perceptions of security and privacy strategies (e.g., encryption, anonymization) adopted by the device for data protection. For each participant, the above process was repeated for three other devices. At the end of study, participants answered a set of demographic questionnaire. On average, each session took around 45 min.

---

[1] List of IoT Devices, compiled by Mozilla Foundation: https://mzl.la/2zOK4II.

[2] Qualtrics is an online survey platform used to create, distribute, collect, and analyze survey data (www.qualtrics.com).

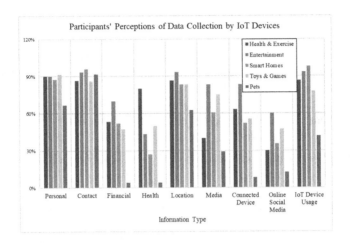

Fig. 1. Participants' perceptions of data collection by IoT devices

Analysis. We went through the privacy policy of each IoT device, and compared that with participants' perceptions in terms information collection, sharing, and protection. There are four cases resulting from our comparison: a 'Yes-Yes' match, a 'No-No' match, a 'Yes-No' mismatch, or a 'No-Yes' mismatch. Here, a 'Yes-Yes' match for information collection means, the user believes that the information is collected by a device and the privacy policy states that it is indeed collected, where a 'No-Yes' mismatch represents, the user thinks that the information is not collected by a device, but that information is collected according to the device's privacy policy.

3   Results

3.1   Data Collection by IoT Devices

Figure 1 presents participants' perceptions of data collection by the IoT devices, where most of the participants perceive that the IoT devices collect contact (91.07%), personal (86.31%), location (82.74%), and device usage information (82.74%). Participants' perceptions of data collection are related to the category of IoT devices. Considering all data types, IoT devices in "pets" category are perceived to collect least amount of information as compared to the devices in other categories, where the "entertainment"-focused devices are perceived to collect most amount of data from users. In some instances, participants' perceptions of collecting a specific type of information are related to the core service offered by the device, where IoT devices in "Health & exercise" category are perceived to collect more health information as compared to the devices in other categories (see Fig. 1).

Table 1 presents the matches and mismatches between participants' perceptions and the privacy policy of IoT devices in terms information collection. From the perspective of user's privacy preservation, we consider a 'No-Yes' mismatch as the most critical one, where users believe that the IoT device does not collect

Table 1. Match/Mismatch between participants' perceptions and privacy policy: Data collection by IoT devices [*NA: Information is not available in privacy policy]

Information type	(Mis)Match	Health & Exercise	Entertainment	Smart homes	Toys & Games	Pets
Personal	Yes-Yes	74.74%	56.30%	59.88%	77.78%	50.00%
	No-No	3.16%	0.00%	0.00%	0.00%	12.50%
	Yes-No	9.47%	0.00%	25.31%	0.00%	12.50%
	No-Yes	12.63%	43.70%	14.81%	22.22%	25.00%
Contact	Yes-Yes	79.76%	54.17%	64.20%	61.11%	91.67%
	No-No	0.00%	0.00%	0.00%	0.00%	0.00%
	Yes-No	0.00%	0.00%	17.28%	0.00%	0.00%
	No-Yes	20.24%	45.83%	18.52%	38.89%	8.33%
Financial	Yes-Yes	20.00%	27.16%	34.26%	35.19%	4.17%
	No-No	31.43%	35.80%	20.37%	0.00%	0.00%
	Yes-No	20.00%	16.05%	39.81%	0.00%	0.00%
	No-Yes	28.57%	20.99%	5.56%	64.81%	95.83%
Health	Yes-Yes	42.03%	0.00%	0.00%	*NA	*NA
	No-No	14.49%	80.00%	77.08%		
	Yes-No	28.99%	20.00%	8.33%		
	No-Yes	14.49%	0.00%	14.58%		
Location	Yes-Yes	96.43%	63.41%	52.63%	73.33%	58.33%
	No-No	0.00%	0.00%	14.04%	0.00%	0.00%
	Yes-No	0.00%	0.00%	17.54%	20.00%	0.00%
	No-Yes	3.57%	36.59%	15.79%	6.67%	41.67%
Media	Yes-Yes	14.29%	29.41%	37.50%	51.67%	20.83%
	No-No	51.79%	16.47%	33.33%	6.67%	66.67%
	Yes-No	12.50%	25.88%	15.63%	13.33%	8.33%
	No-Yes	21.43%	28.24%	13.54%	28.33%	4.17%
Connected device	Yes-Yes	16.22%	35.71%	11.90%	*NA	*NA
	No-No	32.43%	16.67%	45.24%		
	Yes-No	32.43%	19.05%	26.19%		
	No-Yes	18.92%	28.57%	16.67%		
Online social media	Yes-Yes	15.79%	33.33%	11.90%	50.00%	0.00%
	No-No	26.32%	12.82%	59.52%	0.00%	60.00%
	Yes-No	5.26%	10.26%	19.05%	0.00%	0.00%
	No-Yes	52.63%	43.59%	9.52%	50.00%	40.00%
IoT device usage	Yes-Yes	92.59%	69.05%	48.33%	68.75%	45.83%
	No-No	0.00%	0.00%	11.67%	0.00%	0.00%
	Yes-No	0.00%	0.00%	10.00%	0.00%	0.00%
	No-Yes	7.41%	30.95%	30.00%	31.25%	54.17%

an information, although it is actually collected by that device. For instance, we found a 'No-Yes' mismatch in 95.83% of cases for the devices in "pets' category in terms of collecting financial information. Considering all data types, we found most 'No-Yes' mismatch for the IoT devices in "entertainment" and "pets" category, followed by the devices in "toys & games", "health & exercise" and "smart homes".

As we asked participants about the reasons of information collection by an IoT device, in about half of the cases, they reported that information collection is required for the core functionality of a device. In around one-fourth of cases, participants perceive that information collection is needed for the organizations in IoT business to improve the functionality of their device and offer personalized service to the customers. Some participants believe that the business entities collect user information through their IoT devices for marketing, and advertising their other products to the customers.

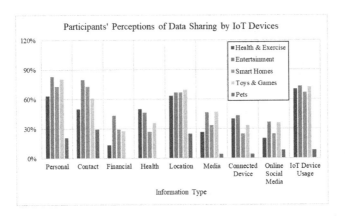

Fig. 2. Participants' perceptions of data sharing by IoT devices

3.2 Data Sharing by IoT Devices

Figure 2 illustrates participants' perceptions of data sharing by the IoT devices. A majority of participants perceive that the IoT devices share users' personal (67.26%), contact (61.31%), location (60.71%), and device usage (61.31%) information with third-party entities. Participants' perceptions of data sharing are related to the category of IoT devices. Considering all data types, IoT devices in "entertainment" category are perceived to share most amount of user data, where the participants perceive that the devices in "pets" category share least amount of user information with other entities. We also found that participants' perceptions of sharing a specific type of information varied across different categories of IoT devices. For instances, the "entertainment"-focused devices are perceived to share user's personal information in above 80% of cases, which is less than 30% for the devices in "pets" category.

Table 2 presents the matches and mismatches between participants' perceptions and the privacy policy of IoT devices in terms of information sharing, where a 'No-Yes' mismatch is considered to be the most critical one from the perspective of user's privacy preservation (see Sect. 3.1 for further details). Considering all data types[3], we found most 'No-Yes' mismatch for the IoT devices in "pets" category, followed by the devices in "toys & games", "entertainment",

---

[3] While considering all data types, the calculations of match and mismatch present a lower limit for the devices in "toys & games" and "pets" category, since some information are unavailable in their privacy policy (see 'NA' in Tables 1 and 2).

Table 2. Match/Mismatch between participants' perceptions and privacy policy: Data sharing by IoT devices [*NA: Information is not available in privacy policy]

Information type	(Mis)Match	Health & Exercise	Entertainment	Smart homes	Toys & Games	Pets
Personal	Yes-Yes	1.11%	26.98%	25.93%	56.48%	23.53%
	No-No	35.56%	30.16%	18.52%	3.70%	0.00%
	Yes-No	57.78%	22.22%	32.59%	12.96%	23.53%
	No-Yes	5.56%	20.63%	22.96%	26.85%	52.94%
Contact	Yes-Yes	3.33%	24.60%	24.62%	34.26%	22.58%
	No-No	48.89%	37.30%	26.15%	10.19%	0.00%
	Yes-No	37.78%	15.08%	20.00%	6.48%	22.58%
	No-Yes	10.00%	23.02%	29.23%	49.07%	54.84%
Financial	Yes-Yes	1.67%	8.33%	9.09%	7.14%	0.00%
	No-No	60.00%	63.10%	42.86%	47.62%	0.00%
	Yes-No	10.00%	15.48%	32.47%	9.52%	0.00%
	No-Yes	28.33%	13.10%	15.58%	35.71%	100.00%
Health	Yes-Yes	0.00%	0.00%	0.00%	*NA	*NA
	No-No	43.33%	80.95%	88.57%		
	Yes-No	56.67%	19.05%	11.43%		
	No-Yes	0.00%	0.00%	0.00%		
Location	Yes-Yes	0.00%	19.61%	18.60%	15.38%	12.00%
	No-No	33.33%	33.33%	32.56%	15.38%	16.00%
	Yes-No	66.67%	31.37%	32.56%	61.54%	20.00%
	No-Yes	0.00%	15.69%	16.28%	7.69%	52.00%
Media	Yes-Yes	0.00%	4.76%	10.94%	12.96%	0.00%
	No-No	81.67%	53.57%	53.13%	27.78%	0.00%
	Yes-No	18.33%	25.00%	6.25%	27.78%	0.00%
	No-Yes	0.00%	16.67%	29.69%	31.48%	0.00%
Connected device	Yes-Yes	0.00%	7.14%	0.00%	*NA	*NA
	No-No	66.67%	54.76%	83.33%		
	Yes-No	33.33%	23.81%	11.11%		
	No-Yes	0.00%	14.29%	5.56%		
Online social media	Yes-Yes	0.00%	4.76%	0.00%	16.67%	0.00%
	No-No	70.00%	59.52%	80.56%	0.00%	0.00%
	Yes-No	30.00%	19.05%	11.11%	0.00%	0.00%
	No-Yes	0.00%	16.67%	8.33%	83.33%	100.00%
IoT device usage	Yes-Yes	0.00%	42.86%	31.91%	17.86%	10.00%
	No-No	23.33%	2.38%	29.79%	14.29%	0.00%
	Yes-No	76.67%	11.90%	10.64%	42.86%	10.00%
	No-Yes	0.00%	42.86%	27.66%	25.00%	80.00%

"smart homes", and "health & exercise". Such mismatches also vary across different categories of IoT devices with respect to information type. For example, we found a 54.84% 'No-Yes' mismatch for the devices in 'pets' category, which is 10% for "health & exercise"-focused devices.

As we asked participants about the reasons of information sharing (with third-party entities) by an IoT device, they mentioned about financial and business gain in about half of the cases. One of our participants said, "*I feel like most companies share whatever they can, so that they can make money.*" Some participants perceive that information sharing with third-party entities are required for improving the functionality of an IoT device.

3.3   Security and Privacy Features of IoT Devices

A majority of participants perceive that the IoT devices in "toys & games", "pets", "entertainment", and "health & exercise" category encrypt user information in process of communication and storage (see Fig. 3). Here, the devices in "toys & games" category are perceived by most of the participants encrypting their information as compared to the devices in other categories. As compared to other categories of IoT devices, the ones in "smart homes" category are perceived by the least number of participants offering security and privacy features.

Table 3 presents the matches and mismatches between participants' perceptions and the practices of IoT devices in protecting user information. Here, we consider a 'Yes-No' mismatch as the most critical one from the perspective of user's security and privacy preservation, where a user believes that an IoT device adopts a secure strategy (e.g., encryption) for information protection, although it does not adopt that strategy as noted in its privacy policy. For instance, we found a 'Yes-No' mismatch in 56.67% of cases for the devices in "health & exercise" category in terms of encrypting user data during storage. That means, in above half of the cases, participants had misconceptions about the secure storage of their information by the devices in "health & exercise" category. A majority of participants perceive that the devices in "pets" category encrypt their information during storage (see Fig. 3), however, the privacy policy of these devices do not mention about their security-preserving steps during storage process. In these cases, we could not compare users' perceptions with the privacy policy of IoT devices.

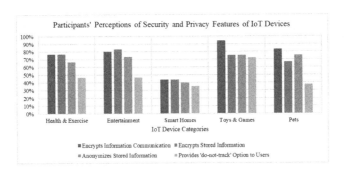

Fig. 3. Participants' perceptions of security and privacy features of IoT devices

4   Discussion

Our study reveals the mismatches between users' perceptions and the data practices stated in the privacy policy of IoT devices. We identified the misconceptions of participants that could potentially impact their privacy behavior. In many cases, participants believe that their information, including financial and health data are not collected by an IoT device, although those information are collected and shared (with third-party entities) by that device. Also, many participants believe that IoT devices protect their information through secure communication and storage, where we identified the mismatches between users' perceptions and actual practices. Such misconceptions could contribute to users' optimism bias [1], where they consider the risks of cyber attacks and information breach as 'distant harms'. As a result, they possess a false sense of security, lack interest and motivation to learn about secure behavior, and fail to take adequate steps to protect their information [1,7].

Table 3. Match/Mismatch between participants' perceptions and privacy policy: Security and privacy features of IoT devices [*NA: Information is not available in privacy policy]

Security/Privacy feature	(Mis)Match	Health & Exercise	Enter-tainment	Smart homes	Toys & Games	Pets
Encrypts information communicated	Yes-Yes	53.33%	45.24%	35.71%	73.33%	77.78%
	No-No	16.67%	2.38%	10.71%	0.00%	0.00%
	Yes-No	23.33%	11.90%	3.57%	20.00%	0.00%
	No-Yes	6.67%	40.48%	50.00%	6.67%	22.22%
Encrypts stored information	Yes-Yes	20.00%	47.62%	33.93%	60.00%	*NA
	No-No	23.33%	2.38%	8.93%	3.33%	
	Yes-No	56.67%	11.90%	5.36%	16.67%	
	No-Yes	0.00%	38.10%	51.79%	20.00%	
Anonymizes stored information	Yes-Yes	0.00%	11.90%	13.11%	*NA	*NA
	No-No	33.33%	45.24%	39.34%		
	Yes-No	66.67%	40.48%	21.31%		
	No-Yes	0.00%	2.38%	26.23%		
Offers 'Do-not-Track' Option	Yes-Yes	3.33%	19.05%	33.33%	*NA	*NA
	No-No	36.67%	28.57%	16.67%		
	Yes-No	43.33%	14.29%	33.33%		
	No-Yes	16.67%	38.10%	16.67%		

The privacy notice often fails to help users with making an informed privacy decision due to its excessive length, complicated language, or poor visualization [6]. As recommended in prior studies [6,11], a privacy notice should preserve the simplicity, brevity, and clarity in design for being understandable to general users. Our findings unpack the misconceptions of users about the data practices of IoT devices. The future research should build upon these results, and conduct further studies if needed, to design simplified privacy notice by highlighting the unexpected data practices, so that users could focus on the privacy aspects they are less informed about. We note that there is no 'one-size-fits-all' solution in this regard, as shown in our study that users' mismatched privacy perceptions vary across device category and information type. So, we recommend to consider each IoT device and information type individually, to identify users' privacy misconceptions and highlight that in a privacy notice to help them with protecting their privacy preferences.

As shown in a recent study [2], users' privacy perceptions of IoT technology could affect their adoption and purchase behavior, where their perceptions are rarely formed through the understanding of privacy policy. So, the design of a simplified and usable privacy notice is important not only for general users, but also for the organizations in IoT business; further emphasized by the findings from our study. We identified instances where participants perceive that a device collects and shares their information, although according to its privacy policy, the device does not collect that information (see 'Yes-No' mismatches in Tables 1 and 2). We also found that some devices adopt data protection strategies, like encrypting user's information during communication and storage, while the participants do not perceive, those devices encrypt their information (see 'No-Yes' mismatches in Table 3). In this context, a usable and simplified privacy notice (see our recommendations in the above paragraph) would provide users with better understanding of the steps taken by organizations in IoT business to protect their customers' privacy interests.

We also recommend to extend our findings through further studies, in order to design usable and effective training materials (e.g., videos, comics, infographics) to raise the privacy awareness of people, where they should be informed about privacy misconceptions and unexpected data practices related to current technologies, including IoT.

5   Limitations and Conclusion

Our sample size is relatively small, where most of our participants were young and university-educated. Thus, our findings may not be generalizable to the entire population. Our selection of IoT devices may not be not fully representative. As our analysis involves comparing user's perceptions with data practices stated in the privacy policy of IoT devices, the devices with better clarity in privacy policy were considered with higher priority in our selection. In this case, different selection criteria might yield varying lists of IoT devices. Despite these limitations, our study provides valuable insights into the mismatches between user's perceptions and the privacy policy of IoT devices in terms of data collection, sharing, and protection. In our future work, we would extend the findings from this study through a large-scale online survey, and leverage our results towards the design of simplified and usable privacy notice for IoT devices.

Appendix

Table 4. List of IoT devices selected for the study

Device category	IoT devices
Health & Exercise	Hidrate Spark 2.0 Water Bottle Peloton Bike Fitbit Charge 3 Fitness Tracker Athena Safety Wearable Samsung Gear Sport
Entertainment	Bose QuietComfort 35 II Google Pixel Buds PS4 Roku Streaming Players Apple TV
Smart homes	Sonos One Mycroft Mark 1 Nest Learning Thermostat Amazon Echo Dot Amazon Cloud Cam Behmor Brewer Coffee Maker Philips Hue Smart Light Kit SmartThings Outlet
Toys and Games	EVO Robot Sphero Mini DJI Spark Selfie Drone CogniToys Dino Dot Creativity Kit Amazon Fire HD Kids Edition
Pets	Tractive 3GS Pet Tracker Tile Mate PetNet Smart Feeder Petzi Treat Cam

References

1. Davinson, N., Sillence, E.: Using the health belief model to explore users' perceptions of 'being safe and secure' in the world of technology mediated financial transactions. Int. J. Hum Comput Stud. **72**(2), 154–168 (2014)
2. Emami-Naeini, P., Dixon, H., Agarwal, Y., Cranor, L.F.: Exploring how privacy and security factor into IoT device purchase behavior. In: Proceedings of the 2019 CHI Conference on Human Factors in Computing Systems, p. 534. ACM (2019)
3. Kaplan, D.: Majority of Americans have an IoT device - and they're open to advertising, December 15, 2016, https://geomarketing.com/majority-of-americans-have-an-iot-device

4. Lau, J., Zimmerman, B., Schaub, F.: Alexa, are you listening?: Privacy perceptions, concerns and privacy-seeking behaviors with smart speakers. In: Proceedings of the ACM on Human-Computer Interaction, pp. 1–31 (2018)
5. Malkin, N., Deatrick, J., Tong, A., Wijesekera, P., Egelman, S., Wagner, D.: Privacy attitudes of smart speaker users. Proc. Priv. Enhan. Technol. **2019**(4), 250–271 (2019)
6. McDonald, A.M., Reeder, R.W., Kelley, P.G., Cranor, L.F.: A comparative study of online privacy policies and formats. In: Goldberg, I., Atallah, M.J. (eds.) PETS 2009. LNCS, vol. 5672, pp. 37–55. Springer, Heidelberg (2009). https://doi.org/10.1007/978-3-642-03168-7_3
7. Naeini, P.E., Bhagavatula, S., Habib, H., Degeling, M., Bauer, L., Cranor, L.F., Sadeh, N.: Privacy expectations and preferences in an IoT world. In: Thirteenth Symposium on Usable Privacy and Security, pp. 399–412 (2017)
8. Page, X., Bahirat, P., Safi, M.I., Knijnenburg, B.P., Wisniewski, P.: The internet of what? Understanding differences in perceptions and adoption for the internet of things. Proc. ACM Interact. Mob. Wearable Ubiquitous Technol. **2**(4) (2018)
9. Patel, K.K., Patel, S.M., et al.: Internet of things-IoT: Definition, characteristics, architecture, enabling technologies, application & future challenges. Int. J. Eng. Sci. Comput. **6**(5) (2016)
10. Rao, A., Schaub, F., Sadeh, N., Acquisti, A., Kang, R.: Expecting the unexpected: Understanding mismatched privacy expectations online. In: Twelfth Symposium on Usable Privacy and Security, pp. 77–96 (2016)
11. Schaub, F., Balebako, R., Durity, A.L., Cranor, L.F.: A design space for effective privacy notices. In: Eleventh Symposium on Usable Privacy and Security, pp. 1–17 (2015)
12. Zeng, E., Mare, S., Roesner, F.: End user security and privacy concerns with smart homes. In: Thirteenth Symposium on Usable Privacy and Security, pp. 65–80 (2017)

Analysis of the 'Open Source Internet Research Tool': A Usage Perspective from UK Law Enforcement

Joseph Williams[1]($^{(\boxtimes)}$) and Paul Stephens[2]

[1] School of Engineering and Computer Science,
University of Hertfordshire, Hatfield AL10 9AB, UK
j.williams30@herts.ac.uk
[2] School of Law, Criminal Justice and Policing, Canterbury Christ Church University,
Canterbury CT1 1QU, UK
paul.stephens@canterbury.ac.uk

Abstract. Internet Intelligence and Investigations (i3) are a fundamental investigative tool of the modern law enforcement official (LEO) in an always-connected online era. Ensuring LEOs follow good procedure for such investigations is critical for both law enforcement and society, as it ensures consistency, rigor and transparency.

Procedural issues lie with online evidential capture, however. For example, it is not feasible to directly apply digital evidence methodologies one would for 'offline' digital forensics; instead, one must apply best practices and a consistent approach. How those best practices and consistent approaches apply will typically fall to individual forces. One such tool in the arsenal of law enforcement is the 'Open Source Internet Research Tool' (OSIRT), a free all-in-one browser that assists law enforcement in conducting i3 in a standardized manner.

This paper analyses and discusses the results of 32 questionnaire responses from serving LEOs in the UK and their use of OSIRT. Results showed that LEOs found OSIRT to be helpful to them and compared to their previous method of conducting online investigations, OSIRT offered an improved system to conduct online investigations in many instances.

Keywords: Internet intelligence and investigations · OSINT · Digital evidential capture

1 Introduction

Law enforcement in the UK conduct Internet Intelligence and Investigations (i3), formerly Open Source Research, as part of their routine inquiries and roles. Previous work in the area of i3 showed that officers used a variety of different tools to conduct online investigations. Tools would often depend upon whatever software would be accessible, largely in relation to cost. This paper discusses Open Source Internet Research Tool (OSIRT), a free all-in-one web browser that was designed in collaboration with the

© IFIP International Federation for Information Processing 2020
Published by Springer Nature Switzerland AG 2020
N. Clarke and S. Furnell (Eds.): HAISA 2020, IFIP AICT 593, pp. 341–352, 2020.
https://doi.org/10.1007/978-3-030-57404-8_26

UK's College of Policing to assist law enforcement of all skill-levels to conduct i3 in a rigorous and standardized manner. This paper continues the discourse from research [1, 2] conducted by the primary author and discusses the need for such a tool and evaluates and discusses 32 questionnaire responses from UK law enforcement that used OSIRT over a period of one month to two years.

2   Background

Knowing why law enforcement conduct investigations online may be obvious in an always-connected Internet-driven world, but matters arise surrounding the capture of such online artefacts. For example, these concerns can range from individual user skillset to legal and ethical issues. This section reviews and discusses prevalent issues UK law enforcement face when conducting i3 from a legal, ethical and practical perspective. The section then provides some background into OSIRT and its use in UK law enforcement.

2.1   Policing and Digital Crime in the United Kingdom

Her Majesty's Inspectorate of Constabulary and Fire & Rescue Services (HMICFRS) issued a report in 2018 outlining the importance of digital crime in policing. Data collection for the report took place over two months by visiting six police forces. The report uses examples of victim statements and how the police handled their reporting of the crime they had suffered.

The report stresses how integral technology is in modern society and how police must respond to the growing demand. The HMICFRS makes clear "[…] it is no longer appropriate, even if it ever were, for the police service to consider the investigation of digital crime to be the preserve of those with specialist knowledge." [3, p. 5]

HMICFRS stresses that all officers must understand handling and managing digital crime. The report from the offset sets out that regardless of job role, whether it is neighbourhood policing or anti-terrorism, officers must have the knowledge and skillset to police in the digital age, and that it is no longer a specialist's domain. The HMICFRS does acknowledge that to achieve the digital skillset required, those officers require to be trained in the technology they are meant to investigate. HMICFRS describe a "mixed picture" [3, p. 12] of officers' understanding surrounding digital crime, particularly highlighted by a response from an officer, "I am 46 years old. I do not have a computer; what do I know about Facebook?" [3; p. 30].

2.2   Legal, Procedural and Ethical Issues

Previous research by the author [2] has shown that law enforcement officials face several issues around online evidential capture. This section seeks to provide a background of the current legal, procedural and ethical issues of i3 and the prevalent statutes surrounding i3 in the context of 'open source' (i.e., publicly available) information.

Regulation of Investigatory Powers Act 2000 (RIPA) [4] is a key piece of legislation to look at when LEOs need conduct i3. However, given that RIPA pre-dates the modern era of social media platforms (e.g. Facebook was founded in 2004, Twitter in 2006) it largely covers covert interception of communications from technology available at the time. Communications like email, SMS messages and telephones all comfortably fall under RIPA's authority but, unsurprisingly, it does not mention anything about social media.

However, RIPA's usage for i3 is necessitated upon the 'level' in which the investigation is being conducted. The levels, in order of 'unlikely to require RIPA authorization' to 'almost certainly requiring RIPA authorization', are: overt, covert 'core', covert 'advanced', network investigation and 'undercover'. For example, a publicly available 'open source' investigation at Level 1 is unlikely to require authorization under RIPA as the investigation makes use of searches using a search engine. The reason for using covert techniques, particularly at levels 2 and 3, is to minimize the 'footprint' of the investigating officer; i.e., the digital trace left behind when visiting a website. For example, an IP address, Internet Service Provider and location could show a law enforcement official from a police computer was visiting a website. "Covert" at these levels of open source capture focuses more on protection for the officer, and police network, as a counterintelligence and countersurveillance measure. Plainly, the higher the level the more training is required. For example, level 1 usually only requires basic training around force policy of computer usage.

Despite no legislation like RIPA to provide concrete structure, and regardless of the 'open' nature of i3, LEOs must still follow procedures and guidelines. The Association of Chief Police Officers (ACPO[1]) in the *Online Research and Investigation* manual lays out one such set of procedures. The 'Guiding Principles' state that viewing open source information "does not amount to obtaining private information because that information is publicly available" [4], and due to this it is "unlikely to require authorization under RIPA" [5]. However, ACPO [4] note that while the open sources may be collected, it must be "necessary and proportionate" and "does not necessarily mean a person has no expectation of privacy" [4]. Expectations of privacy are set out under Article 8, a right to respect for private and family life, under the European Convention on Human Rights (ECHR). Under the Human Rights Act (1998) [6], decisions when handling personal information must be "necessary" and "proportionate". Kent Police use the JAPAN test when handling personal information [7]. While the JAPAN test itself may not be followed by all police forces, its concepts will be. For example, authorization, necessity and proportionality are the backbone of UK policing, and form part of statue laws such as RIPA. Additionally, auditability and justification is guided by NPCC principles, along with data protection laws.

Case law itself provides few guidelines for the digital investigator when conducting open source research. A notable case is Bucknor v R [2010] EWCA Crim 1152, in which Bucknor appealed against his conviction of murder. The judge ruled in the initial case that evidence presented from the social networking sites Bebo and YouTube were admissible. While the initial conviction was upheld, the judgement from the appeal means any evidence taken from the Internet must have full provenance. That is, when (the date and time) and where (the website) the evidential artefact was obtained should be audited.

---

[1] Now the National Police Chiefs Council (NPCC), but the previous ACPO and its guidelines still greatly impact force policies. ACPO principles are still widely used and trained.

The General Data Protection Regulation (GDPR) came in effect in May 2018 and has had an impact on how law enforcement within the UK and the European Union (EU) manage personal data. The GDPR provides citizens (termed "data subjects") with greater control over their personal data from "controllers" (i.e. those who control the data subject's personal data). Data subjects now, trivially, can access and remove personal data upon request.

GDPR provides member states of the EU provisions on how to apply GDPR, and in the UK this brought in the Data Protection Act 2018, superseding the 1998 Act of the same name. The Data Protection Act (2018) [8] covers aspects that "fall out of scope of EU law" [9], such as national security and how "intelligence services" manage personal data; this is covered by Part 4 of the Act. However, Part 3 of the Data Protection Act (2018) covers "Law Enforcement Processing" and provides six "protection principles" in Chapter 2 of the Act for those managing personal data for law enforcement purposes.

Law enforcement are afforded exemptions from the Data Protection Act (2018) but must follow 'protection principles' within the Act as there are themes of necessity and proportionality when handling sensitive data.

2.3 i3 Capture and OSIRT

From both a technical and procedural perspective of conducting i3, officers used a variety of software tools that would vary both in price and quality, with no standard toolset. To bring about standardisation, the College of Policing's Research, Identifying and Tracing the Electronic Suspect (RITES) course recommended several capturing and productivity tools. Trainers on the RITES course soon discovered the cognitive overload this had on the cohort, who would often spend more time learning to use the tools than learning about i3 techniques.

The problem highlighted above prompted the creation of Open Source Internet Research Tool (OSIRT); an all-in-one browser for conducting i3. OSIRT's creation followed the user-centred design (UCD) method, with a two phased development using the software engineering methodologies 'throwaway prototyping', for the prototype version, and 'incremental and iterative development' for the release version.

OSIRT has since been integrated into the RITES course, which trains over 100 officers a year, and provides a feedback outlet for OSIRT. Officers are also using OSIRT back on-the-job.

OSIRT's target audience is those officers, particularly case officers who require a streamlined method of conducting online investigations in terms of systematic evidential capture at Levels 1-3 (overt to covert). However, given OSIRT is a web browser it also has broader uses and can be used for Levels 4 and 5.

2.4 i3 and Open Source Intelligence-Style Browsers

For completeness, this section provides an overview and discussion of several popular OSINT-style 'OSIRT competitor' browsers and applications. Note, the latest version of Forensic Acquisition of Websites and Hunchly came out after OSIRT was released.

Oryon. OSINT Browser. Oryon OSINT Browser (Oryon) is a free browser built using Chromium, making its look and feel much like Google Chrome. The browser itself makes use of a plethora of add-ons and extensions, largely available via the Chrome web store, which makes Oryon extremely feature rich. While Oryon boasts more than 60 pre-installed add-ons, this leaves the interface brimming with icons to the point where it is bordering on overwhelming.

Oryon's overall design leaves the impression it is for those who are advanced computer users who can happily make use of and understand the needs of the add-ons. Oryon does not offer hashing capabilities for files, or report exporting.

Forensic Acquisition of Websites. (FAW - https://en.fawproject.com/) is not a browser designed for conducting open source investigation, but it is a browser designed for law enforcement purposes and reviewed for this reason. Initially, this review focused on the free, and only version, of FAW that was made available in November 2014 and not updated until early-2017.

The 2014 version of FAW was very much a simple, visual website saving application whereby a user visits the page to they wish to capture and clicks the "acquisition" button. FAW would then download the contents of the website and place it within a directory structure. All items acquired were date and time stamped and logged in an XML file. The browser did not offer anything beyond this capturing ability in this version.

FAW lay dormant for several years but came back with an updated version in 2017 that replaced the main browser with CefSharp. While FAW was initially a free product, a tiered pricing model was adopted from FAW version 5. This saw a free, professional and law enforcement licences added. The paid for versions unlock, amongst other features, Tor and user-agent spoofing.

Hunchly. Hunchly (https://www.hunch.ly/) is a paid for extension for the Google Chrome browser. Hunchly costs $129.99USD a year for a single license, or $349.99USD per three licences with a 20% saving for more than three users. This review is based on the major update version of Hunchly released in April 2018.

Hunchly sits within the Google Chrome browser and automatically logs webpages when a user visits by placing them within a local case file; this is the big selling point of Hunchly. Case files can then be accessed by means of the "dashboard", a separate application outside of the browser extension. Additionally, Hunchly contains features such as file attachments, automatic hashing, social media ID extraction and report exporting to both docx and PDF. Hunchly is a very capable addition to the OSINT browsing family, plus has the benefit of being cross-platform because it is a browser add-on.

However, there are several issues with using Hunchly that may impact its use, both from a legal and ethical perspective. In particular, the automated saving of every web-page visited creates an interesting dilemma. The immediate question: is it fair for law enforcement to make automated and automatic copies of webpages they visit without the need to make a conscious decision to do so? Previously, it was shown saving data using an automated means is a breach of Facebook's terms and conditions, but there are ramifications further afield than just a website's policy.

The process of "do first, ask questions later" is, in the opinion of the author, the wrong approach; particularly surrounding law enforcement's collection of personal data.

This chapter has shown that law enforcement need to take a careful and considered approach; one that focuses of necessity and proportionality. Is it then necessary and proportionate to automatically store carbon copies of all websites visited, without any interaction or acknowledgement from the investigating officer? The Data Protection Act (2018) explicitly states that personal data collection must be "Adequate, relevant and not excessive", and debatably, visiting a webpage may be "relevant" to the investigation but arguably that maintaining a copy of every webpage is excessive, particularly with only having to optionally justify that capture with a note. Of course, users can simply delete these traces if not required, but then the audit trail is lost.

3   Method

This paper looks at questionnaire data collected from officer's usage of OSIRT back on-the-job, how they were trained to use OSIRT and their thoughts and feelings.

The questionnaires were distributed to officers via the Police Online Knowledge Area (POLKA)[2] and were completed by 32 participants.

Questionnaires are an indirect method of data collection and are a traditional, efficient method of data collection, as the researcher is not required to be present during their administration. Questionnaires can obtain both quantitative and qualitative data, depending upon the type of questions asked (i.e. open or closed). Questions can generate diverse opinions from respondents, which can then lead to generalisability of any conclusions derived from the responses. Responses are gathered in a more standardised way, particularly when compared to interviews [10].

Limitations surrounding questionnaires are the potential for non-response, particularly for self-administered questionnaires, the consequence of a low/non-response rate may effective generalisability of the results. Additional limitations are that respondents may embellish their answers in order to provide a 'socially acceptable' response; this is known as social desirability bias [11].

3.1   Sample

This section details the officers who participated in the questionnaire and provided details about themselves (Table 1). These responses were optional, so results may not add-up to 32.

As expected, there is a mix of job roles and experience. There is a high proportion of analysts and detective constables, which is not surprising given that OSIRT is a hands-on tool designed specifically for investigators.

4   Results and Discussion

4.1   Previous Tool Usage

These results are typical from what has been previously discovered [1]. Popular tools such as Microsoft Excel and Word would be used to maintain the audit log, and various

---

[2] POLKA closed in January 2020 and was since replaced with 'The Knowledge Hub'.

Table 1. Participant roles and average years active per role.

Role	n	Years active (avg)
Trainer	1	10
Police officer	6	12
Intelligence researcher/analyst	9	3
Detective sergeant	2	17
Detective constable	10	11
Digital media investigator	3	5

other tools and add-ons to capture. In this questionnaire, the browser extension *Fireshot* was the most popular screenshot tool. Even with a pool of 32 responses, it shows the disparate use of different tools that OSIRT has ultimately went on to replace (Table 2).

Table 2. Breakdown of previous tool usage.

Productivity tool	n
Excel/spreadsheet	9
Unspecific add-ons/extensions for browsers	6
Word	5
Fireshot	5
Karen's Hasher	4
Notepad/(++)	3
Camtasia/screen recording	3
Whois? Add-ons	3
Snagit	2
None	2
Ashampoo	1
One note	1
Windows screenshot	1
HTTRACK	1
Tor	1

4.2 OSIRT Usage

Table 3 breaks down the how long the participants have been using OSIRT. Of the respondents, 63% have been using OSIRT for a year or more. Most respondents, 80%, have been using OSIRT for at least 10 months. Those users who have been using OSIRT for two or more years are likely to be users of the prototype and have been using OSIRT around its initial release.

Table 3. How long participants have used OSIRT

How long using OSIRT	n
Over two years	11
Over one - two years	8
four months to one year	9
one to three months	1
Less than a month	2

The interesting aspects of the results of average weekly usage in Table 4 show there are two groups of users. One that uses OSIRT for a not insignificant amount of their work, 11 use OSIRT between 11 and 25 h a week, and those that use it in a more casual manner; 17 use it for two hours or less a week on average. These are not particularly striking results, as not all officers will be tasked with conducting open source research all the time. Some respondents are likely to be "satellite" open source researchers, in that they may start an open source investigation for the dedicated team to start later. For example, starting a case during the night for a Digital Media Investigator to pick up in the morning.

Table 4. The average weekly usage in hours

Average weekly usage	n
Over 25 h	0
16-25 h	2
11-15 h	9
7-10 h	1
3-6 h	1
1-2 h	12
Less than 1 h	5

4.3 How Officers Were Trained to Use OSIRT

While OSIRT is utilised during the RITES course, it is often trained as part of in-house training packages, as seen in Table 5. 25 respondents were either trained directly as part of an internal training package, or by a colleague. Unsurprisingly, internal training is popular as it is cheaper than sending officers to training sessions. Sending officers away will mean losing a resource for a week on top of the cost of the training itself. Additionally, keeping training in-house means officers can be trained to that force's operating procedures and standards. While the RITES course teaches open source research techniques, it can only discuss methods and procedures in a generic manner for the diverse cohort; ultimately this will boil down to force policy. It is not uncommon to see officers attending the RITES course in order to then feedback and train in-house.

Table 5. How respondents were trained to use OSIRT

Trained to use OSIRT	n
Colleague	7
RITES course	2
Self-guided	4
In-house	19

4.4 Does OSIRT Capture All Relevant Data?

This free-form question, with responses in Table 6, offered the respondents a chance to provide feedback on whether OSIRT captures relevant data as part of their open source investigation. Word frequency analysis of the text showed there were 29 occurrences of the word 'yes'. Two respondents noted an issue surrounding video capture.

4.5 Has OSIRT Enhanced the Capability to Conduct Internet Investigations?

This free-form optional question generated 29 responses. Of the responses, 22 started their sentence with "yes" and a further 4 responses were positive in nature. One comment from an officer who has used OSIRT for over two years notes OSIRT's integrated tools and the fact it was designed specifically for law enforcement as a reason for why it has enhanced their capability:

"It has [enhanced my capability], but, it's the fact that this tools places all the relevant functionality of other tools all in one place that is specifically designed for Law Enforcement and the challenges that we face around continuity of evidence.
It also gives peace of mind as we know that all data is locally held and OSIRT is not reporting back to any servers, meaning we can trust it for security around our information."

Table 6. Freeform response for OSIRT's capture abilities

Response	n
"Yes" or "yes"	21
Yes, although the ability to download videos from more websites would be great	1
Yes, the tool is particularly useful for audit and reporting	1
Only current issue is video capture	1
Yes - I always video capture my screen and produce this in evidence	1
For me it does yes	1
Yes. I particularly like the screen recording options and the automatic page logging	1
I struggle capturing video and sound	1
Yes - extremely easy to use and professional means of recording what we do on open source	1
Yes - and more!	1
Yes and then some	1

Of the negative comments, those who said OSIRT has not enhanced their capability, still provided positive feedback "it has enhanced our methods of recording our research and auditing process" and "It has not enhanced - may be user error but it is great at tracking my movements evidentially".

Word frequency analysis showed "easier" was mentioned 6 times. In context, these comments all noted that OSIRT had made conducting Internet investigations easier, with one comment even mentioning it "made my job much easier".

The notion of professionalism OSIRT brings to respondents was also emphasised via word frequency analysis with three participants mentioning how OSIRT provided an output that is "more professional", with another respondent saying, "It has added professionalism to our [Internet investigations]".

It's all I ever knew... For one respondent, they had "only ever used OSIRT" to conduct their open source research. While this is only one respondent, it perhaps shows that for many incoming officers who are required to conduct research, OSIRT will be the de-facto piece of software they use. This will, speculatively, only increase as OSIRT has only been available for several years, so some of those officers who joined the force in 2016 will now be coming off probation into different roles, and perhaps require using OSIRT. This is also highlighted in the Sect. 4.1 (previous tool usage), where several respondents did not list tools as they had only used OSIRT.

4.6 Tool Usage Within OSIRT

Table 7 lists individual tool usage within OSIRT. The usage figures lend credence to the previous discussion during the analysis of SUS results surrounding the 80:20 rule. All tools within OSIRT are used, but of the 20 tools listed seven are used half of the time with only four used at least two-thirds of the time. No individual tool is listed as 100% usage.

Table 7. Individual tool usage within OSIRT (total usage and total usage as a percentage)

Tools	n	%
Video screen capture	22	70.97
Audit log	22	70.97
Full screenshot capture	21	67.74
Snippet capture	21	67.74
Case notes	17	54.84
Report exporting	17	54.84
Tabbed browsing	16	51.61
Full webpage downloading	13	41.94
Timed screenshot	12	38.71
Saving page source code	12	38.71
Attachments	11	35.48
Video downloader	11	35.48
WhoIs? Finder	11	35.48
IP address saver	11	35.48
Facebook and Twitter ID finder	11	35.48
Extracting links on webpage	9	29.03
Tor (dark web browsing)	6	19.35
Exif viewer	6	19.35
Reverse image searching	6	19.35
History viewer	5	16.13

These figures certainly lend credence to Pareto's '80:20' principle as discussed previously. If we consider a tool to be 'popular' that is used by at least two-thirds of respondents, we see a ratio close to 70:30. Given the modest sample size, that is close to the original principle.

5 Conclusion and Future Work

This paper analysed and discussed the results of 32 questionnaire responses from UK law enforcement regarding OSIRT. Results showed that OSIRT greatly assisted officers in their Internet investigations, when compared to previous tool usage. The responses also highlighted the policing spectrum, where OSIRT was used by neighbourhood officers to Digital Media Investigators. For policing to continually be responding to the challenge presented by digital technology they must adapt to their ever-changing surroundings, as the report by the HMICFRS commented.

Future work will look at distributing a similar questionnaire to a broader number of LEOs, as those that chose to fill out questionnaires were, arguably, 'fans' and users of OSIRT. This means that feedback focussed more on positive feedback from OSIRT fans. Access to those who do not use OSIRT, or do not like to use OSIRT, are harder to find because they are unlikely to reach out, or do not visit locations where OSIRT is discussed (e.g. police knowledge exchange forums).

References

1. Williams, J.: Creating and integrating a FLOSS product into UK law enforcement. In: Stamelos, I., Gonzalez-Barahoña, J.M., Varlamis, I., Anagnostopoulos, D. (eds.) OSS 2018. IAICT, vol. 525, pp. 117–127. Springer, Cham (2018). https://doi.org/10.1007/978-3-319-92375-8_10
2. Williams, J.: Legal and ethical issues surrounding open source research for law enforcement purposes. In: Skarzauskiene, A., Gudeliene, N. (eds.) Proceedings of the 4th European Conference on Social Media, Mykolas Romeris University. Vilnius, Lithuania. 3–4 July, 2017. ISBN 9781911218463
3. HMIC: Real lives, real crimes: A study of digital crime and policing (2018). https://www.justiceinspectorates.gov.uk/hmicfrs/wp-content/uploads/real-lives-real-crimes-a-study-of-digital-crime-and-policing.pdf
4. Regulation of Investigatory Powers Act (2000). http://www.legislation.gov.uk/ukpga/2000/23/contents. Accessed 25 Apr 2020
5. Association of Chief Police Officers: Online Research and Investigation, 16 September 2013. http://library.college.police.uk/docs/appref/online-research-and-investigation-guidance.pdf. Accessed 25 Apr 2020
6. Human Rights Act 1998. http://www.legislation.gov.uk/ukpga/1998/42/contents. Accessed 25 Apr 2020
7. Kent County Council: The JAPAN Test. https://www.kelsi.org.uk/__data/assets/pdf_file/0003/26706/Japan-Test.pdf. Accessed 25 Apr 2020
8. Data Protection Act 2018. http://www.legislation.gov.uk/ukpga/2018/12/contents/enacted. Accessed 25 Apr 2020
9. Information Commisioners Office: Data Protection Act 2018 (2018). https://ico.org.uk/for-organisations/data-protection-act-2018/. Accessed 25 Apr 2020
10. Milne, J.: Centre for CBL in Land Use and Environmental Sciences, p. 1. Aberdeen University (2009)
11. Grimm, P.: Social desirability bias. In: Sheth, J., Malhotra, N. (eds.) Wiley International Encyclopedia of Marketing (2010). https://doi.org/10.1002/9781444316568.wiem02057

Critical Analysis of Information Security Culture Definitions

Zainab Ruhwanya[1]([⊠]) [iD] and Jacques Ophoff[1,2] [iD]

[1] University of Cape Town, Cape Town, South Africa
Zainab.ruhwanya@uct.ac.za, j.ophoff@abertay.ac.uk
[2] Abertay University, Dundee, UK

Abstract. This article aims to advance the understanding of information security culture through a critical reflection on the wide-ranging definitions of information security culture in the literature. It uses the hermeneutic approach for conducting literature reviews. The review identifies 16 definitions of information security culture in the literature. Based on the analysis of these definitions, four different views of culture are distinguished. The shared values view highlights the set of cultural value patterns that are shared across the organization. An action-based view highlights the behaviors of individuals in the organization. A mental model view relates to the abstract view of the individual's thinking on how information security culture must work. Finally, a problem-solving view emphasizes a combination of understanding from shared value-based and action-based views. The paper analyzes and presents the limitations of these four views of information security culture definitions.

Keywords: Information security culture · Culture · Shared-value view · Action-based view · Mental model view · Problem-solving view

1 Introduction

In information security culture, the concern is no longer in the technical aspect of information security but the balance between processes and technology with the actors such as individuals, groups and organizations [34]. It is well established that cultivation of information security culture in a social context influences the behaviors of individuals which result in significant effects on the protection of information [15, 45]. This importance of information security culture has resulted in numerous studies centered on "security culture" and its relationship to different information security subjects such as information security, information security privacy, information security management, and security education training and awareness (SETA) [7, 9, 12, 50]. While information security culture is increasingly researched in the information security field, the term "information security culture", lacks a shared understanding of its definition [37].

This lack of shared understanding of the definition of information security culture is not only inherited from "culture" but also from the main field of information systems [2]. Culture is a complex phenomenon that spans from different fields and has numerous

N. Clarke and S. Furnell (Eds.): HAISA 2020, IFIP AICT 593, pp. 353–365, 2020.
https://doi.org/10.1007/978-3-030-57404-8_27

definitions in the literature [31, 46]. These definitions of culture emphasize on different concepts which include values, symbols, knowledge, behavior, attitudes, belief, perception and underlying assumptions [21, 30, 41, 48]. This complexity of culture has also impacted the theoretical clarity and conceptualization of information security culture in the literature. Depending on the culture theory used, researchers in information security culture focus their understanding of information security culture on actions (behaviors) [38, 49], and shared organizational values [7, 10, 11]. Other researchers categorize information security culture as a part of or as a subculture of organizational culture [42]. These different definitions of information security culture also impact the cultural dimensions, concepts, frameworks and type of analysis used to assess information security culture. This lack of clarity brings the need to study further, what information security culture entails.

What information security culture is and what it entails has essential consequences for recognizing information security culture as a contributing domain of knowledge to information security and information systems. As it has been for information systems conceptualizations [2, 5], a definition of information security culture is of interest because it can help in establishing a common ground for understanding and researching information security culture in the organization and different social contexts including cross-cultural studies. Also having a shared understanding will make it easy for researchers to compare and build upon each other's work [2, 5].

Therefore, the goal of this article is to advance the understanding of information security culture, by critically reflecting on how information security culture is defined in the information security literature. The objective is not to provide yet another definition for information security culture or to develop a taxonomy but to review and compare different views of the term information security culture. We recognize that other studies have reviewed the literature on information security culture in terms of dimensions and frameworks used to assess information security culture also provided a short review of different definitions of information security culture [1, 26, 37]. What distinguishes our studies with other studies is that we provide a systematic collection and review of definitions of information security culture categorized in four views of culture.

Since information security culture has its roots in culture, we extend Straub et al. [46] classification of definitions of culture to categorize definitions of information security culture. Straub et al. [46] classified culture into three categories, as (i) shared value views like Hofstede's cultural theory [20] (ii) outcomes-oriented (problem-solving) views like Schein's [40, 41] and (iii) General All-encompassing definitions and distinctions. Enrolling to their school of thought, we extend this categorization of definitions of culture as a framework to differentiate understandings of information security culture in the literature. The review of the literature on information security culture in this article follows a hermeneutic framework by Boell & Cecez-Kecmanovic [4]. The hermeneutic approach is fit for an understanding of the phenomenon of interest while emphasizing on critical engagement [4].

The next section will present the methodology used to identify the definitions of information security culture. Section 3 will present a review of culture theories used as a basis in information security culture definitions. Then Sect. 4 introduces the views and Sect. 5 critically reviews the four views of the definition of the information security culture. Finally, Sect. 6 will conclude the paper.

2   Methodology

The review process and framework followed in this paper is a hermeneutic framework [4]. It was fundamental for this study to follow a hermeneutics approach, as it is appropriate for the understanding of the phenomenon of interest while emphasizing on critical engagement [4]. The enquiry was accomplished by reviewing and analyzing information security and culture literature related to the field of information system. We included a mini review of culture theories since many researchers in information security culture used different culture theories to guide their definition of information security culture. The literature on the theory of culture was drawn from management, anthropology, and ethnography. This review of culture also assisted in increasing understanding and categorizing definitions of information security culture into related themes. The theories used indicated to affect not only the definitions but also the cultural dimensions, constructs, frameworks and analysis method used in different studies.

Searches were done through Google Scholar, Scopus and databases such as JSTOR, ProQuest and Elsevier. The preliminary search started with a Google scholar search engine because of its broader scope of results. To identify relevant literature, we searched the phrase "information security culture" it resulted in 2510 results. To narrow down the search, we used advanced search with a phrase allintitle: "information security culture" and obtained 212 articles from google scholar, and a search in SCOPUS resulted into 154 articles. Because we are following hermeneutics framework, at first, we retrieved a small set of the highly relevant publications. We started our review with 90 articles.

Sorting and selection criteria were done based on the following, publications with a definition of information security culture, with phrases like information security culture "is" or "defined as". We included definitions which have an indirectly implied understanding of information security culture; this was because information security culture is a complex phenomenon that spans from multiple fields. To narrow the scope the definition kept for analysis was from information security and information systems field. To ensure the quality of research, the majority of selected literature were from reputable peer-reviewed journals and conference proceedings articles [53]. More in-depth searches were further done by citation tracking, using backwards and forwards lookup [53]; this process aided to learn more about information security culture and culture theories in the literature. Our initial plan was to include only definitions from 2010; we concluded that definitions older than 2010 must be included in the review because they play an essential role on building the foundation of many current understandings. In the end, we reviewed sixteen distinct definitions of information security culture. For synthesis, analysis and a better understanding of the literature, we did a qualitative research analysis using AtlasTi. The tool helped analyze literature by thematically grouping concepts and adding relationships between concepts.

3 Culture

This section presents theories of culture that contain different and shared concepts such as values, symbols, knowledge, behavior, attitudes, belief, perception and underlying assumptions [21, 30, 41, 48]. These theories of culture formed the basis for many of the definitions of information security culture in the reviewed literature. These culture theories have also been used to develop information security culture frameworks and formed information security culture dimensions.

3.1 Culture

Culture is a crucial but complex phenomenon that spans across different disciplines such as anthropology, ethnography, sociology, psychology, management studies and information systems. One influential definition of culture is that of Tylor [48]. The researcher relates culture to civilization and defined culture in an ethnographic view as '...*that complex whole which includes knowledge, belief, art, morals, law, custom, and any other capabilities and habits acquired by man as a member of society.*' [48]. A different perspective of culture is from social anthropologists Kroeber and Kluckhohn [30] who conducted a critical review of 164 culture definitions. They defined culture as "... *a product; is historical; includes ideas, patterns, and values; is selective; is learned; is based upon symbols, and is an abstraction from behaviour and the products of behaviour*" [30].

Kroeber and Kluckhohn [30], viewed culture as a patterned way of behaving, including implicit behaviours. They further claim that culture influences and shape the behaviours of individuals according to what is expected from them. Thus, culture naturally establishes a system of behaviour rewards and punishment expectations, where members of a group know what type of behaviour can be rewarded or punished [30]. Culture is categorized based on distinct dimensions of shared values at the national level [20], organizational level [6, 21, 41], subunit level [35], and individual level [46]. Majority studies in information security have conceptualized culture based on national and organizational level dimensions.

National culture level. An organizational social anthropologist, Hofstede [21] defined culture at a national level as "*the collective programming of the mind which distinguishes the members of one group or society from those of another*". According to Hofstede [21], values form the core of culture, and an individual acquires culture from his/her group [21, 48] and culture distinguishes one group from another [21]. Although there are myriad of national culture dimensions in the literature [18, 21, 22, 43], Hofstede's [21] theory of culture is extensively used and well endorsed in information system and information security research. Information security studies have used Hofstede's national level dimensions for assessments of cultural values in information security threats, behavioral issue, privacy concerns, data protection [17, 24, 44], and cross-cultural comparisons [9, 23, 31, 46, 52].

Organizational culture level. There are many organizational culture frameworks used in information security research. This study acknowledges organization culture frameworks from theorist such as Schein's [41], Hofstede [21], Kotter & Heskett [28], Detert,

Schroeder, & Mauriel [14], and the competing values framework of Quinn & Spreitzer [36]. This section presents a review of Schein's organizational culture framework and its relation to information security in the organization. Schein [41] defines culture as *"...the pattern of basic assumptions that a given group has invented, discovered, or developed in learning to cope with its problems of external adaptation and internal integration, and that have worked well enough to be considered valid, and therefore to be taught to new members as the correct way to perceive, think, and feel in relation to those problems"*. Also, Schein [41] claims that an organization can have many subcultures depending on their role. Consequently, researchers in information security, also categorize ISC as a subculture of the organization culture [42]. Moreover, the majority of information security culture dimensions have their origin from Schein's organizational culture frameworks [1, 38, 49], fewer with Hofstede [21] organizational culture [47] and the Competing values frameworks (CVF) of Quinn and Spreitzer [36] adopted by [7].

4   Classifications of Information Security Culture Definitions

In the realization of many distinct definitions of security culture and their inheritance from culture definitions, we extended the classifications of the definition of culture based on [46]. Straub et al. [46] classified culture into three categories, as (i) Shared value views like Hofstede's cultural theory [21] (ii) Outcomes-oriented (problem-solving) views like Schein's [41] and (iii) General All-encompassing definitions and distinctions. While this earlier classification of culture by [46] informed the formation of our understanding of categories, our analysis is distinct as we were interested in definitions of information security culture rather than culture. Hence this study categorized information security cultural definitions as follows:

i.   Shared values view: highlights the set of security values patterns shared across the organization
ii. Action-based view: emphasizes the security behaviours of individuals in the organization
iii. Mental model view: relates to the individual's thinking on how information security culture works
iv. Problem-solving view: relates to a combination of understanding from values-based and action-based views

The classification of each definition, as shown in Table 1, is undertaken according to its most prevalent emphasis concerning these views.

4.1 Shared Values View

Definitions in this view emphasized the importance of a set of cultural values as a basis for information security culture in the organization. One exemplar definition is that of [13] who define information security culture from an organization culture definition by [7] as the *"values and beliefs of information security shared by all members at all*

Table 1. Some definitions of information security culture and their corresponding views

View	Definition of information security culture
Shared values view	"reflects the values and beliefs of information security shared by all members at all levels of the organization." [13]
	"a collection of high-level shared security values, beliefs and assumptions in information security." [8]
	"a shared pattern of values, mental models and activities among users or employees" [27]
	"is a specific mode of the organization and development of a subject's information activity, which is represented in the value-oriented models of his information interaction as a sender and receiver of information, under which he determines and controls the unity of existence and development of information objects in their cognitive and communicative manifestations." [3]
Action-based view	"The totality of patterns of behavior in an organization that contributes to the protection of information of all kinds. The prevalence of a security culture acts as a glue that binds together the actions of different stakeholders in an organization" [16]
	"The assumption about which type of information security behavior is accepted and encouraged in order to incorporate information security characteristics as the way in which things are done in an organization" [32]
	"is a subculture in regard to general corporate functions. It should support all activities, so that information security becomes a natural aspect in the daily activities of every employee." [42]
Mental model view	"The way our minds are programmed that will create different patterns of thinking, feeling and actions for providing the security process" [39]
	"a shared pattern of values, mental models and activities among users or employees" [27]
	"a system consisting of interacting framework and content components. Framework contains standardization, certification and measurement of information security. Content includes people attitude, motivation, knowledge and mental models about information security" [19]
Problem-solving view	"the attitudes, assumptions, beliefs, values and knowledge that employees/stakeholders use to interact with the organization's systems and procedures at any point in time. The interaction results in acceptable or unacceptable behavior (i.e. incidents) evident in artefacts and creations that become part of the way things are done in the organization to protect its information assets. This information security culture changes over time." [49]
	"The collection of perceptions, attitudes, values, assumptions and knowledge that guides how things are done in organization in order to be consistent with the information security requirements with the aim of protecting the information assets and influencing employees' security behavior in a way that preserving the information security becomes a second nature." [1]

(continued)

Table 1. (*continued*)

View	Definition of information security culture
	"a patterned way of security-based thinking shared within an organization; based on values, assumptions, and beliefs, which influences the behaviors and actions of the individuals so that, information security becomes a natural aspect in the daily activities in the organization. This ISC is developed, learned and changes with time with the aim to protect information assets and preserve confidentiality, integrity, and availability of information and information systems resources so as meet to the core organization vision" [38]

levels of the organization". These definitions, as seen in Table 1, are driven with the fact that shared cultural values influence information security culture. Different studies have shared values definitions views as a basis for their evaluation of the information security culture in the organizations. These shared values are based on organizational values [7, 11] and also national values [47]. Chang & Lin [7] emphasized that understanding organizational cultural values is a prerequisite in understanding the information security culture of the organization. Understanding of the shared values is necessary for providing security initiatives that prosper in the organization.

The definitions in this view, do not generally deny the importance of other views of information security culture definitions like action-based view or mental models view, but they emphasized on a set of shared values in the organization. For instance, Connolly et al. [10] investigated the impact of organizational values such as people-orientation, solidarity, sociability, task orientation and flat [31] on individual security behaviors. Tang, Li, & Zhan [47] defined information security culture by using values-based dimensions such as accountability, communication, compliance and governance. They used Hofstede's dimension of organizational culture namely process-oriented versus results-oriented, employee-oriented versus job oriented, parochial versus professional, open system versus closed system, loose versus tight control and normative versus pragmatic to qualitatively develop propositions that form the causal linkages between organization culture values and information security culture dimensions.

4.2 Action-Based View

Definitions in action-based view as seen in Table 1 emphasize the behavior and activities in the organization and how these actions contribute to the information security of the organization. The central to understanding information security culture according to the action-based view, are the activities that are performed which support information security culture. These are highlighted by definitions referring to aspects such as behaviors, activities, way things are done [16, 32, 42, 49]. One exemplar definition that many current understandings [1, 49, 51] have advanced is that of [32] where they define information security culture as *"the assumption about which type of information security behavior is accepted and encouraged in order to incorporate information security characteristics as the way in which things are done in an organization."*

The majority of literature in this category adopted [41] definition of organizational culture, and some researchers categorized information security culture as a subculture of the organizational culture [42]. Schlienger and Teufel [42] argue that similar to the organizational culture, ISC must be created, maintained and changed continuously. Other researchers, emphasizes the need to explore the underlying patterns of behavior at the individual, group and organization level [49]. The view supports the cultivation of information security culture as the influence on the behaviors of individuals, which can result in a significant effect in the protection of information [34, 49]. Moreover, Schein's [41] definition of culture emphasizes on learning techniques in order to solve problems in the organizations, and the action-based view makes a significant contribution to information security culture with research on security awareness, training and education (SETA) programs and its influence to information security culture [8, 15, 33].

4.3 Mental Model View

The mental model view as seen in Table 1 is the view of information security culture where the emphasis is on "human's (individuals') thinking about how information security culture should work. One exemplar definition is such as *"the way our minds are programmed that will create different patterns of thinking, feeling and actions for providing the security process"* [39]. Some definitions in the mental model view can also be categorized as a shared view, like [27] defines information security culture as *"a shared pattern of values, mental models and activities among users or employees"*.

These definitions deal with issues of the minds of the individual culture bearers [46]. Similar to the social view of information systems definitions, this view of information security culture is socially determined. Actions on information security culture rely on the individuals' interpretation and meaning creation that makes information security culture [27, 39].

4.4 Problem-Solving View

A problem-solving view definition of information security culture presents a combination of understanding of the shared values and action-based view definitions as seen in Table 1. One exemplar definition is that of [38] where they define information security culture as *"a patterned way of security-based thinking shared within an organization; based on values, assumptions, and beliefs, which influences the behaviors and actions of the individuals so that, information security becomes a natural aspect in the daily activities in the organization. This ISC is developed, learned, and changes with time to protect information assets and preserve confidentiality, integrity, and availability of information and information systems resources to meet to the core organization vision."*

A problem-solving view of information security culture is the most promising view. This view looks at what information security culture as a solution can accomplish in the organization [46] by also considering specific organizational values and required actions (behaviors) of the individual. According to Schein (2004), organizations strive for internal integration and external adaptation to ensure business continuity. Similarly, the purpose of information security is to ensure business continuity by preventing the impact of security incidents [16, 45]. Hence with information security culture organization must survive from the external and internal security threats. Internal threats are such as humans (employees) with malicious and non-malicious intents. Humans are bound to consciously or unconsciously cause security violations [29]. Non-malicious intent also categorized as human errors include poor security practices such as opening an unsafe attachment or accessing unsafe URLs, sharing a password, using weak passwords, loss of devices, unclear security policy and procedures, using a known faulty system, and improper systems configuration. As a consequence, information security culture is necessary to make sure an organization can cope with organizational problems of external adaptation and internal integrational for business continuity [41].

5   Discussion

The views are used with different underlying theories or frameworks of culture. However, there is still a need for a critical reflection on each of these views. The objective is not to provide another definition of information security culture but to review and compare the view and their practicality in pushing forward information security culture understanding. How is each view contributing to the understanding, assessment and cultivation of information security culture? To engage in the reflection, we use Alter's [2] framework to assess definitions based on criteria for judging the merits of conceptual models adopted from [25] as seen in Table 2.

Table 2. Criteria for judging information security culture definition based on [2, 25]

	Shared values view	Mental model view	Action-based view	Problem-solving view
Simplicity	Yes	No, definitions are abstract	Yes	No, definitions are complex
Clarity	No	No	Yes	Yes
Scope	Yes	No	No	Yes
Systematic power	Yes	No	Yes	Yes
Explanatory power	Yes	Yes	Yes	Yes
Reliability	No	No	Yes	Yes
Fruitfulness	Yes	Yes	Yes	Yes

- Simplicity: Definitions under the information security culture view are simple other things being equal.
- Clarity: Definitions under the information security culture view contain concepts that are clear and explicit.
- Scope: Definitions under the information security culture view cover the scope of the area of interest and do not overlook essential phenomena and issues.

- Systematic power: Definitions under the information security culture view helps in organizing concepts, relationships, and information related to whatever is being defined.
- Explanatory power: Definitions under the information security culture view helps in describing and explaining the phenomenon and predicting outcomes.
- Reliability: Definitions under the information security culture view lead to relatively similar observations and under-standings when applied to the same situation by different observers.
- Fruitfulness: Definitions under the information security culture view lead to essential questions for research and practice, and help in answering those questions

The shared values view. This view of information security culture encourages research that contributes to the understanding of the role of organizational or national values on influencing information security culture in the organization. This view is simple, has systematic power, explanatory power and covers a broader scope. However, the view lack of clarity because the information security culture assessment focuses on the core cultural values concepts than information security. Moreover, this view lacks reliability due to the lack of consensus on the shared cultural values for the assessment of information security culture. This view has an added value of fruitfulness as it contributes to the development of research that is based on national cultures [24] such as cross-cultural studies [52] and those based on organizational culture [10, 47].

The action-based view. The definitions in this view are simple, and they focus more on individual behavior and activities than holistic organizational security. Programs such as a SETA are seen as the primary drive in the cultivation of information security culture [8, 15, 33]. Research in action-based view focuses on how behaviors influence information security culture. Moreover, this view contains clear concepts, explanatory power, reliability and fruitfulness. The limitation of this view is the lack of scope in terms of the holistic organizational need for security.

The mental model view. The drawback of this view is that conceptualization is abstract and unconscious [52]. Furthermore, the view is challenging in formulating practical information security culture strategies due to the idiosyncratic interpretation of security. Nevertheless, the mental model view has the potential to lead towards new insight by looking at the psychological and social aspect and cultivation of information security culture in the organization.

The problem-solving view. This view has the potential to overcome the limitations of shared values, action-based and mental model. The problem-solving view provides a more practical definition of culture. It opens a scope for researchers to create studies with the combination of identified values specific to the organization, action appropriate for the organization and the perceived outcome on the information security culture.

The definitions in problem-solving contain clear concepts, cover a broader scope, have systematic power, explanatory power, reliability and fruitfulness. Reviewed literature have shown that understandings of information security culture in a problem-solving view have a potential to produce research to investigate information security culture holistically in terms of understanding, assessment, cultivation and improvement of information security culture in the organization [38, 49]. The only limitation on this category is that it lacks simplicity, although definitions are understandable, they are not simple.

6 Conclusion

The review of information security culture definitions shows that information security culture is a complex phenomenon, inheriting its complexity from culture. By using the hermeneutic approach and extracting themes from the definitions in the reviewed literature, we extended the classification of Straub et al. [47]. We thematically categorized information security culture definitions into four views; shared values view, action-based view, mental model view and problem-solving view. The review has shown that each understanding of information security culture contributes to useful research in information security. These views can be applied to investigate specific research problems, such as core values (organization or national level), SETA based research, behavioral, and holistic organizational information security culture. These views also allow researchers to explore information security culture from specific viewpoints, and in combinations of different views. The problem-solving view, for instance, creates an opportunity to use a combination of shared values, and action-based understanding to create a well-rounded information security culture research.

The discussion included analysis of the information security culture definitions using criteria for evaluating information systems definitions, on simplicity, clarity, scope, systematic power, explanatory power, reliability, the fruitfulness of the definitions [2, 25]. These criteria show that each view has its limitations. A shared values view lacks clarity and consensus on the set of patterned values used for the assessment of culture. The problem-solving view lacks simplicity. An action-based has a limited scope, while the mental model view is abstract and challenging in assessing information security culture. Future research should consider exploring these definitions in detail using alternative assessment methods such as the ontological and epistemological assumptions to uncover new and exciting research directions.

References

1. Alhogail, A.: Information Security Culture: A Definition and A Literature Review. IEEE (2014)
2. Alter, S.: Defining information systems as work systems: implications for the IS field. Eur. J. Inf. Syst. **17**(5), 448–469 (2008). https://doi.org/10.1057/ejis.2008.37
3. Astakhova, L.V.: The concept of the information-security culture. Sci. Tech. Inf. Process. **41**(1), 22–28 (2014). https://doi.org/10.3103/S0147688214010067
4. Boell, S.K., Cecez-Kecmanovic, D.: A hermeneutic approach for conducting literature reviews and literature searches. Commun. Assoc. Inf. Syst. **34**(1), 257–286 (2014)
5. Boell, S.K., Cecez-Kecmanovic, D.: What is an Information System? March 2015. https://doi.org/10.1109/HICSS.2015.587
6. Cameron, K.S., Quinn, R.E.: Diagnosing and changing organizational culture (2011)
7. Chang, S.E., Lin, C.-S.: Exploring organizational culture for information security management (2007). https://doi.org/10.1108/02635570710734316

8. Chen, Y., et al.: Impacts of comprehensive information security programs on information security culture. J. Comput. Inf. Syst. **55**(3), 11 (2015). https://doi.org/10.1080/08874417.2015.11645767

9. Chen, Y., Zahedi, F.M.: Individuals' internet security perceptions and behaviors: Polycontextual contrasts between the United States and China. MIS Q. **40**(1), 205–222 (2016)

10. Connolly, L., et al.: Organisational culture, procedural countermeasures, and employee security behaviour a qualitative study. Inf. Comput. Secur. **25**(2), 118–136 (2017). https://doi.org/10.1108/ICS-03-2017-0013

11. Connolly, L., Lang, M.: Information systems security: The role of cultural aspects in organizational settings. Inf. Syst. Secur. (2013)

12. Crossler, R., et al.: Future directions for behavioral information security research. Comput. Secur. **32**, 90–101 (2013). https://doi.org/10.1016/j.cose.2012.09.010

13. D'Arcy, J., Greene, G.: Security culture and the employment relationship as drivers of employees' security compliance. Inf. Manag. Comput. Secur. **22**(5), 474–489 (2014). https://doi.org/10.1108/IMCS-08-2013-0057

14. Detert, J.R., et al.: A framework for linking culture and improvement initiatives in organizations. Acad. Manag. Rev. (2000). https://doi.org/10.5465/AMR.2000.3707740

15. Dhillon, G., et al.: Interpreting information security culture: An organizational transformation case study. Comput. Secur. **56**, 63–69 (2016). https://doi.org/10.1016/j.cose.2015.10.001

16. Dhillon, G.: Managing Information System Security. Macmillan International Higher Education (1997)

17. Dinev, T., et al.: User behaviour towards protective information technologies: The role of national cultural differences. Inf. Syst. J. **19**(4), 391–412 (2009). https://doi.org/10.1111/j.1365-2575.2007.00289.x

18. Hall, E.T., Hall, M.R.: Understanding Cultural Differences. Intercultural Press (1989)

19. Helokunnas, T., Kuusisto, R.: Information security culture in a value net. In: IEEE International Engineering Management Conference, pp. 190–194 (2003)

20. Hofstede, G.: Cultural dimensions in management and planning. Asia Pacific J. Manag. **1**(2), 81–99 (1984). https://doi.org/10.1007/BF01733682

21. Hofstede, G., et al.: Cultures and Organizations: Software for the Mind. McGraw-Hill, New York, NY (2010)

22. House, R.J., et al.: Culture, Leadership, and Organizations: The GLOBE Study of 62 Societies. Sage Publications (2004)

23. Hovav, A., Arcy, J.D.: Information & management applying an extended model of deterrence across cultures: An investigation of information systems misuse in the U.S. and South Korea. Inf. Manag. **49**(2), 99–110 (2012). https://doi.org/10.1016/j.im.2011.12.005

24. Ifinedo, P.: The effects of national culture on the assessment of information security threats and controls in financial services industry. Int. J. Electron. Bus. Manag. **12**(2), 75–89 (2014)

25. Järvelin, K., Wilson, T.D.: On conceptual models for information seeking and retrieval research. Inf. Res. **9**(1), 1–20 (2003)

26. Karlsson, F., et al.: Information security culture – State-of-the-art review between 2000 and 2013. (2016). https://doi.org/10.1108/ICS-05-2014-0033

27. Karyda, M.: Fostering information security culture in organizations: A research agenda. In: Mediterranean Conference on Information Systems (MCIS), pp. 1–10 (2017)

28. Kotter, J.P., Heskett, J.L.: Corporate Culture and Performance (1992). https://doi.org/10.1080/15367100903202706

29. Kraemer, S., Carayon, P.: Human errors and violations in computer and information security: The viewpoint of network administrators and security specialists. Appl. Ergon. **38**(2), 143–154 (2007). https://doi.org/10.1016/j.apergo.2006.03.010

30. Kroeber, A.L., Kluckhohn, C.: Culture: A critical review of concepts and definitions. Pap. Peabody Museum. **47**(1), 223 (1952)

31. Leidner, D.E., Kayworth, T.: A review of culture in information systems research: toward a theory of information technology culture conflict. MIS Q. **30**(2), 357–399 (2006)
32. Martins, A., Eloff, J.: Information security culture. Secur. Inf. Soc., 203–214 (2002)
33. Menard, P.: Proposing SETA program design based on employee motivational fit. In: Americas Conference on Information Systems, pp. 1–5 (2016)
34. Van Niekerk, J., Von Solms, R.: Information security culture: a management perspective. Comput. Secur. **29**(4), 479–486 (2010). https://doi.org/10.1016/j.cose.2009.10.005
35. Quinn, R.E., Rohrbaugh, J.: A spatial model of effectiveness criteria: towards a competing values approach to organizational analysis. Manage. Sci. **29**(3), 363–377 (1983)
36. Quinn, R.E., Spreitzer, G.M.: The psychometrics of the competing values culture instrument and an analysis of the impact of organizational culture on quality of life. Emerald (1991)
37. Ramachandran, S. et al.: Variations in information security cultures across professions: A qualitative study. Commun. Assoc. Inf. Syst. 33(1), 163–204 (2013). https://doi.org/10.17705/1CAIS.03311
38. Ruhwanya, Z., Ophoff, J.: Information security culture assessment of small and medium-sized enterprises in Tanzania. In: Nielsen, P., Kimaro, H.C. (eds.) ICT4D 2019. IAICT, vol. 551, pp. 776–788. Springer, Cham (2019). https://doi.org/10.1007/978-3-030-18400-1_63
39. Sabbagh, B. Al, Kowalski, S.: Developing social metrics for security modeling the security culture of it workers individuals (case study). In: The 5th International Conference on Communications, Computers and Applications, vol. 3(1), pp. 112–118 (2012)
40. Schein, E.H.: Coming to a New Awareness of Organizational Culture. Sloan Manage. Rev. **2**, 3–16 (1984)
41. Schein, E.H.: Organizational Culture and Leadership. Jossey-Bass (2004). https://doi.org/10.1080/09595230802089917
42. Schlienger, T., Teufel, S.: Information security culture – from analysis to change. South African Comput. J. **31**, 46–52 (2003)
43. Schwartz, S.H.: Beyond individualism/collectivism: New cultural dimensions of values (1994)
44. Smith et al.: Information privacy research: An interdisciplinary review. MIS Q. **35**(4), 989 (2011). https://doi.org/10.2307/41409970
45. Von Solms, B., Von Solms, R.: The 10 deadly sins of information security management. Comput. Secur. **23**(5), 371–376 (2004). https://doi.org/10.1016/j.cose.2004.05.002
46. Straub, D., et al.: Toward a theory-based measurement of culture. J. Glob. Inf. Manag. **10**(1), 13–23 (2002). https://doi.org/10.4018/jgim.2002010102
47. Tang, M., et al.: The impacts of organizational culture on information security culture: A case study. Inf. Technol. Manag. **17**(2), 179–186 (2016). https://doi.org/10.1007/s10799-015-0252-2
48. Tylor, E.B.: Primitive culture: researches into the development of mythology, philosophy, religion, art, and custom. J. Murray (1871)
49. Da Veiga, A., Eloff, J.H.P.: A framework and assessment instrument for information security culture. Comput. Secur. **29**(2), 196–207 (2010). https://doi.org/10.1016/j.cose.2009.09.002
50. Da Veiga, A., Martins, N.: Defining and identifying dominant information security cultures and subcultures. Comput. Secur. (2017). https://doi.org/10.1016/j.cose.2017.05.002
51. Da Veiga, A., Martins, N.: Information security culture and information protection culture: A validated assessment instrument. Comput. Law Secur. Rev. **31**(2), 243–256 (2015). https://doi.org/10.1016/j.clsr.2015.01.005
52. Warkentin, M., et al.: Cross-cultural IS research: Perspectives from Eastern and Western traditions. Eur. J. Inf. Syst. **24**(3), 229–233 (2015). https://doi.org/10.1057/ejis.2015.7
53. Webster, J., Watson, R.T.: Analyzing the past to prepare for the future: writing a literature review. MIS Q. **26**(2), xiii–xxiii (2002). http://dx.doi.org/10.1.1.104.6570

Author Index

Ahsan, M. A. Manazir   329
Al-Ameen, Mahdi Nasrullah   329
Alkhamis, Esra   123
Alotaibi, Mohammed Khaled N.   85

Botha, Reinhardt A.   97

Camp, L. J.   109, 211
Chauhan, Apoorva   329
Crowley, Michael   3

Da Veiga, Adéle   16, 144, 300
Das, S.   109, 211

Freudenreich, Jan   233
Fricker, Samuel A.   289
Furnell, S. M.   47

Gangire, Yotamu   144
Gopavaram, S.   211
Gritzalis, Stefanos   315
Grossklags, Jens   233

Herkanaidu, R.   47
Herselman, Marlien   144

Johnson, Graham   259
Johnstone, Michael N.   3

Kalloniatis, Christos   269
Kävrestad, Joakim   71, 224, 247
Kim, A.   109
Kocabas, Huzeyfe   329
Kruger, H. A.   133

Lennartsson, Markus   247
López-Bojórquez, Lucia N.   30

Magklaras, Georgios   30
Maguraushe, Kudakwashe   300
Marsden, Simon   58
Martins, Nico   300
Mokobane, Ntsewa B.   97
Momenzadeh, B.   211

Nohlberg, Marcus   71, 224, 247

Ophoff, Jacques   16, 259, 353

Papadaki, M.   47
Petrie, Helen   123

Renaud, Karen   123, 259
Ruhwanya, Zainab   353

Shanley, Leah   3
Shojaifar, Alireza   289
Sideri, Maria   315
Snyman, D. P.   133
Spruit, Marco   161
Stephens, Paul   341
Szewczyk, Patryk   3

Thomson, Kerry-Lynn   186

Unchit, P.   109

Van Niekerk, Johan   186
Vasileiou, Ismini   175
von Schoultz, Dean John   186

Weidman, Jake   233
Williams, Joseph   341

Yigit Ozkan, Bilge   161

Zagouras, Panagiotis   269

Printed in the United States
by Baker & Taylor Publisher Services